Tomas Termote

WAR BENEATH THE WAVES

WAR BENEATH THE WAVES

U-boat Flotilla Flandern 1915-1918

Tomas Termote

Uniform

Uniform
an imprint of Unicorn Publishing Group

Unicorn Publishing Group
101 Wardour Street
London W1F 0UG
www.unicornpublishing.org

First published by Uniform 2017
© Tomas Termote, Unicorn Publishing Group 2017

The moral right of the author had been asserted.

All rights reserved. No part of this publication may be reproduced, stored in a retrieval system or transmitted, in any form or by any means, electronic, mechanical, photocopying, recording or otherwise, without prior permission in writing from the publisher.

A CIP catalogue record for this book is available from the British Library

ISBN 978-1-910500-64-4

Printed and bound in Slovenia

Contents

PREFACE 9

HISTORICAL OVERVIEW 11
    PREWAR POLITICS CONCERNING THE USE OF SUBMARINES 11
    A GENERAL VIEW OF THE U-BOAT CAMPAIGN OF THE FIRST WORLD WAR 12

THE BELGIAN COAST 19
    ITS LOCATION AND STRATEGIC IMPORTANCE 19
    THE CAPTURE AND OCCUPATION OF BRUGES, ZEEBRUGGE AND OSTEND 21
    THE POTENTIAL OF GHENT AND ANTWERP 23

THE U-BOATS 27
    GERMAN DOCKYARDS 27
    U-BOAT TYPES DURING THE FIRST WORLD WAR 28
        Long distance U-boats: U-type 28
        Coastal patrol submarines 31
            UB-I 31
            UB-II 40
            UB-III 43
        Minelayers 45
            UC-I 45
            UC-II 52
            UC-III 55
    TECHNICAL ANALYSIS 56
        Structure of a U-boat 56
            Hull, pressure tanks and rudders 56
            The conning tower 59
            Internal division, watertight doors and accommodation 61
            Hatches 65
            Colour, recognition marks and camouflage 65
        Engines 68
        Instruments and navigation 72
            Navigation and positioning 72

Compasses	73
Telegraphs and other instruments	75
Periscopes and optics	75
Communication	79
Radio-telegraphy	79
Hydrophone	81
Other signalling devices	81
Armament	82
Torpedoes and torpedo tubes	82
Deck guns	88
Ammunition	91
Mines	93
Sprengpatrone M/03	95
Small arms	97
Hand grenades and firebombs: the Goldschmidt-system	97
Salvage and safety	99
Dinghies	99
Telephone and light buoy	102
Lifting hooks and salvage vessels	103
Escape apparatus	104
Other safety measures	105

UNTERSEEBOOTSFLOTTILLE FLANDERN — 109

Development of a unit	109
Two Flotillas	111
Modus operandi	112
Results	113
Officers and men	115
Requirements and training	115
Uniforms	119
Decorations	121
A few U-boat officers	122
In the service of a U-boat flotilla	129
Life on board	129
Water and victuals	132
Sickness, hygiene and poisoning	134
Life on shore	142
Morale, propaganda and war trophies	146
The reverse of the coin: the sinking of a U-boat	152
The bases	155
Zeebrugge	156

  Bruges 164
  Ostend 176
  In the harbour: alarms against air attacks and camouflage 182
 U-boat Bunkers, concrete half shelters and other protective infrastructure 184
  Kragunterstanden 184
  U-boat pens 189
  U-boat bunkers 192
  Dry dock 195
  Other buildings 198

ALLIED COUNTERMEASURES 202
 Interception of radio messages, espionage and prisoner interrogation 202
 Nets, mines and fields 203
 Patrol vessels 206
 Depth charges 207
 British submarines 207
 Aircraft 207
 Explosive paravane 208
 Hydrophone 208
 Decoy vessels and Q-ships 208
 Convoys 212
 Royal Naval Divers 212
 British invasion plans and blockades 215

OPERATIONS OF THE U-BOATS OF THE FLOTILLA FLANDERN 219
 Nautical Archaeology as a means to discovering lost U-boats 219
  Wrecks and their lifespan 219
  Identification 220
 The U-boats of the *U-Flottille Flandern*, careers and fates 221
  UB-Boats 221
  UC-Boats 287

THE EVACUATION OF THE FLANDERS BASES 343

BIBLIOGRAPHY 347
ACKNOWLEDGEMENTS 349
NOTES 350

Preface

The literature of the Second World War gives ample room to the history of the German U-boats. Large amounts of information are readily available in archives and libraries. The patrols of the U-boats are well documented by means of photo and film. At this moment there are still living witnesses and many experiences were (even during the war) recorded. Some countries own and display some surviving U-boats, which attract a large amount of visitors. For the movie industry the subject has proven to be an attractive theme. Undoubtedly, there is a certain fascination and afinity for the lives of the U-boat captain and his crew.

After the First World War this was not the case. The U-boats which operated from the Flanders ports were depicted by the Allies as treachorous and vile weapons. This stood stark in contrast with the idea of British submarines and Q-ships, which in fact had been camouflaged as innocent merchant vessels.

War always has two sides. In this book, the story of the 'other' side is told: the history of German U-boats and their crews, a story that, up to present, barely has been described from an objective point of view. This publication gives an impartial view on German practices of war on the high seas.

Tomas Termote, a nautical archaeologist and skilled diver, has managed to combine historical research work with many years of 'on site' exploration, although this must be considered in a wider context.

The first part of the book relates the historical evolution and technical description of the German U-boat division during the First World War. With endless patience the author has analysed dozens of builders' plans and leafed through many archival files and managed to orderly pen down findings and corrections. He also describes in detail changing naval tactics and techniques in their historical context.

In the second part of the book, attention is given to the U-boats which were based in Flanders. With painstaking accuracy the author has described the development, the commanders, the patrols and (in most cases) the fates of every U-boat.

Termote has surpassed what is expected of a historian. As a nautical archaeologist he has spent, together with his father Dirk, an impressive amount of hours at the bottom of the sea and has closely studied many of these U-boat wrecks. This research work alone can already define the distinct originality of this book. Historical sources were approached with the necessary scepticism and checked in situ. Often findings were made which did not concur with what was found in archives. Some locations were not correct. Damage observed on U-boat wrecks sometimes was more relevant than information mentioned in sinking reports (or in some cases the opposite). Historical interpretations had to be adapted. With every U-boat, the author makes an evaluation. The help of international fellow-divers was essential and Termote combines and verifies their experiences with the discovered historical facts.

The author has given much importance to the illustrations. The descriptions, much of which will sound very technical to some readers, were illustrated with photos which are meant to give a clearer view. In his non-relenting search Termote has been able to source exceptional unpublished material. Many of the photos have been published for the first time, here, in this book. This make this publication a crucial reference book on the study of the Flanders coast in the First World War, complementing the (not so numerous) publications which focus on the coast and the sea.

Alex Deseyne
Honorary Curator Domain Raversijde

A U-boat slowly cruises away from a sinking Norwegian ship (TT)

Historical overview

PREWAR POLITICS CONCERNING THE USE OF SUBMARINES

During the First World War the submarine experienced a rapid technological evolution which had a big impact on the way the war at sea was fought. It would be the most potent weapon Germany had at its disposal and which brought Great Britain to the brink of capitulation.

This development is surprising because Germany's prewar politics toward U-boat construction was one of caution and even hostility. Admiral Alfred von Tirpitz, commander of the navy and advocator for the building of large U-boat fleet, was of the opinion that the U-boat would never play a key role in the war. Before 1906 both Britain and France had already constructed a fleet of submarines. In the early part of the 20th century the submarine was considered by the Royal Navy as a cheap weapon to safeguard coastal stretches and harbours. During the war it would evolve from a defensive to offensive weapon and threaten the superiority of the battleship. This became clear when a single U-boat, *U-9*, torpedoed and sank three British cruisers, *HMS Cressy*, *HMS Aboukir* and *HMS Hogue* on 22 September 1914 off the coast of Ymuiden. Because of the threat the U-boats posed, large ships could not operate independently anymore without having a fleet of guard vessels to protect them. The modern battlefleet was born.

At the dawn of the First World War the Royal Navy consisted of a fleet of more than 2.2 million tons, which amounted to about double that of the German High Seas fleet. Germany had no choice but to develop the U-boat if she wanted to defeat Great Britain at sea.

This new weapon would not necessary be built to tackle the navy of an opponent, but mainly to disrupt its supply routes.

The Industrial Revolution of the 19th century had made Great Britain totally dependant on the import of raw materials and food as well as the export of industrial products. If it would lose its superiority at sea, it would also mean hunger for its population.

Germany produced about 80% of its own food. Coal could be found in abundance in its own territories and iron ore was imported from Scandinavia. Even though Germany had better means at its disposal to feed its own population, a British blockade of its sea-routes and ports would mean a slow strangulation.

In the summer of 1914 the world's merchant fleet consisted of 42.4 million tons, a total of 22,000 ships of more than 100 BRT each. Germany possessed the second largest merchant fleet in the world with 4.4 million tons, but Great Britain took the lead with almost 21 million tons. Its later Allies, Russia, Italy, Japan and France, possessed together 6.4 million tons in ships. Austro-Hungary had only 1 million tons of shipping at its disposal. Important neutral countries, such as the United States, Holland, Scandinavia and South America, disposed of 10 million tons.

Even before the war had started, calculations were made to use the submarine as a weapon against the merchant fleet. In theory the Royal Navy would only need 36 submarines to keep the German North Sea ports in a constant blockade. Due to the enormous coastline of the British Isles, a blockade of Great Britain would be much more costly for the German Navy. It would need more than 200 U-boats to blockade ports and disrupt major shipping routes if it was to obtain any form of success. Great Britain could do this with ease as she already possessed 72 submarines in 1914. When the war started, Germany had only 28 U-boats at its disposal and many more would have to be produced.[1]

A GENERAL VIEW OF THE U-BOAT CAMPAIGN OF THE FIRST WORLD WAR

The German navy took on a more positive view of the U-boat as an offensive weapon from 1912 onwards. This was mainly because it wanted to break through a projected British blockade and even besiege the British Isles.

SS *Glitra* was the first British merchant ship sunk by a U-boat, on 20 October 1914, off the Norwegian coast. It was sunk in a way which generally typified the U-boat war. The ship was ordered to stop, the crew was given ample time to evacuate, the seacocks were opened and the ship sunk. The U-boat even towed the lifeboats as close to the coast as possible to guarantee the safety of the crew. Similar actions followed in the North Sea and the English Channel and marked the first part in the U-boat campaign. From August 1914 until February 1915 Germany wanted to stop and sink as many merchant ships as possible which headed towards the British Isles. It would mean much more for the outcome of victory than a major confrontation with the Royal Navy in a battle at sea. But the Royal Navy did not lie idle and early on in the war it started its blockade of the German North Sea ports. By December 1914 Germany began to feel the toll which the British blockade took on the severing of its overseas shipping routes. German high command discussed a change in U-boat tactics at sea.

By the 1 February 1915 the second fase of the campaign was launched. Germany declared that all troop transports and ships carrying munitions toward France would be torpedoed on sight. Neutral shipping was warned to keep away from the northern and western coasts of France. Shortly afterwards,

A U-boat crew looks on as a merchant ship has fallen prey to them (Claus Bergen)

Hüte Dich, England!

Es heult in den Lüften, wild schäumt das Meer,
Am Himmel jagt wütend ein Wolkenheer.

Ein Brite, beladen mit Körnerfrucht,
Den Weg durch das Toben und Schäumen sucht.

Die Flagge flattert: „Platz da, ich bin
Die Flagge der Meeresbeherrscherin!" –

Da plötzlich, den Torpedo im Rohr,
Ein U=Boot taucht aus den Fluten empor.

Gesichter darauf, wie Bronze=Metall;
Ein kurzer Befehl, – dann drüben ein Knall!

Der Frachter neigt sich, sinkt nieder zum Sand. –
Hüte dich, stolzes Engelland!

Wiener-Braunsberg.

German recruitment propaganda for the U-boat division (TT)

Germany declared the entire area around the British Isles and Ireland a warzone. All enemy shipping which would be found within would be sunk on sight, without guarantee of the safety of the crew. This was Germany's answer to Britains' hunger blockade of their country. The same fate would await neutral ships which ventured in this warzone. This, Germany said, was due to the abuse of neutral flags by Great Britain. But Germany did not want to be totally indifferent to the basic principles of International Law at sea. U-boat commanders were ordered not to torpedo ships without warning and to check ships' documents if possible. This renewed campaign had immediate results. U-boats sunk more than 100,000 BRT at a monthly rate and ventured further from their own bases. The German Admiralty had an optimistic view of an unrestricted U-boat campaign and expected Great Britain to sue for peace in six months time. In March 1915 it was decided to postpone unrestricted warfare because there were only 80 U-boats at its disposal. Germany also wanted to evade all out war because of the negative publicity that it received due to the sinking of neutral shipping. On 7 May *U-20* torpedoed *RMS Lusitania* with the loss of 1,198 lives. Among the casualties were many American citizens. The United States severely warned Germany of this act of war. Finally, Germany had to reign in its campaign after the sinking of *RMS Arabic* on 19th August in which 41 people died. Germany had to promise the United States not to attack any more passenger vessels and to wage a war according to the rules of International

A general picture which illustrates the U-boat war: a merchant ship makes her final voyage (TT)

Law of the Sea. The German navy was now forced to concentrate on waging war by means of U-cruisers against merchant shipping and the laying of mines by U-boats. The latter part of 1915 passed without major incidents and the new rules of combat frustrated U-boat commanders. Only the UC-boats which operated from the Flemish ports obtained many successes in the eastern part of the Channel and on the British east coast. There were almost no activities in the home waters, but a doubling of attacks on shipping in the Mediterranean had begun.

It was early 1916, a year had passed, and still the promised victory over Britain had not come. The number of British ships sunk kept climbing, but the Royal Navy held fast. Germany intensified its campaign by issuing the order to sink without warning all vessels which happened to be in the warzone.

It would not be a large liner, such as *RMS Lusitania* or *Arabic*, which would call an abrupt stop to the renewed campaign, but a cross-channel ferry. 50 people lost their lives when the French cross-channel packet *SS Sussex* was torpedoed and damaged on 24 March 1916. There were no American citizens amongst the casualties, but the incident enraged the American public. In their eyes the murderous U-boats had once more targeted innocent civilians. After heated diplomatic negotiations, Germany was forced to abandon an unrestricted submarine war.

Besides carrying out the function of warship and destroyer of merchant vessels, the U-boat attained the function of a peaceful cargo vessel. The large merchant cruiser *U-Deutschland* crossed the Atlantic to buy raw materials in the United States. This method had only limited succes because the loading capacities were small. *U-Deutschland* only made two trips to the other side of the Atlantic and after the loss of its sistership *U-Bremen*, which disappeared with all hands, further trips were cancelled.

From the summer of 1916, a limited U-boat campaign was restarted where ships were stopped and the manifest was checked. *Korvettenkapitän* Karl Bartenbach, commander of the *U-Flottille Flandern*, demanded from High Command that his unit could re-commence an unlimited campaign from October 1916 onwards. This was only allowed with caution as diplomatic incidents with neutral countries such as the United States wanted to be avoided.

President Woodrow Wilson attempted to mediate a peace between the Allies and Germany towards the end of 1916. Germany was divided internally. The workers wanted a peace through negotiations or *Verständigungsfrieden* which would end the war through a 'status quo ante bellum' and return to the geographical boundaries before the war. This would be unheard of for the Prussian nobility in the army, the naval officers, the industrials and most of the rightwing oriented middle class. The only way there could be peace would be to win the war or by means of *Siegfrieden*. Admiral Henning von Holtzendorff was convinced that Great Britain would beg for peace when an unrestricted U-boat campaign had been unleashed. *Siegfrieden* meant the continuation of the old regime and would guarantee stability for the country. *Verständigungsfrieden* would bring about social revolution, upset the internal hierarchy of the country and bring about a mountain of debts from war reparations. On the military side Germany still held the upperhand on land as well as in the U-boat war. After Fieldmarshal August von Mackensen captured Bucharest on 12 December, Germany and the Axis powers held out their hand sincerely for peace toward the Allies. This was bluntly rejected.

When the last hope for a negotiated peace had passed, unrestricted submarine campaign recommenced on 31 January 1917 that all vessels - enemy, neutral, armed or unarmed - would be sunk. Even hospital ships were considered legitimate targets if they were found to be in the warzone. Germany said it had undisputable evidence of the misuse of hospital ships as munitions- and troop transports. There followed a period of considerable more successes as there were much more U-boats on patrol and above all any shipping could be attacked in the warzone. The shipping around the British Isles consisted of up to 30% neutral vessels.[2] By sinking neutral ships in the warzone, Germany wanted to stop Scandinavia and Holland trading with Great Britain. Britain's answer was a policy of blackmail towards neutral countries, whereby a neutral ship would only be let free from a British port after another neutral ship had entered one.

The unrestricted U-boat campaign against Great Britain seemed to bear results. In April 1917 the campaign reached its climax in which a record number of 122 merchant ships were sunk in just two weeks. This meant that a quarter of all ships which left Britain bound for a foreign port were sunk.

The U-boats of the Flanders Flotilla could sink up to an average of 21 ships per month in the Channel, reaching a peak of 37 in December. This meant that not only food and arms were at risk of depletion, but also oil supplies for the naval fleet were at an all time low. The actions of the U-boats did not only bring the British people to the edge of starvation but also forced the navy to remain in their harbours.

Not only the British suffered from the campaign, many U-boats and their trained crews were lost. The Flanders Flotilla alone lost 29 U-boats in 1917 through the actions of patrol vessels, minefields and steel nets.

Many American vessels were destroyed during the unrestricted campaign and it is not surprising that President Wilson declared war on Germany on 6 April 1917.

In the end it would be the introduction of the convoy system and overwhelming American support which would turn the tide against the U-boats. Towards the end of 1917 all trans-Atlantic shipping was organised in convoys and in 1918 the convoy system was also introduced to coastal shipping around the British Isles. Convoys proved to be a huge success. They brought the percentage of shipping lost to U-boats from 10% down to just 1%.

The German people were deeply disillusioned that their fleet had not broken the British blockade. Still, faith in the U-boat as an ultimate weapon existed until the spring of 1918. After that it was realised that the U-boat had failed in the destruction of enemy shipping and could not stop the constant flow of American troops to the battlefields of France. This disillusionment ignited the fuse of revolution within the navy. Only the men of the U-boat division remained loyal to the Kaiser.

A U-boat has spotted a sail on the horizon: the chase begins! (DT) ▶

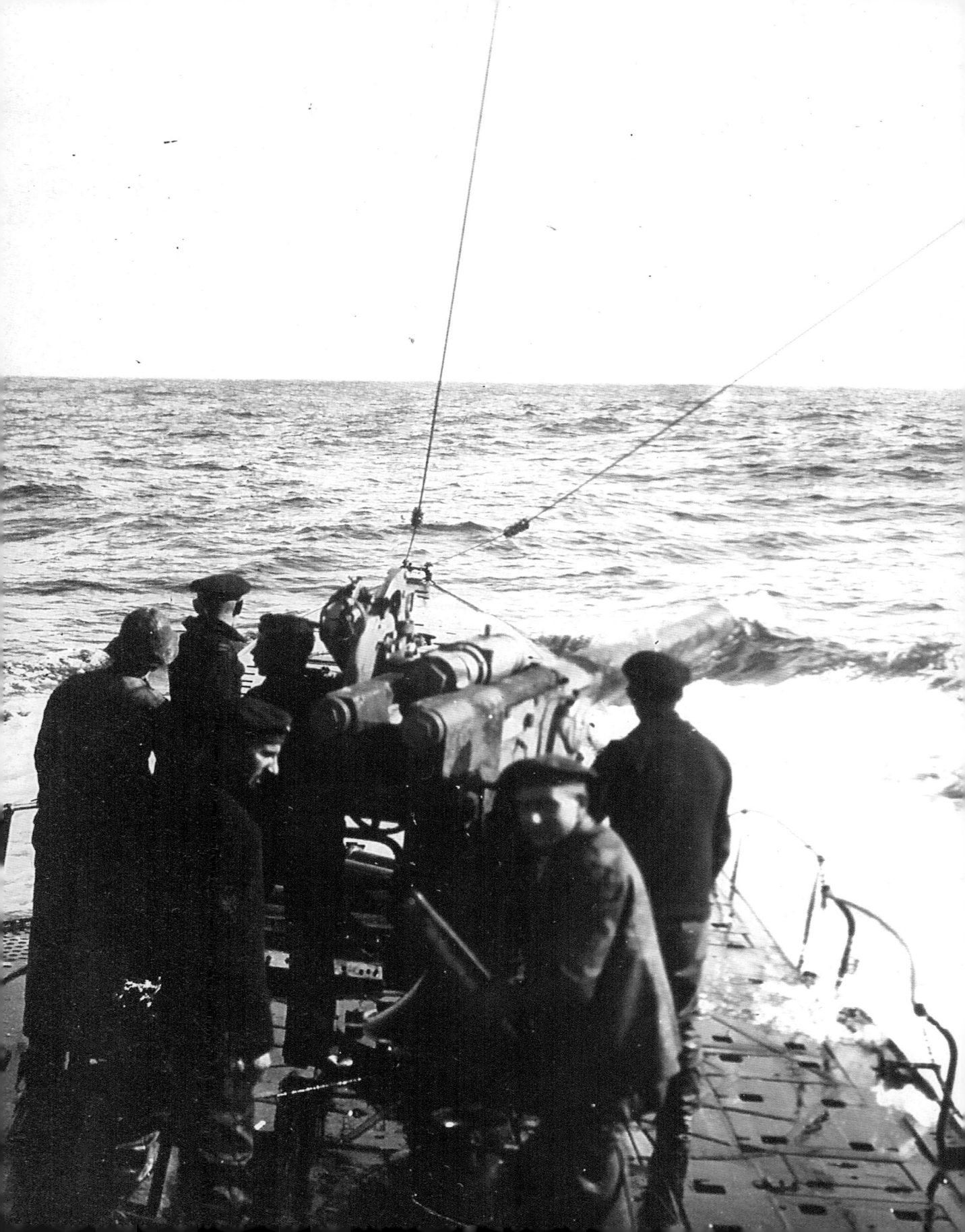

The Flemish coast was defended by all kinds of calibre of guns (TT)

The Belgian coast

ITS LOCATION AND STRATEGIC IMPORTANCE

The geographic situation of the Flemish coastline differs totally from the German war harbours in the North Sea and the Mediterranean. Only 30 km of coast lay between the enemy in the west and a neutral country in the east, just at the doorstep of the Royal Navy's strongest ports of war. Only the changeable weather situations at sea and the heavy fortifications on land kept it securely in German hands for four long years.

The Belgian army had to surrender the majority of Flanders after five weeks of heavy fighting against a diehard German army. The first occupational troops, known as the von Beseler division, marched victoriously into Bruges on 14 October 1914. Troops from a naval division followed a week later and dug themselves in between Knokke and Lombardzijde. A few months later they were organised as the *Marinekorps Flandern*. Their ranks were thickened by 20,000 troops of the *Seebataillon*, crack naval troops, which stood under overall command of Admiral Ludwig von Schröder.

When the Germans reached the Flemish coast in October 1914 they found the harbours of Ostend and Zeebrugge virtually untouched. Most of the ships had been taken, but harbour installations had not been destroyed. At the beginning of the conflict the Allies had hoped that the French would be able to force a breakthrough at the Yser river to recapture Ostend. There was opposition against bombing Ostend as its harbour could be used to land British troops.

Soldiers of the Marinekorps Flandern carrying out an exercise in the dunes of Mariakerke (TT)

19

Due to this mishap the German navy could almost immediately make use of the available facilities and started to build frontline bases for its U-boats. This small stretch of Flemish coastline, just barely 30 km in length, would decide in the next four years the general outcome of the war.

The German Admiralty had two reasons for obtaining this small bit of Western European coastline. It knew that the Channel and the Bay of Biscay were the most important supply routes for the enemy. Geographically, the Channel was also the shortest crossing from one point on the mainland to another. To build protected harbours in Flanders meant that U-boats had 300 miles less to sail in comparison with a departure from Helgoland, Wilhelmshaven or Cuxhaven. A return voyage for a submarine leaving from Flanders to the western part of the Channel would amount to 1,800 miles, to the Irish Sea 600 miles and to the western coast of France 2,000 miles. The distance to the Thames Estuary and the British Eastcoast was just under 100 miles. U-boats departing from the German North Sea ports and Helgoland had to also contend with mined areas in the German Bight. To avoid these areas, they had to sail a more northerly course, along the Jutland coast or through the Baltic via Skagen. This meant that the closest enemy territory was the British east coast which amounted to a round trip of 700 miles, and one of the furthest parts, the French Atlantic coast came to 2,600 miles. These distances would not be feasable for the small UB-I and UC-I types and even the middle-sized UB-II and UC-II types would be stretched to their limits. The German Admiralty also wanted to re-supply the large *Unterseebootkreuzers* [3] in Belgian ports before sending them on missions in the areas around the Azores and Madeira. In comparison with a departure from the Mediterranean or the German Bight, this meant a shortening of the voyage by five days. This plan was never put into action because the shallows of the southern North Sea and the size of the U-cruisers in question.[4] The harbours would be reserved for the smaller and middle-sized U-boats and there was even preference for the small UB-I types because of the shallows in this part of the world.

The Germans feared losing the strategic potential of the Flemish ports if the Royal Navy was successful in sealing off the area between Dover and Calais, the most important passage for U-boats, with mines and nets.

Another important reason for building a U-boat base in this part of Europe was that it was located only two days sail from important shipping lanes, supply dumps for the British and French armies and the Royal Navy's main ports. This meant that war could be waged on Great Britain's doorstep. The disruption of the supply routes would be the mainstay of the U-boats leaving on patrol from the Flemish bases.

Besides the danger to their shipping routes, the British anticipated the danger that Holland posed if it ever fell into German hands. It would mean that the German Empire would possess a coastline which matched that of the British east coast.

Admiral Sir Reginald Bacon, commander of the Dover Patrol between 1915 and 1917, knew of this danger:

'*to any thinker the Flanders coast was the only strip of territory that the enemy had in his possession which was of direct and vital interest to this country. With Flanders German territory, Holland would have been isolated from the Continent, to fall like a ripe plum into the lap of Germany. The whole coast from Wilhelmshaven to Nieuport would then have been German territory. For this reason every endeavour was made to facilitate an advance by our army should it take place.*'

From November 1914 onwards numerous plans for landing in the area of Westende-Middelkerke-Ostend were devised in an attempt to eliminate this danger. These never materialised as there never was sufficient support from the landfront. An army would have to make a breakthrough at the Yser river and push towards the coast to cover an assault by landing craft. In April and May 1918 this took effect when the Royal Navy attempted to block the harbours of Zeebrugge and Ostend.

German High Command understood the importance of this coastal stretch and ordered its immediate fortification during the first months of the war. From the frontline at Nieuwpoort to the Dutch border in the Zwin, enormous fortifications were built. Coastal batteries of all calibres were supported and protected by bunkers, trenches, machinegun nests and barbed wire emplacements. At a later date airbases, anti-aircraft batteries, telecommunications posts, enlargement of the batteries and flotillas of torpedo boats and minesweepers were added in strength. These defensive structures had as sole function the protection of the harbours of Bruges, Zeebrugge and Ostend against a possible landing or attack from the sea.

THE CAPTURE AND OCCUPATION OF BRUGES, ZEEBRUGGE AND OSTEND

An important meeting was held in October 1914 between *Korvettenkapitän* Karl Bartenbach*, *Marine-stabsingenieur* Schultz and *Marinebaumeisters* Krankenhagen and Ahsbahs. The aim was to discuss plans for the construction of a U-boat base in Bruges with connections to Zeebrugge and Ostend. The available facilities thwarted their decisions.

At the beginning of the war Bruges was not considered to be an optimal war harbour as it did not possess decent facilities, hangars or workshops. It only had certain lengths of quayside within the lock area where warships could safely berth. Its only trump was its location: at a distance of 12 km from the sea it could function as a refuge from bombardments from ships. U-boats which took shelter here would be able to reach Zeebrugge and open sea via the connecting canal. The Canal Bruges-Ostend was unusable in 1914 because of the narrow lockgates, but this could be adapted in a later phase.

---

* Bartenbach would become Flotilla Commander in 1915 of the newly created Untseeboots Flottilla Flandern

At the start of the war Zeebrugge was a relatively modern port. On its western side was a seawall or Mole of 1.5 km, with a protected anchorage within. On the land side of the lockgates there were large lengths of quayside with numerous workshops and hangars.

Even with these available facilities, the group of surveying naval officers was not content with what they saw at Zeebrugge. The facilities did not seem apt enough to protect berthed submarines. The inner part of the lockgates had a great deal of good quays, but it took 20 minutes to reach the beach area from here which did not have a single berth to its disposal on the seaward side. Near the workshops there were also no safe mooring spaces. The long seawall, which had a parapet and a large width could protect an anchored fleet against westerly and northwesterly winds, but an easterly gale could create problems. All described areas lay spread out which made them vulnerable to espionage and prohibited watertight security.

In the first instance, an extensive reorganisation was necessary. The most pending was to protect the

A German aircraft makes a reconnaissance flight over the Ostend area (Dirk Termote)

The young port of Zeebrugge with its characteristic 'Mole' (Dirk Termote)

At Bruges, there were many docks and quays available, making the construction of the Imperial Dockyard possible (TT)

The port of Ostend seen from the air, 1916. Top right is the herring hall (called 'cirk' or circle in local dialect), bottom right is the east bank with the foreship of a minelayer, probably *UC-14* (Dirk Termote).

infrastructure with a perimeter lined with guns. The function of artillery would be threefold. Firstly it had to protect a small fleet of minesweepers which would be working to clear a minefree zone on the seaward side of the Mole. Secondly, U-boats leaving on patrol had to receive protection until they reached deeper water, which was at least 6 miles off the coast. And lastly its own installations at Zeebrugge had to be protected against enemy bombardments from the sea.

U-boats could reach the Bruges canal and the sealocks, which were sited at a sufficient distance from possible attacks from the sea. There was much potential for the port of Zeebrugge, but much work had to be done. From the beginning, German High Command realised that the lockgates were the weakest point in its entire fortification. If this would be put out of action, no ship could leave the canal for open sea.

Of all three bases Ostend seemed most fitting to develop as a U-boat base. There were good berths in the western and eastern parts of the harbour and wharves, workshops, hangars, living space and dry docks were readily available. Far beyond the city, on the eastern side of the harbour lay the shipyard. This could be totally sealed off by a system of locks and bridges. The site had been constructed on a peninsula, which was walled, making security simpler. All kinds of machinery and equipment were at hand to maintain a fleet of submarines. The wharf was ready to be used and loading facilities could be constructed from existing buildings belonging to the Ostend Electricity Works. Only a circle of gun emplacements had to be dug to protect the area. The command of the Naval Division also pointed to Ostend as the most opportune harbour for U-boats. As soon as it was possible, a protective belt of artillery had to be made and men, infrastructure and materials could be delivered.[5]

THE POTENTIAL OF GHENT AND ANTWERP

The same group of officers who was entrusted with the coastal cities had to also look at the potential of the facilities at Ghent and Antwerp.

The facilities at Ghent were considered to be poor with just a machinery factory of the Carels and a small dry dock with neither workshops nor cranes. Everything would have to be newly constructed or imported from Germany. It was here that the idea blossomed to transport the small dismantled submarines by rail from Germany and reassemble them at the Ghent shipyard. Here a passage for ships with a maximum draught of 2.5 m was possible

Antwerp had by far the largest facilities for a fleet than all other harbours combined. It had six large dry docks, but without cranes or workshops. All necessary provisions, such as facilities for shipbuilding, engine maintenance tools, a slipway, a crane and a dry dock, were available at the Cockerill yard in Hoboken. This yard would prove to be perfect to reassemble the small U-boats which would be arriving by rail. This was the positive part of the harbour, the negative part was the size of the area which would jeopardise secrecy and bring about the possibilities of sabotage. The Antwerp Naval Dockyard proved to be better suited for this function as it had the necessary infrastructure to build and repair large merchant ships. At maximum capacity it could set to work about 800 workers. The Imperial Navy's *Baudivision* would have four large slipways with a length of 110 m to its disposal.[6]

Completed ships which had maximum measurements of about 48 m length, 6 m in breadth and a draught of 2.5 m could make the passage from Antwerp to Ghent, Bruges and even Ostend. The whole journey could only be possible after the repair and widening of a number of locks in Ostend. Ships with larger dimensions would have rudder guards and bows simply cut off. This would not impede their buoyancy as it would be the section in front of the first watertight compartment which would be removed. Cut off sections would be re-attached on the Bruges yard.

By March 1915 the Germans had also installed accommodation for crews of five U-boats. Officers had been assigned private residences at ten minutes' walking distance from the shipyard. Meals were served in several hotels in the Hoboken area. Non-commisioned officers and men stayed in the barracks of Fort VIII, which was just 15 minutes from the yard. Their meals would be served by the kitchens of the fort.

By mid 1917 the shipyard had increased its capacity and there were also lodgings in the empty spinnery. Even though Antwerp possessed a large shipyard with extensive facilities, it still only remained useful for long-term repairs for smaller vessels. If the war had lasted beyond 1918 the balance of importance would have moved from Bruges to Ghent.

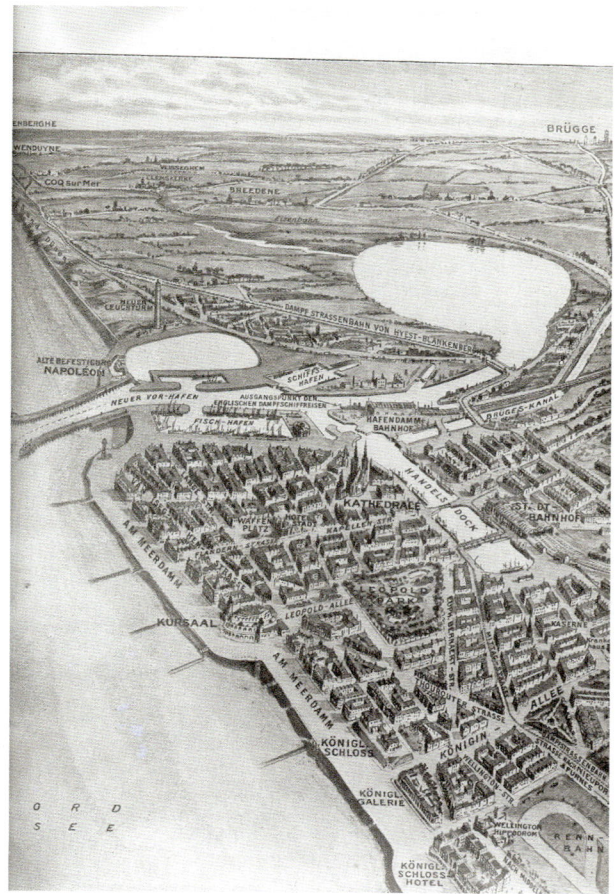

A view of Ostend (Illustrierte Kriegszeitung)

Aerial view of central Ostend, with a German military parade in front of the town hall (TT) ▶

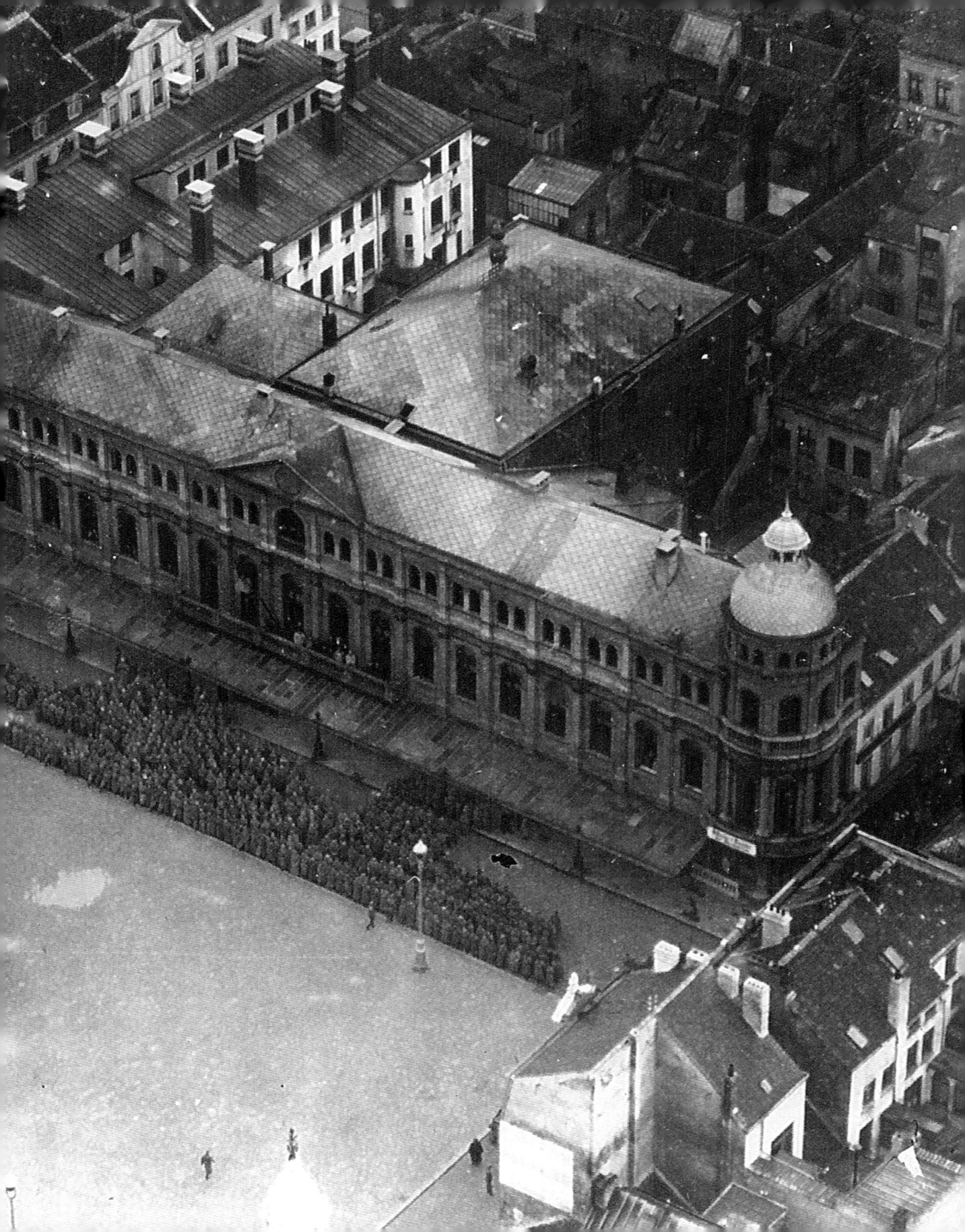

UB-I on the slipway of the Kiel dockyard, 22 January 1915 (U-boot-Archiv Cuxhaven)

The U-boats

GERMAN DOCKYARDS

In the pre-war years only the Germaniawerft Kiel and the Kaiserliche Werft Danzig were equipped to build U-boats. During the war four more dockyards were added for U-boat construction. These were Blohm & Voss and Vulkan in Hamburg, the Weserwerft in Bremen and the Bremer Vulkan Werft in Vegesack. The large U-types were mainly built in Kiel and Danzig, whilst Blohm & Voss and the Weserwerft took care of the UB- and UC- boats. By the end of the war they had designed a new type of U-boat: the UF-boat, but it was not completed in time and did not see any action. The plan was to build 50 of this new type U-boat at Schichau in Elbing, on the Neptune yard in Rostock and at Seebeck and Tecklenburg in Geestemünde.

Construction time of a single U-boat varied from type to type and yard to yard. A large U-type took from nine to 30 months to build, with an average of 20 months. The speed of completion of the first UB-I and UC-I types was extraordinary: three to four months. The middle sized to large UB- and UC-boats took a period of eight to ten months to complete.

From the start of the war up to a few months after the Armistice, the German government ordered a total of 810 U-boats at several yards. Less than half of this number were actually finished, a total of 391. This consisted of 144 U-boats, 143 UB-boats and 104 UC-boats. At the time of the Armistice in November 1918 there were 160 U-boats in half-finished condition on the yards. During four years of war 329 U-boats were put into action in four zones: the North Sea, Flanders, the Mediterranean and the Black Sea.

A UB-I type U-boat in the Weserwerft, Kiel (U-boot-Archiv Cuxhaven)

U-BOAT TYPES DURING THE FIRST WORLD WAR

Three main classes of U-boat were developed: U-boats, UB-boats and UC-boats. U-boats fit the original concept of the submarine: large, twin-hulled high seas' vessels with large range. UBs were built to fit the profile of vessels which would be on short patrols and UCs would have the capacity to lay mines.

At the start of the war Germany's U-boat fleet consisted of 28 U-boats of the classic U-type. The U-boats *U-1* to *U-18* were provided with Körting-Paraffin engines and it was only from *U-19* onwards that they had heavy diesel engines fitted. At the outset a U-boat belonged to a specific series which consisted of three to five U-boats of similar construction. Later on a larger standardisation was implemented to assure a faster and more efficient production. A certain series of the U-type could comprise up to ten of the same U-boat. With the UB- and UC-types, a series meant the same type of submarine. Every series, with a couple of exceptions, had an increase in size to the previous one.

In contradiction with what the word 'submarine' suggests, U-boats stayed as long as possible on the surface. They would only submerge during bad weather, if they had to shadow an enemy or if they attacked or when they themselves were being attacked. Their endurance underwater was usually about 12 hours, with a distance of 75 miles stretching to 100 miles if necessary. By rule, a U-boat captain would never go to the limit for fear of damaging the batteries.

All modern German U-boats were tested up to a depth of 65 m, but in an emergency they could reach 100 m without sustaining damage. If they wanted to rest the submarine and its crew this would be done on depths up to 55 m. The preferred cruising depth for a submerged U-boat would fluctuate between 22 and 27 m, except in circumstances where heavy swells would force them to seek deeper water.

LONG DISTANCE U-BOATS: U-TYPE

Of this type none were permanently allocated to the Flanders Flotilla. U-types mainly left from the northern German bases and the Mediterranean, but some would

The ocean-going U-boat *U-29*, under command of *Kapitänleutnant* Otto Weddigen, leaves the harbour of Ostend in March 1915. She would be lost with all hands off the British coast. In the background lies the mail boat *Princess Joséphine*, which would later on be turned into an accommodation vessel for U-boat crews (TT).

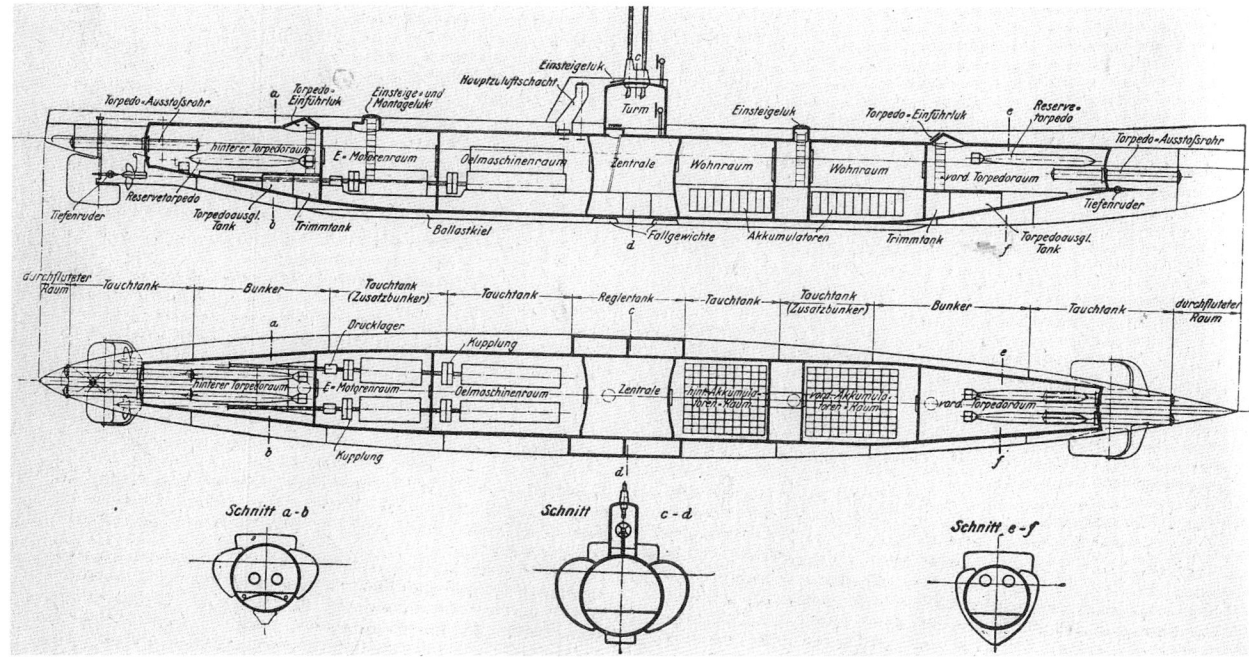

Schematic of a double-hulled U-boat (Techel)

stop at Ostend and Zeebrugge as a refuge from their trip from Germany towards the Western Approaches and on their return journey. They would run into the Flemish ports to undergo hasty repairs, hide during extreme weather and take on victuals and fuel. *U-12* was the first ever U-boat to enter a Flemish port. *U-5* and *U-11* had departed Zeebrugge in 1914 on their final mission towards the British coast and were lost with all hands. *U-22* had to undergo urgent repairs and had entered the sanctuary of Zeebrugge for necessary spares. *U-29*, under command of the famous *Kapitänleutnant* Otto Weddigen[*] had departed Ostend on 8 March 1915 for his final voyage. *U-29* and her entire crew would be lost ten days later after they had been rammed by *HMS Dreadnought* off Scotland.

Germany's first U-boat, *U-1*, was completed in 1906 and had a length of 45 m and a displacement of 235 BRT. The series *U-2* to *U-18* was driven by petrol engines had little or no other armament besides torpedoes. Their Körting engines proved to be their largest handicap. The often poisonous smoke had to be released through a funnel which was mounted on deck. During the daytime hours white plumes of smoke would be visible for miles around and during the night escaping sparks would give away the U-boat's position. They were also slow in submerging and making a U-boat dive was only in utmost necessity when they were under attack or if there was another danger. From this series, a total of 11 boats were lost and a third were used as training vessels in the Baltic. It was only with the series *U-19* to *U-138* that a larger size of U-boat was constructed which had a longer endurance at sea. With their new diesel engines and a supply of 120 tons they could remain away from land for up to five weeks. Their displacement was 640 BRT and their maximum speed varied between 14 and 17 knots on the surface to 8 and 9.5 knots beneath the waves. The average length was 70 to 75 m, with a width of 7 m and a draught of 4 m. Besides having torpedo tubes as armament they were also fitted with one or two artillery pieces of the 8.8 cm or 10.5 cm calibre. All these submarines were twin-hulled, with the outer hull giving the U-boat its 'ship shape' and interior one being the pressure hull. The series *U-71* to *U-80* proved to be an exception as they were minelayers with just a single hull and carried cargoes of 34 to 36 mines and had slow cruising speeds of just 6 knots. The following series, *U-117* to *U-126*,

---

[*] In September 1914 Otto Weddigen commanded *U-9* and managed to torpedo and sink three British cruisers – *HMS Hogue*, *HMS Aboukir* and *HMS Cressy* – in just one and a half hours off the coast of Ymuiden.

were designed as large minelayers of 1.500 BRT, but proved to be unsuccessful. *U-105* to *U-114* consisted of large submarines with an increased displacement of 820 BRT. The true titans amongst the U-boats were the series *U-135* to *U-150* and were known as U-boat cruisers. They measured more than 100 m in length and had a displacement of up to 2.125 BRT. Armament consisted of two 15 cm guns and eight torpedo tubes which turned them into veritable floating fortresses. These U-boats were based at Kiel and could stay away from home for up to almost half a year without needing to touch land. They operated off the American east coast, the Azores and Africa's west coast.

The last series, *U-151* to *U-157*, were built as merchant submarines to be able to trade with the United States. These twin-hulled U-boats measured 70 m in length, on a width of 10 m and had a displacement of 1.490 BRT. They were as long as the normal U-boats, but much broader to give more cargo loading facilities. The U-boat minelayers were slow boats with cruising speeds varying between 6 and 8 knots, whereas a merchant submarine could only reach 6 knots at its maximum speed. Bad diving qualities and the slow speed of three minutes to submerge designated them as cumbersome boats. The principle of the merchant submarine ended in 1917 when the United States entered the war on the side of the Allies.

The early U-types were manned by 22 to 28 officers and men, the larger ones had crews of 35 and the minelayers 40. The large U-cruisers and merchant submarines were crewed by 83 seamen.

COASTAL PATROL SUBMARINES

The German Admiralty wanted to design a submarine which was highly manoevrable in shallow waters and could operate near an enemy coastline. The UB-I or Coastal patrol U-boat was developed and evolved to the middlesized UB-II and larger UB-III type submarines.

UB-I

On 8 August 1914, just two days after the war had started, the German Admiralty had the design of a small U-boat in mind which would be quicker in construction than the usual submarine which took almost a year to build. It would not be until February 1915 that UB-I could be launched in Kiel. Earlier on the U-boat inspectorate had rejected the idea of a small U-boat because it considered that small armament and a limited range would not inflict enough damage on the enemy. This thinking changed after Antwerp had fallen on 10 October 1914 and Germany controlled a stretch of coastline which was close to Great Britain and the Channel.

The southern North Sea and the Channel bristle with sandbanks and shallows which made it difficult for big U-boats to seek shelter and remain undamaged in large swell and storm. The new U-boat design had to be small and manoeuvrable but still be suited as a good sea-going vessel. On 15 October 1914, the *Reichsmarineamt* approved 'Project 34' which was the building of 15 units of the UB-I type boat. The Germaniawerft in Kiel started with the construction of *UB-1* to *UB-8* and AG Weser in Bremen took on *UB-9* up to *UB-15*. An extra order for the building of *UB-16* and *UB-17* went to the Weserwerft on the 25 November 1914 because the Austro-Hungarian navy was alotted *UB-1* and *UB-15*.

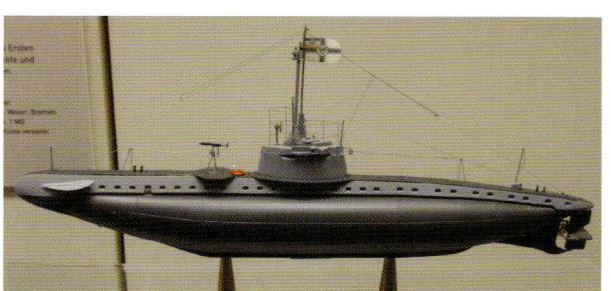

Model of a UB-I type submarine (International Maritime Museum Hamburg)

◀ A spectacular view on the forward deck and conning tower of the large U-cruiser *U-157*, taken from the top of her extended radio mast. (TT)

The UB-I type was the smallest submarine which Germany had built during the First World War. It had an overall length of 28,10 m, on a width of 3,15 m, a draught of 3,03 m and a displacement of 127 BRT surfaced and 142 BRT submerged. Because of its small size it only needed a single pressure hull and one propellor. Originally, U-boats were built with an interior pressure hull and an outer hull. In between these two hulls lay the diving tanks, trim-and stabilisation installation and also the fuel tanks. With the UB-I type all this had to be fixed within the pressure hull. Optically this U-boat was a pressurised cylinder on to which a bow, an aft section and a small tower were added.

For surface cruising, the UB-I type was provided with a Daimler- or Körting 60 HP 4-stroke (*Beibootdiesel*) engine which gave it a speed of 6.47 knots. A Siemens-Schuckert 120 HP electric engine was used for submerged cruising and gave it a maximum speed of 5.51 knots. Within the small hull there was storage room for 2.4 tons of diesel oil and 112 battery cells. The diesel engine gave it a remarkable range of 1,650 miles if run at a constant speed of 5 knots. Underwater it was more restricted and the electric propulsion gave it only a range of 45 miles at a speed of 4 knots. The most remarkable point of this U-boat was its 22 second diving speed to reach a test depth of 50 m.

A view of the stern of a UB-I in the Kiel dockyard (U-boot-Archiv Cuxhaven).

UB-I boats were supplied with two 45 cm bowtorpedotubes and only had a supply of two torpedoes due to the lack of space. An 8 mm-machinegun could be mounted on deck on a tripod. The U-boat was crewed by one officer and 13 seamen. Space was so limited on board that there were berths for only seven men, making two crewmen each share one bunk.

The first three boats of this series were launched in Germany and underwent trials in home waters. Every newly constructed UB- and UC-boat had to undergo trials in the Baltic lasting 10 days with a range of 70 miles. This consisted of submerged cruising, grounding

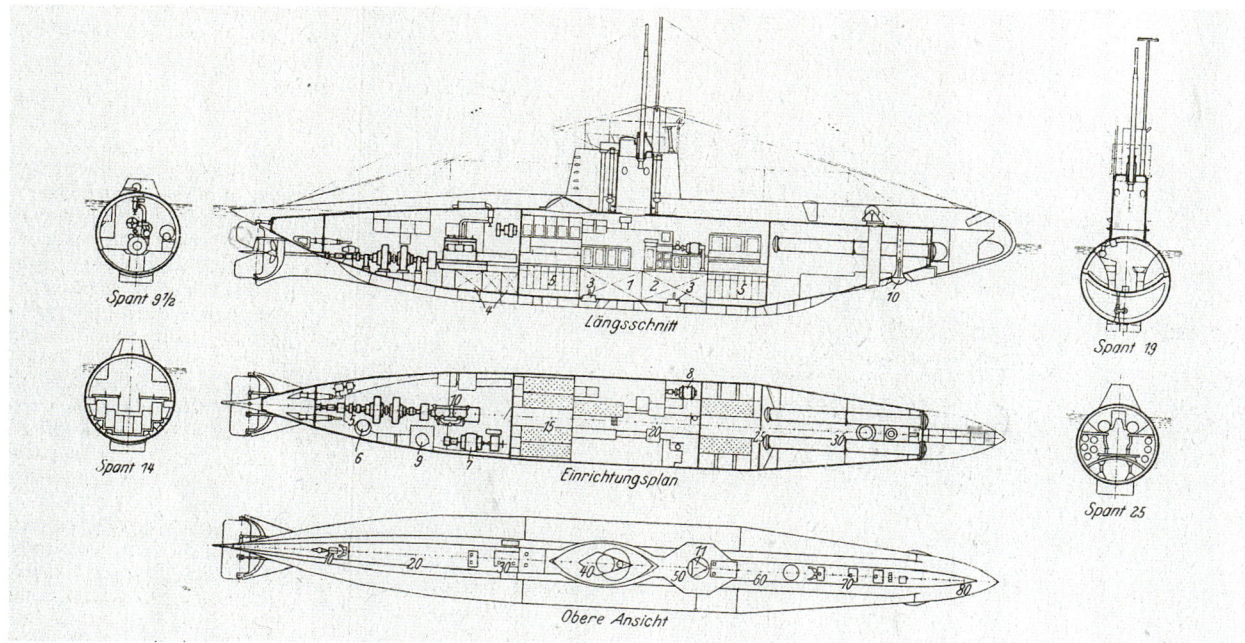

Schematic of UB-I class U-boat (Techel)

◄ A view of the bow of *UB-I* in the Weserwerft (U-boot-Archiv Cuxhaven)

33

UB-9 and part of her crew (TT)

A UB-I type U-boat on a return from a patrol passes the coast of Blankenberge, before reaching the Zeebrugge Mole (TT)

The crew of a UB-I U-boat prepare to moor their vessel alongside a quay in Zeebrugge (TT)

the submarine, regular loading and firing of practice torpedoes, loading the tubes whilst ascending and descending, nigthtime and surfaced target practice, avoiding obstructions and navigation which would take them back home. After being content with her performance, the U-boat would get a new crew assigned which had two days to accompany the original crew and learn everything about their boat as soon as possible.

In the beginning it was the idea to let these small U-boats reach the Flemish coast on their own accord, which took eight days to enter Zeebrugge Harbour after sailing along the northern coast of Germany, the Dutch islands and along the Dutch coast. This would give the crew enough time to know their U-boat optimally.

But the Admiralty soon learnt that this process was not so advantageous after near disastrous experiences of *UB-2* in the North Sea. *UB-2* had left Kiel at the end of March 1915 via the Kiel Canal and set a course to the Borkum Roads via Cuxhaven. She was under command of *Oberleutnant z. S.* Werner Fürbringer and his endurance was immediately put to the test when *UB-2* encountered a northwesterly storm force 10 when rounding Den Helder. The enormous waves buffeted the stern and constantly swamped the tower. *UB-2* was in for a rough time and the U-boat rolled and pitched heavily with moments were the top of the tower touching the surface of the sea. Both the giro and spare compass on the bridge were put out of action due to the incessant shaking. Moisture which had entered the compass made the compass-card illegible. In the end Fürbringer had to settle his U-boat on the seabottom to let the storm blow over

before continuing the journey. *UB-2* roughly touched bottom at 28 m and even at this depth it rolled violently through the effect of the heavy swell. To keep the U-boat settled on the bottom for the next 12 hours enough water ballast had to be pumped out.[7] When *UB-2* was finally able to resurface after the storm had abated, a course had to be set using the sextant and to calculate the correct direction towards Zeebrugge.

Despite the difficult circumstances, *UB-2* managed to reach its destination - also because it had a capable captain - but the Admiralty decided not to take any more risks and had all other UB-I boats transported by rail. Upon arrival they would be unloaded and reassembled in the shipyard and do their trials locally. By July 1915 all 17 UB-I types had been finished and commissioned.

UB-10 was the first UB-I type boat to be commissioned with the newly created Flanders Flotilla in March 1915. After *UB-10*, another eight UB-I boats followed and by the end of April the fleet consisted of *UB-2, UB-4, UB-5, UB-6, UB-10, UB-12, UB-13, UB-16* and *UB-17*. The remaining UB-I type boats were sent to the Mediterranean and joined the Austro-Hungarian navy.

Generally, crews of UB-I boats were assigned tough tasks. A tour of duty usually started out with a three-day patrol off the Belgian coast. After

◂ *UB-9* lies next to her mothership, with crew assembled on top and in front of the tower. The seaman in the front stands on the telephone and lightbuoy (TT)

completing this first mission, a UB-I boat would remain in port for five days, followed by a hunting patrol or *Feindfahrt*. In a seven month service span, a UB-I boat would spend on average 150 days at sea, which would put heavy pressure on the crew. *UB-4* had the honour of sinking the first enemy ship for the Flanders Flotilla. This was the British merchant ship *SS Harpalyce* which was torpedoed near the Northhinder Lightship. The chosen area of operations for the UB-I boats was in the area between the British east coast and Dutch coast, known as the Hoofden.

They would venture a little further to Yarmouth, up north to the east coast and some daring commanders went as far as Calais and the Dover Straits.

UB-4 and *UB-13* were lost with all hands in their first year of service, *UB-2* and *UB-5* were transferred to the Baltic. *UB-6* ran aground in shallows off the Dutch coast in March 1917 and was interned, together with its crew, for the rest of the war. *UB-12* was converted into a minelayer but went missing whilst on patrol in 1918. *UB-16* and *UB-17* also failed to return from their respective patrols. Only *UB-10* survived the war in Flanders and was scuttled off the coast of Heist just before the Armistice.

UB-I boats received much criticism as being too slow, too small and not powerful enough with their single propulsion. On the surface they could not catch up with fleeing merchantmen and they did not have enough endurance to remain submerged for longer periods of time. After an hour under water the batteries usually ended up depleted. On 21 June 1915, *UB-6* had to make its way to the Boulogne area to spy on shipping movements. *UB-6* passed successfully through the net barrage at Cap Gris Nez during the night after following in the wake of an unsuspecting cargo ship. The next day commander *Oberleutnant z. S.* Erich Haecker observed a couple of ships in the Boulogne Roads and decided to return back to base. *UB-6* had to battle a heavy opposing tide which made it impossible for the 60 HP diesel engine to pass through the Dover Straits. Surfaced, the U-boat made an easy target for British patrol vessels, so Haecker decided to ground *UB-6* and wait for the turning of the tide. As soon as *UB-6* could take advantage of the tide, she had to pass through the most difficult area under water on electric engine, which rapidly drained the batteries.[8]

U-boats ran another great risk when being in enemy territory: UB-I boats were rife to engine failures and the shearing of the shaft which could put them totally out of action. UB-I boats also had the nasty habit of breaking trim after having fired a torpedo. They were equipped with compensation tanks which were designed to flood and buffer the loss of a C/06 torpedo which weighed 770 kg. This system did not always work, making the bow shoot to the surface. If too much water was pumped into the tube at once, the U-boat would almost immediately sink to the bottom. One of their commanders compared the irregular actions of the UB-I to a sewing machine after an 'iron tadpole' (or torpedo) had been fired.[9] Heavy swell and stormy circumstances proved to be impossible to keep an UB-I type at periscope depth. The constant vibrations, pitching and rolling made the compass deviate and put delicate instruments out of action. The navigator had to depend on the presence of either the sun or stars to find their way back to base. The UB-I boat also proved to be an easy target for armed merchantmen or Q-ships when they could not answer back with a deckgun.

Criticism of the UB-I boat was rife, but it gained a large amount of success even during the tougher anti-U-boat campaign. Until 18 September 1915 they had managed to complete 90 patrols and sink 84 merchant ships and fishing vessels as well as three warships, amounting to a total of 48.902 BRT. After this date the U-boat campaign came somewhat to a standstill after America protested against the actions of the U-boats. From 1917 this would be changed to harder actions in which ships were sunk without warning. In this campaign the use of the smaller, underarmed UB-I type lost a lot of its use. *UB-10* proved to be the most successful of all UB-I types as it managed to carry out 100 patrols and sink a total of 36 civilian vessels and one warship in a career spanning almost four years. Despite its waning efficiency in battle, the UB-I was converted to a practical training vessel for new captains and crews. Famous U-boat captains such as *Oberleutnant z. S.* Otto Steinbrinck, *Kapitänleutnant* Henno von Heimburg, *Kapitänleutnant* Fürbringer and *Oberleutnant z. S.* Reinhold Saltzwedel all started their careers in UB-I boats and managed to be successful in later commands.

UB-10 and UB-13 lie side-by-side under the protection of a half shelter along the inside of the Zeebrugge Mole. They have been painted with camouflage colours and the typical 'eye' of the Flanders U-boats (TT) ▶

The detached stern section of *UB-10* sits on a railway truck, ready for transport to Flanders (U-Boot-Archiv Cuxhaven)

The bow of *UB-10* (U-boot-Archiv Cuxhaven)

The conning tower of *UB-10* (U-boot-Archiv Cuxhaven)

The stern section of *UB-10* (U-boot-Archiv Cuxhaven)

A UB-I U-boat is dismantled in four large sections for transport towards Flanders (U-boot-Archiv Cuxhaven)

U-boats on the Schelde River: a very rare photo taken in the Hoboken naval yard shows two UB-I boats nearing completion on the slipway. There was a great need for secrecy and a canvas wall had been erected to shield the work (TT)

U-BOATS TRANSPORTED BY RAIL

After the negative experiences with small U-boats, such as was the case with *UB-2* and *UC-11* (see p. 49), the German Admiralty decided in March 1915 to ship the small U-boats by rail to Flanders and reassemble them there in the local shipyards.

The small UB-I and UC-I boats were dismantled after their trials at sea and loaded on several railwaytrucks. The four largest segments, bow, midships, tower and aft sections were transported on 40-ton trucks. The keel and superstructure were easily dismantled so as not to overload the transport. Lifting hooks and exhausts were taken off and battery cells were stacked on smaller trucks which had a 20 ton load capacity. The loading of the trucks took 24 hours to complete in the yard and the unloading almost double that. All parts were covered with tarpaulins to guarantee a certain level of secrecy. Via northern Germany they made their way through Altona and Essen to end up five days later in Flanders.

By the end of March 1915 the Hoboken shipyard had changed into the rallying point for all parts and sections of the UB-I and UC-I boats. After arriving at the yard, the parts were unloaded and assembled by the Antwerp Naval Yard or *Marinewerft Antwerpen*. 840 labourers of the 59th *Württembergischen Armierungsbataillon* were set to work on assembly. Belgian labourers were not allowed to be used due to fear of sabotage and the threat to secrecy.

A UB-I U-boat is being re-assembled in the Hoboken yard (TT)

The engines of these U-boats were delivered by the Schlummberger foundries of Ulm and Mauser of Oberndorf. The main parts were constructed by French prisoners of war, but assembly was enthrusted to German specialists.

On average it took 15 to 20 days to complete a reassembly, after which the U-boat could be launched. Another two to three days had to be added for necessary tests and trials. The appointed crew was kept as long as possible in Germany for thorough schooling. Only when their alotted U-boat had been finished and launched, would they be sent to Belgium.

In the early part of 1915 there were nine U-boats in the Hoboken dockyard. Two were launched by the end of April and one was bombed and damaged by a British aircraft. The six other boats were finished some time later and towed by canalboats toward their final destination: Bruges.

A heavy lift deposits the newly arrived stern of a UB-I boat on the slipway (TT)

Work environment on the Hoboken yard was generally poor, as the German labourers who had originally served on the Eastern front were put on heavy rationing. All 840 were housed in the St. Joris barracks. Their day started at 6.30 am when they were each issued a piece of sausage, bread and black coffee as breakfast. Every third day they had to eat 'heavy' bread which just fell apart after two days because it was made of compressed potato peels. No lunch was issued and the main meal was served at 7 pm and was officially called soup but was just a gruel of liquidised potatoes. Twice a week, on Wednesdays and Sundays, a small piece of meat was added to the gruel. The labourers could add to their diet by buying food at the local canteen which was run by Belgians. Every tenth day the workers were paid their daily 53 Pfennigs, which was usually totally spent in the canteen.[10]

UB-II

Despite its weaknesses, the UB-I type had proven to be a valuable weapon against Allied shipping. The German Admiralty decided to improve on this model and asked the shipyards to design more advanced U-boats. The UB-II type would have a greater surface speed, a larger range and better armament. On 20 April 1915 the U-boat Inspectorate gave the green light to build a series of twelve units, *UB-18* to *UB-23* at Blohm & Voss and *UB-24* to *UB-29* at the AG Weser yard. Displacement had increased to 263 BRT on the surface, a length of 36.13 m, a width of 4.36 m and a draught of 3.7 m. This also meant that construction time increased to eight months per unit and the new fleet would not be ready before the end of 1915.

The UB-II type had a double propulsion consisting of two 140 HP dieselengines (Körting, Daimler or Benz) and two Siemens-Schuckert electric engines. They gave the U-boat a surface speed of 9,15 knots and submerged 5,81 knots. The hull was single and a second periscope was added. On the bow a netcutter and anti-minecables (*Minenabweiser*) had been

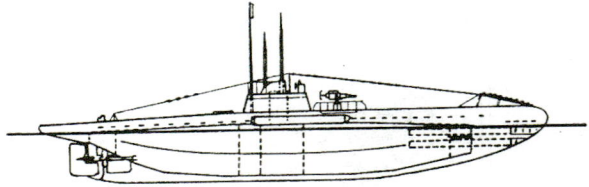

Profile of a UB-II boat

mounted, which had to keep the superstructure free of entanglement. There was a 29 ton fuel supply and 112 battery cells fed the hungry electric engines. Armament consisted of two 50 cm bow torpedo tubes with a supply of four torpedos. On deck, just in front of the tower, a 5 cm- or 8.8 cm deckgun was added with a supply of 120 shells. Commanders appeared to be satisfied with the diving speed of the UB-II type: in 30 seconds it could disappear from view and reach a test depth of 50 m. Complement consisted of one officer and 22 men.

By the middle of 1915 it was realised that the war would certainly outlast 1916, which forced the U-boat Inspectorate to search for new shipyards to build

U-boats on Flemish canals: a UB-I-Boat is transported on a floating dock, pulled by two steam tugs in the direction of Bruges (TT)

A UB-II class submarine enters the lock at Zeebrugge (TT)

UB-24 and another UB-II class submarine lie as training ships in Eckernförde (TT)

more U-boats. On 22 July 1915 the Reiherstiegwerft in Hamburg received the order for building the next series of twelve U-boats, *UB-30* to *UB-41*. At the end of July AG Weser would be ordered to build *UB-41* to *UB-47*. The UB-II boats would mainly operate out of bases in northern Germany and Flanders.

On 16 February 1916 *UB-18* entered Zeebrugge as the first UB-II type submarine. *UB-19, UB-29* and *UB-26* followed suit in March. The arrival of this new type meant a serious change in results for the Flanders Flotilla. For almost a year they had to make do with the small UB-I types which could undertake little action in the area to the west of the Dover Straits. Priority now went out to employing the UB-II boats in attacks on enemy troop transports which were arriving in the French part of the Channel. The UB-II had a maximum range of 6.650 miles with a surface cruising speed of 5 knots. Its theatre of operations had now been broadened to the Scottish coast and the western part of the Channel. The range submerged was still only 45 miles with a top speed of 5.8 knots.

In the month preceding the Battle of Jutland (31 May and 1 June 1916) the U-boats of the Flanders Flotilla were partly engaged in harassing the Royal Navy so as to try to subdue its dominance of the sea. In theory it was to give the German High Seas Fleet even chances of success. The UB-II boats made attacks on the harbours of Great Yarmouth and Lowestoft to entice the surface ships out of port. But it did not have the desired effect.

By March 1917 nine UB-II boats were based in Flanders: *UB-18, UB-20, UB-23, UB-31, UB-32, UB-36, UB-38, UB-39* and *UB-40. UB-33* was added to the fleet in October 1917. In the first three months of 1917 UB-II boats were able to sink 158.123 BRT in enemy shipping at the cost of just one U-boat, *UB-37. UB-32* proved to be the most successful by sinking 16 ships (38.054

The crew of a stranded UB-II class submarine calmly await the falling of the tide (Dirk Termote)

Stamping, rolling, bobbing like a cork and an atmosphere of constant moisture. Life on board a submarine was not for the faint-hearted (TT)

BRT) in just three patrols. The period from May to July 1917 was a dark one as four UB-II boats, *UB-39*, *UB-36*, *UB-20* and *UB-27*, were lost. On 10 June 1917 *UB-32* was the first U-boat to encounter the new Allied anti-submarine system: the convoy. *UB-32* would fall victim to a depth charge attack in September of the same year. The high losses were mainly due to the efficiency of the Allied patrol vessels, aircraft and airships. Use of depth charges, mines as well as armament on 90% of the merchantmen had a big influence in losses and in 1918 *UB-31* and *UB-33* were also lost.

Even though the UB-II type had been built with many improvements, it still proved to be a difficult U-boat to handle in stormy weather. Werner Fürbringer, commander of *UB-39*, experienced difficult circumstances when his U-boat was in the western area of the Channel and got caught in a hurricane which appeared out of nowhere and remained in the area for 24 hours. He let his U-boat dive to the safety of 40 m, but even at this depth the middle-sized U-boat was not fit for the large swell. As he had experienced earlier on in his career with *UB-2*, *UB-39* was similarly tossed around like a cork. After 12 hours they had to surface to replenish the air and were confronted by a monstrous sea. Fürbringer and the watchman had to be secured to the tower so as not to be swept overboard. Both compasses were put out of action and the U-boat could only cruise on the electric engines because the diesels only functioned with an open hatch to draw in fresh air. When a merchant vessel was spotted, they did dare not go into battle because *UB-39* was simply sucked passed their prey by the stormy circumstances. After sighting another cargo ship, the gun crew quickly went to their action stations. But a freak wave broke over the bow and landed on the 8.8 cm gun, washing away the entire gun crew of whom only one could be saved.

UB-III

Due to larger distances, more Allied countermeasures and the losses which the U-boatfleet was suffering, the need came up to build a larger type of U-boat at a quicker production rate. In the spring of 1916 the U-boat Inspectorate ordered the newly designed UB-III type. This was a better and more agile boat than the pre-war U-type and had a displacement of 516 BRT, which was 300 tons less. Because of its agility, the UB-III also managed to be totally submerged in just 30 seconds and reach a testdepth of 50 m.

The first series of the UB-III, *UB-48* to *UB-53*, were built by Blohm & Voss between January and March 1917. In comparison with the construction time of the U-type, the six months for the UB-III boats proved to be a record. In total 89 UB-III type boats were built for the Imperial Navy and consisted of *UB-48* to *UB-132*, *UB-142*, *UB-143*, *UB-148* and *UB-149*.

The exterior of the U-boat had evolved rapidly in just over two years. A UB-III type submarine had a length of 55.3 m, a width of 5.8 m and a draught of 3.7 m. It could obtain a maximum speed of 13.5 knots

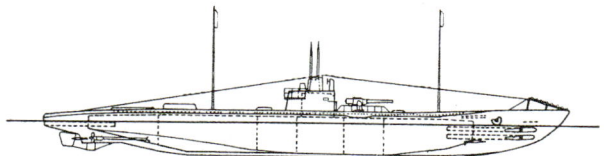

Profile of a UB-III class submarine

on the surface, driven by two 550 HP six-cylinder diesel engines. For submerged cruising two Siemens-Schuckert electric engines gave it a speed of 7.5 knots. The UB-III boat fell into the category of a coastal patrol submarine, but was able to cover a range of 9,000 miles at an average speed of 8 knots on the surface. The battery supply was only sufficient enough to give it a range of 55 miles at 4 knots speed below the surface. This new type of U-boat was capable of reaching the major approaches to the British Isles from German bases. The UB-III type was capable of operating in the Irish Sea, the North Channel, St. George's Channel, the Bristol Channel, Cornwall and the Western Approaches.

By 1918, U-boats had evolved to heavily fortified ships of war: a U-cruiser and a UB-III class submarine lie side-by-side in Helgoland Harbour (TT)

The crew man their 10.5 cm deck gun on a UB-III boat (TT)

Three sailors pose in the forward tubes of a UB-III submarine (U-boot-Archiv Cuxhaven)

Its armament was formidable and consisted of five 50 cm torpedo tubes, four in the bow and one aft, with a supply of ten torpedoes. On deck, in front of the tower, a deckgun of the 8.8 or 10.5 cm calibre was fitted, with a supply of 160 shells stowed above and below deck. Complement consisted of three officers and 31 men.

UB-54 was the first UB-III type to be added to the *U-Flottille Flandern* on 8 August 1917. Two weeks later it torpedoed and sank the Q-ship *Vala* and the cargovessel *SS Friga* in the Western Approaches. Throughout 1917 there were 20 UB-III types active in the North Sea and eight of these U-boats had joined the Flanders Flotilla: *UB-54, UB-55, UB-56, UB-57, UB-58, UB-59, UB-80* and *UB-81* whilst the 12 others were based in ports in Germany. *UB-57* proved to be the most successful UB-III and managed to sink 17 ships (43.561 BRT) in five patrols.

In 1918 another 17 UB-III boats entered the Flemish bases: *UB-74, UB-78, UB-88, UB-103, UB-104, UB-106, UB-107, UB-108, UB-109, UB-110, UB-111, UB-112, UB-113, UB-114, UB-115, UB-116* and *UB-117*. All the other numbers left for the Mediterranean, the Baltic and the German North Sea ports.

They had been introduced to a period of the war where it had become difficult to do damage to Allied shipping, mainly because of the organisation of coastal convoys. The eastern entrance of the Channel was guarded much closer, forcing the larger U-boats to take the northern route, via Scotland, to reach the Irish Sea.

In the end the Flanders Flotilla would suffer gravely with the loss of 16 UB-III type submarines: *UB-54, UB-55, UB-56, UB-57, UB-58, UB-74, UB-81, UB-103, UB-104, UB-107, UB-108, UB-109, UB-110, UB-113, UB-115* and *UB-116*.

UB-70 during excercises in home waters. On the bow are the net cutter and erected radio mast (U-boot-Archiv Cuxhaven)

A UB-III boat at full speed. Forward of the tower stands her 8.8 cm deck gun (Dirk Termote)

MINELAYERS

From the start of the war a blockade against Germany's supply routes was imposed by the Royal Navy. Neither the actions of the High Seas Fleet and their own commerce raiders in foreign waters could do enough damage to Britain and its Allies to force it to stop the blockade. The spectacular results which the U-boats achieved against warships and the torpedoing of numerous merchant vessels at the end of 1914 made the belief grow in Germany in the U-boat as the ultimate weapon of salvation. Admiral Hugo von Pohl, commander-in-chief of the Imperial Navy, declared the seas around the British Isles and Ireland to a warzone. In the early period of the war, ships were boarded and documents were checked before sinking them, but later on they were just torpedoed on sight.

British propaganda against the German mining offensive. Mines were portrayed as cowardly and unfair weapons (TT)

The sinking of *RMS Lusitania*, on 7 May 1915, in which a large number of civilians were drowned, provoked heavy protest from the United States against the German 'barbarities' at sea. So as not to provoke the United States too much, the German Admiralty had to change its tactics at sea and revert to the sea mine as a possible weapon.

From the beginning of the war the navies of both nations had laid out defensive minefields to protect homewaters. Mineclear passages in the fields were created to ensure the safety of their own vessels. Offensive minelaying operations had been limited from the start. On 5 August 1914 a desperate attempt had been made by the auxiliary minelayer *SS Königin Luise* to lay 180 mines off the Thames Estuary and Northhinder. *SS Königin Luise* was sunk by the light cruiser *HMS Amphion*, but the next day the cruiser struck her mines and sank after two explosions with the loss of 169 men and 18 German prisoners. In the same month the mine cruisers *SMS Albatross* and *SMS Nautilus* laid several hundred mines off the Tyne and Humber estuaries, but without much result. Further plans to engage surface ships in minelaying operations were immediately cancelled after the disastrous loss of four torpedo boats. *S-115*, *S-117*, *S-118* and *S-119* of the *7e Torpedo-Halbflottille*, which were on their way to lay mines in the Thames Estuary on 17 October 1914. They were intercepted by a superior force of British warships and totally destroyed in what was known as the battle of Texel.

Even though the surface minelaying operations suffered disastrous results, the German Admiralty still thought it possible to wage an 'invisible' mine warfare. This chance presented itself with the occupation of the Flemish ports.

UC-I

On 8 August 1914, two months before the Flemish coast succumbed to the German onslaught, the naval arm had ordered the U-boat Inspectorate to build coastal patrol submarines with torpedo tubes and the capacity to carry mines.

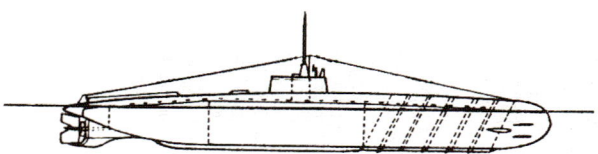

Profile of a UC-I type minelayer

The newly developed type, the UC-I, had a length of 33.99 m, a width of 3.15 m and a draught of 3.04 m. Its displacement of 168 BRT could be compared with the UB-I type. Fifteen units of the UC-I type were built, the series *UC-1* to *UC-10* by the Vulkan yard in Hamburg and *UC-11* to *UC-15* by AG Weser in Bremen. It was a novel U-boat design. The aft section and tower matched the UB-I type, but the bow had a totally different construction. The bow had been fitted with six vertical shafts measuring 1 m in diameter and providing room for two mines placed above each other. The shafts were vertical with a forward slant so that the mines could drop out easily whilst the U-boat slowly made its way forward. The loss of buoyancy which naturally followed the release of the mines was adjusted by filling compensation tanks between the shafts. It was therefore possible to drop the mines without breaking trim and shooting to the surface. Being one-hulled boats, the UC-I type had the cargo

Two UC-I boats lie mcored in the Small Merchantdock in Bruges (TT)

Model of a UC-I type submarine (International Maritime Museum, Hamburg) ▼

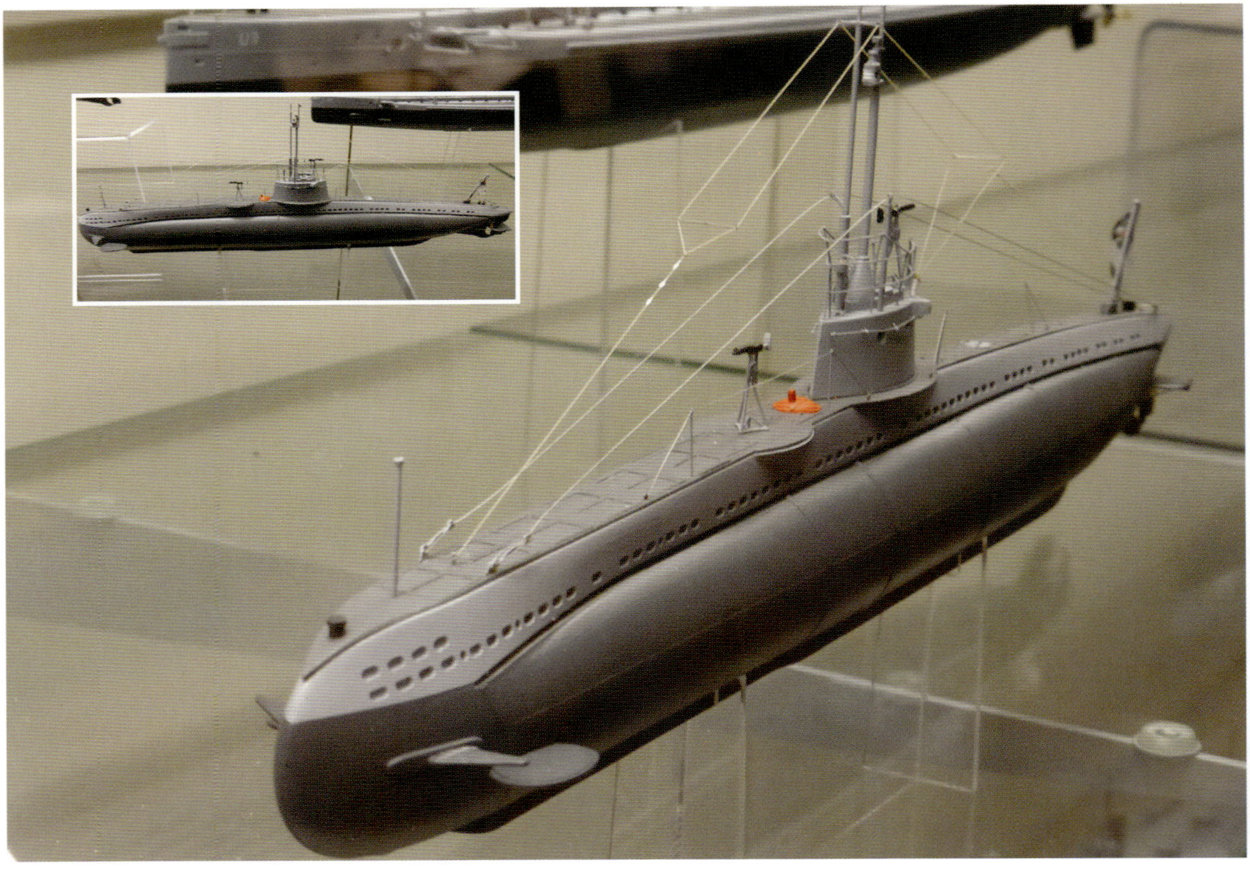

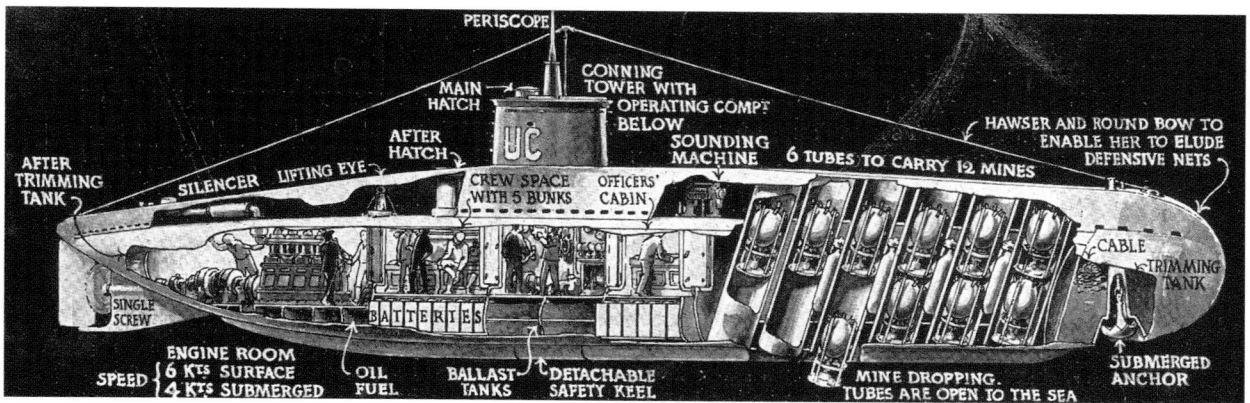

Simplified British description of a minelayer (The Sphere)

of mines stored outside her pressure hull. This meant that the mines permanently remained submerged and could not be reached from within. Necessary depth settings had to be made before leaving port. A UC-I boat could only lay mines in a pre-designated area where the depth was known. It would be out of the question to change to a different target area during a voyage, unless it had exactly same depth as the previous area. Laying mines was a work of enormous precision and demanded skill from the captain. They only could have effect if they were dropped in a fairway or near the entrance of a harbour. Navigation was of utmost importance to follow the planned course and tides had to be taken into account. Mines would be dropped at low tide so as they would remain below the surface and would not be observed too quickly.

In the first model of the UC-type it was not possible to provide torpedo tubes because of its small dimensions. But engineers weer soon looking at plans to combine a UC-I with a UB-I type U-boat in October 1915. UC-I boats did not have any offensive weapons besides a deck-mounted machine gun and were quite vulnerable vessels. They were driven by a single screw and a 90 HP diesel engine gave it a maximum speed of 6.5 knots on the surface. The 3-ton diesel supply gave her a range of 800 miles. She only had a range of 45 miles at a speed of 5 knots when using the Siemens-Schuckert electric engine for submerged cruising. Diving speed was remarkable, she could be totally submerged in 22 seconds and reach a test depth of 50 m. For the crew, life on board was even harder than on the UB-I boats as one officer and 13 crew had to make do with living quarters in the stern and central area only. The former bow was totally occupied by the mineshafts and remained inaccessible throughout a voyage. Just forward of the command area was a small space alotted to a radio-installation above which was placed a telescopic, wooden radio mast. Regular communication with the base was of importance because the survival of the U-boat and its crew depended mainly on its propulsion system which would quite often fail. As with the UB-I type U-boat, one of the main weaknesses of the UC-I was that the batteries only gave an hour of power to the electric engine when the diesel would not function. If this would fail, the U-boat would drift helplessly and could not defend itself against enemy vessels. Pigeons were brought along in the early part of the war as a primitive method of communications, but proved not to be so reliable at sea when faraway from home. Even though the UC-I boat had many mechanical problems it still proved to be well suited for the southern North Sea.

UC-11 entered Zeebrugge on 26 May 1915 as the first minelaying submarine. Two days later she made history as the first U-boat to lay a minefield in open sea. The results not only surprised the British but also the High Command of the Flanders U-boat Flotilla. Twelve mines lay unnoticed near the South Goodwin lightship. In the following three weeks they damaged the destroyer *HMS Mohawk* and sunk two torpedo boats, a patrolship and two cargo vessels. Because of these successes the UC-I type submarine would become a true *Flandernboot* and immediately an order was placed to have all the other boats brought over to strengthen the Flotilla. Not much later *UC-1, UC-2, UC-3, UC-5, UC-6, UC-7* and *UC-9* were put on railwaytrucks and transported to Belgium. *UC-4* was assigned to the *U-Flottille Kurland* and *UC-8* served

Two seamen stand on the bow of their UC-I type boat ready to moor in the Zeebrugge lock (TT)

as a training vessel in the Baltic, but both would be assigned to the Flanders Flotilla by winter time. *UC-12*, *UC-13* and *UC-15* were permanently stationed in the Mediterranean, with *UC-14* only operating in the Adriatic until early 1917, after which she would be transported to Belgium.

UC-minelayers had to work in all kinds of circumstances and face big risks in enemy territory. Besides the threat of enemy attacks, there was the constant possibility of engine failure which put heavy physical and psychological pressure on its crew. Tasks on a minelayer were often monotonous and seemingly unrewarding: leave port, lay mines and return. In the interim period the enemy would sweep the mines all or partially after which the same modus operandi would be undertaken. Weeks and even months could go by before a ship hit a mine and often it was not known to which U-boat it could be credited to. Many questions played in the captain's mind: were the mines set to a good depth? Were they discovered too early? Did I drop them in the fairway or just beside it? Was there a mechanism defect? Had corrosion disrupted the release gear? The threat of previous mines not being swept in an area was also very real. Each UC-I boat usually had its own area of operations to which it would return, but faced the danger of running into its own minefields. The British were alerted of this manner of operating and left some German mines unswept to trap a returning U-boat. This cunning scheme was the reason for the sinking of *UC-11* on 26 June 1918 near the Sunk light vessel, in the Thames Estuary.[11]

The area of operation of these minelayers lay not more than one day sailing from their bases. It stretched from the Flemish coast up to Yarmouth on the British east coast and westerly to the Dover Straits. Their main activities were in the area off Dover known as the Downs and the Estuary of the Thames*.

UC-2, sunk in July 1915, would be the first UC-I type submarine lost whilst on patrol. Its sinking would also inform the Royal Navy of the source of the mysterious minefields which had been popping up everywhere during the hours of darkness. On 2 July *UC-2* had been accidently rammed and sunk by a cargo ship. After the wreck was located and dived on by Chatham dockyard divers it was clear that *UC-2* had run into one of its own mines which had blasted off its stern.

Even though the UC-I type was vulnerable and had no secondary armament, this small flotilla managed to make 42 minelaying missions up to September 1915. Twenty-five enemy ships were damaged or sunk in 39 minefields. *UC-7* was the most successful and destroyed a total of 14.501 BRT in shipping. Pressure increased on commanders of the small minelayers from August. After the loss of American lives with the

---

* This was the anchorage off Dover.

sinking of *SS Arabic* by *U-24*, the Allies declared the unannounced torpedoing of defenceless ships as a barbarous way to wage a war. To calm down heated international feelings the U- and UB-boats had to operate more cautiously. Pressure increased on the commanders of the minelayers to book more results in the war against enemy shipping. During October 1915 the Fleet lost *UC-9* and *UC-8* got stranded and interned in Dutch waters. From the autumn of 1915 until the spring of 1916, *UC-1, UC-3* and *UC-5* operated in the triangle of the Sunk, Kentish Knock and Galloper areas. *UC-6, UC-7* and *UC-10* laid mines in the shipping routes to the north of the Thames up to the Humber. During this period 52 enemy and 23 neutral ships were sunk, amounting to a total of 154.176 BRT. *UC-6* was the most successful, sinking 38.946 BRT. On 24 March 1916 *UB-29* torpedoed and damaged the cross-channel ferry *SS Sussex* on which more American lives were lost. The United States issued an ultimatum to Germany after which the Admiralty had no choice but to place the U- and UB-boats as support vessels of the High Seas Fleet. A new series of minelayers was developed, the UE-I types (amongst them *U-71* to *U-80*) to operate in more northern waters around the British Isles. The UC-I boats of the Flanders Flotilla continued their operations unperturbed, but losses were suffered.

UC-5 was captured by the Royal Navy when it grounded on the Shipwash. *UC-3, UC-7* and *UC-10* disappeared and were presumed lost with all hands. Between May and August 1916 they had been able to destroy 17 ships, a total of 27.367 BRT. The fleet had almost been bled dry in 1917 and only two U-boats, *UC-4* and *UC-11*, remained. The demand for minelayers was big and *UC-14* was shipped from the Adriatic to Belgium. *UC-14* would be lost to a mine only nine months later. In 1918 *UC-11* also was lost, leaving *UC-4* as the only surviving U-boat of the UC-I minelayers. The chart with losses obviously shows that 5 UC-I types were lost between Dover and Yarmouth and five others near to Walcheren, on the Dutch coast. Even though historical sources blame the losses of most UC-I types to detonation of their own mines, present day research of the wrecks contests this theory. Most of the surveyed UC-I type wrecks were sunk on their return voyages as all wrecks were void of mines.

The results of the UC-I minelayers were not to be ignored. This small unit managed to sink 172 merchant- and fishing vessels (320.522 BRT) as well as 112 warships. The minelayer had made its name and its success would lead to the creation of a U-boat which was better equipped for operating in the southern North Sea: the UC-II type.

Four UC-I boats lie alongside their flotilla ship (possibly the trawler SMS Frigg) in Bruges Harbour. All crewmen stand to attention, to great Kaiser Wilhelm II, who is steaming past on the yacht. The emperor had just presented *Oberleutnant z. S.* Steinbrinck with the *Pour le Mérite* (Jörn Jensen)

THE SINKING OF UC-2 AND THE SOLVING OF THE MINE-MYSTERY

In the early hours of the morning of 1 June 1915, the destroyer *HMS Mohawk* was mined 6 miles to the northeast of Dover. She could be saved but had suffered heavy damages to the forecastle. The origin of the mine and the field were a total mystery for the Dover Patrol. No enemy vessels had been sighted and neither had British mines been laid. The solution presented itself a month later on the east coast in which *UC-2* was involved. The appearance of mines and the sinking and the study of a German minelayer brought about a change in British submarine design. Up to now the Royal Navy was convinced that the minefields which had started to appear on the east coast and in the Thames Estuary were the work of German surface craft.

Oberleutnant z. S. Karl Mey took command of *UC-2* on 17 May 1915 and brought her a month later to Zeebrugge. During her first and only minelaying operation *UC-2* lay in the Stanford Channel, off Lowestoft, on 2nd July. The previous day Mey had laid a small minefield near Great Yarmouth. On the same day, around 14h50, the cargo ship *SS Cottingham*, on its way from Calais to Leith, hit a submerged obstruction. Captain Colin Mitchell felt a heavy bump, first to starboard, then to port and eventually in the middle of the bow area. The lookouts observed a large rush of air, accompanied by a strong smell of gas and a large oilslick on the surface. The captain radioed to a nearby patrol vessel and told them of the strong possibility that they had hit a U-boat. Minesweepers came on site and set out a sweep with cables. Not long after they snagged an obstruction, buoyed it and kept watch on the location. At 21h40 a heavy underwater explosion was detected. The Admiralty decided to send in divers as soon as possible to search for the sunken U-boat. By the morning of 3rd July, chief diver Dusty Miller descended along the shotline to the target. At 14 metres depth he touched bottom but could not distinguish much because of the limited visibility. But even through the murky circumstances he managed to identify the tower of the U-boat. It was definitely *UC-2* and he continued his path toward the bow. About 3 m in front of the tower he nearly fell into a deep gash which went right through the pressure hull and had been caused by the bow of *SS Cottingham*. After the gash Miller stumbled upon the mineshafts of which three still contained a mine each. It would be the first time someone from the Royal Navy would lay eyes upon a minelayer. *UC-2* lay at an angle of 45° to starboard and the curve of the hull made it a difficult task for the diver to

After *UC-5* had been captured by the British, the Admiralty was given idea of the workings of a minelayer (Dirk Termote)

keep a grip. After some difficulties he managed to reach the stern, which had been totally severed from the front part about 4 m abaft the tower. Miller could glance into the opening, towards the command area of the submarine. Severed cables and wiring hung down and started to sway up and down with the increasing tide. Miller wanted to get inside to get a closer look. The sharp edges of the thorn steel threatened to cut his airhose, but in the end he managed to open a watertight door and reach the command area. Miller was surprised to find no bodies of the crew. He had a good look at the periscope and on the bottom he spotted a metal box. Miller had found paydirt as the chest contained several books, which contained secret codes as well as a High Seas Fleet signal book. Amongst the books was also a chart which showed the location of the recently laid minefield.

It was the secondary explosion which the patrol vessels had witnessed which had damaged the stern section. After *SS Cottingham* had struck *UC-2* in front of the conning tower, the U-boat had sunk to the bottom, near one of its own mines. The sweep set out by the minesweepers had dragged one of the mines closer to *UC-2* and subsequently detonated it later on. The bodies of Mey and the rest of his crew were all found in the stern section. After the collision with *SS Cottingham* they had managed to escape to the engine room where they were trapped and drowned by the water which flooded the last compartment.[12]

On 13 July 1915 all diving operations ceased and commanding Admiral Oliver asked to blow up the remains of the U-boat. Captain Ellison, in charge at Lowestoft, was against this idea and suggested to raise the wreck to study the construction of the shafts in more detail on land. The Admiralty was not interested and ordered him to blow up the wreck with guncotton instead of an explosive paravane. Ellison persisted and wrote a letter to Admiral William Hall on 8 August underlining the importance of recovering the wreck. Hall did not show any interest either and was curt with Ellison. In the end Ellison had to fold and ordered 25 kg of explosives placed in the tower and within two shafts. The explosion decimated *UC-2* and only a mangled wreck remained on site.[13]

The information obtained from the site of *UC-2* had big consequences. Everybody in the fleet received the latest German codes and were able to decipher their communications. The mine system was to be copied in six submarines of the E-Class which were still under construction. Twenty vertical shafts were fitted in the submarines *E-24*, *E-34*, *E-41*, *E-45*, *E-46* and *E-51* instead of torpedotubes amidships.[14] By the spring of 1916 it was possible for the Royal Navy to also wage an invisible war with mines at the doorstep of Germany's bases.

Sketch of the wreck of *UC-2*, drawn by commander Ballard of *HMS Halcyon*. The British would be confronted with a U-boat-minelayer for the first time (Grant).

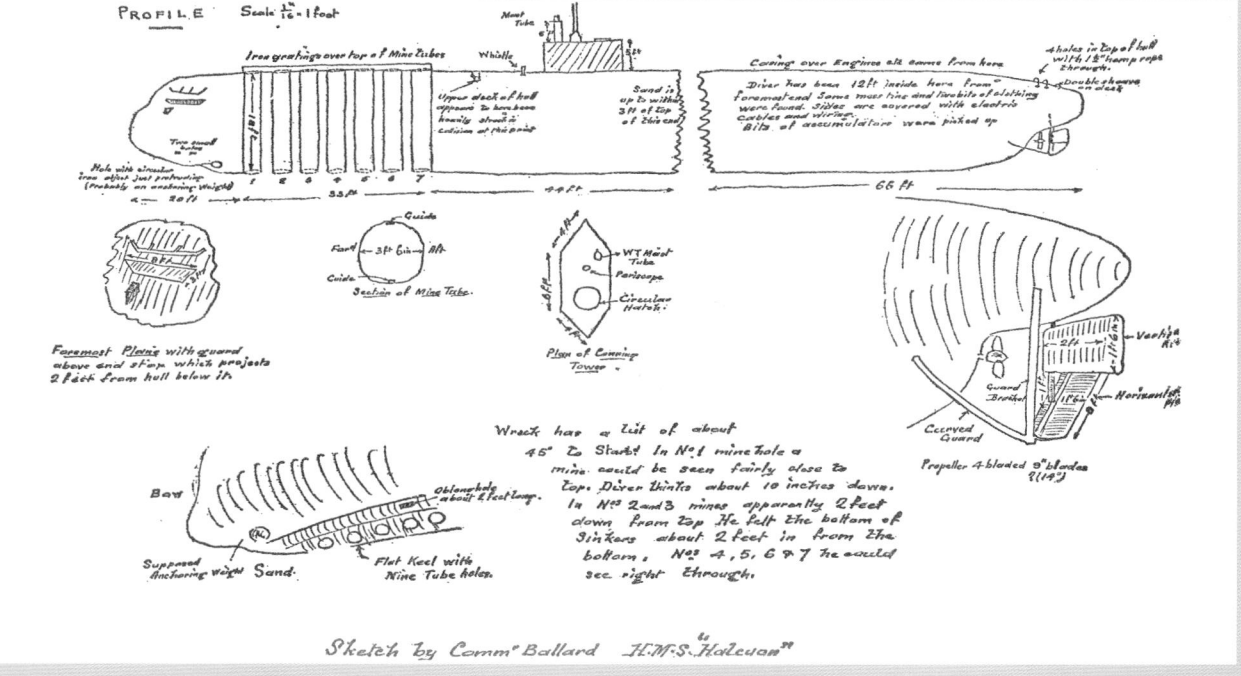

UC-II

Even though the UC-I type was quite successful in most of its mining operations, many captains still remained unhappy about her faults. *Oberleutnant z. S.* Matthias Graf von Schmettow, commander of UC-6, wrote in his *Kriegstagebuch** on 8 November 1915 about how frustrating it was to have an enemy troopship in the crosshairs of his optics at a distance of just a mile and have to let it just sail by because one did not have the armament to attack. His patience would be rewarded less than a year later when he was posted to the newly built *UC-26* on 18 July 1916. The UC-II type would be the most efficient submarine design produced during the First World War.

The Reichsmarineamt issued an order to the U-boat Inspectorate on 28 August 1915 to start construction of the improved minelayer. Blohm & Voss was given the series *UC-16* to *UC-24* and AG Vulkan in Hamburg built the following series, *UC-25* to *UC-33*. The new minelayer had a displacement of 417 BRT surfaced and 511 BRT below the waves, a length of 52.7 m, a width of 5.2 m and a draught of 3.7 m. This double-hulled submarine could reach a test depth of 50 metres. Construction time would take less than eight months per U-boat.

The bow, which was still designed with six vertical shafts, had been heightened to provide room for 18 mines of the type UC/200. The top sides of the shafts were covered with hinged, iron frames and the mines were partly in dry storage which made it possible to arrange depth settings from within the submarine.

---
* KTB or war diary.

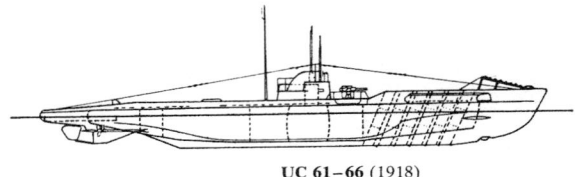

Profile of a UC-II type submarine

UC-II class submarine, type n° UC-25 to UC-33 (Jörn Jensen)

On both sides of the heightened bow were two 50 cm torpedo tubes, each charged with one torpedo. Abaft the engineroom was the stern torpedo room provided with one tube and a supply of five torpedoes. On deck, in front of the tower and just abaft the mineshafts was an 8.8 cm canon with a supply of 133 shells.

Not only had there been an improvement in the armament, but the UC-II type was given double propulsion with two 500 HP six-cylinder diesel engines which gave her a surface speed of 11,5 knots. Two 230 HP electric engines gave her a cruising speed of 7 knots submerged. Maximum range had increased to 9,400 miles on the surface at an average speed of 7 knots and 54 miles at a speed of 4 knots under water.

A UC-II class submarine in dazzle paint (Dirk Termote)

Even with its high superstructure, the UC-II managed to dive at a speed of 35 to 40 seconds and it proved to be a remarkable U-boat. It had a complement of three officers and 23 men.

The first UC-II type minelayers were available during the spring which also was a period when the U-boat campaign had very much quietened down. The U-boat Inspectorate already knew what would be at stake and in the autumn of 1915 had already ordered 15 extra units: *UC-34* to *UC-48* were being constructed at three different yards. The Naval Command wanted a production of *UC*-boats which would supercede the losses of 1916. By October 1916 two new shipyards had to be engaged to build 31 extra UC-II types. *UC-49* to *UC-54* were being built by Germaniawerft Kiel, the Kaiserliche Werft Danzig had *UC-55* to *UC-60* and AG Weser was committed to *UC-61* to *UC-64*. Blohm & Voss took on *UC-65* to *UC-73* and AG Vulkan the final series of *UC-74* to *UC-79*. Blohm & Voss proved to be the best in answering the demand of building multiple series, which shortened the construction period by a month. Between October 1916 and January 1917 27 UC-II boats came *Frontreif*[*] from the training schools and were sent to three different

[*] Literally, 'Ripe for the front'. This meant that the U-boat and its crew were ready and trained for battle.

View from the tower on the gun platform, which is being flooded by a wave (Dirk Termote)

A misty November morning 1916 in Bruges Harbour. Two UB-I boats lie alongside a UC-II type minelayer with open torpedo tube. Behind them lies a captured mail boat, which has been used as a depot ship. (Jörn Jensen)

A UC-II boat at sea. Abaft the tower lies the up-ended dinghy, tied down to the deck (TT)

theatres of war. A total of eight boats, *UC-16* to *UC-19*, *UC-21*, *UC-26*, *UC-46* and *UC-47* were sent to Flanders. Later on their numbers were strengthened by four more UC-II boats. Their area of operation was mostly situated in the southwestern approaches to the Channel, with the French Atlantic ports such as Cherbourg, Dieppe and Brest and on the British side Plymouth, Portland, Falmouth and the entrance to the Bristol Channel being targeted. The harbours of Cork and Waterford, in the southern part of Ireland, were also being mined. Between October 1916 and January 1917 a total of 45 fields of 219 mines had been laid successfully. On the east coast this numbered almost double with 83 fields and 734 mines. During this period it was *Oberleutnant z. S.* Graf von Schmettow, commander of *UC-26*, who proved to be the most successful in his missions. In just three months his U-boat was responsible for sinking 37.598 BRT in shipping.

But it would be *UC-65*, under command of *Oberleutnant z. S.* Otto Steinbrinck, which would reach a record of 60.159 tons of shipping sunk in early April 1917. But during this period four UC-II boats, *UC-39*, *UC-46*, *UC-18* and *UC-68* were lost with their seasoned crews. Despite the losses of numerous UC- and UB-boats, the tonnage of British shipping being sunk kept on rising by the middle of 1917. Mines of *UC-61* had sunk the French cruiser *Kleber* off Brest and *UC-65* torpedoed and sank the British cruiser HMS *Ariadne* off the Royal Sovereign light vessel.

But, even with the mounting monthly losses in ships and the possibility that Great Britain stood on the verge of famine, it refused to capitulate to Germany. The declaration of war by the United States on 6 April 1917 also had an influence in this decision. With America entering the war, an enormous fleet joined in to fight the U-boats in all kinds of ways. *UC-26* and *UC-36* were lost in May 1917 and *UC-61* was accidently beached on the French coast and had to be blown up. The organisation of shipping in convoys in the Western Approaches made it almost impossible for a U-boat to achieve much success and they started to hunt for single ships in the Channel. The demand for more minelaying submarines increased with the growing fleet of minesweepers in British waters. In 1916 the Royal Navy cleared about 180 mines per month. In 1917 this amount had almost doubled to 355 on a monthly rate. But it was not a job without danger: in the last half of 1916 the British lost 35 minesweepers and in the early part of 1917 this had risen to 84 sunk.

The UC-boats suffered heavy losses because they had to operate close to shore. In 1917 a total of nine UC-II type U-boats failed to return: *UC-16*, *UC-21*, *UC-38*, *UC-47*, *UC-51*, *UC-62*, *UC-63*, *UC-65* and *UC-69*. In the first half of 1918 a further six were lost, *UC-48* and *UC-56* being interned in Spain, *UC-50*,

UC-75, *UC-78* and *UC-64* being lost at sea. In the second half of 1918 *UC-49* and *UC-70* failed to return from their patrols. By 20 October 1918 there remained only three UC-II boats in the Bruges base. *UC-17*, *UC-31* and *UC-71* were ordered back to Germany and stationed with the 1st U-boat flotilla in Helgoland.

The UC-II had been an improved version of the UC-I and proved to be one of the best submarine designs of the war. It combined all necessary offensive weapons in a single vessel: torpedoes, mines and a deck gun. It also had a good range and satisfactory surface speed.

Even though it was a well designed war machine, complaints came in about its agility and the general conditions on board. Due to the large superstructure on the bow, necessary to house the extra mines and the twin torpedo tubes, the U-boat would prove to be unstable and difficult to submerge in conditions which exceeded force 5. In a choppy sea the waves would crash into the bow and tower which made it very wet and uncomfortable for the watchkeepers. Even with calm seas in wintertime the spray would hinder a steady watch. Gun crews had problems keeping their footing around the 8.8 cm gun during a heavy swell, let alone hit a moving target. Many illnesses, such as reumatism and facial neuralgia, were caused by cold draughts within the U-boat.[15] These discomforts would be tackled in small changes to a new design: the UC-III.

UC-III

As the UC-III type was developed at a very late stage of the war, none of the series saw any action. It was an improved version of the UC-II, so it is still worth having a closer look at this vessel.

By the end of 1917 the U-boat Inspectorate ordered 43 UC-III type submarines with the Kaiserliche Werft Danzig, AG Weser and Blohm & Voss. None of them every reached the status of *Frontreif*. The unfinished *UC-80* to *UC-89* were demolished on the slipways and *UC-106* to *UC-114* were launched, but after the Armistice went to the Allies without engines. *UC-115* and *UC-138* were half finished and dismantled in their yard. The UC-III had the same overall characteristics as the *UC*-II, only its silhouette was slightly different. The bow of the UC-III was more stretched out towards the front, lowered and on frontdeck level reached the same height as the base of the tower. The bow torpedo tubes were moved to the middle, to the sides of the tower. The gun platform had been widened and there was enough room for a 10.5 cm gun. Because the bow had been lowered, only 14 mines could be carried, but the U-boat seemed much more stable in a heavy sea state. The fact that the 3-ton torpedo tubes were located in the centre gave the U-boat more stability. Even in quite rough circumstances the gun platform would remain dry. There were larger diesel tanks giving a higher supply of fuel and letting the U-boat reach up to 10,000 miles on a single voyage at an average speed of 7 knots. Dive depth was now 75 m.

The better-developed UC-III type was too late to be of any use and saw little action. She was much more stable at sea than the UC-II, as torpedo tubes had been shifted amidships (WZ Bilddienst)

TECHNICAL ANALYSIS

The U-boat had evolved rapidly during a short period of time from an unimportant vessel to an infamous weapon which brought Britain almost to the verge of surrender. It also changed the way of thinking and the manner in which battles were fought at sea. Large battleships were not invincible anymore and neither did they dominate every sea battle. The submarine is automatically associated with a vessel that only moves below the surface and is armed with just torpedoes. We have learnt that U-boats mainly had to cruise on the surface and only dived when attacking or being attacked. Torpedoes represented only a small part of its offensive arsenal, because mines and the deck gun caused many successful losses to enemy shipping. Structurally and technically the U-boat was a well-thought of machine and a lot can be said about its functions. For the technical descriptions, the publications of engineer Hans Techel and Julius Küster were excellent. During the war British intelligence had built up an enormous knowledge concerning all different aspects of its enemy. The survey reports written by the Royal Navy concerning sunken U-boats, the discovery of technical manuals and the interrogation reports of prisoners proved to be of great value. The work of Norman Friedman summarises the extensive knowledge about U-boats which the British had amassed up to 1918. The interrogation reports of prisoners held in the National Archives and the technical files in the Militärarchiv of Freiburg gave insights in the technical details of the workings of a U-boat.

STRUCTURE OF A U-BOAT

HULL, PRESSURE TANKS AND RUDDERS

The submarine's design is basically that of a cylindrical body tapering towards each end. In this steel tube are contained all necessary parts for steerage, navigation and accommodation. When submerged, this body, called the pressure hull, has to be strong enough to resist the surrounding water pressure. The hull had a thickness between 9 and 12.5 mm and was tested to a depth of 60 m. To be able to submerge, the weight of the submarine had to be reverted to zero.

This photo shows U- and UB-III type U-boats after the surrender in Harwich (TT)

The conning towers of U-boats differed a lot. Here the much smaller tower of a UC-II type submarine is overshadowed by that of a large U-type (TT)

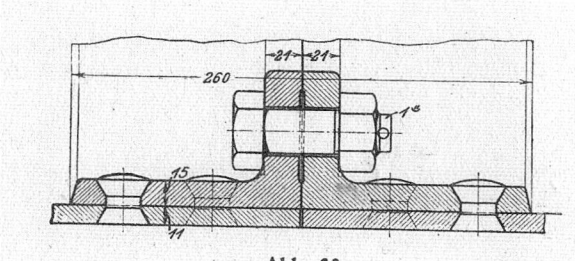

Profile of a connection between the various sections of the pressure hull (Techel)

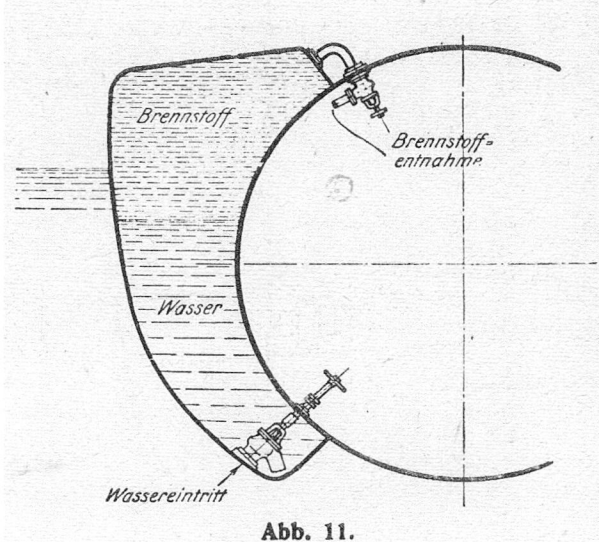

Diagram of the fuel tanks. An ingenious design made it possible that, with the help of a vent at the bottom, seawater would replace the spent diesel fuel, which kept the U-boat stable (Techel)

This would be made possible by taking in seawater in specially designed ballast tanks. Small U-boats were built as single-hulled vessels in which all the tanks for ballasting, fuel and fresh water were situated within the pressure hull. Its bobbin-shaped exterior would make it cruise well under water, but cruising on the surface would be cumbersome.

To improve on this shape the large types - U-, UB-II, UB-III and UC-II were fitted with double hulls. Ballast tanks, fuel tanks and pressure cylinders were arranged on the outside of the pressure hull. Because the ballast tanks would be totally filled with seawater during submerged cruising and the flood vents stood open, the outer hull did not have any problem with resisting pressure. Therefore the outer hull could be made to whatever shape and thickness. The outer hull

'At the depthrudder' (Unsere Marine im Weltkrieg)

was designed to give the U-boat maximum possible speed on the surface. Thickness of this part of the vessel was generally around 4 mm and served only to improve its streamline.

At both ends of the U-boat there were trimtanks which were interconnected by pipes. When sluicing

Helmsmen stand in the heart of the U-boat: the depth rudders, depth gauges and steering post (TT)

water through these tanks, from fore to aft and vice versa, this movement could influence the balance of the U-boat to make it dive faster.

The other important tanks were those for torpedo-compensation. When a U-boat fired an 800 kg torpedo in just under a few seconds it would lose its all important trim. These tanks had to take care of the trim after firing.

The fuel for the diesel engines was stored in tanks which were also sited on the outer hull. A fuel tank was constructed according to an ingenious principle. Diesel would float above water, as it is lighter. The interior of the tanks was connected to the sea and as the fuel would be spent, the tank would slowly fill with seawater by means of a valve at the bottom of the hull. The intake of seawater made the U-boat heavier but compensated at the same time for the use of grease, victuals, fresh water and ammunition. If the U-boat needed to be compensated further, then the compensation tanks could be filled.

The depth setting of the U-boat was kept by two sets of rudders, one pair forward and another aft. The U-boat could move underwater in wavy movements depending on the angle of the rudders. The four depth rudders were connected and controlled by steel cables which led to the control room. In the first U-boats, *U-1* to *U-4*, the depth rudders could only be moved manually. From *U-5* onwards they were controlled by hydraulics which made submerged cruising less labour intensive for the helmsmen. This system was also adapted in the UB- and UC-boats which made it possible for the NCO and seamen at the helm to set their own depth.

In the larger U-boats both top and bottom of the bow had been provided with a steel netcutter. The top one measured 1.5 m in length, had a saw-edge and was mounted it an angle of 30°. The netcutter was supported by steel strengtheners which were bolted

Interior views of the control room of *UB-110* (Tyne Museum)

to the deck. The bottom netcutter was of similar construction but directly attached to the hull. The sawtooth had a width of 5 cm and a height of 4 cm. Theoretically, the sharpened teeth would be able to saw through taut steel nets which had trapped the bow of the submarine.

Two *Minenabweiser* or anti-mine cables ran across the whole length of the U-boat from the bow, over the top of the tower and back down to the aft section. These double steel cables had a thickness of 3 cm and were meant to keep mines, cables, nets and other obstructions away from the tower and the other parts of the superstructure during its time under water. Part of the cables were insulated to serve as auxiliary antenna for radio-communications.

THE CONNING TOWER

Every submarine was provided with a tower or command bridge situated in the middle of the hull. The shape and size differed with each type of U-boat. Generally, the small to mid-sized U-boats had round towers whilst the U- and UB-III types had towers which were more oval in diameter from 1915 onwards. It measured 3.5 m in height with a diameter from 1.5 to 2 m. The pre-war conning tower designs consisted of three smaller, circular towers which were interconnected. This tight construction would make it sturdier to withstand a large amount of water pressure.

The conning tower proved to be each U-boats' Achilles' heel, besides the torpedo-loading hatches on deck and the smaller deck hatches. These were all protrusions which had to take a lot of resistance from the sea. Because the tower had to ensure a constant passage for the crew, and was also built to provide necessary space, it would also have a limited resistance to pressure. For the designers it was a hard job to build a tower which was tough enough as the rest of the hull, give enough room for movement in the interior but also have a superstructure which would not suffer too much from external pressure. The conning tower was made up of two sections: a pressure cylinder and a superstructure of steel plate which gave it its streamline form. The pressure part of the tower was made of nickel steel and had thickness of 40 mm in the early submarines. Nickel steel not only gave it the necessary toughness, but was also non-magnetic. This was crucial for the installation and function of the compasses which were inside and on top of the tower. Naval engineers managed to calculate the exterior pressures on the steel more acurately which brought the thickness of the tower to between 16 and 22 mm with the small to large U-boats. One or more portholes were fitted to simplify steering. On port- and starboard sides a number of built-in navigation lights were provided because the U-boat had to also function as a normal surface craft. The top of the tower was lightly domed,

Top view of the conning tower of *UB-13*, in Bruges, 1915. At the front is her compass and helm. In the middle of the tower are two retracted periscopes and the opening for the hatch (TT).

UB-13 and *UB-10* lie beside the Zeebrugge Mole (TT)

Oberleutnant z. S. Ernst Müller-Schwarz and his officers enjoy a cup of coffee on the tower of *UC-64*. Their U-boat is on the canal, heading towards Zeebrugge (TT)

On a U-boat, a bridge watch consisted minimally of four persons to check for enemy ships and aircraft. The U-boat pictured here seemed to be in friendly water, as three engineers took the liberty to catch some air on deck (TT)

with an access hatch to the back of the superstructure. The hatch could be shut from inside by turning a handwheel which had four internal locking arms. At the bottom inside of the tower (except with UB-I, UC-I and UC-II types) there was a second hatch which could isolate the tower from the rest of the submarine. The second locking hatch was not built in UC-minelayers, which made the rest of the U-boat vulnerable. Proof of this vulnerability was found on the wreck of *UC-62* which was sunk on the Thornton Bank. German sources state that *UC-62* was lost in the Channel. But the wreck of the minelayer was found in 1993 much closer to home. Besides evidence of a heavy explosion on the bow, there were several holes in the pressure hull of the conning tower. *UC-62* had probably been under attack from a surface vessel which had fired on her and damaged the tower. *UC-62* had escaped, but the holes had hindered its diving capabilities. This damage had made it fatal for *UC-62* when she was spotted on the surface on the Thornton Bank by the British submarine *HMS E-45*, and torpedoed and sunk.[16] If *UC-62* would have been provided with a hatch at the bottom of the tower then she might have been able to return back to base.

The inside of the conning tower was equipped with a depth-indicator, an inclinometer, one or two enginetelegraphs*, a torpedo launch mechanism, a gyrocompass and a steering position. Contact between the tower and the central control area was kept with a system of voicepipes which had to manually shut before diving. All U-boats, except the UB-I and UC-I types, had magnetic compasses mounted on the tower and were housed in a water-resistant bronze casement, made by the firm Carl Bamberg of Friedenau, Berlin. A steering column would be fitted

---

* The amount of telegraphs depended on whether the U-boat was fitted with either one or two engines. U-boats were provided with a steering position on top of the tower and in the command area. Sometimes it was possible to steer the U-boat from inside the tower, but that was not possible with UB-I and UC-I boats.

UB-22 in a heavy sea. In the foreground is the steering column and compass (TT)

Four officers and two seamen stand watch on the tower of *UB-41* (TT)

near or on the compass casement. On the smaller UB-I and UC-I type U-boats there was only a steering installation which looked like a steering wheel from a car mounted on a slender pillar. The periscope system was constructed within the pressure hull of the tower. An extra periscope could be present in front or abaft the tower. The top of the tower had railings on which a heavy canvas tarpaulin could be attached. In the pre-war U-boats this tarpaulin had to be removed with every dive, which made it a time-consuming and dangerous endeavour. During the war a robust screen was designed which could resist the pounding of the waves and the sudden wash of water when diving. During rough weather it gave the bridgecrew reasonable protection. In theory, the helmsman would steer the U-boat from within the tower by using the available compass and steering gear and by gazing through the portholes. But in practice the lookouts and the helmsman had to have a perfect overview of all sides around the U-boat and in the air at any given time. On the exterior of the tower was a steam whistle and a manually operated sounding device.

INTERNAL DIVISION, WATERTIGHT DOORS AND ACCOMMODATION

Watertight compartments divided a U-boat internally. The safety of a U-boat depended on the correct division and location of these watertight and partly pressure-resistant compartments. Within each watertight bulkhead was a convex, round door of 70 cm diameter. Its convex shape made sure it was pressure resistant and these doors underwent the same tests as the pressure hull. One compartment could be shut water- and airtight by means of turning a handwheel.

The normal bulkheads were provided with rectangular steel doors, with a height of 1.5 m. In a standard submarine there was a torpedo room in the bow and sometimes in the stern too. In minelaying submarines the forward torpedo room had been replaced by mineshafts. The larger UC-II type was provided with

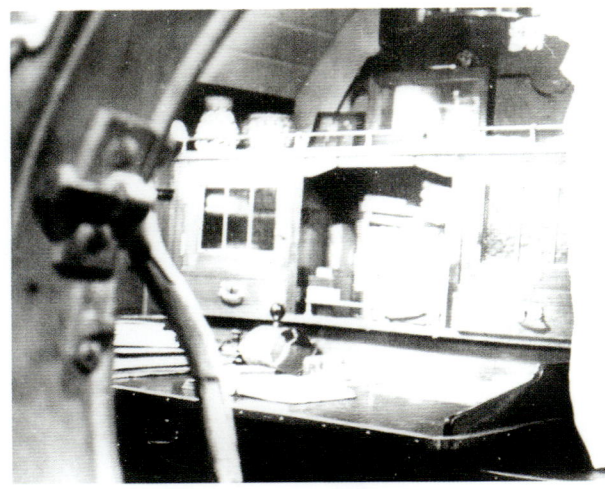
Desk in the officers' mess of *UC-39* (U-boot-Archiv Cuxhaven)

Wood panelling and cupboards made the mess of *UB-105* more comfortable. A portrait of Kaiser Wilhelm II made it feel even more 'homely'! (U-boot-Archiv Cuxhaven)

an aft torpedo room. In the forward torpedo room provisions were made for spare torpedoes, workbenches, cupboards and sleeping facilities for part of the crew. Abaft of the the forward section there was a galley, the officers' mess and the radio room. A radio unit was fitted in a small, separate cabin just aft of the first mineshaft. In the central command area of the submarine was the steering installation, depth- and pressure gauges, the main compass, navigational instruments and the periscopes within their wells. From the heart of the U-boat there was a section of accommodation for the rest of the crew, mainly for engine room personnel. In the section in front of the aft torpedo room lay the engine room, with diesel engines and the electric engine room. If the U-boat was designed with a second torpedo room this would be situated in the stern. Its set up would be similar to that of the forward torpedo room with a storage for spare torpedoes and bunks for the crew.

In contrast with what the terminology of cabins and rooms suggests, we would rather describe the compartments as areas then cabins. Crew spaces were very cramped and narrow and their design was well thought of to make optimal use of the available space. On the small- to middle-sized U-boats the sleeping facilities for the crew consisted of two metal-framed bunks fixed above one another on both sides of the vessel. If the top bunk was not in use it could be collapsed and serve as a back for the bottom bunk which was turned into a seat. Hammocks could also be rigged if there was little other space. Cupboards and racks were built into the side and under the bunks so as to provide every crewman with a couple of square decimeters of personal storage space. In between the bunks was the central passageway, a narrow avenue. The officers did not fare much better as they also had no privacy due to the central passage. Only the large U-boats were provided with a separate, private area which served as a mess. This was mostly situated behind the bulkhead of the forward torpedo room, so that the officers would be disturbed as little as possible by passing crewmen. Officers also had to be situated as close as possible to the control room to react and be on station in an emergency. In the officers' mess there also was storage for spare torpedoes which made its design as moveable as possible. The accommodation for the petty officers was located just abaft the control room and the rest of the crew was spread over the rear compartments.

In the small- to middle-sized U-boats a watercloset was provided, but no washing facilities. The larger U-boats had a second watercloset as well as a collapsible basin to fulfill basic hygiene necessities. In the UC-II type the watercloset lay on the starboard side of the mineroom and a second was kept as a spare in the control room. There was little privacy for the crew, with just a small curtain to shield off the watercloset.

A view in the officer's space in the bow area of *UC-39*. This area lay in front of the watertight compartment of the control room, right below the forward hatch (U-boot-Archiv Cuxhaven) ▶

A rare moment of relaxation: U-boatmen have erected a table in the passageway of their U-boat, and are sharing beer and food with comrades from the army (TT)

In the control room of a U-boat (TT)

On a UB-III type submarine there was only one toilet for more than 30 seamen. This example was photographed on the wreck of a UB-III type submarine on the Fairy Bank (TT).

As a rule the watercloset was not to be used during submerged cruising.

The sides of the U-boat were coated with light cork mats which had to check the constant flow of condensation and make the compartments a little bit more comfortable. Floors which were situated just above the batteries would be fairly hot. This stood in stark contrast with floors in the torpedo rooms as there were no batteries there. These compartments were heated by mobile electric heaters. All compartments were also designed with steamheaters, which would heat the interior when a U-boat lay in port.

Cooking inside a submerged U-boat was only possible with an electric cooking pot. The galley lay between the accommodation for the petty officers and other crew. In the early U-boats there was an electric stove built in which could be used after fixing the bunks up against the wall.

There was no natural light in the interior of a submarine and all compartments were illuminated by electrical power. Later in the war there was experimentation with cylindrical lightshafts fitted in the deckhead. The idea stayed with an experiment because the heavy covers on the in- and outside of the glass were not practical.

A constant supply of fresh air was an important necessity in submarines. On the surface, air would mainly be sucked in through the opened tower hatch. An arrangement of vertically fixed pipes around the conning tower gave extra ventilation to the interior and fed the diesel engines with fresh air. When underwater, alkali air filters would purify the air every five or six hours, recycling the air in the submarine and making it breathable for a certain period of time.

HATCHES

Round hatches were fitted in different areas of the deck of the U-boat. In principle, every watertight compartment had a hatch which made exit to deck level possible during surface sailing. Because of their close proximity to the waterline, these hatches also had to be closed during a slight seastate. The only hatch that would remain dry or not have any problems with flooding would be the one on the top of the tower. Hatches could be closed with a half turn of a handwheel which was fitted on the in- and outside. The number of hatches would depend on the size of the U-boat. The large or long distance submarines, U- and UB-III types, usually had five external hatches, with three around the tower: one on top, one in front and one just abaft. A fourth and fifth hatch lay just above the forward and aft torpedo rooms. The round hatches of the torpedo rooms were placed on a second, larger, oval hinged hatch which was fixed by bolts and nuts to the deck. The larger hatch could be opened in the harbour and was intended for loading torpedoes in an oblique way. The middle sized UB- and UC-type U-boats had three hatches: one on the tower, one just in front of the tower near the deck gun, and one above the engine room. The UB-I and UC-I type U-boats only had two access hatches, one on top of the tower and one just abaft, above the engine room. The UB-I type did have an oblique hatch at the foot of the tower in order to load its torpedoes.

COLOUR, RECOGNITION MARKS AND CAMOUFLAGE

The hull of a submarine which had to operate in the North Sea or Atlantic Ocean was usually painted a light grey colour. The deck was painted black or left natural and the conning tower was a dark grey colour. This stood in stark contrast with a dark blue deck for submarines which had to dive in the clear waters of the Mediterranean where a submarine could be spotted by an aircraft to a depth of 30 m. U-boats were not usually camouflaged, but often waves would be painted over the grey of the hull to confuse an enemy.

To be able to load a torpedo in a torpedo room, a hatch had to be totally opened. The crew of *UC-64* is busy with manhandling a torpedo into their U-boat in Bruges docks (TT)

Oddly painted camouflage on the periscopes of *UB-105* (U-boot-Archiv Cuxhaven)

U-boats were painted with recognition marks for their own aircraft, one of which was a white circle on the foredeck. This U-boat obviously was suffering a leak in the fuel tank and floating in a sea of oil (BArch)

Bizarre stripes and colourful patches had eminated from Kubistic ideas to distort and disfragment the shape of a ship. The enemy would find it more difficult to judge size, shape, speed, direction and followed course of a vessel. A painted bowwave was to give the impression that the U-boat was cruising at a high speed and there were some instances known of the superstructure retaining a black and white chessboard pattern. Periscopes would also be camouflaged with flowing green lines eminating waves. Light grey would mostly remain a standard colour[17]. Attempts were also made to camouflage a U-boat against air attacks. *UC-4* had been painted in irregular patches of red and white,[18] but this had only been an experiment.

Flanders Flotilla U-boats did not carry any standardised recognition marks for warning friendly aircraft. During the war the large U-boats had painted white rings on deck to avoid being bombed by German aircraft or airships who would mistake them as British targets.[19] By the middle of the war it was usual that all U-boats of the Flanders Flotilla had been given 'eyes' on both sides of the bow. This had been introduced by an officer who had served in China where it was traditional to paint eyes on local junks* to ward off evil spirits. In the beginning it served as a talisman, but later it functioned as a recognition mark to avoid being attacked by a friendly U-boat. With the later U-boat models, the UB- and UC-types, it would not be necessary anymore to have recognition marks as they totally differed from British submarines. The eye that typified the Flanders U-boat proved to be a marker for Royal Navy diver Dusty Miller, who had dived on more than 20 sunken U-boats, usually just after their loss.[20] The British compared the eye with the German Kokarde - black, white and red. In combination with the forward hydroplanes, which resembled fins, the small UB-I boat looked like a whalehead. *'Ihre Augen gefallen mir'*, said *Oberleutnant z. S.* Valentiner to *Oberleutnant z. S.* Fürbringer after he had saved *UB-2* by towing it back to Zeebrugge with his own boat, *UB-16*. Valentiner went even further by having eyes painted above a grinning, shark's mouth.[21] The eyes and obvious convex nose gave the UB-I boats a funny, whale-like appearance.

---

* A wooden sailing ship with two or three masts and a gaff-rigged sail.

Two UB-I boats lie under the protection of a half shelter in Bruges docks (Jörn Jensen) ▶

ENGINES

Almost all of the newly developed U-boats were driven by diesel engines on the surface. A one or two stroke engine provided 300 to 1.700 HP. When a U-boat had to submerge, the diesel engines would be disengaged and the electric engines would take over. Before the early 1920s it was technically impossible to build fuel injection pumps which would supply enough pressure to atomise fuel efficiently. Fuel was injected with pressurised air at 70 bar. The necessary compressor was built into the engine and was driven by the main shaft on the front. All large engines were started by injecting 30 bar of pressurised air from a starter tank. The pressure capacity of the tank would be topped up again after every start of the engine. MAN and Germaniawerft/Krupp were the most famous manufacturers of U-boat engines. During the war more U-boat engines were produced than the actual number of U-boats available.

Large scores of batteries had to supply energy for the electric engines and had to be charged when the diesel engines were running. An enormous supply of batteries was built in under the central pathway of the accommodation. Small U-boats would carry about 350 kg of batteries, whilst the larger U-boats had about 800 kg. Battery cells proved to be dangerous and deadly when seawater would flood

Near the wreck of an unidentified UB-II boat, sunk west of the Fairy Bank (see *UC-66*, Wreck I) lies a mushroom-vent for the diesel engines' air intake (TT)

A rare view in the electric engine room of a UB-III type boat, seen from the diesel engine room (TT)

A crewman stands near the controls of the diesel engine of a UC-II class submarine (TT)

View of the footplate of the diesel engines of a UB-II boat. The many gauges served to keep an eye on the various parts (TT)

68

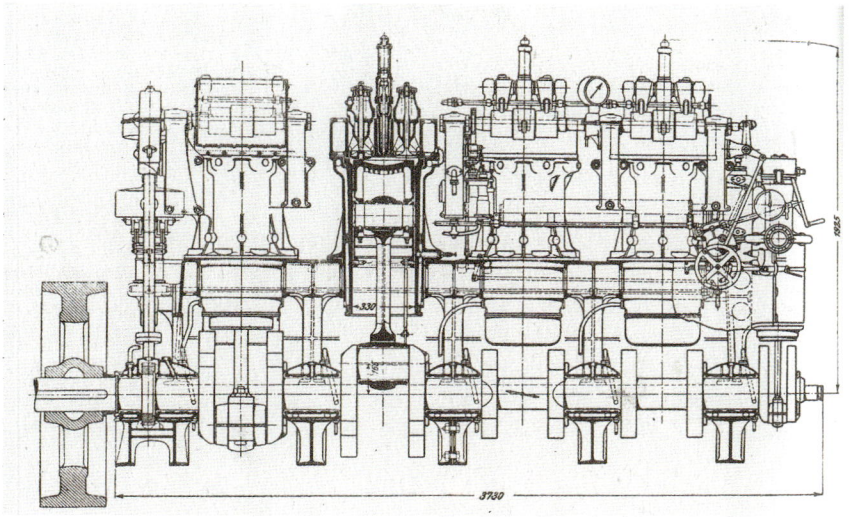

Profile of a standard four-stroke diesel engine of 300 HP (Techel)

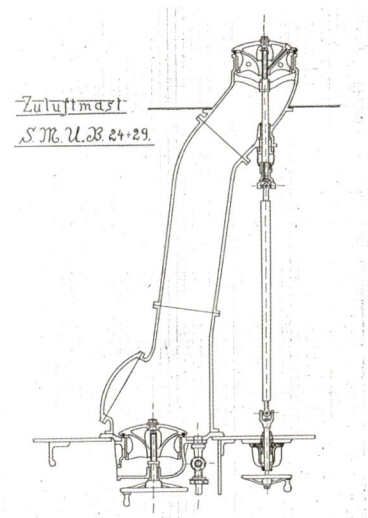

Air intake for the diesel engines to the upper deck, showing watertight shut-off vents (Rössler)

them and so release poisonous sulphuric acid gas. To prevent this from happening the batteries would be well insulated and kept in sealed containers in which the bottoms and sides were coated with rubber. Between the rubber and the wall of the container was a thin lead strip to counteract corrosion in case of any spillage.

German U-boat engines proved to be of such high calibre that even after the war they were being used in merchant ships and in factories. The fact that it had to generate maximum power with limited weight and space was what made a U-boat engine so sought after. This was all possible on board a U-boat because the periods of maximum power were short and there was highly trained personnel on board to tend to them. In stark contrast to the U-boat division, factories and industry had the necessity for prolonged and incessant power and the number of engineers had to be kept as low as possible to keep it all cost effectual.

View of the control panel of the electric engines of UB-110 (Tyne Museum)

U-boat manuals for engines and compass (TT)

GERMANIAWERFT-ENGINE NUMBER 1203, 1916

It was not only the post-war German Industry that eyed the top quality U-boat engines, but British factories were also being supplied with surrendered German constructions. In the years which followed the Armistice, dozens of decommissioned U-boats were towed to the Medway river and beached in the shallows. Private firms bought the large U-, UB-III- and UC-III boats from the Ministry of Defence and recovered as much of the non-ferrous metals and re-usable parts as possible. Engines remained the main point of interest. Proof of this activity is still visible today in the remaining wrecks which partly re-appear at lowtide. Most of the hull remains untouched, whilst tower and superstructure have been removed to gain easier access to the engine room. The recovered engines went to replace the old steam engines in local cement factories. Engines were also delivered to the Southend Electricity Works, the Wembley Exhibition of 1924 and the power supply for a radio station. Two engines even made it to the other side of the world, to New-Zealand, where they were incorporated in a hydro-electric project.[22] To this day, the majority of these engines have been scrapped, so the chance of finding an authentic U-boat engine in working condition seemed to be impossible.

Until a catalogue of the auction house Hermann Historica of München appeared in May 2011 with an extraordinary lot. An original six cylinder U-boat-diesel engine, made in 1916 by the Germaniawerft Kiel-Gaarden of Friedrich Krupp AG, was offered for sale. It weighed almost 15 tons, had a length of 4.85 m, a width of 2.1 m and a height of 3.1 m. This specific engine had been bought by the company C. Döllgast & Söhne for use in the electric works of Partnach in Partenkirchen. The engine was obviously of high quality and very reliable because the company ordered more diesel engines from Krupp in the 1920s. In 1939 the engine

received an overhaul and important parts were replaced. The MAN company had to repair minor damages in 1959 because Krupp did not produce any more engines of this size. In the early 1990s it had another overhaul, but in the meantime Partnach had been taken over by Isar-Amperwerke. It was only in 1995 that this former U-boat diesel engine was decommissioned and found its way to a privately owned engine collection.[23] A lifespan of 80 years is definitely proof of high-quality German engineering!

All U-boats were propelled by single or double propellers. Three-blade propellers were made of manganese nickel bronze and had a diameter of around 1.25 m. The propellers were protected by horizontally placed, perforated steel plates. These propeller guards were mounted about 30 cm above the waterline and also served as rudder guards.

U-boat engine (Hermann Historica Auktionshaus)

INSTRUMENTS AND NAVIGATION

NAVIGATION AND POSITIONING

A U-boat captain usually left the tasks of chartwork and calculations to a specially appointed petty officer such as a *Steuermann* or *Obersteuermann*. As a rule the *Steuermann* would be given the task of plotting a course so that the U-boat would reach its goal at a certain speed. This higher petty officer would serve as the right-hand man to the captain and would also advise him when having to set course and deflection for a torpedo during an attack. These were usually ex-merchant navy officers whom, in peacetime, had gained years of experience of Allied ports and routes. Navigation in the Channel and North Sea often depended on light vessels and buoys, as well as soundings.

When war had been declared, most parts of the Allied coastline went into total darkness. Buoys and other beacons were doused to, in theory, inhibit the U-boat's navigation. In an interrogation report of a German U-boat commander, it proved that a blackout did not add to any extra difficulties. When they doubted their position, a U-boat would be taken to the bottom to make a sounding. In the North Sea and the eastern part of the Channel a U-boat could always get a positional fix on the surface by locating direction finders for wireless telegraphy. During the night there was always some kind of illumination which would give the captain enough cross references to indicate the position of a minefield.[24]

Every U-boat was assigned a number of sextants, one being part of the ship's inventory, the others belonging to each officer in question. A sextant could only be used during the day or night when the U-boat

The control room of a U-boat: a seeming chaos of valves, tubing, instruments, gauges and controls (Felix Schwormstadt)

72

An officer shoots a position with his sextant amidst his bridge watch (Dirk Termote)

lay on the surface. It measured the vertical angle of the sun and the horizon to be able to determine position on earth. When date and time were known it was able to calculate longitude. The best timing would be to shoot the sun at its zenith, which was at noon. It was possible to calculate latitude by measuring the height of the north star. Exact time would not be of importance, just the longitude of the observer. So-called *Schutzbrillen* or protective glasses were used against the glare of the sun when taking a position.

Besides latitude, a navigator had to know the longitude one was on to determine his position on earth. This was calculated with the ship's chronometer, fitted in gimballs in a wooden case, which had to neutralised the constant movement of the ship. The chronometer gave the exact time in port (or Greenwich) and this would be compared with local time. The local time was determined by the state of the sun or the culmination time of a star. The first watertight U-boat chronometer for the Imperial Navy was delivered in November 1916 to *UC-34*. The instrument had been constructed by the *Kaiserliche Chronometer Observatorium* and was fitted in a double iron case. This casing was supposed to stop the influence of magnetic deflection on the mechanism. From the end of 1916 onwards, all large U-boats were supplied with three chronometers. UB- and UC-boats only received one example, due to the lack of storage space on board.[25]

COMPASSES

A U-boat would mostly be equipped with four compasses. A gyrocompass had to tackle the problem of magnetism in a complete metal 'atmosphere' during the navigation process from within the hull. The compass housing and the gyro were made watertight and filled with hydrogen. The gyros made 30,000 revolutions per minute, which created a larger and more specific directional force than the normal magnetic compasses. The company Anschütz was the main supplier for the Imperial Navy.

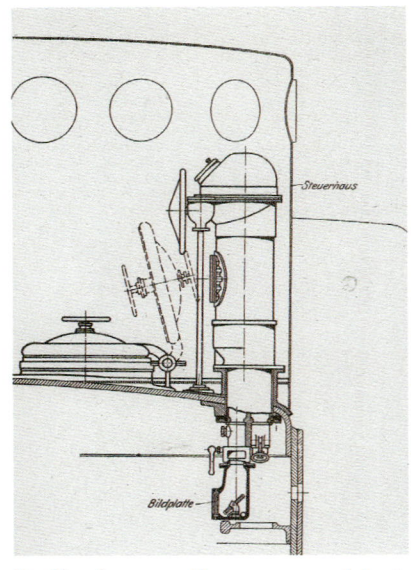  

Profile of a magnetic, pressure-resistant compass housing (Techel)

Pressure-resistant compass housing (Dirk Johansen)

A view on the front of the conning tower of a UB-I type submarine (TT)

A mother compass was installed just below the conning tower, in the control room, whilst there were two secundary compasses in the tower and engine room.

We assume it to be totally natural that a compass can function without any problems in the iron bowls of a U-boat. But in 1906 finding a sollution to this problem proved to be an enormous headache for German engineers. A hull had to be of steel as it was the strongest and cheapest metal which exists to build a ship. Ferromagnetic materials in ships have always caused problems for a compass to work satisfactorily. The magnetic field which ferrous materials creates interferes with the instrument or makes it malfunction totally. A compass fixed in the conning tower would only work when the steel of the tower was combined with an alloy of nickel, making it non-magnetic.[26] The British were never able to solve this problem and had to keep building bronze towers for their submarines right up to the Second World War.

The company Carl Bamberg of Friedenau, Berlin built the magnetic bridge compass. The compass itself was fitted in a bronze pressure- and waterproof housing on the front of the conning tower. This kind of compass had the advantage that it could be used during surface navigation as well as submerged cruising. The compass had a perforated compass rose which would be projected by a system of lenses and prisms, making it legible to the helmsman on the inside. If the housing would be damaged, then an influx of water could be stopped by a shut-off valve. On the top of the tower, just abaft the compass was a steering column which was either mounted on a separate foot or integrated as part of the compass housing with its indicator and wheel, such as was the case with the UB-III type.

A gyrocompass would be used when navigation had to be conducted from within the submarine. This is a type of non-magnetic compass which is based on a fast-spinning disc and rotation of the earth to automatically find geographical direction. The gyrocompass has a gimballed suspension, is electrically driven and keeps its position to true North by using the effect of gyroscopic precession. Gyrocompasses would sometimes fail because of the constant pitching and rolling of a U-boat.

The batteries and the main electric engine could also hinder the workings of the compass. Batteries were stored below the footplates forward. Cables would run from the batteries to the main engine and run beneath the centrally positioned compass. Electric cables which were too close to the compass created a magnetic field which disrupted the compass. To avoid this magnetic field, the builders had the cumbersome task of re-routing the cables.

CHURCH BELLS FOR COMPASSES

Chief Engineer Luc Commeine pointed out an interesting fact from the war. I was shown an official German document, kept in the Episcopal Archives in Bruges, which concerns the requisition of church bells. The German *Kommandantur* issued an order in November 1917 to requisition 16 bells from seven churches from the area Ostend-Mariakerke. Automatically one would assume that the bronze from recycled bells would be used for the production of shell casings for munitions. Nothing is less true. The metal from which a bronze bell is made is much too precious to be used just for munitions. It contains an alloy of copper, tin and sometimes lead, which gives it the sharp tone when ringing. This alloy was the most adequate material for the housing of a U-boat compass. It could withstand the magnetic influences of the ferrous hull and protect the compass against other factors such as the magnetic field which would be created once the electric engine was started. Because of this specific alloy in the compass housing in a new generation of U-boats, magnetic fields did not have any more effect on compasses.

TELEGRAPHS AND OTHER INSTRUMENTS

Every U-boat was fitted with a telegraph system which had to pass on orders from the control room to the engineer to reduce, pick up or stop the speed of a U-boat. Telegraphs were fitted in the conning tower (for giving orders when on the surface), just beneath the tower in the control room and in the diesel- and electric engine rooms. A telegraph consisted usually of a flat-faced, ingraved or enamelled plate onto which an indicator hand and bell system was fitted. When an order was given, the bells sounded and the

The steering position on a U-boat (U-boot-Archiv Cuxhaven)

indicator hand would point to the order on the plate. This order had to be confirmed by, for example, the engine room, which then would put a second, smaller indicator hand to the same order. The larger U-boats of the UC-II type were provided with a system of electric telegraphs. The ones destined for the conning tower would be illuminated by a built-in light.

Other instruments in the tower and control room consisted of level indicators, which showed the inclination of the submarine, rudder- and hydroplane indicators, revolution counters, torpedo-firing and mine-release mechanisms, ampère- and voltmeters and all kinds of switches, valves and wheels.

PERISCOPES AND OPTICS

The number of periscopes in a U-boat could vary between one and three. The larger U-boats of the Flanders Flotilla had two periscopes, one of which would slide in a cylindrical protective tube in front or just abaft the tower and another would be mounted in a second tube on top of the tower. The periscope itself consisted of a 7 cm thick tube in two sections. The top part was made of brass or steel and had a length of 120 cm. The bottom half was thicker, with a diameter of 15 cm, a length of 6 m and was made of nickel steel. The companies Goerz and Zeiss were the main suppliers of periscopes to German shipyards. At the bottom of

75

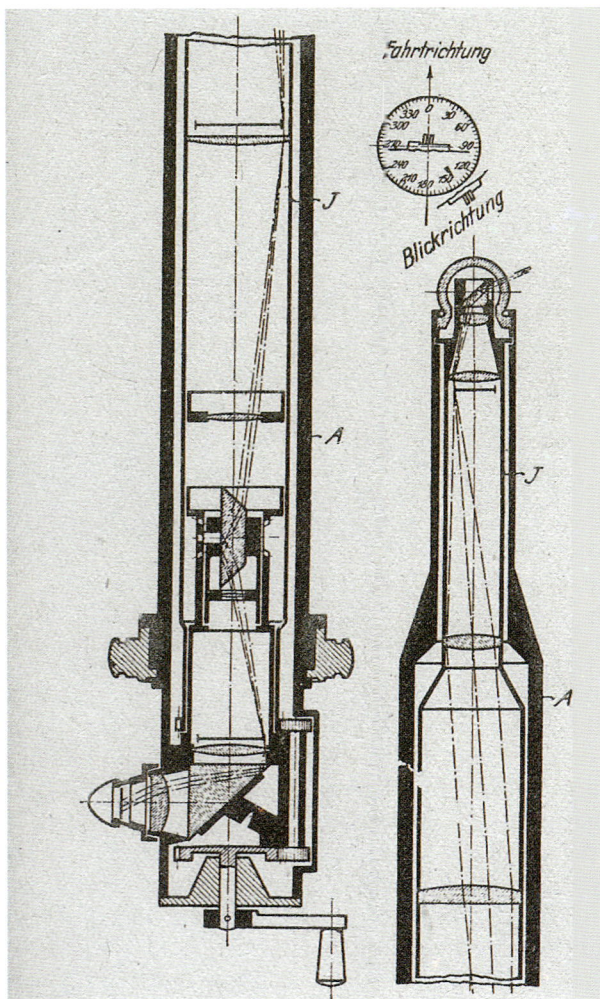

the instrument was the eyepiece with degree indication marks and on both sides there were handles to be able to turn the periscope 360°. At the top was a lens which could sight up to 40° in height. Two or more periscopes were constructed for navigational use and to search the sky for any enemy airplanes or airships. To enable an upward view, a top prism could be switched by tugging on a lever. A periscope could be used in the control room as well as in the conning tower. A small electric engine lifted the periscope upwards or downwards and in an emergency it could be manually operated. The bottom of the more than 7 m long tube was housed in cylindrical well which reached to the keel. Signal lamps were fitted in the top of the periscope and could be activated from within by means of a morse signalling device.

During the war, three Berlin based companies, Voigtländer, Zeiss and Leitz, were responsible for the production of binoculars and other optics for the U-boats of the Imperial Navy. The large UB- and UC-boats were provided with 6 7x50 and 2 12x60 prismatic binoculars. The smaller UB- and UC-boats only received half of this number for the watchkeepers.

The multi-ocular of a periscope (Techel)

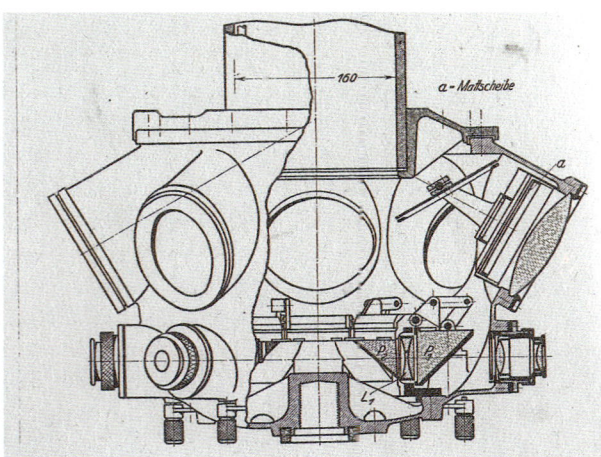

Technical drawing of ocular and lenses of the observation periscope (Techel)

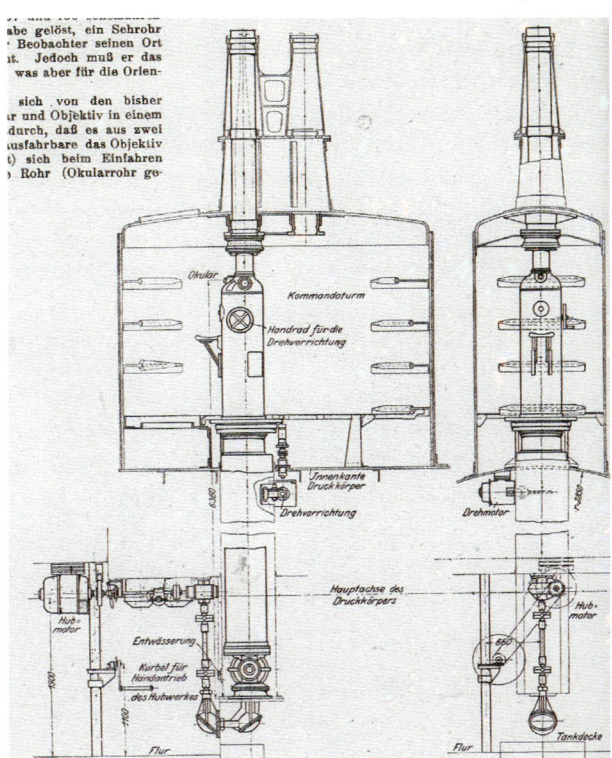

Profile of the pressure hull of the tower and its periscopes, on a UB-III type submarine (Techel)

This interesting photo shows ten crewmen of *UC-60*, who stand, squashed together on the tower. On the rear of the tower one of them is handling a manual sounding device (right), in the centre of the tower the footing on which a machinegun is mounted, is visible (TT)

The bridge watch on board the tower huddles behind the screen and the retracted attack periscope (TT)

By mid 1916 the Admiralty received multiple complaints concerning Voigtländer's double prismatic binoculars. During rainy and adverse weather conditions binoculars used by the *U-Flottille Flandern* and Mediterranean divisions would get damaged because of moisture seaping through the seals.[27] As a solution to this problem, Zeiss and Leitz immediately produced watertight 7x50-binoculars, which replaced all the Voigtländers in the *U-Flottille Flandern*.

Normally, when a U-boat had to dive, all binoculars were taken below deck to prevent loss or damage. The Admiralty toyed with the idea of mounting fixed binoculars of the so-called von Busch-type. These would be mounted on a small platform on the bridge for observation during calm weather and cruising speed. In rough or stormy conditions this type of binoculars would be useless, as the U-boat would be rolling too much. These binoculars were also impractical, as they had to be taken below before every dive, even though they were watertight. In an emergency, when left outside, they would normally withstand the pressure from a single dive.

The artillery pieces of a U-boat were provided with two telescopic, prismatic sights from the company Zeiss. Both sights were internally lit for night-time operations and light filters for the eyepiece. The sights were pressure-resistant and could be left on the deck gun when the U-boat had to suddenly dive. Normally they would be removed before the U-boat dived and were stored in the control room.

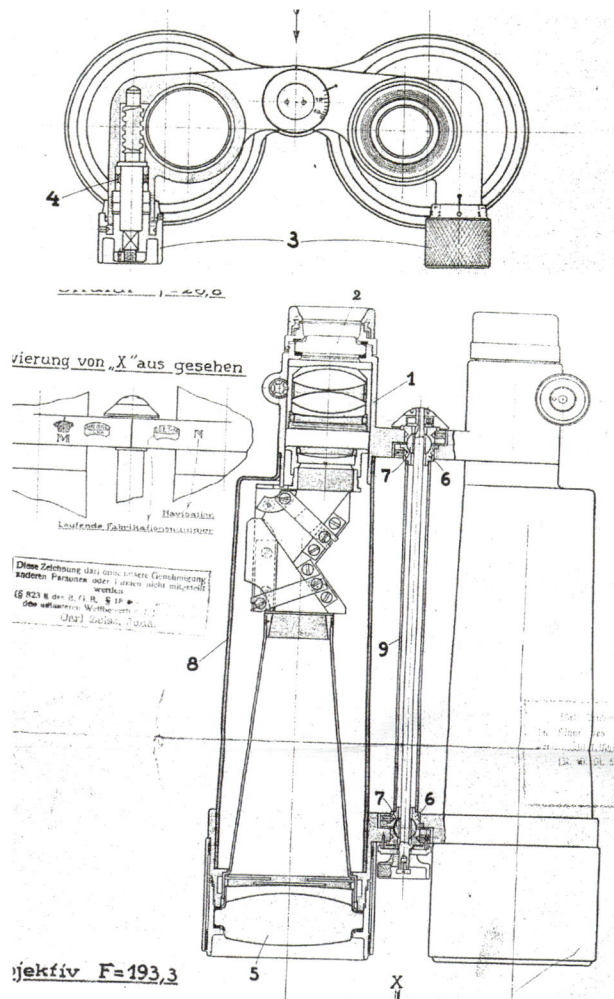

Technical drawing of the Carl Zeiss-binoculars (BArch)

COMMUNICATION

RADIO-TELEGRAPHY

It was during the Great War that wireless telegraphy or radio was extensively used for the first time in history. U-boats would not be so isolated from the their bases and could communicate with friendly units from fairly large distances. By the spring of 1915 directional signals were emitted by Sylt, Borkum, Norholz and Bruges. These messages could be received by a U-boat, but also by a listening enemy. To be able to keep messages 'secret', these were coded by two means. Firstly, the text was translated in an artificial language with the aid of a codebook. After that, the language of this codebook would undergo a number of changes and replacements to hinder the enemy translating an intercepted message. A codebook in the base and on the U-boat were indispensable, but more knowledge was necessary to decode a message. One had to know the meaning of certain numbers and symbols in the message to fully understand it. By the middle of 1918 a standard message from a U-boat could look like the following example: '1-2-4-068a-UB37'. This meant that *UB-37* had sunk a ship of 2.000 BRT, had four torpedoes in reserve and was located in the western part of the Channel. The position was communicated by chart reference, in this case quadrant 068, area alfa. U-boat numbers were often also disguised further in code with letters instead of numbers. Messages to U-boats were sent out at regular periods in time with orders coming from Bruges at 01h, 10h, 15h and 20h. The base at Bruges would also keep an eye on changing weather circumstances, and intercepted Allied radio traffic and communicated this with patrolling U-boats.

In the beginning of the war the large U-, UB-II, UB-III and UC-II type submarines had two hinged masts in front and abaft the conning tower. When erected they had a height of 10 to 12 m and a radio antenna would be strung up between them. These masts could only be employed when a submarine was on the surface and it would take several minutes for the crew to install and replace them. This would be done by a screw and tackle system which could either be

◀ The crew of a UB-III submarine have just put up the forward radio mast, to be able to send and receive messages (TT)

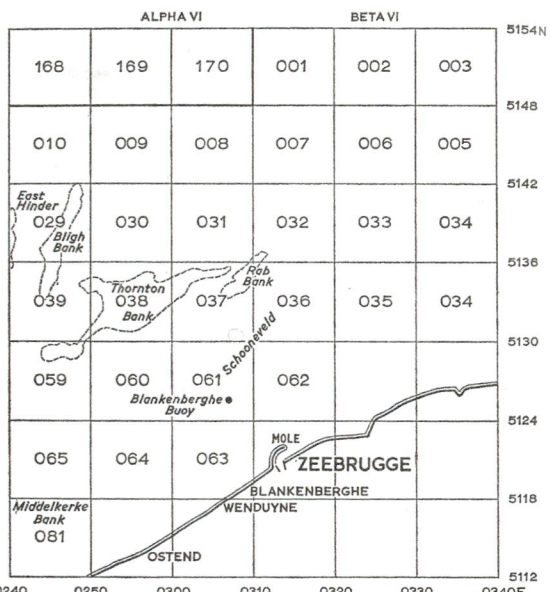

Example of the divisions used on a chart representing the sandbanks and coast of Flanders. The areas are coded, to give secrecy if a message was intercepted (Grant)

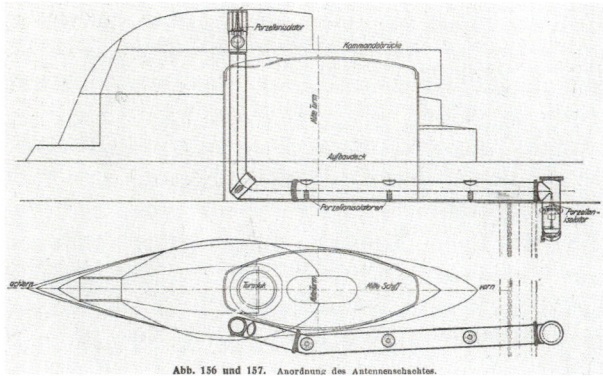

Technical drawing of the location of porcelain insulators on a UB-III boat tower (Techel)

On the wreck of UC-62, which was sunk on the Thornton Ridge, lies a broken off antenna protector (TT)

79

Two UC-I boats in the Klein Handelsdock in Bruges Harbour. The jumping wires, which run from forward, over the tower, up to the stern, serve as auxiliary antennae, enabling them to receive radio signals (Jörn Jensen)

A peaceful moment at sea. An officer takes advantage of this to smoke his pipe whilst on watch (TT)

operated electrically or manually. During the day the high masts gave a range of 100 to 300 miles and during the night and during good weather this could be more than doubled to 700 miles. The increased range was due to the sun not interfering with the radio waves. The masts did make the U-boat extremely vulnerable as she would not be able to dive quickly when there was an unexpected attack. The masts proved also to be impracticle during rough weather and would not be set up totally straight up for fear of breakage due to the swell. To counter this problem a reserve antenna was placed on the *Minenabweiser*, but this only gave half of the reach in comparison with the fully erected mast. The antenna did prove its use, as a surfaced U-boat could almost immediately receive messages without the necessity of setting up a mast.

The smaller UB-I and UC-I boats were provided with a telescopic radio mast in front of the tower. The antenna consisted of two wires which ran forward as well as aft. The UB-III and UC-II types had a small radio room, or more rather 'a quiet corner', in the control room or - in a minelayer - just abaft the mineshafts to port. Special acoustic insulation was fitted around the radio room to deaden the sound of the engines. UB-I, UC-I and UB-II class submarines did not have a separate radio room because of the lack of space and only were provided with a small wireless set which measured 1.2 m on 0.6 m and was placed in the control room. The transmitter in the radio room was connected via a 30-cm wide tube to the antenna on the bridge. In the tube there were at regular intervals insulators onto which the thick copper conductor was attached. The duct ended in a bronze foot with a porcelain insulator protected by a basket-shaped top. This was situated on the conning tower. Another conductor left from here to the

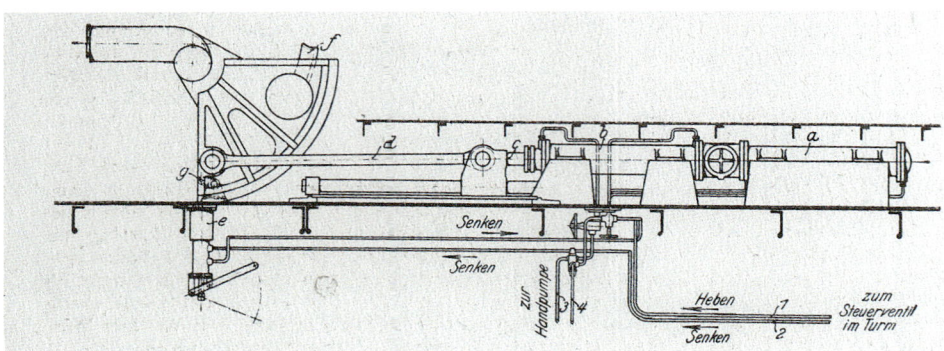

Technical drawing of the hydrolic-pneumatic system to hoist a radio mast to its vertical position (Techel)

Two seamen demonstrate the use of a double- and single-barrelled flare pistol (TT)

higher antennamast. It was a rule that minelaying submarines used the wireless as little as possible, except for listening to general radio passage. But, in general, U-boats used the radio as little as possible so as not to betray their position to the enemy. Only important messages, such as the progress of a patrol, the expected return to base and the occurance of defects were transmitted.

HYDROPHONE

Underwater signalling and reception devices were extremely primitive during the First World War. Only the large U- and UB- class U-boats were equipped with receivers and signalling instruments. Minelayers only could receive sounds underwater. The receiver was a hydrophone or *Unterwasser Geräusch Empfänger* and could detect all sounds in a radius of about 10 miles around the submarine. To be able to listen to and distinguish various underwater sounds and judge their respective distances, an operator had to be experienced enough. The hydrophone would work optimally when the U-boat lay on the bottom and all onboard sounds, such as talking, movement and the running of auxiliary engines had ceased. The instrument consisted of three pairs of microphones which were fixed on the outer hull. Inside it was connected to a battery, a control panel and an adaptable resistor and a telephone receiver. The receiver was perfect for picking up the sounds of fast-moving ships in group, such as torpedo boats.

OTHER SIGNALLING DEVICES

UB- and UC-boats were each provided with nine fire-signals and 60 shells for flareguns.[28] In September 1914 the recognition signal for a surfaced U-boat was a starshell fired from a double-barrelled pistol. The starshell exploded as a white star and fell further apart as two red stars.

Smokepots or *Nebel Unterwasser Bomben* were also part of the signalling arsenal on board a U-boat. These were green painted metal cylinders with a thin

Officers on the conning tower of *UB-41*: commands are given through voice-pipes to the steering position below (TT)

spiral-shaped spring and a detonator on the top side. Inside was a highly flammable liquid which would ignite skin and clothes on contact. When they were ignited and thrown overboard they gave off a white or grey smoke.[29]

Early on, the Flanders Flotilla experimented with pigeons on board U-boats. The pigeons were normally attached to the Zeebrugge seaplane base, but did not seem apt enough for communication at sea. When they would be about 60 to 70 miles from Zeebrugge, in full sea, they were able to find their way back home. In proximity to the British coast they usually did not return home, but chose the safety of the nearest land. Even though they were not very reliable, pigeons were kept on board as a kind of back-up and it was on 29 August 1918 that the British could intercept a pigeon. The winged messenger had come from *UB-109*, which had completed a patrol in the western part of the Channel and was on the return leg of her patrol. On its leg was a handwritten note which had to inform the base of Bruges of the arrival of *UB-109*.[30] The British were able to trap the U-boat that same morning and destroy it by electrically firing mines in a field off Folkestone. Eight crewmen and the pigeon were the sole survivors of *UB-109*.

Crewmen carefully load a torpedo from a barge into the hatch of their U-boat. The photo is taken in Bruges Harbour (Dirk Termote)

ARMAMENT

TORPEDOES AND TORPEDO TUBES

All Imperial Naval U-boats, except those of the UC-I class, were fitted with torpedo tubes. The large U- and UB-classes had a maximum of four tubes in the bow and two in the stern.

Torpedo tubes were installed in two ways, mainly fitted within the pressure hull with a loading hatch towards the inside. By these means it was easier to maintain and inspect each tube separately. The tubes were shut on the outside with a hinged door made watertight with a rubber seal. The doors could be opened from within with a worm mechanism or via conical gears. Torpedoes were fired manually or electrically from the conning tower, control room or torpedo room. The UC-II class minelayer was the only submarine to have two external torpedo tubes fitted on the bow. These lay alongside the six vertical mineshafts. They were built into the superstructure of the secondary hull and only the forward door was visible. Firing was done electrically or manually from the tower or control room with a firing pistol. A small cartridge filled with black powder was ignited, whereafter the power of the explosion pushed on to an ignition and fired the tube.

The company Schwarzkopff* supplied G/7-, G/6-, C/06-, C/03-, G/125- and K III-torpedoes with diameters of 45 and 50 cm. They had an overall length of 5 m and with a range of 1000 m they could reach speeds of up to 35 knots. At a setting of 2,000 m they still could obtain 25 knots speed. The explosives of a 45 cm torpedo consisted of 100 kg of wet, moulded guncotton. The weight of the explosive charge doubled in a 50 cm torpedo. Funnily enough

---

* Funnily enough its British counterpart and producer of torpedoes was called Whitehead.

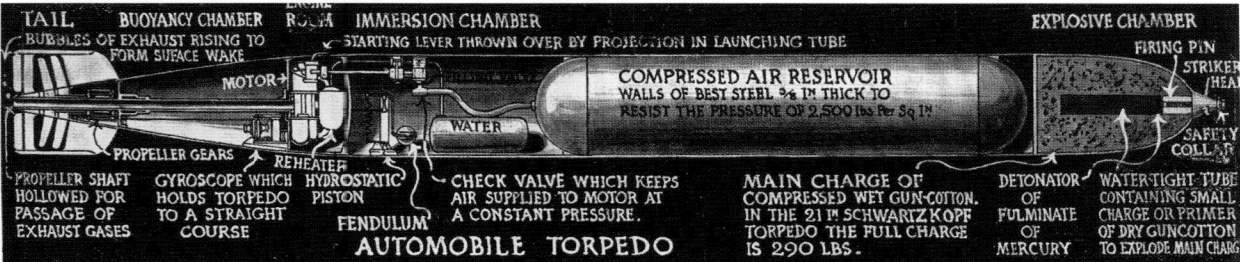

Schematic diagram of the active parts of a torpedo (The Sphere)

A rolling crane on the dockside in Bruges Harbour (Klein Handelsdok) brings a 45 cm torpedo over to the deck of a camouflaged UB-I type boat (TT)

The same location in the harbour of Bruges. Only the bollards and the cornerstones of the quai bear witness to the once very busy dockyard (TT)

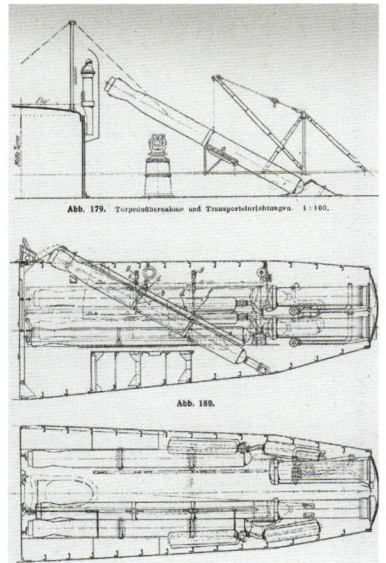
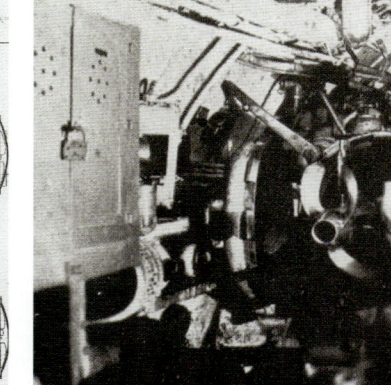

Technical diagram of the loading procedure of a torpedo (Techel)

A crewman shoves a greased torpedo in its tube, ready to fire (TT)

the half-rounded, bullet-shaped design of the torpedo did not have any influence on its speed. This rounded shape had the important advantage to put the centre of the charge as close as possible to the object which had to be destroyed. Torpedoes had counter-rotating propellors* installed which initially were driven by compressed air. The disadvantage of this propulsion system was that when expanded air cooled down under influence of high pressure it brought the danger of ice formation in the engine of the torpedo. This was solved by heating the air with seawater before it was fed into the engine. To make pre-heating of compressed air possible, steam installations in the torpedo chambers had to be fitted. This had the added advantage that a 'steam torpedo' could run faster and have a larger range. Engineers developed another idea to inject liquid fuel, such as kerosine, in the air and let it ignite. The air would be heated much faster, expand more and increase range and speed of the torpedo. These developments eventually led to the use of water in the explosive chamber to cool down a fuel-driven torpedo. This torpedo was called 'wet-heated' and was the most used type of torpedo in the war.

Torpedoes normally exploded when the firing pistol on the head of the torpedo came in contact with the hull of a ship. It aimed to create an opening near the waterline of a ship under attack which resulted in a 50% chance of flooding and sinking. The following explosion expanded in the atmosphere, which constricted the damage. If a torpedo was fired too deep, then the explosive would never hit the ship. There was also the chance of a torpedo hitting a hull sideways and failing to explode if a ship had a rounded or concave hull. To counter this problem the Germans developed a magnetic firing pistol on the head of the torpedo early in the war. This ingenius system let the torpedo explode beneath the ship, instead of directly impacting against the hull. The magnetic influence of the steel ignited the detonator on the head when the torpedo came close to the hull. An explosion beneath a vessel would damage its hull much more as the sudden expansion was caught between the water-column and the hull. The force of the explosion would lift the vessel out of the water and break its back, which resulted in the vessel ripping in half. A hole created in the bottom by such an explosion would have more chance of sinking the enemy vessel.

To determine depth and distance settings for a torpedo, a shaft within the body had to be turned left

---

* Both propellers turn in opposite directions on the same shaft.

This photo shows the bodies of two stowed torpedoes in the forward torpedo room of a UB-II type boat (TT) ▶

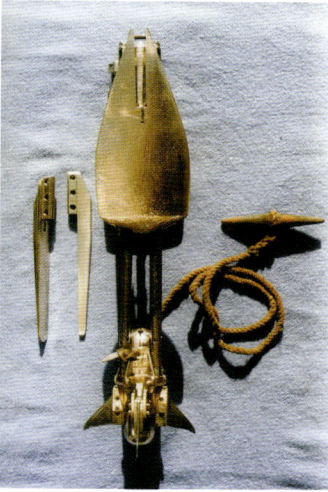

A very necessary instrument: the stopwatch. This shows the rear with its Imperial Naval marking (TT)

In 1917 the very secret Nettschneider (or net cutter) for G-torpedoes was developed. After firing it from a torpedo tube it was intended to slice through steel nets which had trapped a U-boat (TT)

This photo shows the open door of the starboard tube of a UC-II type submarine (U-Boot-Archiv Cuxhaven)

Torpedo. Los! (TT)

A heavily rusted, but virtually intact Imperial Naval torpedo. This example was trawled up out of the North Sea by the Dutch fishing vessel *TS 6* in 1997 (Dirk Johansen)

◄ In 1999, a Dutch trawler ended up with a remarkable find in its trawl: the outer torpedo tube of a UC-II minelaying submarine (Dirk Johansen)

Return from a long patrol: around the forward hatch lie all kinds of galley items, kitbags and clothing ready to be offloaded when the U-boat reaches Bruges docks. It is a photo of *UC-64* which is cruising on the Canal Zeebrugge-Bruges (TT)

Damage caused by an impact of a torpedo on the bows of a merchant ship (Der Seekrieg)

or right with a spanner. This could be done before or after loading the torpedo into the tube. A built-in gyroscope kept the torpedo running on its course after it had been fired.

The amount of spare torpedoes depended on the U-boat in question. Torpedoes were a burden in the cramped confines of a U-boat and in some cases, like with the UC-II class, had to be broken up in three parts to be able to stow them away. Loading of torpedoes was always done in port, where they were manhandled obliquely via hatches to the torpedo room. First the tubes would be filled and after that the remaining space would be taken up by the spare torpedoes. The amount of spares varied from one to 12. Spare torpedoes were mainly stored inside the submarine, but sometimes they were lashed to the deck or sides, above the ballast tanks.

Barriers made of steel nets proved to be a big problem for submerged U-boats. The netcutter on the bow was not of much use to help the whole submarine through a barrier if it would get caught. Only an explosive charge could remove an obstruction satisfactorily. By 1917 the top secret *Nettschneider* for G-type torpedoes was developed. This was an explosive charge which was mounted on the torpedo and had detachable arms with cutting sides.

DECKGUNS

At the beginning of the war a U-boat had not been provided with armament on deck, besides a Maxim-machine gun which had to be taken below when diving. This machinegun could be mounted on top, in front or just abaft the conning tower on a detachable pedestal. A machinegun could compel a crew of a small vessel to surrender and destroy floating mines. They were mostly useless against aircraft or airships because they could not be angled high enough. Many captains urged for heavier anti-aircraft guns on

 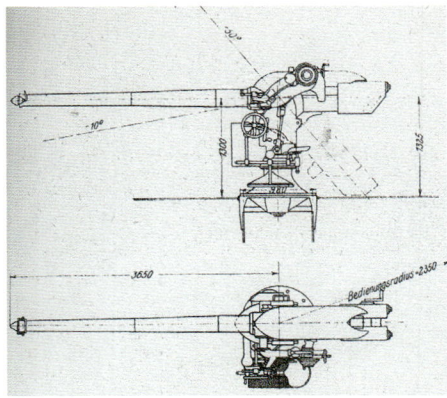

Two crewmen fire at a merchant ship with their deckmounted machinegun (Dirk Termote)

Drawing of a 10.5 cm deckgun (Techel)

An 8.8 cm gun on UB-22 (TT)

An officer guides his UB-I boat through the lock gates at Zeebrugge. On the rear of the tower a Maxim machinegun is set up on a pedestal (TT)

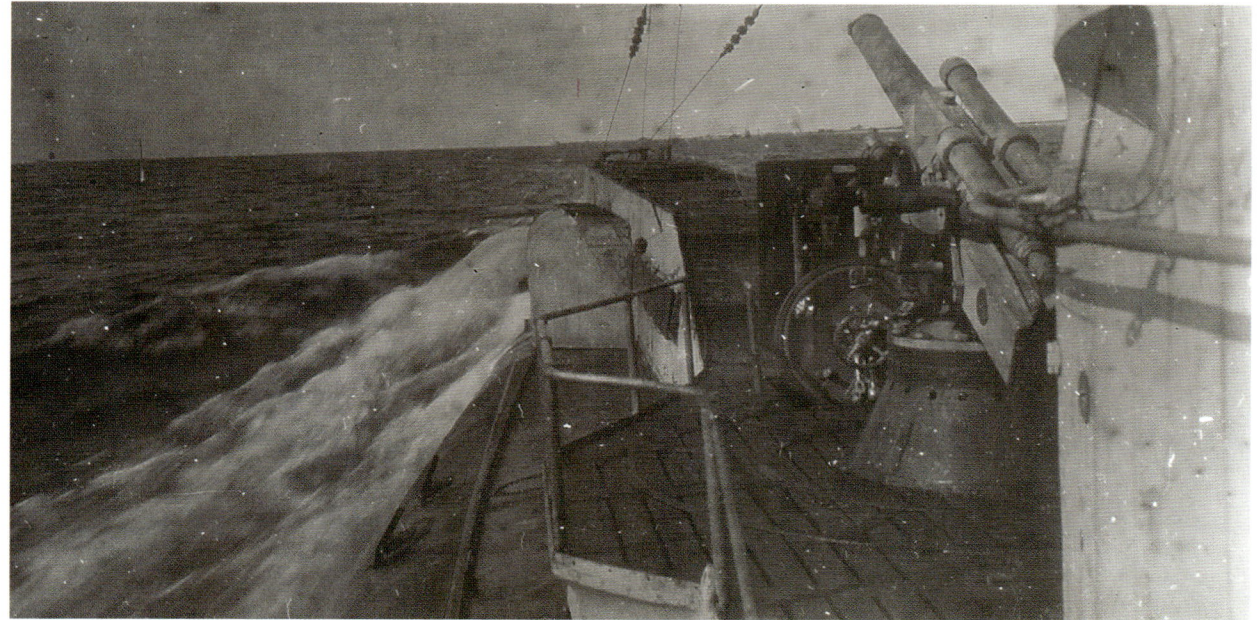

A view on the bow of the cruising *UC-64*, with Zeebrugge in the distance. The forward hatch is open, to give air to the compartment below and the 8.8 cm gun is unattended (TT)

The upkeep of a gun was important. Two crewmen clean the barrel of a 10.5 cm gun (U-boot Archiv Cuxhaven)

Watertight canisters for shells are hauled from beneath the deck to feed the 10.5 cm gun (TT)

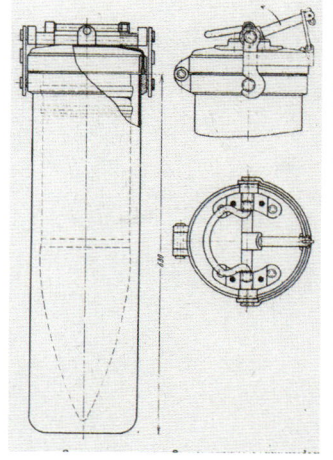

Drawing of a watertight shell container (Techel)

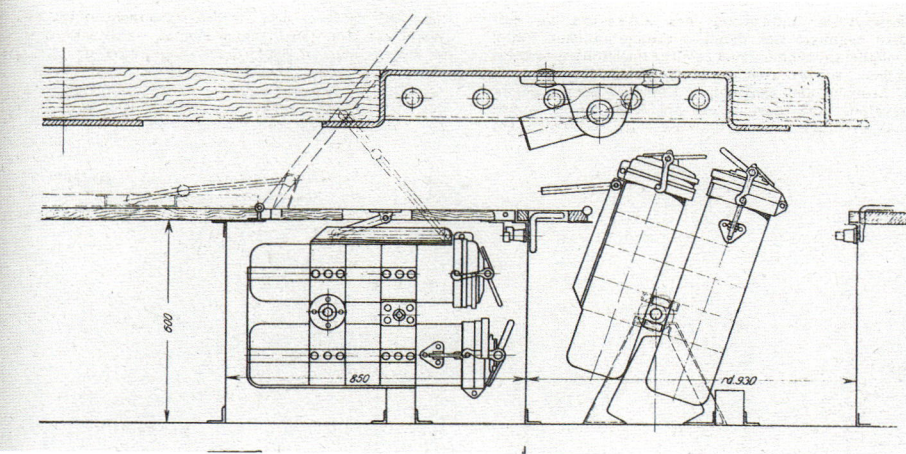

Drawing of the stowage of watertight shell containers beneath the upper deck of a U-boat (Techel)

the rear of the tower to counter any threat from the air. These requests were never answered by the Admiralty.

The companies Krupp and Ehrhardt delivered the first artillery pieces for the U-boat fleet in 1914. The most used calibre guns were 8.8 and 10.5 cm, which had a range of 13 to 14 km. In theory a U-boat had to approach to about a third of this distance to have even a slight chance of hitting a moving target. The deck gun was positioned on deck, in front of the tower, on a slightly raised platform protected on both sides with railings. The gunners could reach the gun through a hatch located close by on deck. The gun barrel could reach an angle of 45° and had no protective shield for its crew. All barrels and recoils were provided with wooden tampions which had to be inserted before diving. The company Zeiss provided every gun with pressure-resistant, double telescopic sights.

Crews of the *U-Flottille Flandern* did not perform exercises with their own deck guns. An 8.8 cm U-boat gun was mounted on a platform on the Mole at Zeebrugge. A mechanism had been built under the platform which made it sway and imitate the waves and a crew had to practice firing at targets which were towed by a tug or torpedo boat.[31]

AMMUNITION

The ammunition supply varied from U-boat to U-boat. For a 10.5 cm calibre gun with the U-type there was a supply of 400 shells, for an 8.8 cm gun it would almost double to a supply of 750 shells. If a U-boat had both types of deck gun, then there would be an equal amount of 200 shells for each piece. The middle to large UB- and UC-boats had 150 rounds for an 8.8 cm as well as an 10.5 cm calibre gun. The magazine was located in front or just aft of the control room, in the vicinity of the deck hatch, to allow a rapid to deck-level. During an action the ammunition would be manhandled to the gun platform via the deck hatches, or during rough weather through the tower hatch. If the shells had to be lifted out through the tower hatch the crew would sometimes use the *Minenabweiser* as a shell hoist to the lower platform.

An example of the underside of a 8.8 cm shell, with typical markings. Manufacturer: 'Patronenfabrik Karlsruhe', owner: 'Kaiserliche Marine' (crown over M), date: 'Mai 1906', detonator type: 'C/12' (TT)

Artillery practice on board, with the 8.8 cm deck gun (TT)

A seaman takes out a 8.8 cm shell out of its watertight container (TT)

A number of U-boat shells were stored as ready-use ammunition on deck or around the tower and kept in zinc containers. The containers were watertight and pressurised and did not get damaged when a U-boat had to submerge. The use of zinc had to prevent a charge in shell case from exploding when a fire was raging. Fire tests proved that the contained powder and detonator did not explode. There was no danger of explosion until the outer part of the container had totally melted away. This was not the case with iron containers. The resulting heat of a fire was conducted almost immediately through to the shell which would explode and do heavy damage to the U-boat and her crew.[32]

The supply of shells on the outside numbered between 12 and 24 and was stored in racks. After a shell had been fired, the lid of the container was kept open so it could fill with water. All expended rounds were held above or below deck to be sent back to the factory for refilling.

The German Admiralty had also thought of using gasmunition, but the idea was cancelled as most targets at sea lay close to a surfaced U-boat. The released gas could be sucked up by the U-boat's air intakes, depending on the direction of the wind. There was also the danger to use gasmunition fired into enclosed spaces on surface ships, especially the areas below the waterline.[33]

MINES

The function of a mine was to sink an enemy ship or to damage it in a way that it had to be salvaged to undergo repairs. But this was not its only purpose. It was as important that the threat of mines could occupy an entire fleet of enemy minesweepers in minesweeping activities so they could not be used in actions against U-boats.

UC-I and UC-II boats were issued with the specially designed U-boot-Mine UC/200 type. It was a small EMA* with rounded anchor plate (also known as 'chair') which had a drum attached which held the anchor cable. Four arms of 1.75 m in length were attached to the chair and made it easier for the mine to slip from the shaft. The hinged arms opened up once the mine hit the bottom and gave it the necessary anchorage and stability to remain upright. The

---
* EM = Einheitsmine, A = status of development.

◂ The captain of *UB-21* leans leisurely against the conning tower and cradles a K98 rifle in his arm. To his left are several watertight shell containers (TT)

93

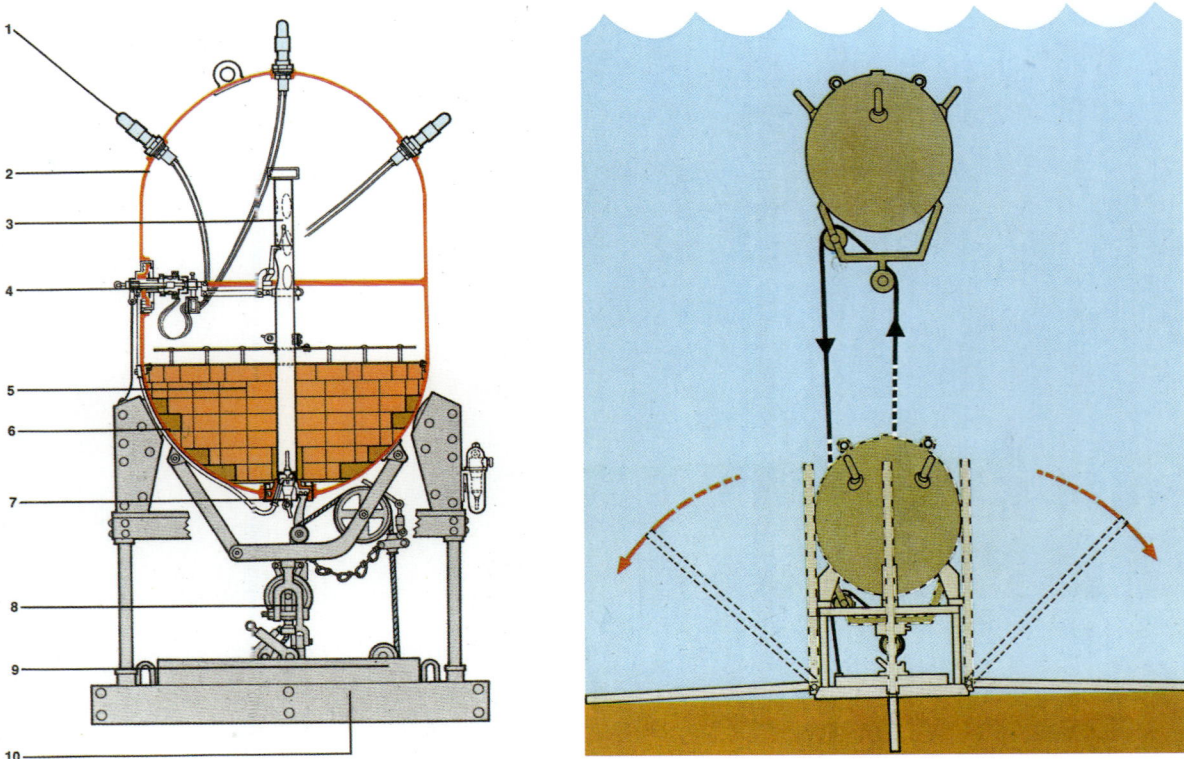

Schematic diagram of a U-boat mine and its working: Hertzhorn (1), iron casing (2), detonator (3), safety (inactive when the mine is layed) (4), TNT-charges (5), wood supports (6), electrical controlled firing mechanism (7), hydrostat (8), anchor cable fitted in a horizontal drum (9), mine chair (10) (Fitzsimmons)

Crewmen watch on while a mine, mounted on its chair, is carefully lowered into the bow of a UC-II class U-boat (TT)

The loading of mines in the narrow shafts of a UC-II class boat was a painstaking job which needed precision and caution (U-boot Archiv Cuxhaven)

explosive charge consisted of 120 kg of TNT,[34] which had a higher explosive power than the previously used nitrocellulose. The shell of the mine had to be pressure-proof, because it would be stored outside the pressure hull of the U-boat. Mines could be deposited to a maximum depth of 100 m. When it left the shaft, the mine was weighted down to the bottom by its chair and the extended arms would secure it upright. The mine would not be immediately released to its pre-set depth, but a salt capsule functioned as a timer. This was meant to give the U-boat laying the mines enough time to escape before the mine left its anchor. Eventually the mine drifted to its pre-determined depth and was kept hooked by the anchor cable.

German contact mines enduced an electric current from the moment they were touched by a vessel. Inside there was a dry-charged battery without any acid. On the top of the outer shell there weer four or more lead horns or caps (*Hertzhorn*[35]) which covered a glass file filled with chromium acid. In the acid there was a zinc-coal element floating around. After a ship hit the mine, the horn bent and the glass file broke causing the zinc-coal element in the acid to make an electric contact with the battery.[36] The battery produced an electric current which ignited the charge of TNT. Because of its separate, enclosed circuit the German mine did not have the same problem of corrosion as the British contact mine.

SPRENGPATRONE M/03

A *Sprengpatrone* or explosive cartridge was a charge put into a cylindrical brass or iron container. It had a diameter of 12.5 cm and a length of 32.5 cm. Its total weight was 2.5 kg, of which 1.8 kg was TNT. The cartridge was provided with a detonating mechanism and a fuse of about 2 m. The detonator was ignited by means of a wooden system which could be pressed like a plunger. After removing the safety pin, the fuse would ignite by bashing the plunger hard onto the detonator. Depending on the total length of the fuse, it would burn for five to ten minutes. On board the U-boat, detonators and charges were kept in separate areas of the vessel. Detonators were kept in wooden boxes and the charges in round iron barrels which had been welded shut.

The *Sprengpatrone* was mainly designed to destroy an enemy vessel in the most economic way. This stood in stark contrast with the use of torpedoes or a large expenditure of shells to sink an enemy ship

A Sprengpatrone was an amount of explosive fitted in a cylindrical container which was detonated by a plunger (TT)

A somewhat simplified depiction of the detonation of a Sprengpatrone (TT)

by gunfire. The explosive charge could only be used in ideal circumstances, with a calm sea and when the targeted ship had surrendered itself. There could not be an immediate threat from other vessels, such as fast warships or airships, because the crew of a U-boat had to reach the intended vessel with a small skif to be able to place the explosives. Only after the enemy crew had been ordered to leave their ship in their own lifeboats could the vessel be entered by a prize crew. A prize crew consisted mainly of an officer or petty officer and two or more seamen. The explosive charges were attached to each other in clusters and grouped in two or three areas which lay beneath the waterline, with a preference to the outside of the hull, in front or just aft of a bulkhead. Depending on the size of the ship and the type of cargo it carried, the usual choice was the engine room. Because the detonating mechanism had to be fired from deck level, this meant that the crew had enough time to depart the doomed ship. It was advised not to attach the charge to the inside of the hull as there was a chance that the force of the explosion would be directed inwards and not do enough damage to the hull. By tying charges to the outside of the hull, the explosion would be aided by the water pressure to make a larger hole in the hull. If this was impossible to position, then the charges had to be placed as deep as possible against the hull, in a location beneath the waterline, and covered sufficiently by heavy weights such as bags of sand or coal. With smaller ships the charges netted the best result when they were placed between the condenser and the hull or near a seacock or pump. The prize crew had to thread carefully through boilers and coal bunkers as accumulated coal dust could make too large an explosion. If there was time and the circumstances allowed it, seacocks and hatches would also be opened to let air circulate within the ship and let it sink quicker. From 7 April 1915 it was the rule that every U-boat had to possess a minimum of six *Sprengpatrone* and six time fuses in its arsenal.

The second reason to have explosive charges on board was that they were perfect for the self-destruction of the U-boat. This action would be necessary when the U-boat threatened to fall into enemy hands. The charges were most successful when attached to the warhead of a torpedo or near a seacock, so as to guarantee the U-boat's destruction for sure. A supply of six to 12 explosive charges was reserved for this function alone.

Sprenggeräte were designed for larger U-boats, such as U-cruisers, which operated far from land. This was a normal *Sprengpatrone* which had a time mechanism. The prize crew would place the charge in the hold or another compartment and set the time

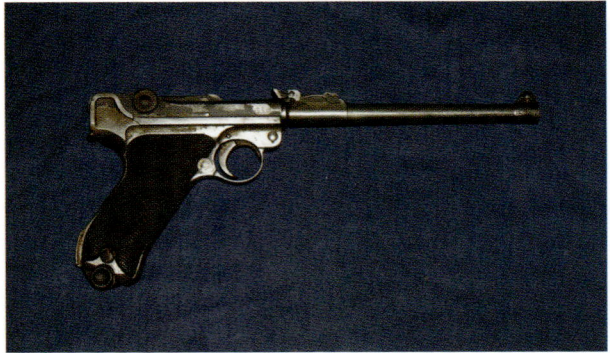

A typical, long-barrelled naval Luger (Provincial Domain Raversijde)

96

mechanism from between one to 15 days, enabling the enemy crew to reach land and evacuate the ship safely.(37) When the time had come, the time fuse would detonate the charge and sink the ship. This system was not in use with the U-boats of the Flanders Flotilla because they operated close to their own ports and the enemy.

SMALL ARMS

By the end of the war all U-boats were supplied by the AG Weser yard with M/1904-pistols. The amount of pistols on board a large U-boat could be as many as 30. Half of them were kept in a locked cabinet in the forward torpedo room and the other half in the aft torpedo room.(38)

Besides pistols, there were also K98 Mauser carbines on board which were mainly used to riddle and sink drifting mines. Their length made them unhandy weapons for stowage and preference went to the *Marine-Lüger* or Naval Lügerpistol. The *Marine-Lüger* or P04 was the standard pistol of the Imperial Navy and had a longer barrel than the normal P08-pistols. It had a wooden grip and special leather holster and belts. The small arms arsenal was completed with a *Seitengewehr M1911* or *Entermesser*, which, together with the pistols was used for man-to-man fighting if on a boarding action. The blade of the boarding knife resembled the standard bajonet 98/05, but had a longer blade. Around the hilt was a basket-shaped protection, which made it look like a boarding sabre. The *Entermesser* was produced by the company Simson & Co. from Suhl.

HAND GRENADES AND FIREBOMBS: THE GOLDSCHMIDT-SYSTEM

In 1915 all U-boats had a supply of a hundred hand grenades. Later this was limited to only the larger U-boats which had prize crews on board. Prize crews were put on board enemy cargo ships which had a valuable or very useful cargo after which an attempt would be made to sail them to a friendly port. Hand grenades would be used together with small arms in boarding actions. Grenades proved to carry certain risk as they could damage the U-boat or its crew. *Kapitänleutnant*

A crew pose after finishing their basic U-boat training. They are armed with boarding knives and naval Lugers (TT)

An officer keeps watch with a drawn naval Luger, on the conning tower (TT)

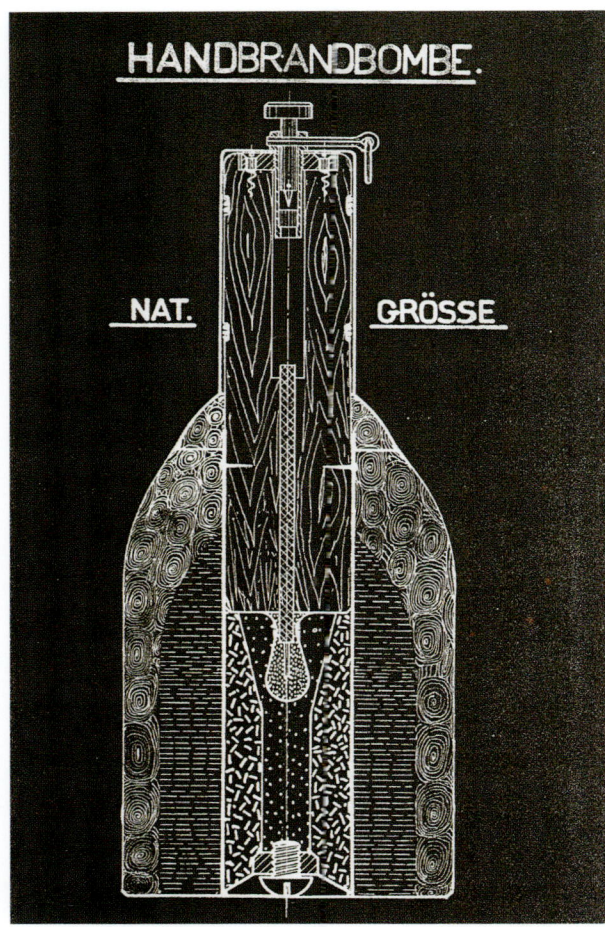

Drawing of the manual firebomb (BArch)

z.S. Gerdes wrote a letter to the High Command of the Navy in Wilhelmshaven in 1916 where he pleaded for them to scrap hand grenades in the list of the stores. Gerdes said that the explosive of the grenade would not do enough damage to an enemy and only became a threat to their own vessel. Grenades thrown manually only had a maximum range of 30 to 40 m and an impact on living targets. A stick grenade would not do any damage to a vessel because of its light construction. Fragments of the grenade could end up 100 m away and wound its thrower or the crew which was on deck. There was also the risk that an enemy crewman reacted quickly enough to pick up a thrown grenade and throw it back at the U-boat.[39] Gerdes' advice was taken and by January 1917 there were no more hand grenades on board U-boats.

From July 1915 German Naval Command introduced firebombs as a cheap alternative weapon for sinking sailing ships and vessels laden with wood or flammable materials. It meant another means of saving torpedoes and shells. Just as with the explosive charge it could only be used in ideal weather conditions.

By the end of the same year the command of the *U-Flottille Flandern* put in an order with the company Th. Goldschmidt of Essen. This firm was already supplying materials for the airships of the Imperial Navy. The ordered device was quite simple in design and composition. It consisted of a wooden stock with an iron container designed to carry a flammable liquid. The container was filled with thermit and covered with a hardened, flammable coating. The stock, which fitted perfectly in the metal container, had a cylindrical stem in to which the detonating system was fitted. In the interior was the main detonator and on the outside there was a manual detonator. The explosive was lit by removing the cap and breaking the pin which held the exterior detonator. This would ignite in the stem and the main detonator would make the liquid burn and so start the fire. The whole process would take just five seconds.[40]

A firebomb would not be effective if just thrown anywhere on an enemy ship. The prize crew had to first go on board and place the bombs in areas below decks. After that, the deck and cargo had to be doused in petrol to increase the effect of the firebomb. This was theory, practice proved to be a totally different story.

In an extract from the wardiary of *U-35*, dated February 1917, a note was found concerning experiences with the Goldschmidt-system. *Kapitänleutnant* Lothar von Arnauld de la Perriere wrote that the flammable liquid in the bombs did not preserve. Two of the four bombs used refused to burn, even though the detonators had ignited. The bombs that did burn were extinguished shortly afterwards, as they lacked a constant supply of fresh air. Thick clouds created at the ignition would suffocate the bombs and douse them. The bombs could not be used in compartments where there was no free-flowing air. On deck there was no shortage of fresh air, but the wet atmosphere at sea mostly did not let the bombs burn out. Even though the Command of the Flanders Flotilla had placed an order for these weapons from Goldschmidt, there is no written evidence of this weapon actually being used in the North Sea. The simpler explosive charge proved to be a more effective weapon.

SALVAGE AND SAFETY

DINGHIES

At the beginning of the war the U-class had an iron dinghy lashed upside down to the deck, just in front of the tower. Later on, this was replaced by a small canvas dinghy which could carry four men. This type of dinghy was only supplied to the larger UC-II and UB-III class submarines which had sufficient deck space. For most U-boat captains the dinghy proved to be more of a nuisance than an aid. When contact had to be made with a detained merchant ship, usually the enemy was ordered to use their lifeboats to come alongside the U-boat. A dinghy was unwieldy as a lifeboat because it took a lot of time to detach and turn it over. Many captains were in favour of leaving the dinghy behind in harbour.

Crewmen row out on a rubber dinghy towards an enemy ship in order to search for supplies (TT)

This photo shows a signaling pistol held by the officer left, and at the bottom the top of the telephone and light buoy is visible on deck (TT) ▶

TELEPHONE AND LIGHT BUOY

All pre-war U-boats had been fitted with a telephone and light buoy. With this a sunken U-boat could come in contact with a surface vessel and possibly be provided with fresh air. The brass buoy, which was mounted in a recess at deck level in front of the tower, was filled with air under pressure. A steel cable on a drum connected the buoy to the U-boat. A steel spring in the bottom part kept the buoy in place being secured with a pin. When the pin was removed, the buoy shot towards the surface. The spring system made it possible for the buoy to detach itself from the U-boat even if it lay on its side.

The telephone was fitted in the watertight compartment of the buoy which could be opened by using a handwheel. The buoy could be illuminated by a watertight electric light. On the side of the buoy was a bakelite push button which could be used to signal morsecode to the trapped crew. As well as the cable there was a hose which could provide fresh air to the U-boat if necessary. A marked plate was visible on the top of the buoy which read: *'Hier liegt ein deutsches Unterseeboot'*, with the concerning U-boatnumber. During the war most commanders had the buoy removed and left on land as the position of a U-boat could be jeopardised if a buoy was accidently released by the shock from an explosion.

Worldwide, there are hardly any of these buoys still in existence. The former Zeebrugge museum had one on display, but after the museum closed down the buoy was lost and is only known from old photographs.

By means of a telephone buoy it was possible to talk with the crew of a sunken U-boat (Der Seekrieg)

A photo taken in one of the rooms of the former Zeebrugge Museum. In the centre of the photo stands a very rare example of a telephone buoy (TT)

Details of the telephone and light buoy for U-boats (International Maritime Museum Hamburg)

A heavily overgrown lifting hook on the stern of the wreck of *UC-62*, sunk on the Thornton Bank (TT)

A U-boat is lifted up into the belly of the salvage ship *SMS Vulkan* (TT)

LIFTING HOOKS AND SALVAGE VESSELS

If a crew of a sunken U-boat had the luck to be discovered in time, then a salvage ship could be sent to the site. Hardhat divers descended along the cable of the telephone buoy to the wreck and would attach steel cables to lifting hooks which were fitted in front and aft of the conning tower. Later lifting hook types were constructed in such a way that automatically two or four buoys would float to the surface after the U-boat had sunk. These buoys were connected to each other by a pully system of thin cables. The salvage team could pick up one of these buoys and replace the lighter with a heavier cable. By reeling in the second buoy, the heavy cable would be led to the hook on the U-boat hull via the cable of the first buoy. Once on the U-boat it would arrive automatically on the saddle-shaped hook. The same system was used for the second hook. Because the cables were evenly connected to bow and stern, the U-boat could be brought horizontally to the surface. With this system there was no necessity to use a diver and chances of success were much higher. The Imperial Navy possessed two specially designed ships for the salvage of submarines: the twin-hulled *SMS Vulkan* and *SMS Cyclop*. They were in fact a primitive version of what we know today as the catamaran. They had a displacement of 1.500 BRT and in between the two hulls was a space wherein the salvaged U-boat could be lifted. These large salvage vessels could only be used in home waters. If a U-boat was sunk at the battlefront, the crews had to make their own way out.

A diver on *SMS Vulkan* descends into the water to inspect the salvaged U-boat (TT)

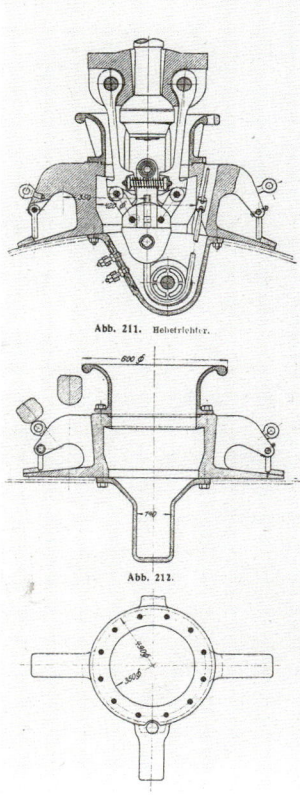

Technical drawing of a lifting hook on a U-boat (Techel)

ESCAPE APPARATUS

Naval surface ships usually had an extensive aray of diving gear on board to be able to carry out immediate repairs or checks at sea. The gear consisted of pumps, divesuits, helmets, weights and many metres of rubber air hose. In the limited interior of a U-boat it was not possible to stow much of this kind of gear and another type of diving gear had to be devised. In 1913 a 'hoseless' apparatus was introduced, designed by the companies Dräger of Lübeck and Westfalia-Gelsenkirchen. The diving apparatus worked satisfactorily to depths up to 30 m. It was light and compact, which made it easy to stow in small vessels. It functioned on small cylinders filled with pure oxygen which circulated through a purification cartridge. At a depth of 20 m a dive of about one hour could be made.[41] The device had a kali cartridge for air purification, an inflatable life vest, a nosepincer, a mouthpiece and goggles. The kali cartridge purified the exhaled, poisonous carbon dioxide by adding an amount of oxygen from the oxygen bottles so the air could be recycled. The kali cartridge was a cylindrical tin in which were 20 layers of kali- and natron

Every crewman of a U-boat had a Dräger escape apparatus at his disposal (TT)

A sailor, equipped with a Dräger-breathing apparatus is preparing himself to make an inspection of the underwater part of the hull of his U-boat (TT)

purification matter. In certain areas there were exits to let poisonous gasses escape from the aircycle. The tin gave the user about half an hour of breathable air. The oxygen tank had a contents of 0.6 l and the oxygen supply had to be regulated manually. The same had to be done with the compressed air tank of 0.4 l, which was necessary to inflate the life vest. The cartridge and all the tanks were fitted in a brass frame which was protected by a rubber cover and could be attached to the chest of the diver with canvas straps. A 5 kg lead weight on the bottom of the apparatus had to prevent the diver's head from falling backwards. By regulating the airflow in the life vest with a vent, the diver could determine his ascent speed (in theory!). Besides being used for quick surveys of the hull and repairs at sea, it was introduced as the main escape apparatus of the U-boat. The first U-boats had a supply of these apparatus for every single crewmen and could be used without danger up to depths of 60 m. The Dräger-apparatus weighed 24 kg, which was a fraction of what a hardhat diver had to carry. It took up only a small area and every crewman could be issued with one. The apparatus was also easy and quickly to use in an emergency. The diver could be totally independent from the U-boat, because he carried his own air supply. Watertight handlamps were not issued to everyone, but every compartment was provided with one.

OTHER SAFETY MEASURES

From March 1915 a safety line was introduced on all U-boats. This was a heavy rope which ran from the tower to the netcutter on the bow. On the rope slid a strengthened rope eye with a belt and quick-release clip. This sliding rope would prevent anyone from being swept overboard during rough weather and with little purchase on the slippery hull. His comrades could also guide the rope to which the seaman was attached from front to back and vice versa. The belt on the rope eye had sewn-in pockets which could carry a hammer or spicing equipment.

Swathed in oilskins, a sailor holds on to the jumping wires on the stern of his U-boat (TT)

105

ESCAPE FROM THE SUNKEN *UC-26*

U-boot Matrose Rudolf Eickhoff and his brother pose for the photo. Rudolf would be killed when his U-boat, *UC-26* was sunk on 2 June 1917 (TT)

Finding evidence of the use of the Dräger-apparatus during the war has proven to be a hard undertaking. During the war there were probably less provisions for all crew members than in pre-war U-boats. Reports from surviving U-boatmen state that they mainly had to risk an ascent from a stricken U-boat without the help of any escape gear. Most of the survivors would suffer pulmonary problems.

In the morning of 8 May 1917, *UC-26*, under command of *Kapitänleutnant z. S.* Matthias Graf von Schmettow, was rammed and sunk by a British Destroyer off Cap Gris Nez. *UC-26* sank to a depth of 50 m and water started to gush in through a rent near the radio room. The surviving first officer, *Oberleutnant z. S.* Heinrich Petersen, testified that the U-boat had a slant of 50° to starboard after the explosion and that afterwards all power failed. Several times the crew tried in vain to blow the ballast tanks and release air into the U-boat. The engine room was flooding and all surviving crew members had gathered in the control room. In this compartment the water level was gradually rising to the survivors' chest levels. Petersen crawled up into the tower to try to open the tower hatch and make an escape possible. Oil from the ruptured tanks had mixed with the rising water and drowned several men. The last thing that Petersen heard was von Schmettow encouraging three hurrah's for the Emperor from his men. The pressure from the rising water increased the pressure in the tower which ended up in the tower hatch being blown open. During his escape Petersen hooked his foot on the tower ladder, but could free himself and get to the surface. The captain and a apprentice engineer were also able to escape through the tower hatch. Petersen knew he was under six atmosphere of pressure at this depth and he tried to slow his ascent as much as possible. He exhaled twice and reached the surface and breathed in the cold air. At first instance he felt he had not suffered any wounds, felt no pain and no blood came from his mouth. He heard several cries for help around him, but could not see anybody because of the high waves. Twenty minutes later a British destroyer, which was heading against the sea, was sighted, and its crew threw life belts to the survivors. Petersen managed to hold on to one of the life belts with the last of his strength. Because the destroyer was drifting eastwards with the tide, it distanced itself further and further from the survivors. The British launched a lifeboat and were able to pick up Petersen and *Maschinistenmaat* Axel. Another group of survivors were still floundering some way off. When Petersen was landed on the deck of the destroyer he heard one of the officers say: '*I think, that will do it.*' He still heard cries for help coming from seven or eight crewmen in the water. In the meantime, the British crew had stowed the lifeboat back on board and the captain gave orders to continue their patrol. Petersen approached one of the officers and begged them to save the others and not to let them drown. He did not get any further but fell unconsciously to the deck and was taken to the officers' mess, after which the destroyer picked up speed. After two hours Petersen awoke to a severe headache and pain in his ears, head and kidneys. After eight hours the ear- and kidney pain eventually subsided and Petersen was well treated on board the destroyer. The rescued engineer stated later on that he and five others had escaped through the engine room hatch. Once on the surface they were able to stay afloat by hanging on to pieces of debris, but one by one they had drowned. The destroyer continued its patrol until 8 am the following day, when it entered the port of Dover. The uniforms of both survivors had been drenched with oil and they were replaced with hospital fatigues. Under escort of six armed men they were taken to HMS *Terror* and locked up below deck. After interrogation they were sent to prisoner-of-war camps. Petersen ended up in Donington Hall, the camp for officers, where he still suffered a year later from chest pains caused by his rapid ascent. When at Manchester camp he was overcome by tuberculosis.

Despite all the sufferings, Petersen managed to survive and after his release after the Armistice he got permission to recuperate from his tuberculosis at Bad Reichenhall spa. But even in 1919 he still suffered from problems which had damaged his lungs during his escape from *UC-26*.[42]

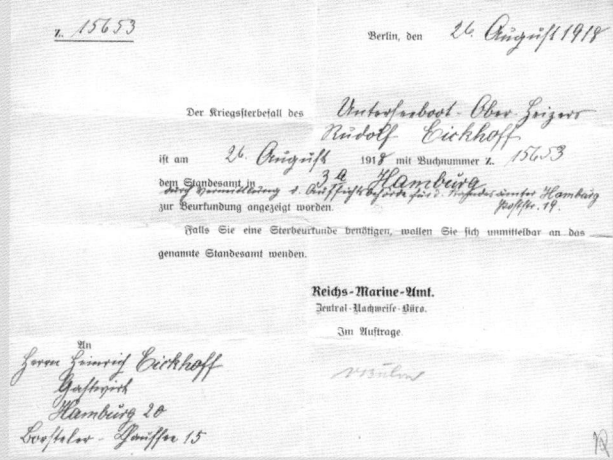

Notice sent to his family concerning the death of *Unterseeboots-Oberheizer* Rudolf Eickhoff of *UC-26* (TT)

A handwritten letter from Rudolf Eickhoff to his family, dated 23 February 1917, three months before his death (TT)

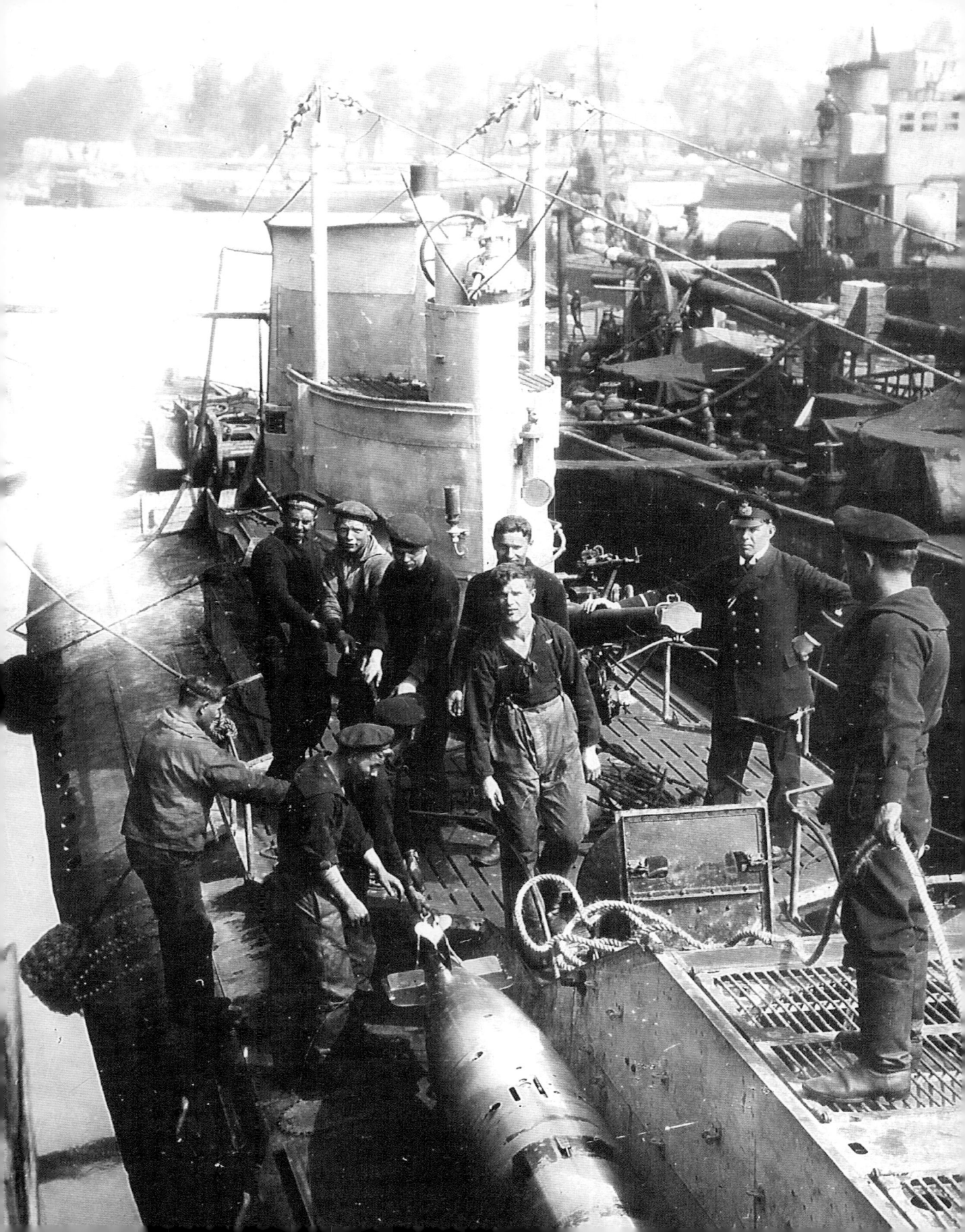

UNTERSEEBOOTSFLOTTILLE FLANDERN

DEVELOPMENT OF A UNIT

From December 1914 the Germans started to transform the Flemish ports as protective harbours or supply points mainly for U-boats, but also for small surface craft. The Admiralty could not berth large warships in these ports because they ran too much risk when crossing the North Sea from the German ports to Flanders. Due to its proximity to the British coastline, Flanders was seen by the Germans as a possibility to increase the war with U-boats against Allied shipping and therefore these ports were transformed to permanent berths for an entire fleet of U-boats.

The supreme command of the German Naval forces was led by Admiral Ludwig von Schröder who had his headquarters in Bruges. The *Unterseebootsflottille Flandern* was created on 29 March 1915, with *Korvettenkapitän* Karl Bartenbach as its commanding officer. He was generally seen as capable and well liked. U-boat captains were usually totally independent, they could leave and return with their U-boat when they wanted, but had to give a date for their return.

The area of operations for the Flanders Flotilla bordered in the east with the line that stretched from Flamborough Head to the Terschelling lightvessel. In the west it stretched from the longitude of 7° W and the latitude of 56° N.

The UC-boats would carry out their minelaying operations within this demarcation. As a rule, mines had to be laid within 3 miles of land. Minelayers also would make sure their mines were sown near harbours or busy coastal routes. The area around Wissant, the Scillys and the western entrance of the Channel around Land's End were not to be mined.

Officers of the II. U-Flottille Flandern, taken on 29 March 1918, the third anniversary of the U-Flottille Flandern. They have gathered on the steps of Bartenbach's residence (TT)

◄ A 50 cm Schwarzkopf torpedo is loaded in the starboard tube of *UC-64* in the Bruges docks. On the right stands first officer Lt. d. Res. Braue (TT)

The U-boats used torpedoes and deck guns to engage enemy shipping in the Channel, the Western Approaches, the Thames Estuary, the Northhinder, the east coast, the Irish Sea and the Scottish coast. Although there was a specific area which was assigned to the U-boats of the Flanders Flotilla, its captains still stayed relatively free for movement. The captured *Kapitänleutnant z. S.* Claus Lafrenz declared to the British that he could roam freely with his *UC-65* as far as the southern coast of Ireland and the northern area of Spain. For U-boats from the five flotillas based in the German North Sea harbours, it was strictly forbidden to intrude in the area designated to the Flanders boats.[43]

The length of a patrol at sea was defined by the size of the U-boat. The small UC-I and UB-I types mostly remained three days up to maximum one week away from home. The middlesize UB-II and UC-II types returned after two to three weeks. *Kapitänleutnant z.S.* Lafrenz had the habit of remaining 14 to 16 days at sea, depending how fast his supply of mines and torpedoes was depleted. His shortest patrol he carried out with *UB-18*, with which he only remained 69 hours at sea. During this time he had fired all five torpedoes and sunk five merchantmen. The absolute record-holder for the briefest patrol was *Oberleutnant z. S.* Otto Steinbrinck who only remained 55 hours away from home. After he had sunk the light cruiser *HMS Ariadne* and three merchant ships in quick succession, he returned home to load five new torpedoes. The larger submarines were able to stay up to a month away, depending on their fuel- and munition supplies.

A seaman hands over the manifesto to a U-boat officer of a stopped American cargo ship (Claus Bergen)

TWO FLOTILLAS

The U-boats of the Flanders Flotilla managed to gain large successes in just one year. Up to October 1915 a fleet of 16 U-boats had sunk a total of 140 Allied ships. From 1st October 1915 until 30 April 1916, the small fleet destroyed 84 Allied and 28 neutral vessel whilst its own losses were limited to two U-boats. From the end of April 1916 came a longtime ban on attacking merchant ships. This was to avoid incidents where American civilians might be killed. During this time six small UC-I boats continued their minelaying operations in the Thames Estuary and on the British east coast. In September 1916 the U-boat fleet increased in strength with the improved minelayer, the UC-II type. From February 1917 U-boat activities increased and by July 1917 38 U-boats were permanently based in Flanders.

In August 1917 the fleet was split into *U-Flottille Flandern I* and *II*. The first flotilla came under command of *Oberleutnant z. S.* Hans Walther and the second under *Oberleutnant z. S.* Otto Rohrbeck. As aides they had *Oberleutnant z. S.* Fritz von Twardowski (*I U-Flot. Flandern*) and *Oberleutnant z. S.* Kawelmacher (*II U-Flot. Flandern*).

By 1918 supreme command was still in hands of *Korvettenkapitän* Bartenbach with *Kapitänleutnant* Steinbrinck as admiral staff officer. *Kapitänleutnant* Günther Suadicani was assigned to Bruges as his second staff officer.

U-boats often changed flotilla and it was difficult to determine a fixed berth for certain U-boats. This

Korvettenkapitän Karl Bartenbach (TT)

Another merchantship on her final plunge to the bottom (TT)

was due to the high losses which the fleet suffered and the monthly replenishments of new U-boats.

The situation on 15 October 1917 was as following: *U-Flottille Flandern I* consisted of 16 boats with *UC-4, UC-11, UC-16, UC-17, UC-50, UC-51, UC-77, UC-79, UB-54, UB-55, UB-56, UB-57, UB-58, UB-59, UB-80* and *UB-81*. *U-Flottille Flandern II* was made up of 21 boats with: *UC-47, UC-48, UC-62, UC-63, UC-64, UC-65, UC-69, UC-70, UC-71, UC-75, UB-10, UB-12, UB-16, UB-17, UB-18, UB-30, UB-31, UB-33, UB-35, UB-38* and *UB-40*.

By May 1918 *U-Flottille Flandern I* numbered 15 U-boats: *UC-4, UC-11, UC-17, UC-56, UC-77, UC-78, UB-55, UB-57, UB-59, UB-74, UB-78, UB-80, UB-103, UB-107* and *UB-109*. *U-Flottille Flandern II* only had ten U-boats remaining: *UB-10, UB-12, UB-16, UB-30, UB-31, UB-40, UC-64, UC-70, UC-71* and *UC-75*. More than half its number had been decimated and were lost at sea.

The total number of U-boats in active service with the Flanders Flotilla throughout the war was 93. By early 1917 the losses were so high that the flotilla never possessed more than 30 boats at one moment.

111

MODUS OPERANDI

U-boat captains had a reasonable independence concerning their patrol grounds. Mutual agreements were usually made with fellow commanders when two or more U-boats would have to operate in the same area, for example the British east coast or the Thames Estuary. Otherwise there was no instance where U-boats worked in 'packs', such as was the habit in the Second World War. When two captains did decide to cooperate, it was the seniority in rank which brought the greatest problem and it would constrict the junior officer's initiative.

Minelayers were assigned sectors of divided areas of coast. Usually a captain evolved into an expert for a certain area and he alone would operate there with his U-boat. This had been the case with *UC-65*, in which *Kapitänleutnant z. S.* Claus Lafrenz and his predecessor would lay mines off Le Havre, on the coast of France. Mines were preferably laid at tidestop at a maximum depth of 30 m. Minelayers would often operate on the surface during the night or early morning where they would count on a lessened enemy vigil. Theoretically, a group of four mines had to be laid per harbour or zone. In practice, this usually proved to be quite different. A captain was mostly too pressed to run long distances with a boat full of mines and was prone to laying fields closer to each other.

If information was at hand, then there was a preference to mine areas which had previously been cleared. When the Royal Navy discovered a field of six to 12 mines, shipping was diverted to 2 miles away from the area. It normally took two to three days to clear a whole area of mines and it would take the same amount of time to clear groups of four or 18 mines.

This way of operating was known to U-boat captains who tried to sow irregular patterns when releasing their explosive cargo. On one side five mines were dropped, whilst only three or none were dropped the another side.[44] By doing this they could confuse and prolong the job of the minesweepers.

The routes which U-boats followed towards the open sea had a set pattern. To reach the western area of the Channel they had to pass many hazards. First they had to make sure not to get entangled in the anchored mine nets off the Flemish coast and the smaller fields between Dunkirk and the Goodwin Sands. After that they had to endure the most dangerous part of the journey: the Dover Barrage. Once they had passed the Barrage was a third obstacle: the deeper minefield of the Varne Bank. On the surface the whole area was protected by dozens of armed trawlers which were waiting to chase a cornered U-boat to deeper water and into the minefield.

To reach this area from Zeebrugge, the U-boats took a northwesterly course from the end of Zeebrugge Mole to a buoy off Blankenberge. From Blankenberge buoy a course of 330° was set. This course was kept for 18 miles, and was also taken by U-boats leaving of Ostend, after which they submerged to the bottom and remained there until night had come.[45] Captains usually preferred to cross a mined area on the surface, near high tide and during the night. Preference was taken for the British side of the Dover Barrage as this had deeper water.

It was a said rule that a small- or middle-sized U-boat would be turned over to the *Werft Division* (or wharf division) after every trip of five to 10 days

A relaxed atmosphere on board a homeward bound U-boat (TT)

112

for a general inspection, overhaul and to carry out repairs. Docktime for larger U-boats, which had remained at sea up to a month, was three weeks. Because the Germans had created large facilities, six to eight U-boats were able to be taken into dry dock simultaneously. After July 1917 trials were limited to the harbours of Ostend and Zeebrugge. This was implimented after *UB-20* was lost with all hands in a minefield whilst on trial in the Kwintebank area on 28th July 1917.

Theoretically only 20% of the 30 U-boats in service with the Flanders Flotilla, a total of six U-boats, were at sea at one time. The other 80% were spread out over the three ports for repairs and rest, and the division was as follows: six U-boats in Ostend, 12 in Zeebrugge and six in Bruges. This was the situation in 1915-1916 and the amount of operational U-boats would double in the last two years of the war.

RESULTS

In comparison with the three main German bases in western Europe, Flanders proved to be proportionally the most successful. By 1 May 1918 the Flanders Flotilla had sunk 2,501,000 tons of shipping with an average presence of 22 U-boats. The North Sea port - with 55 operational submarines - were able to sink 4,219,000 tons in shipping and the 31 U-boats stationed in the Mediterranean destroyed 2,480,000 tons. During the months of October 1917 to May 1918, which saw some of the hardest actions of the war, the Allies increased the pressure on the U-boats. They adapted the convoy system and made much use of depth charges to combat U-boats. This period also made it more difficult for the Flanders' boats and proved to be the lowest months of Allied sinking results. In seven months they only managed to destroy 105,000

A sailing ship is ordered to hove to for an approaching U-boat (Dirk Termote)

The entire crew of *UB-22*, including the ship's dog, gathers for the photo after a successful mission (TT)

tons, whilst the North Sea U-boats sank 1,431,000 tons and the ones in the Mediterranean 1,173,000 tons. The U-boats of the Flanders Flotilla were under enormous pressure to perform successfully and it was clearly visible in the results of their monthly actions. Figures for the beginning of 1918 show that a total of 24 U-boats had to carry out 20 patrols per month. In the North Sea ports 54 U-boats undertook 27 monthly patrols and in the Mediterranean 35 U-boats were on average 12 times per month out of port. This meant that the U-boats based in the Flemish ports sank an average of 41,500 tons in shipping. This was a mere 24,600 tons per U-boat for the ones in the North Sea ports and 32,900 per U-boat in the Mediterranean.

By the end of the war the Flanders Flotilla was able to sink a total of 2,554 Allied ships. But for this result a high price was paid: the *U-Flottille Flandern* lost a total of 73 U-boats at sea and five were interned by neutral countries. This was a loss rating of 80%! 145 officers and more than 1,000 crewmen perished in this Flotilla alone. It was mainly in the last two years of the war that the highest losses were suffered. Between October 1917 and May 1918 19 U-boats failed to return out of a total of 146 operations carried out. The U-boats based in the North Sea ports had to endure a loss of 27 U-boats out of 194 missions. The patrols which the U-boats had to carry out from German ports were much longer than those of the Flanders boats, but they were exposed to the same amount of danger. In terms of percentage, 13% of the Flanders boats and 14% of the North Sea boats were lost during their respective operations.

OFFICERS AND MEN

REQUIREMENTS AND TRAINING

In the run up to the first year of war potential U-boat crews were selected from volunteerss who had to correspond to a long list of demands. By 1917 the system of volunteers was dispensed with and U-boat crews were just selected. They did not necessarily even have to come from the navy, a branch of the army would do. If one was to be accepted in the U-boat division one had to meet the demands which were high. The selection was mainly based on physical requirements, but psychologically candidates also had to fit a certain profile. Many officers and petty officers would already have a background in the merchant navy.

A candidate had to be healthy and not have a history of heart- or vascular diseases. A muscular body was preferable, just as a healthy skin, good teeth and a perfect ear, throat and nose system. It was crucial to possess a good hearing, especially for radio operators, as well as good eyesight without colour blindness. Lungs and respiratory channels had to function well, as well as the digestive system and a candidates' speech had to be perfect without signs of stuttering. Strangely enough it was also decided to withhold a command to men who had throat and nose problems, such as inflammation of the tonsils or blocked nasal cavaties. A person had to be able to present a family history which would hold an indication to heriditary diseases. If there were symptoms of tuberculosis, then even a seemingly healthy candidate could be refused.

An applicant was allowed to weigh minimum 60 and maximum 80 kg. As the war progressed this criterium was dropped to a minimum of 55 kg in cases where the man was fit and firmly built. Maximum body length was set at 180 cm. Even healthy, strong men were refused if their weight and length did not meet the requirements. Too tall and heavily built persons found it difficult to move quickly through the hatches and watertight bulkheads and after a certain period of time would feel unhappy and more than usually cramped in limited spaces.

Age limitation was set at a minimum of 18 and maximum of 30 years. But even during the third year of the war there was no shortage of volunteers for the U-boat division. By then most of the volunteers had some form of experience in battle and were usually quite healthy. Usually the choice for the U-boat service was not based on idealism, but eminated out of a form of opportunism. They were mostly attracted by a higher wage and better food. By 1917 the bar for maximum age was raised to 35 years, but that would be the limit. Persons who were much older did not possess the elasticity and adaptability to survive in the confines of a U-boat.[46]

Applicants were also not permitted to have a criminal record and to carry out a crime during their service in the U-boat division meant immediate transfer back to 'normal' units of the navy or army.

Before candidates were sent to the Flanders front or elsewhere, they had to undergo months of

The crew of a UB-boat in oilskins. On the rear of the postcard, there is the date: 22 March 1918 (TT)

Officer cadets stand around the foredeck of the training U-boat *UB-24* in Eckernförde (TT)

training in the Baltic. For this purpose there were several training U-boats, *U-1, U-2, U-9, U-24, UB-9, UB-24* and *UB-60*, attached to the U-boat school in Kiel. Command was based on the salvage vessel *SMS Vulkan* and gunnery practice was carried out on the light cruiser *SMS Danzig*. The light cruiser *SMS Thetis* gave enough opportunity for future gunners. All seamen destined for U-boats went through six weeks of mandatory training in a naval infantry division. After completing their basic training all ranks would spend the following period on a training U-boat to learn the ropes of their specialisation. This would consist of a real patrol in the Baltic with accompanying docktime before and after the trip. Petty officers were sent on further specialisation courses to learn more about the diesel and electric engines and the functions of the gyroscopic compass.[47] After this extensive training they were ready for service in a newly appointed U-boat. A crew would always consist of a core of experienced seamen who had the task of keeping up morale and passing on their expertise.

Before the war U-boat officers had to follow a course lasting eight weeks, which consisted of three main parts: theory, torpedo firing exercises and navigation. Theoretical lessons were spread over a period of three weeks and got them familiar with general U-boat knowledge, set up of a U-boat, compass, engines, handling of secret documents, diving regulations (*Tauchretter*), taking command, roleplaying, knowledge of signals, radiotelegraphy and decoding.

This course was varied with practical exercises in the Baltic on *SMS Grille* which had to train them in seamanship, morsecode, anchoring, rules and regulations and the use of torpedoes. Navigation was highly important in a U-boat officer's course and two weeks were specially assigned in the course. Cadets were taught terristrial navigation, lessons on the compass, sounding, triangulation, chart navigation and recognition of landmarks. They also had to learn the use of astronomical navigation through sun and star navigation, deviation control and the use of the sextant. By the end of 1915 this course had been compressed to six weeks and new officers proved to lack important knowledge of navigation. Navigation course was a serious package and if it was shortened it could prove to be an important problem to the safety of a command. In the end it was *Korvettenkapitän* Bartenbach who insisted that more practice should be obtained in navigating from smaller ships than *SMS Grille*, such as a torpedo boat. Cadets would be forced to train more intensively on charts and calculations whilst accustoming themselves to the usual inconvenient movements of the sea. It seemed in the end that the small steamer *Admiral von Knorr* was the most suited for this job.[48]

For officers, petty officers and seamen there followed months of practical training after they had received their basic education, before they could be accepted as ready for action. Training an officer for command would take up to seven months, a

UB-24 and two other training boats lie alongside their depot ship in Eckernförde (TT)

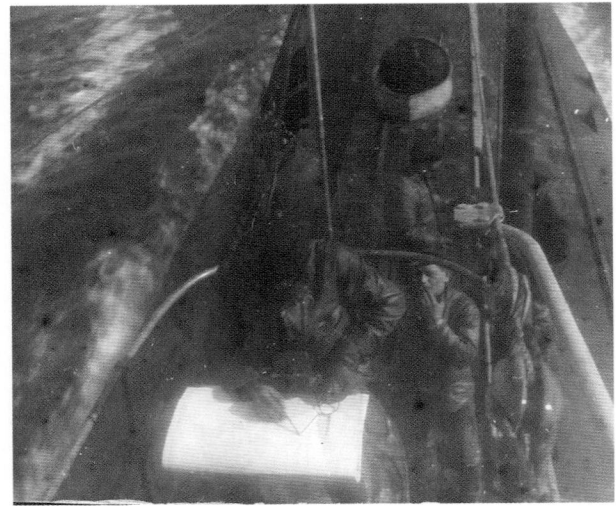

Leutnant z. S. Eduard Hillers, first officer of *UC-64*, takes markings on the chart (TT)

first officer (*Wachoffizier*) and chief engineer took six months; a petty officer and telegraphist seven months; a stoker three months; an engineer cadet eight months; an engineer nine months; a torpedo specialist eight months and a boatswain 14 months.

The analysis of a Prisoner of War report of five survivors of the torpedoed *UC-65* gives a perfect idea of the different types of seamen who were attached to the U-boat division. On 3 November 1917 *UC-65* was torpedoed and sunk by the British submarine *HMS C-15*. Out of a crew of 29 there were only five survivors: *Kapitänleutnant* Claus Lafrenz, *Leutnant* Diedrich Braue, *Obermatrosen* Willy Ostergaard and Erich Fügner and *Funkentelegraphie Gast* Theodor Bremer. Although *Obermatrose* Ostergaard only was a petty officer in the U-boat division, he used to be first officer on *SS Adorna* before the war. In April 1915 he managed to reach Germany from Peru after he had joined as a crewman on a Norwegian sailing ship. In stark contrast stood the other *Obermatrose*, Erich Fügner, who had served in the naval infantry from 1914 up to 1917 after which he was immediately enrolled for service on *UC-65*. The telegraphist, Bremer, who was only 18 years old, had been called up in September 1916. His course in radiotelegraphy in Kiel lasted until March 1917 and he was able to finish his U-boat course by August 1917. After this he was sent to the Flemish front and only took part in two trips with *UC-65* after which he was taken prisoner. *Leutnant z. S. d.R.* Braue had come forward as volunteer, eventhough he was older than 40 years. He was born in a middle class family and before the war had been an officer with the Norddeutscher Lloyd. When the war had started he was in the United States and took it as his duty to his fatherland to find a way home. As reward for his return he was assigned to the U-boat division. Braue was usually brutal to his crew and they thought him unsuited for work on board submarines. Most of the crew of *UC-65* hated him.

The captain of *UC-65*, *Kapitänleutnant* Claus 'Lala' Lafrenz, was considered a perfect example of the classical German Naval officer. He came from a prosperous family who owned an estate on the island of Fehmarn. Against his father's wish he joined the navy. His father wanted to convince him to leave the navy by offering him a substantious amount of money and proposed him to travel for 18 months. In the end Lafrenz was convinced, left the navy and spent time in Spain, France and Edinburgh. At his return he still wanted to enlist in the navy and entered at the age of 19 and finished second in a class of 200. At the beginning of the war he served two years in torpedo boats and in May 1916 he volunteered for the U-boat division. He followed the U-boat course and in October of the same year was promoted to *Oberleutnant* and immediately assigned to the command of *UB-18* in Flanders. His results must have been extremely good, because he did not have to undergo the usual period of *Wachoffizer* or first officer. By August 1917 he had been promoted to *Kapitänleutnant* and Lafrenz was considered as one of the most successful captains of the Flanders Flotilla. He would also be the first person to take a photo of a British Q-ship. His father and two of his brothers would be killed on the Western Front.[49]

As was normal with seafarers, U-boatmen were also superstitious people. No U-boat would depart to

Leutnant Braue and *Leutnant* Wille photographed in the Bruges market in the summer of 1917. Friedrich Braue, first officer on board *UC-64*, would be taken prisoner in November 1917 after his U-boat was sunk in the Channel (TT)

117

Besides dogs and parrots, monkeys were also classed in the family of exotic animals taken from captured ships. The frescoes in the U-boat casino at Fort Lapin, Bruges, show images of monkeys partaking in all kinds of mischievous acts (TT)

sea on a Friday or on the 13th day of the month. There was one case where a captain was able to convince his crew to leave on Friday the 13th. His argument was that two lots of bad luck could only result in good luck. Not much later, the concerned U-boat was lost on patrol with all hands. Superstition and ill luck seemed to follow Oberleutnant z. S. Hans Joachim Emsmann, commander of UB-40. It was believed if another U-boat would leave the harbour at the same time, one would not return. U-boat crews believed that the loss of UC-75, a very successful U-boat, was caused by this coincidence.[50]

A lot of pressure lay on the shoulders of a captain to be successful. Captains who could not produce sufficient results after three missions were usually forced to leave the U-boat division. They were relocated in a posting with the High Seas fleet or on shore, an action which would serve as a demotion.

A U-boat crew would often keep an animal on board as a mascot, usually a ship's dog, a rabbit or a bird. A cat was out of the question as superstition dictated it as an omen of bad luck. It was not uncommon that exotic animals, such as a parrot or monkey, were kept as pets. These usually came from boarded ships which had come from foreign harbours. *Leutnant z. S.* Friedrich Siegel, first officer of *UC-64*, brought a parrot back to land and left it as a pet in his accommodation in the Spaanse Loskaai, in Bruges. The parrot had been taken from a sunken ship, most likely the French bark *Ville de Dieppe*, during one of the patrols of *UC-64*. The animal was called Roku and would survive his owner,

Leutnant Friedrich Siegel sits on a balcony accompanied by his pet parrot Roku, in his residence near the Spaanse Loskaai in Bruges. Siegel, first officer on board *UC-47*, would be killed when his U-boat was sunk (TT)

Every U-boat had to have a mascot: on *UB-22* this was a small black dog (TT)

because Siegel failed to return from his last mission. Exotic animals such as monkeys were also portrayed in the frescoes of the U-boat mess in Fort Lapin.

The Portuguese sailing ship *Maria de Molenos* was stopped by *U-20* about 200 miles to the west of the Irish coast. The U-boat captain let the crew, which was totally made up of lascars, take to the lifeboats. After they had evacuated, the deck gun was used to sink the small schooner. After some well-placed rounds the bark dissapeared beneath the waves. Moments later a large airbubble welled to the surface, accompanied by fragments of floating wreckage and cargo. Incredibly enough a live cow had managed to escape the sinking ship, shot to the surface and was frantically trying to clamp on to a piece of wreckage. The crew of *U-20* noticed a small wooden chest and next to it a black head which wallowed on the waves. The black head belonged to a small dog which was trying to hang on for dear life. The struggling animal softened the sailors' hearts and they took her on board. The dog was baptised Maria, after the doomed sailing ship, they fed and fussed over her. But Maria proved to be pregnant and not much later a litter of six puppies was running around in the U-boat. In the end the crew of *U-20* had to give away three dogs to other U-boats because they proved to be too much for the confined spaces of *U-20*.[51]

UNIFORMS

Sailors on U-boats were equipped with the same uniform as their colleagues on the surface ships. This was white (usually for summer or tropical climates) and blue dress, with a *Colani* or peacoat which had a double row of four buttons. They carried markings such as BAW (*Bekleidungsamt Wilhelmshaven*) or BAK (*Bekleidungsamt Kiel*), a date and sizemark. Officers and petty officers also had blue clothing, with a white shirt, black tie or bowtie. An Imperial crown above gold stripes on the sleeves indicated the rank of the officer. Buttons were brass and had an embossed anchor surmounted by a crown. Seamen and petty officers had white or gold coloured buttons, those for the officers would be gilded (*Feuervergoldet*) and garlanded with a border imitating rope.

Crewmen on board a U-boat wore a mixture of non-regulation clothing: oilskins, leather jerkins, wool pullovers, peacoats and shirts (TT)

Wandschneider
Kanalstr 36
Holtenau Kiel

Telegraphie des Deutschen Reichs.

Telegramm aus Rüstringen 1 13 W. den 1 um 12 Uhr 15 Min.

herzl. glückwunsch zum eisernen kreuz sofort anlegen

löck

C. 187.

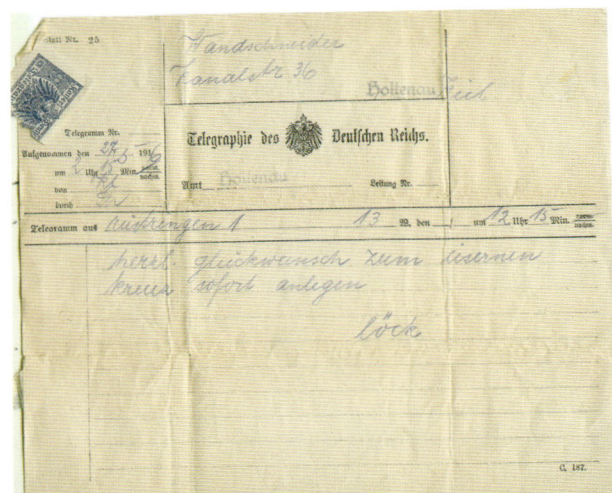

Telegram sent to U-Boot *Steuermann* Wandschneider for his Iron Cross (TT)

11. Auf S. M. Schiffen bezw. auf Ablösungstransportdampfern: 8

S. M. Schiff bezw. Ablösungs-transportdampfer	Entsendung nach dem Auslande (Bezeichnung der Reise oder Station) bezw. Aufenthalt in heimischen Gewässern	Eingeschifft vom	bis	mithin Jahre	Tage	Datum des Passierens a) d. Linie Dover Calais bezw. b) des Breitenparallels von 60° Nordbreite c) des Meridians v. 3° Westlänge von Greenwich bei der Ausreise	Rückreise	Dauer des Aufenthalts außerhalb der Ost- und Nordsee Jahre	Tage	Mithin nach Artikel I des Gesetzes vom 24. 5. 87 bei der Pensionierung doppelt zu rechnen Jahre	Tage
U. Fland.		22. 8. 16.	30. 9. 16.								
U. B. 17		1. 10. 16.	27. 12. 16.								
U. Fland.		28. 12. 16.	13. 2. 17.								
" "		28. 2. 17.	23. 3. 17.								
U. B. 38		24. 3. 17.	8. 7. 17.								
U. B. 40		9. 7. 17.	28. 2. 18.								
U. Fland.		1. 3. 18.	4. 3. 18.								
U. C. 76.		22. 3. 18.	4. 8. 18.								

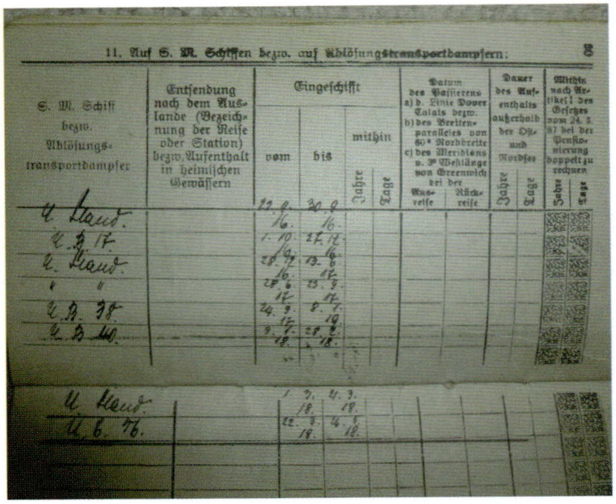

Military pass for *Unterseeboots-Funkentelegrafie-Obergast* Mack, U-Flottille Flandern. Mack served on *UB-17*, *UB-38*, *UB-40* and *UC-76* (TT)

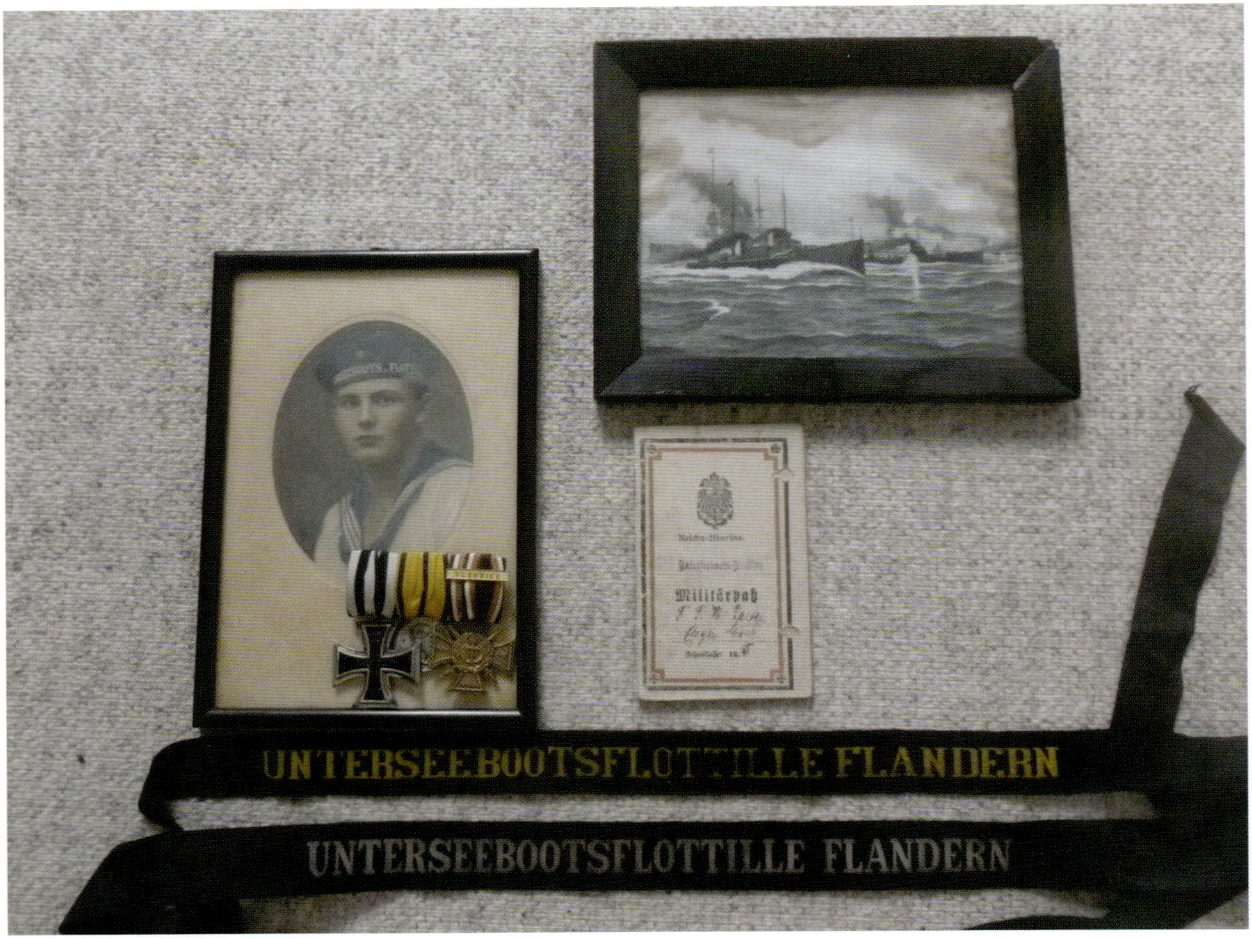

Unterseeboots-Funkentelegrafie-Obergast Mack: military pass, captallies, medals and photos (TT)

Officers, NCOs and seamen stand gathered to the rear of the tower (TT)

The sailor's cap was a round, dark blue seaman's cap, known as a *Tellermutze*, sometimes with a white cover or made from canvas or leather cloth to make it impermeable. On the front, top, there was kokarde with Germany's national colours: black, white and red. The bottom of the cap held a black silk tally with a length of 150 cm. The unit was embroidered in Roman script, such as *Unterseebootsflottille Flandern, Unterseeboots Abteilung, Werft Division, Kaiserliche Marine*... Gilded embroidery indicated sailing personnel, silver was for technical units. Petty officers wore a peaked cap with an emblem consisting of an Imperial crown above a kokarde with two flowing ribbons. Officers also wore a dark blue peaked cap, but with a Kokarde emblem held in a wreath surmounted by a crown and embroidered in gold thread. Although there were little variations to these kinds of headgear, there were examples known which were made of water-resistant material such as sailcloth or leather.

Living in an atmosphere which was damp and cold demanded sturdy, waterproof clothing. This consisted of a pair of brown leather trousers and jacket and a southwestercap, for officers as well as for normal ranks. The jacket closed in the middle with a single row of four buttons and was fitted with a collar or V-shaped neckline. Officers would sometimes wear leather coats with a double row of buttons. These leather jackets would be the predecessors of the typical, light grey leather jackets which the U-boat crews in the Second World War would be wearing. Their wardrobe would be completed by a wool sweater, scarf and warm socks.

Once a seamen went into service he was provided with several pieces of clothing, such as a parade uniform, a work outfit and a uniform for sea service. In practice, each crewman only had one set of clothing with him at sea, which he would wear constantly. This was not only due to the lack of space, but it was also inconvenient and impractical to change clothes or even wash during a patrol. Officers usually had to pay for their own kit. Other uniforms and arms used on parade were left in port on the accommodation ships or lodgings on land, although there are cases known where daggers, swords and belts were stowed aboard.

DECORATIONS

U-boat crews would be issued with different kinds of decorations. This depended on the number of patrols, how successful their U-boat was and personal cases of merit or bravery.

The Iron Cross, First or Second class, was the most common medal awarded to crews. From 1918 onwards the *Verwundetenabzeichen für die Marine*, or wound badge, in black, silver or gold was awarded according to the number of times the person had been wounded. This badge was decorated with an embossed anchor with two crossed swords surrounded by a chain.

Also in 1918, the *U-boot-Kriegsabzeichen*, or U-boat badge, was designed specifically for U-boat crews. This was an oval badge with the image of a U-boat in the centre surrounded by a wreath and topped with an Imperial crown.

The highest award would be the *Pour le Mérite* or *der Blaue Max*. This was mostly awarded to commanding officers, such as Admiral Ludwig von Schröder and garlanded U-boat captains, such as *Oberleutnant z. S.* Otto Steinbrinck. In the beginning the award was made of gold with blue enamel, but as the war progressed the gold was substituted by gilded silver. This award was worn at the throat on a broad silver and black ribbon.

All decorations were accompanied by a document stating the name of the recipient, his unit, vessel, date and place of the award. The document for the *Pour le Mérite* would be personally signed by the Emperor.

A FEW U-BOAT OFFICERS

OBERLEUTNANT Z. S. ERNST MÜLLER-SCHWARZ

Oberleutnant z. S. Müller-Schwarz was born on 8 May 1889 and entered the Imperial Navy in April 1908. He started his career as first officer of *SMS Zahringen*, but his calling would eventually lead him to the U-boat division. At the end of 1915 he was transferred to the U-boat school and seven months later he served as first officer of *U-28*. There was a pressing demand for commanders for the Flanders Flotilla and in August 1916 he got command of the small *UB-16*. In early 1917 he was promoted to command the large minelayer *UC-71*. The longest and for us the most important part of his career in Flanders was as commander of *UC-64*, between February and November 1917.

Müller-Schwarz would never develop a major career within the Flanders Flotilla and stayed amongst the ranking of 'average' captains. He was no Otto Steinbrinck or Johannes Lohs, but a window into his life from the spring to autumn of 1917 gives us an idea how a mainstream U-boat officer spent his days. To encounter personal information such as documents and photos of a U-boatman or officer is a rarity. One hundred years of history and two World Wars have wiped out a lot of

Oberleutnant z. S. Ernst Müller-Schwarz (TT)

Some rest in his residence near the Spaanse Loskaai 20 (TT)

Lt. Hillers, first officer of *UC-64*, stays in the same lodgings as his captain, Müller-Schwarz (TT)

A photo taken in the officers' mess in the St. Joris straat, Bruges. There is a party ongoing as *Oberleutnant z. S.* Friedrich Dönitz (sitting in centre) and *Oberleutnant* Simon (left next to him) have just received the Iron Cross first class. From the ceiling hangs a lifebelt used as chandelier, on it is the homeport 'Ipswich' legible and has most likely come from a sunken vessel. The officer on the left, *Oberleutnant z. S.* Max Viebeg is playing with a monkey (TT)

UC-64 on the Canal Bruges-Zeebrugge. Between February and November 1917 the U-boat was commanded by *Oberleutnant z. S.* Müller-Schwarz (TT)

This photo shows the Spaanse Loskaai and the residence (with the balcony) for the officers of *UC-64*. (TT)

The same location in 2014 (TT)

information. When two photo albums, which belonged to the first commander of *UC-64*, surfaced there was an influx of information, mainly thanks to the fact that every photo had been meticulously described. They not only cast a light on the life of Müller-Schwarz, his first officer *Leutnant z. S.* Eduard Hillers and his crew, but also of *UC-63* and her commander *Oberleutnant z. S.* Karsten von Heydebreck. It illustrates their daily life in Bruges, in their lodgings on the Spaanse Loskaai 20, situated between the Burg and the fish market, the relaxing moments in the U-boat mess in the Sint-Jorisstreet and meetings with other officers. In a photo taken in the dining room of the U-boat mess we make out 20 partying officers. In the middle are seated *Oberleutnant z. S.* Friedrich Dönitz (brother of the well-known Karl Dönitz, also U-boat commander and later Admiral) and *Oberleutnant z. S.* Wilhelm Simon. There is a reason to party as they have both just received the Iron Cross First class from *Korvettenkapitän* Bartenbach. Both held the posting of first officer, Dönitz on *UC-65* and Simon on *UC-71*. Around them are other U-boat officers: Max Viebeg, Thomas Bieber, Adolf Feddersen, von Holm, Friedrich Siegel, Paul Hundius, von Mangold, Hermann Glimpf and Kurt Ramien. Five of the afore named would perish in the same year. Faces could be put to names which were encountered in books or on monuments. But they are sad faces as the description on the photo carried a cross and the date they died. In the 'action' photos it was obvious that *UC-64* was closely connected to *UC-63*. Müller-Schwarz and his first officer Eduard Hillers were close, not only as colleagues on *UC-64*, but also as friends. We can see the same in the photos with the captain of *UC-63*, Karsten von Heydebreck, and his first officer Max Brandt.

Müller-Schwarz belonged to the minor group of lucky ones who survived U-boat service. After commanding *UC-64* he was posted to *UB-24* until November 1917. 1918 was spent as training officer on *SMS Stralsund* and *SMS Königsberg* for new recruits. He would make it as far as *Kapitänleutnant*, but died on 22 April 1920. Eduard Hillers would be transferred at the same time as his commander to the U-boat school, but acted as instructor for the hydro-plane operators. *UC-64* would have two more captains until she was lost with all hands in the Dover Straits.

Von Heydebreck and Brandt would both be killed on 1 November 1917 when *UC-63* was torpedoed by the British submarine *HMS E-52* in the Channel.

KAPITÄNLEUTNANT MATTHIAS GRAF VON SCHMETTOW

Just as Müller-Schwarz was a lesser known captain, so was von Schmettow. But it did not mean he was less successful. In a career with the U-boats which lasted a year he sank almost 80 ships (111.000 BRT). Von Schmettow managed to prove himself with the Flanders Flotilla and was well liked by his men and fellow officers. Born on 9 November 1887 in Pommerzig, Prussia (now Pomorsko, Poland), he enlisted in the Imperial Navy at the age of 18 in April 1906. When war was declared he was serving as first officer on board the torpedo boat *S-148* and in January 1915 he volunteered for the U-boat division. He finished his schooling in May 1916 and subsequently commanded *UC-6* and later *UC-26*. He was killed in action on 9 May 1917 when *UC-26* hit a mine and sank in the Dover Straits.

KAPITÄNLEUTNANT Z. S. OTTO STEINBRINCK

Steinbrinck was born on 19 December 1888 in Lippstadt to the son of a professor. He enlisted with the Imperial Navy in 1907 and a year later he became an ensign. By 1910 he had been promoted to *Leutnant z. S.* during his service on the cruiser *SMS Berlin* and in 1911 he took a specialisation course in torpedoes. By the start of the war Steinbrinck was in command of *U-6* and on 15 March 1915 he was transferred to Flanders to command *UB-10*, one of the first U-boats of the newly created flotilla. He stayed in command of *UB-10* for about one year after which he was issued the larger *UB-18* in January 1916. During this period he achieved fame by sinking nearly 75.000 BRT in enemy shipping during 14 missions. On 29 March he was awarded the *Pour le Mérite,* Germany's highest military decoration. His next command was *UC-65* in which he managed to sink 100.000 BRT of shipping and a British cruiser in only eight patrols. Because of his success he was promotod to the rank of *Kapitänleutnant* and issued the large U-boat, *UB-57*. *UB-57* was his last command, in which he served from 1st August 1917 until 2 January 1918. Steinbrinck was highly regarded not only by his colleagues, but also by his British counterparts. He was no daredevil and not reckless by nature, but dutiful, hardworking and reliable. In the last war year he ended up as staff officer for *Korvettenkapitän* Bartenbach in Bruges. In his entire career he had sunk a total of 250.000 BRT,

This photo, taken outside the U-boat casino shows three captains of UC-boats, from left to right: *Oberleutnant z. S.* Graf von Schmettow (+ *UC-26*), an army officer, *Oberleutnant z. S.* Georg Haag (+ *UC-7*) and *Oberleutnant z. S.* Alfred Nitsche (+ *UC-19*). (Haag)

Kapitänleutnant z. S. Otto Steinbrinck (TT)

which were 205 merchant ships, two warships, one of which was a submarine.

After the war he worked in the *Verein Deutscher Eisen und Stahlindustrie*, mainly as chairman. His efforts for German industry earned him the honorary title of *Standartenführer der SS* in 1935. During the Second World War he was once more active within the navy, but now as *Fregattenkapitän* as well as continuing his duties in the industrial career. During the Flick-trials in 1947 he was condemned for his honorary title in the SS and received five years' incarceration. During his imprisonment he became ill, but the British refused to have him treated. Finally he was allowed to be operated on in August 1949, but died four years later, on 16 August 1953, due to a weakened body. He was buried in Lippstadt.

OBERLEUTNANT Z. S. JOHANNES LOHS

Johannes Lohs was born in 1889 in Einsiedel, Saxony, the son of a factory owner. He entered the navy as, cadet in 1909 and served from October 1912 in the cruiser *SMS Strasburg*, on which he also made a world cruise. He actively partook in the war from 28 August 1914 and was promoted in the autumn of 1915 to *Leutnant z. S.* Lohs was admitted to the U-boat school and after his training finished in March 1917, he was to command *UC-75*. *UC-75* was a minelayer serving in the Flanders Flotilla and carried out nine patrols in British waters. On 2 January 1918 he took over command of the larger *UB-57* from Otto Steinbrinck, who had become somewhat of a legend. But Lohs was also enjoying an increased notoriety. He boasted good ideas of waging war with U-boats and thought of new plans of attack. For his perseverance and successes he was awarded the *Pour le Mérite* in April 1918. In his career he managed to sink 150.000 BRT (77 ships) and damage 90.000 BRT (16 ships). He had a self-confident nature and was known as a risk-taker. This was the reason why he managed to obtain so many successes and evade detection by the patrols. He despised the Dover Barrage, boasting: '*Immer feste über Wasser durch. Die Wachboote sind alle blind. Die sehen überhaupt nichts. Ich laufe ihnen direkt vor der Nase vorbei.*[52] Time and time again he made true his boast and would arrive at Zeebrugge laughing and successful after playing his game with death. On 3 August 1918 *UB-57* left Zeebrugge for her final patrol. Lohs managed to complete a semi-successful patrol for about ten days. On 14 August, when passing the Sandettiebank, *UB-57* made radio contact with Bruges to let command know that they were on the return voyage. After that, all contact with *UB-57* ceased. A week later the bodies of Lohs, *Oberleutnant z.S.* Siegfried Fuchs and a few other crew members washed ashore in Walcheren and Zeebrugge. The number of corpses and grades of the deceased, amongst whom where two officers, suggested that it concerned a bridge watch on the conning tower. We can assume

A UB-III boat cruises on the surface (TT)

Oberleutnant z. S. Johannes Lohs (TT)   *Kapitänleutnant z. S.* Hans Howaldt (TT)   *Oberleutnant z. S.* Reinhold Saltzwedel (TT)

that *UB-57* had been mined and sunk whilst cruising on the surface. Lohs was initially interned in Section III 'Unknowns' at the military cemetery of Flushing. On a later date his brother, Heinrich, and his wife were able to identify the body through the socks, which were marked Lohs, the initials 'J.L.' in his jacket, the wedding ring and the four gold crowns in his back teeth. He left behind a wife and daughter. At the end of 1937 the Kriegsmarine honoured him by creating the *U-Flottille Lohs*.[53]

KAPITÄNLEUTNANT Z. S. HANS HOWALDT

This remarkable U-boat ace was born in 1888 in Kiel. He joined the Imperial Navy and by September 1913 had obtained the rank of *Oberleutnant z. S.* During the war he served in the U-boat division and subsequently took command over the U-boats *UC-4*, *UB-40* and *UB-107* with the *U-Flottille Flandern* between 21 October 1916 and 16 May 1918. During the transfer of *UB-107* from Germany to Flanders he nearly perished due to a wrong diving manoeuver. Howaldt managed to hold on to the extended periscope whilst a British armed trawler had opened fire on him (the full story is told under '*UB-107*'). In just 11 patrols and in one and a half years he was able to sink 65 ships, a total of 130.000 BRT. By 1 February 1917 he had accounted for 8% of the total tonnage of shipping sunk by the *U-Flottille Flandern*. For this accomplishment he received the *Pour le Mérite* on 23 December 1917. He survived the war and passed away on 6th September 1970 in Bad Schwartau.

OBERLEUTNANT Z. S. REINHOLD SALTZWEDEL

Reinhold Saltzwedel was born in 1889 in Rosenberg, Oberschlesien. When war was declared Saltwedel was serving as a *Leutnant z. S.* in the battleship *SMS Kaiser*. He was promoted to *Oberleutnant z. S.* on 19th September 1914 and about half a year later entered the U-boat school and was sent to the Flemish front. He received his first command on 13th January 1916, which was *UB-10*. After serving in *UC-10* and *UC-11* he was transferred in the same year to the larger *UC-21* and *UC-71*. He would sink a total of 173.000 BRT (111 ships) and was considered an ace. On 20 August 1917 the young officer with blond hair and blue eyes was awarded the *Pour le Mérite* for his achievements. He was well liked in the Flotilla and his humour and easy manner stood in stark contrast with the stereotype of the barbaric Hun. On 18 September 1917 he took command of his sixth and last U-boat, *UB-81*. During the night of 2nd December 1917, *UB-81* was mined and sunk off the Isle of Wight. Six crewmen could be saved from the wreck, but Saltzwedel was not amongst the survivors. In the 1930s the second U-boat flotilla of the *Kriegsmarine* in Wilhelmshaven was named after this extraordinary captain.

This photo shows happy U-boat officers in their mess in Bruges. Müller-Schwarz, the original owner of the photo, had mysteriously marked some persons only with their nicknames. Herbert Sauer (2) (POW in UK after sinking of *UC-55*), Nickel (3), Staff (4) Simon (5), Hinkelmann (6), Friedrich Siegel (7) (+ *UC-47*), Adolf Feddersen (8) (+ *UC-14*), Charli Braun (9), Bruno Seemann (10) (+ *UC-36*), Friedrich Dönitz (11) and Hermann Freudendahl (12) (POW in UK after sinking of *UB-81*)(TT)

KAPITÄNLEUTNANT Z. S. PAUL HUNDIUS

Paul Hundius was born in 1889 and just before the outbreak of the war promoted to *Oberleutnant z.S.* whilst serving as flag officer on board *SMS Lothringen*. In July 1915 he transferred to the U-boat school and after just under a year of training was sent to Flanders. He got his first command on 5 April 1916, which was the small *UB-16*. Six months later, in October, he was transferred to *UC-47* and with the UC-II class minelayer he carried out a year long of successful patrols. Hundius was awarded the *Hausorden von Hohenzollern* and promoted to *Kapitänleutnant* in July 1917. By December 1917 naval command realised his ability and he was given command of the large *UB-103*. On special demand from *Korvettenkapitän* Bartenbach he was decorated on 18 August 1918 with the *Pour le Mérite*. This was after he had managed to sink 70 ships, totalling almost 100.000 BRT. Sadly his luck did not last perpetually, because he would perish almost a month later, on 16 September 1918, in *UB-103* together with his entire crew in the Dover Barrage.

KAPITÄNLEUTNANT WERNER VON ZERBONI DI SPOSETTI

Not only Prussian officers coloured the ranks of the Imperial Navy. Many German officers boasted a foreign heritage, such as Lothar von Arnaul de la Perrière, with French roots, and von Zerboni di Sposetti, who originated from an Italian family. He was born on 8 July 1890 and entered the Imperial Navy as a cadet, just before the outbreak of the First World War. Von Zerboni di Sposetti served on the Torpedo boat *G-11* and was promotod to *Oberleutnant z. S.* in September 1914. In November 1915 he decided to enlist with the U-boats and after his basic training he was sent to Flanders in November 1916. There he received command over *UC-6* and later *UC-21*. He would die in action on 27 September 1916 after *UC-21* was lost with all hands in the Dover Barrage, in the area known as the Downs.

His father and four brothers were all German officers and earlier on in the war the sea had claimed the life of one of the Sposetti family. His brother Günther, who also carried the rank of *Kapitänleutnant*, drowned in the Baltic in October 1915 when his ship, *SMS Prinz Adalbert*, was torpedoed and sunk by a British submarine.

IN THE SERVICE OF A U-BOAT FLOTILLA

LIFE ON BOARD

The U-boat division could not be compared with any other branch of the navy. It truly was a different world. Life for crewmen was cramped in small, unventilated compartments, which lacked any form of privacy and often led to nervous breakdowns and mental problems. Therefore the naval high command made it top priority to structurally plan enough free time on land. Leave would correspond with a submarine's repairs or docktime. Usually a skeleton crew (this was in the rule one-third) was kept on board to carry out general maintenance and guard duty.

Before they were allowed on leave after a long patrol, the entire crew had to report to the flotilla's doctor for a general check-up. When they had been a month or longer at sea they would be transported as far away from the battlefront as possible to enjoy long needed rest. This rest consisted of a well thought out programme with long nights of uninterrupted sleep and brisk walks

A seaman finds a moment to smoke a pipe on deck (TT)

Amidst the turmoil of war, the crew of a UB-III boat takes a moment to enjoy the sunset (TT)

Front and stern views of the Bruge-Zeebrugge Canal, seen from a UC-II class boat (TT)

during daytime. During the summer it had been advised to bathe in open air and in the winter they would spend days in heated facilities. Visits to family back home in Germany would be arranged as well.

By 1917 the periods of leave had been shortened significantly and U-boat crews would only be allowed to go home or away from the frontline after carrying out three or four patrols, which amounted to six or eight months. Losses in the U-boat division increased exponentially after this year because naval command exerted an enormous pressure for results. Generally, crews from sunken U-boats captured by the British expressed relief to be released from the constant threat of death which daily hung above their heads, even though they would stay a prisoner of war for the remainder of the war.[54]

Returning U-boats would enter the harbour of Zeebrugge and make their way via the canal towards Bruges. By 1917 it had become a habit that U-boat crews took their kitbags with limited possessions and clothes with them to the accommodation vessel or barracks. All facilities would be awaiting them upon their return. They could bathe in a warm tub and scrub two or three weeks of dirt from their bodies. After which they could enjoy as much sleep as they wanted in a comfortable and clean bed.

Relaxed atmosphere on the foredeck of a returning minelayer. The crew has just been on a mission and enjoy listening to a record whilst their boat is cruising towards Bruges docks (TT)

Officers usually had to head unwashed and in their seaclothes to the officers' mess in the Sint Joris-street, which was near the center of Bruges. A U-boat captain was to report to Bartenbach, the commander-in-chief of the flotilla. Only after the necessary report, could he relax, wash and enjoy a change of clothes. Fürbringer gives an adequate description of his condition after returning from a mission, in his book '*Alarm, Tauchen!!*':

I set off for the officers' mess alone, pounding through the silent streets of late-night Bruges in heavy seaboots with wooden soles. Clad in the thick U-boat gear one felt so disinclined to shed, I was soon sweating like a polar bear in the Sahara. Worse still, I had not yet reaccustomed myself to walking. At sea one strolled a U-boat's deck only in the finest weather and far from the enemy's shore. As both were rarities, one exercised by shifting weight from one foot to the other rather in the manner of the stork. Thus I was close to exhaustion when I arrived at the officers' mess. I found the street doors open and went up a short flight of marble steps into the corridor which led to the mess halls. The bar was shuttered, which was a great pity since I could easily have sunk a litre bottle of beer forthwith. I knew that the Flotilla commander would be in his office and I made a few improvements to my appearance in the washroom, pulling my scarf across my throat, raising the neck of my sweater high to hide the filthy shirt I had on. My hair was matted and unkempt and I combed it across with my fingers after scrubbing furiously at the nails for several minutes. Finally I made another adjustment to the red peasant-kerchief I was never without.[55]

In the U-boat service there was always a tight form of discipline. There were differences in punishment for newcomers or for old hands who had survived a number of patrols. Petty crimes by old hands were usually wavered because replacement became harder to find as the war progressed. Habitual offenders were usually put to work in submarine dockyard depots or on board accommodation ships. When a newcomer had done wrong than he was immediately banned to another branch of the Navy.

The threat of a horrible death always hung above the head of a submariner. The older petty officers in service with the Flanders flotilla knew it as the *Absaufkommando*,[56] which indicated an accepted pessimism surrounding death.

WATER AND VICTUALS

A daily provision of 2 l of fresh water was alotted to each crewman. Of this amount 1.2 l had to be reserved for basic hygiene, 0.3 l for brushing teeth and 0.5 l for drinking water. The consumed amount largely depended on the weather, the work environment and the length of the journey. After being stored for some time at sea, water would turn a rusty colour and it tasted like lead. The inner lining of the tanks started to rust and the constant rolling and pitching of the U-boat did not let the sediment settle and was always present in their rations. This minor discomfort could only be tackled by filtering and boiling the water before consumption.

Canned food as well as fresh victuals were taken on board. Fresh food consisted of potatoes, appels, pears, cabbage, beans and all kinds of meat. The disadvantage of fresh food was that always a part would spoil during the voyage. Meat was and is high on the menu of any self-respecting German and sausage was a much loved product. On longer trips it had to be skinned, resalted and hung to lengthen its lifespan. It must have been an odd sight to see whole lengths of sausages hung from pipes and valves in the cramped confines.

Besides meat, butter and coffee were favoured extras. Butter could not be kept fresh on long trips and most often they had to satisfy themselves with only dry bread. When the crew could board an enemy ship the opportunity was given to search for butter, meat and other fresh provisions. By 1918 the population in Germany had to be satisfied with ersatz or replacement coffee which was made from chicory. This usually was not the case in U-boats where they were issued with real coffee.

Canned food such as capers, peas, jam and butter seemed to preserve well although they were submitted to rusting because of the constantly moist atmosphere in all compartments. Although canned food was a necessity as victuals, crews were appalled at having to eat the same food on long trips. Bread survived surprisingly enough up to five weeks when it was wrapped in paper and kept dry. Canned bread would also last longer, although mould would start to appear after a month. Prunes where taken on board in large quantities and preserved in cans.[57] Stewed fruit was always popular as a desert.

The interrogation report of petty officer Fritz Marsal, the only survivor of *UC-63*, showed that U-boat crews in November 1917 still had a relatively good diet. For breakfast they would be served with bread, butter and sausage, lunch consisted of meat and soup, and dinner was a plate of egg and bacon. This was a diet rich in cholesterol! Butter was mostly only available when they were in port. With all meals there was a choice between coffee and cocoa.[58]

A crew makes use of a sunny moment to have their food above deck (TT)

132

Supplies have just arrived. Crewmen break open transportation crates holding canned food and sausages to enable them to be stowed below (TT)

The British thought differently about German supplies on U-boats. When *UB-18* torpedoed the British submarine *HMS E-22* on 25th April 1916 near the Brown Ridge, two survivors were hauled out of the sea. They were cared for and taken to Zeebrugge where they were interrogated. Second Engineer Frederick Buckingham said that the German sailors treated them well, but that the food on board was awful.[59] His commentary possibly mirrors the situation of the second year of the war when supplies started to dwindle, but it is more probable that the taste of the Royal Naval seaman totally differed from that of the average German.

German prize crews were usually eager to board enemy ships to take in fresh food and add to their own supply. *UB-39*, commanded by *Oberleutnant z. S.* Werner Fürbringer, sank the British merchantman *SS Tagus* on 16 September 1916. Before the explosive charges were detonated in the hold, the prize crew transferred 3,000 fresh eggs to their U-boat. They were at the beginning of a patrol and eggs had to be stowed in the already filled compartments. During the first week each seaman was given daily liberal helpings of 12 to 14 eggs! After the initial desire for eggs had waned, the remaining stock was absorbed in all kinds of manners, such as coffee with four whipped eggs.[60] The cargo would not keep for long as they were susceptible to the temperature fluctuations on board and everything had to be consumed as fast and as well as possible.

There were a few cases known where a U-boat would surface amidst a fleet of fishing vessels, friend as well as foe, and the crew would be asked to sell or trade fresh fish for canned food. A case was known were an unnamed UB-II class U-boat surfaced amidst a fleet of French trawlers. The French fishermen were taken by surprise and feared for their lives, but the U-boat had no ill intentions towards them and only wanted to resupply its dwindling stock of food with all kinds of fresh fish. When the Frenchmen realised that their was no danger in losing their boats, they gave great quantities of fish to the Germans. During the following days it was a virtual feast on board the U-boat: fish of all types and sizes were boiled, fried, cooked in butter, grilled, fried with breadcrumbs...[61]

If it was safe for a U-boat to appear on the surface after it had torpedoed a merchant ship, the captain would certainly take the opportunity. Usually there

In so far it was possible, a U-boat would surface after sinking an enemy ship and scour the sea for usuable items (TT)

Christmas Eve in War and Storm (Illustrierte Kriegszeitung)

Beneath spare torpedoes in the torpedo room of a UB-II type boat several electrical cooking pots are stacked. It is very possible that it concerns *UB-20* (TT)

was an assortment of usuable items amidst the flotsam, such as wood, bales of cotton, livestock and fresh fruit and vegetables. This had been the case for Werner Fürbringer and the crew of *UC-17* after he brought his U-boat to the surface on 24 June 1917. They had torpedoed and sunk the cargoship *SS Clan Davidson* off the Isles of Scilly. The vessel had been on a voyage from Sydney and had a large cargo of butter and other goods on board. After the ship had disappeared from the surface, some wooden barrels shot to the surface, followed by a large sheep that floated amongst the barrels. The crew of *UC-17* was amazed to see the sheep paddling through the waves as if it was its natural environment. After the amused crew had dragged the exhausted animal from the sea it clearly was suffering from decompression sickness as it had ascended rapidly from several meters. The animal was put out of its misery, skinned and the meat was taken to the galley where it was turned into a tasty roast.[62]

Cooking at sea was a difficult undertaking. It had to be done in a closed compartment under water, without much ventilation and usually in circumstances where the U-boat would be pitching and rolling. Electric cooking pots and pans had to be used, as a gas cooker was extremely dangerous in bad weather and in a confined area.

SICKNESS, HYGIENE AND POISONING

Seasickness was normal with any newcomer in the navy, especially in U-boats. Usually this annoyance

An example of an electric cooking pot used at sea (Johansen)

Due to their heightened bows, UC-II type boats were fairly unstable vessels. Even during moderate weather gun deck and stern would be awash (TT)

would occur during the first part of the patrol. All kinds of medication, such as *validol* or drops of atopic sulfate, were issued in an attempt to lessen its effects, but all to no avail. Seasickness had to be overcome by body and mind and usually this was cured after a number of days on patrol.

Hygiene on a U-boat was difficult to keep up, especially on long voyages. There were no real wash facilities and most U-boats only had one toilet on board. The crew seldomly got the chance to change their clothes and would wear the same attire during the whole patrol. A swim and wash in the North Sea were uncommon, unlike circumstances in the Mediterrean. This was not only due to the harsh weather, but also because of the constant threat from the air and attacks from enemy ships. The odours of sweat, unwashed bodies, oil and stale air were all too common in the bowels of a U-boat. In contrast to surface ships, the officers' facilities were the same as those of the crew. *Oberleutnant z. S.* Johannes Ries, captain of *UC-77*, was secretly nicknamed the unflattering name *Hein Schniefelig*. This was a popular name in Germany for a person who emitted distateful odours. Ries was not known for his personal cleanliness! The unfortunate Ries would not make it to the end of the war and perished on 26 July 1918 when *UC-77* was lost in the Channel. He had experienced an extensive career in the U-boats of the Mediterranean Fleet and almost two years in the Flanders Flotilla.

Nerves and bowels caused annoying sicknesses in the U-boat division. Stomach cramps and colonic problems were caused by the irregular and adverse circumstances in which a U-boat crew had to have his dinner. Before the war, a flotilla doctor would test all operational men from the U-boat service. Between October 1910 and October 1911 this numbered only 126 men. From this small amount 36, which was 35%, suffered colonic problems and this was in peacetime, when U-boats were only used during exercises and limited patrols.[63] During the war more than 50% of the crew would suffer from painful cramps. Cramps were usually combatted by taking *lecithinalbumin*, which was a liquid issued in the standard medical kit.

Headaches too were common and could be soothed by taking aspirin. In the same pre-war tests it was also clear that 24% of operational crews suffered from some kind of nerve-related illnesses. Even a fraction of this percentage could not be traced in crews of surface ships, such as torpedo boats. During the early part of the war, in November 1914, the pressure to achieve started to weigh high on a crew. Medical personnel thought it important to develop special health resorts for crews who came back from a patrol. These resorts would have to be in the vicinity of the base and not more than six to eight hours travel by rail. Ideal circumstances dictated a rural facility or a converted farm, large enough to offer necessary relaxation to wounded as well as healthy men. To send them immediately home to friends or family would not be advisable as they never had the chance to relax and usually occupied themselves with chores at home, work and family-related issues.[64]

An officer found a moment to have a shave on deck (TT)

Two offcers relax beside the deck gun (TT)

Many U-boat officers suffered from nervous breakdowns caused by the circumstances on board and the stress which went with the responsibility of command. The 36-year old *Kapitänleutnant z. S.* Paul Schwerdtfeger had to be taken in to care for 30 days on 3 January 1918 as he had been mentally drained and suffered from cardiac problems. Schwerdtfeger was a traditional officer and had served in the navy since 1910 and would have never admitted to this kind of problem.[65] The flotilla doctor had ordered a forced leave after he saw him deteriorating rapidly.

Even after the war, cases of mental problems appeared. The successful *Kapitänleutnant z. S.* Hans Howaldt was struck by a nervous breakdown. He had been part of the navy since the start of the war and in 1916 he was training future U-boat crews. During the war he had commanded subsequently *UC-4*, *UB-40* and *UB-107* of the Flanders Flotilla. In a letter dated 27 December 1918 he asked the German Admiralty for a leave of 45 days. After an intensive life as U-boat captain in Flanders he suffered from cardiac problems and nervous breakdowns and wanted to be assigned to a posting on land.

During the same month, on 18 December 1918, *Kapitänleutnant z. S.* Tornow applied for 30 days of leave in an area on the border of the German Empire. Otto Heinrich Tornow was a loyal officer to the Emperor and had served in U-boats since 1916. He had commanded the minelayer *UC-42* until the end of the war. The spread of Communist revolt amongst the fleet had struck him deeply. Physically and mentally he had become very depressed when he heard the news and wanted to be far away from it all.[66]

The flotilla commander *Kapitänleutnant z. S.* Hans Walther made it his job to convince Naval Command to send the successful ace Otto Steinbrinck to a health resort. By January 1918 he had served continuously since 1912 on U-boats. Steinbrinck was replaced as captain of *UB-57* by Johannes Lohs, but it would not be before the end of August 1918 that he was admitted to a hospital in Mittenwel in Bavaria to enjoy a forced rest. It would only be on 5 April 1919 that he had his first two-week holiday![67]

Older crewmen, such as petty officers, had to cope more with rheumatic ailments caused by the wet and cold atmosphere during watches. But the interior of the U-boat proved to be constantly damp and the thinly insulated metal sides were a long-term health hazard.[68]

Officers find a moment to play a game of backgammon (Dirk Termote)

Seamen in the forward torpedo room of *UB-22*: mail from home has arrived ! (TT)

NCOs and seamen stand ready between the diesel engines (Thomas)

Engine room and deck gun crews suffered from hearing problems. The Admiralty had provided them with cotton earplugs, but usually these were not used during quick actions. Due to the proximity of the gun to the tower, the watch keepers would also suffer after many rounds had been fired. These were relatively minor inconveniences and would dissipate after some time.

Engine room personnel suffered more physical problems than the other crew members due to having to work and live in a world of constant noise and vibrations. The diesel engines were particularly noisy, but the electric propulsion could not be described as totally mute. The hardest was the constant fluctuation in air pressure due to the high necessity of air for the engines. Hatches opening anywhere in the U-boat proved to be specially troublesome. This motion let air move from front to back and cause an under pressure in the engine room. Watertight doors were shut as much as possible to keep the pressure stable, but it would not make much difference when they had to be opened again.

Visual problems were rife with U-boat crews. Engineer Arthur Enigk, from *UC-5*, had served before the war on several surface ships such as *SMS Schwaben*, *Wettin*, *Hessen* and *Vulkan* before entering the U-boat division in June 1915. He would serve for one year on *UC-5* before his U-boat was captured by the Royal Navy and he became a prisoner of war. During his career he mainly worked in the engine room, solved technical issues and was responsible for the maintenance of diesel engines and searchlights. During his service he suffered loss of sharpness of sight as well as diminished vision due to the constant life in the closed confines of *UC-5*, which was lit by electric bulbs.[69]

Poisoning or gassing were not frequent occurances. Leakage of calcium phosphor from torpedo war heads could enduce cramps, dizziness, headaches and nausea with crewmen. The best remedy to this was a brisk walk on deck in the fresh air. Poisoning by the deadly CO^2 gas was only experienced by crews who were trapped in shut-off areas in a sunken U-boat. The absence of a constant supply of fresh air could ultimately lead to death. In 1916, the crew of the small *UB-I* type, *UB-13*, were being assailed by a

In the forward torpedo room of *UB-52*: eyesight of crewmen working in a constant atmosphere of artificial light, suffered a lot. (TT)

Four engineers pose for the camera after coming up on deck for some fresh air (Dirk Termote) ▶

Time for a haircut! (TT)

U-boat Engineer Fritz Kasten finds a moment to come on deck in order to catch some air (Dirk Termote)

Wounded sailors and soldiers were cared for in Marine-Kriegslazarett III, which was not far from the Minnewater in Bruges (TT)

number of British torpedo boats off the east coast. To avoid detection they had to remain silently on the seabottom for two following days and nights. Her captain, *Oberleutnant z. S.* Arthur Metz, had no choice but to keep his U-boat silent and in the same position until they would eventually depart. After a day the air became stale and disgusting. A stoker witnessed that his comrades were gasping for air, whereupon their eyes would literally start bulging out of their sockets. In the end, the British torpedo boats gave up the hunt and *UB-13* made it safely back to Zeebrugge. After that experience every one of the crew had cardiac problems. Air lacking oxygen was a constant phenomenon when a U-boat had to spend long periods submerged.

On 27th September 1917, *Oberleutnant z.S.* Hans Howaldt, captain of *UB-40*, wrote in his diary that the lack of oxygen put a lot of strain on his crew. Whilst on patrol in the Channel they could not be allowed on deck for air, not even during the night, as there was the constant risk of being attacked. Only the most necessary personnel were allowed on the tower during their watch. Howaldt had suggested to incorporate an extendable airmast in the design of the new UB-type. This mast could be raised simultaneously with the periscope and give the crew the essential fresh air. High command gave him a curt answer to his request. From a military point of view the mast was seen as an extra threat against discovery of the submerged boat and it was not feasable to construct.[70] Although his suggestion was shelved, it would be used a quarter of a century later in the shape of the *Schnorkel*, at the end of the Second World War. This airmast would allow a U-boat to be submerged at all times whilst giving air to the engines.

It was not only the lack of oxygen in the air, but also heated gasses would eminate from the diesel engines. These gasses would cause a type of fever. The crew of *UC-17* would undergo this unpleasant experience during the last week of one their patrols. Almost the entire crew felt sickly, suffered headaches and a weakness in all limbs. The serious cases showed fevers up to 39.8°C, accompanied by fear and heart palpitations. The symptoms appeared after a forced underwater patrol of more than 20 hours when it had not been possible to ventilate the U-boat. This was normally an improbable occurance as kalicartridges purified the exhaled air.[71]

There were also victims who suffered from ruptured eardrums. About half of the crews would suffer from permanent wounds and were discharged from service.[72]

By the end of 1917 crewmen started to suffer from a skin disease which was baptised to 'Petroleum sickness'. Small sores would appear all over the body and were ascribed to poor quality oil from Galicia.

Victims would be cared for on shore in the many field hospitals or *Kriegslazarette*. The first major hospital was installed in 1914 and situated in Bruges in de *Vlamingenstraat*. It was housed in the present public school and named *Kriegslazaret I*. As the war progressed, the need for more hospitals increased. By 1918 two more had been added. These were the *Marine Kriegslazaret II*, near Bruges station and *Marine Kriegslazaret* III in the *Minnewatercentrum*.[73]

Sailors paddle through Bruges on canoes as a way to spend their off-duty time (TT)

LIFE ON SHORE

Seamen pose in their number 1 uniforms, in the countryside around Bruges (TT)

A game of discus throwing (TT)

A Sunday service is held in the church of Leffinge, near Ostend (Dirk Termote)

Not only the population of an occupied country such as Belgium had to abide to the rules imposed by the occupying force. The German military and naval personnel were also disciplined by hard regulations imposed by high command.

It was not uncommon to see war time romances developing between German sailors and local women. There were even known cases were members of the *Marinekorps* officially wed Flemish women in churches or at townhalls. Of course this happened without the knowledge of their superiors. From the middle of June 1916 these marriages were forbidden by Admiral von Schröder, as it was unacceptable to have weddings with people whose nation was openly fighting Germany.

It was not surprising that U-boat crews would create havoc once back on land after spending weeks at sea, whilst death had hung above their heads. Excess consumption of alcohol was a release to the omnipresent stress, fear and anxiety. Higher command was suspicious of the consumption of huge amounts of beer and gin (*Schnaps*) by sailors as well as officers. Public drunkenness was commonplace and it led to inappropriate excess. But in the eyes of the Admiralty it was mostly the reputation of the occupation force which would suffer. A reputation which had to be kept high toward the local population. As said, not only sailors indulged themselves in public drunkenness. Pressure of command must have weighed heavily on *Oberleutnant z. S.* Reinhold Salzwedel. After a three-week patrol he was assigned one week of leave, but did not manage to spend a single day of it sober. It was one of the only cases were *Korvettenkapitän* Karl Bartenbach had to personally drag him out of bed and order him to prepare to leave for his next mission.[74]

Hard punishments were issued to keep necessary discipline. Belgian publicans would be prosecuted if they were found guilty of administering alcohol to already drunken military personnel. The court of law on the Burg was used by the *Kommandatur* and the *Strafkammer*. In 1918 a *Kriegerheim*, a casino for U-boat crews, was created in the Dweerstraat in Bruges.[75]

At the beginning of the war higher command would turn a blind eye to German troops (these mainly concerned younger officers) practising their

Seamen and officers of the *Seebataillon* and navy celebrate Christmas 1917 in the cellar of the Palace Hotel in Zeebrugge (TT)

In Germany, women are sorting through mail destined for the front (TT)

Off-duty time could consist of all kinds of activities, such as taking a dip in a local ditch (TT)

A funny sketch made by Richard Fiedler of a grounded U-boat (An Flanderns Küste)

knowledge of French with the local population (as always there was no mention of Dutch or Flemish, but of the all-dominating French). After 1 October 1916, the war hardened and a prohibition on the use of the languages of enemy nations such as French and English was enforced.[76] Exceptions were granted if urgent requests had to be made if it was of military significance.

Receiving mail and packages from home was an important boost to the morale of U-boat crews and other units which were at the front line. Packets usually contained pieces of equipment, clothing (such as gloves, socks, knee- and wristwarmers, ear- and breastprotectors, neckerchiefs), but also fruit, chocolate, cigars, cigarettes, canned food, fresh and smoked meat and of course all kinds of sausages. It was forbidden to send matches, lighters with fluid and all kinds of flammable acids. Christmas (*Weihnachten*) and Easter (*Ostern*) were very important occasions for the German soldier. In December 1915 the *Marine-korps* received a total of 58,000 parcels, dubbed as '*Weihnachtsgeschenke*', for free distributions amongst naval personnel. These had been constituted and sent by different patriotic organisations such as *Damen in den Marine-garnisonen, Herren von Hamburg,* Hanseatic cities such as Rostock, Lübeck and Bremen as well as the *Abnahmestelle* Berlin.[77] Parcels would arrive in Bruges in the *Feldpost Amt* of the *Marine-korps*, situated in the present *Groeninge Museum*.

Different towns such as Ostend, Bruges, De Haan, Wenduine and Zeebrugge were provided with libraries for naval troops. Sailors and officers could leaf through literature and relax during their free time. Magazines such as *Jugend, Illustrierte Zeitung* and *Die Woche* gave them an obviously censored and one-sided view on the general progress of the war.

Sketch of a UC-II boat by the artist and seaman Richard Fiedler (An Flanderns Küste)

U-boatman Paul Belt found a moment in 1915 to make a couple of sketches of Bruges (TT)

On 15 March 1916 the first example of the Naval Corps' own newspaper was produced: *An Flanderns Küste*. Its responsible publisher was *Korvettenkapitän* Erich Schulze. The newspaper was filled with poetry, charicatures, sketches and historical contributions about Flanders, and Bruges in particular. Articles such as *Schilderungen von der Front, Anekdoten, gute Photographien* etc... were written by sailors and soldiers. Illustrators and artists such as Franz Eichhorst, Walter Poetsch and Richard Fiedler took care of cartoons and illustrations. A total of 62 issues were published (up to 1 October 1918), eventually being printed in an edition of 8,000 copies which ran up to 15,000 copies in 1918. Sailors could purchase the newspaper for 10 Pfennig in the *Feldbuchhandlung* in the Steenstraat in Bruges or the *Marinebucherei* in Ostend. Books could be lent from the Marinekorps Library located on the Van Eycksquare in Bruges.

MORALE, PROPAGANDA AND WAR TROPHIES

Besides the fact that the largest part of the U-boat crews were volunteers, it was also known that they were very loyal. Discipline seemed to be maintained even during the period of Communist revolt in October 1918. U-boat crews would even protect their officers against mutineering torpedo boat crews.

In the first two years of the war a total of 6,000 naval personnel would eventually desert to neutral Holland where they would be interned.[78] It did not seem likely that U-boat crews formed part of the desertions, but mainly concerned sailors from the naval regiments. Their main reason seemed to be the fact that they were seamen who wanted to serve on ships rather than trenches in a war on the front.

A sluicemaster from Zeebrugge witnessed the last U-boat to leave the harbour in October 1918 had its crew lined up on the foredeck. The captain called for

Self-portrait of U-boatman Paul Belt, in Bruges (TT)

A propaganda poster for war support, to increase pressure on the blockade of the United Kingdom (TT)

146

three hurrahs and declared it to be the last of Flanders that they would see.

British interrogators of the survivors of the crew of the sunken *UB-72* were impressed by the loyalty they showed towards their commander who had been killed in action. On 7 and 8 May 1918 *UB-72* was hounded by two surface vessels and an airship which dropped a total of 51 depth charges on the unfortunate U-boat. His crew said that he only had one fault: he always wanted to stay too long on the surface to be aware of everything which went on around him. It was this habit which brought them into trouble and had them eventually sunk. The interrogators concludes that to be able to justify the death of their comrades he obviously had other qualities.[79]

Propaganda remained an important element throughout the war to keep the morale of the German people high. One of these methods was through organising several expositions of *Kriegsbeute* or war trophies. In the first years of the war these were filled with objects which sporadically had been brought back by U-boats. These pieces were used as decoration in the casino or mess buildings. There was a cut-open British mine centrally placed in the officers' mess and served as a punchbowl! This had been recuperated by a U-boat captain from a net in the Dover Barrage. From 1916 onwards systematic collecting of souvenirs was begun and shipped to Germany to be displayed in permanent and travelling expositions.

UB-12 brought several hundred pieces of machine gun ammunition home in the spring of 1917. These had been taken from a float plane which had been forced to land on the water. *UC-17* brought back the sight of the deck gun of a British merchantman in the summer of 1917. *Oberleutnant z. See* Otto Steinbrinck had to be seen as the king of collectors when he was captain of *UC-65*. After one voyage with his U-boat he brought back a 15 cm breachblock, six compasses, two binoculars, three speedlogs, three sextants, a compass housing and a ship's bell as souvenirs. But also Werner Fürbringer, nicknamed 'Fips' by his fellow officers, would not be underdone concerning the collecting of trophies. In July 1916 he had made a wager with *Oberleutnant d. Res*. Schütte of the coastal naval artillery division. Schütte was responsible for the 8,8 cm battery at the end of the Zeebrugge Mole. Due to his isolated existence at the end of the Mole, in the lighthouse, he was also known as 'the Pope of the Mole'. Zeebrugge

MARTIN BERGERHAUSEN, TORPEDO OBERMATROSE, MISSING WITH THE LOSS OF UB-37

During the search for information concerning U-boats, one comes in contact with all kinds of accounts. Diaries, photographs, souvenirs and albums sketch a human image behind a brutal and cruel war. By chance I stumbled upon an amount of handwritten letters and poems which had partly been written in ink or typed with a typewriter. It concerned Martin Bergerhausen, a senior petty officer from *UB-37*, which called Bruges as its base during 1916. In the lot of material there was also a photo and a death certificate of the person in question. The part which grabbed my attention were the numerous stamps of the *U-Flottille Flandern* and signatures of Bartenbach and Suadicani. The correspondence covered the period from August 1912 until the end of 1917 and concerned letters which Bergerhausen wrote to his parents from the ships on which he served. He started as 17-year old on a training ship in 1912, in Kiel, and served aferwards on a torpedo boat in Stettin until 1915. At the end of 1915 he was transferred to the U-boats and travelled to Bruges and the Flanders' Front. In January 1917 the letterwriting stopped and his father, Wilhelm, wrote several times to the High Command of the *U-Flottille Flandern*. The replies were that of a missing in action up to a confirmation of his death with the sinking of *UB-37*.

U-boot Matrose Martin Bergerhausen (TT)

> **Kommando**
> **der 11. Flottille Flandern**
> B.-Nr. 783
>
> den 25. Februar 1917.
>
> Herrn Wilhelm Bergerhausen! Horrem, Bez. Düsseldorf.
>
> In Beantwortung Ihrer beiden Schreiben wird Ihnen mitgeteilt, dass es laut Gesetz nicht möglich ist, Ihnen die Nachlasssachen Ihres Sohnes direkt zu übersenden. Bares Geld war beim Nachlass Ihres Sohnes nicht vorhanden und es muss angenommen werden, dass er es mitgenommen hat. Etwa 35 M Restgebühren werden Ihnen nach der gesetzlichen Abwickelung durch die U-Abteilung übersandt werden.
>
> Ueber das Schicksal des Bootes ist bisher nichts bekannt geworden; falls aber noch irgend welche Nachricht eintreffen sollte, wird Ihnen dies von hier sofort mitgeteilt werden.
>
> Suadicani
> Oberleutnant z. See und Flaggleutnant.

A letter written by *Oberleutnant z. S.* Suadicani to father Wilhelm Bergerhausen. It concerns the return of personal items of his fallen son Martin (TT)

After the confirmation of his son's death, the letters concerned the repatriation of his personal effects, the payment of a back pay, 56,92 Marks and clothing money. It was noteworthy that a lot of the correspondence was handled personally by the staf and High Command. There was, for example, a long, handwritten letter written by Korvettenkapitän and Flotilla leader Bartenbach to Wilhelm Bergerhausen. He wrote that he was saddened by the loss of his son, but that he loyally had fulfilled his duty to the very end. It was evident that a lot of care was taken in bringing this terrible news of his loss to the family.

Next to the letters were a large number of unpublished poems which Martin Bergerhausen has written during his free time. They attested a mentality which remained unaltered as the war progressed. In his poem '*Unserer Nummer 1*' he praised the first officer of *UB-37* who had recently been decorated with the Iron Cross first class. Not for his personal courage, but for his sense of responsability which the officer had shown during his service and the conduct which also brought the U-boat safely back to port. The poem indicates a close camaraderie and group spirit, aimed at the demise of the enemy (England). The poem ends with the typical praise and the expressing of '*Hurra : Unser Nummer I, sie lebe! Hurra! Für Alle*'.[80] In his '*Gedanken bei der Wacht*',[81] he praises his fatherland and despises Britain's Navy and speaks of the endurance of U-boat and torpedo boat crews during the performance of their duties. In this particular poem one feels the coming of difficult times and the monotony of watchkeeping duties and the difficult moments on board with little rest. Despite these moments there was no complaining, as Bergerhausen literally says, but perseverance in their mission. A melancholy side surfaces when he talks about missing his family and the homefront, known as '*Trennungsschmerz*',[82] and the memory of his brother who was killed in action.

Several war museums were created and opened during the war, in which the public was given a chance to view war booty. This photo shows the 'Deutsche Kriegsausstellung' of 1916 (TT)

Mole was in fact the most western part of the First World War frontline. Schütte was known to U-boat crews as a person who could obtain certain 'extras', one of which was alcohol. It was with him that Fürbringer had made a wager. Fürbringer promised to capture the bell of every ship he would stop and sink on his next patrol. If he won this wager, this had to be paid for by a bottle of Magnum champagne. It is not sure which trip it concerns, but possibly one he made early August 1916. On this trip the lifebelt of the trawler *King James* was captured and brought home[*]. Fürbringer was able to sink a total of 16 ships on the British east coast with his *UB-39* during a week-long patrol. The ships were lawfully stopped, investigated and sunk, but before they made their last plunge to the depth they had enough time to gather the bell of every vessel. Just before arriving back at Zeebrugge he had 16 bells hung in two rows on the railings between the conning tower and stern. When Flanders came into view all the British and Dutch company flags of the sunken ships were suspended from the flagstaff. Above the flags the signal 'Total of 16' was made. In between the suspended bells stood eight of *UB-39's* crew and Fürbringer ordered them to sound the bells once the U-boat rounded the lighthouse into the Zeebrugge Roads. Schütte and his artillerymen were impressed by the feat and the officers of *UB-39* were bestowed with the promised champagne.[83] It was one of the rare occasions when there was no hurry for them to reach their base at Bruges via the canal. It is most likely that the bells found their way to the U-boat casino in Fort Lapin and were hung as souvenirs. It is not known what happened to the trophies after the war. For a diver this would be a dreamt-about situation. It would be a large mystery if the wreck of a U-boat was discovered and a dozen bells of different ships would be scattered on the seabed beside the wreck!

As the war progressed, the collecting of trophies from the enemy was seen as useful instrument of propaganda. A *Reichsmarinesammlung* was created for which *Kapitänleutnant z. See a.D.* Max Wittmer

---

[*] This remarkable piece was displayed as trophy in the U-boat mess in Bruges. After the war it was kept and displayed at the Zeebrugge museum and when the museum was closed down it was taken into care by Bruges Musea.

The German public was sporadically allowed to visit U-boats in order to give them an idea of the weapon which was severely damaging the Allies (TT)

was responsable for the *Flandernfront*. He was assisted by *Hauptmann* Dening as *Sammlungsoffizier* of the *I Marine Division*. In Germany *Major* Sterzel was *Sammlungsleiter des Kriegsministeriums* and looked after the division and display of the captured pieces pieces.[84] On 6 January 1918 the headquarters of the *Sammlungsamt* issued a pressing request for new pieces. Since 1917 it had become difficult to obtain souvenirs from enemy ships due to the changes in the war at sea. Ships were usually torpedoed on sight and crews did not have the time to board them to search for items.

Even at the end of the war, in September 1918, there were numerous demands for war relics from the *Reichskriegs*musea and war museums of the *Bundesstaaten*.

Relics taken at sea not only served as decoration or propaganda. Complete radio units were taken out of the wireless rooms of the captured ships *SS Colchester* and *SS Brussels*. One was installed in the *Oststand* of the artillery battery *Deutschland* in Bredene, the other in the battery *Kaiser Wilhelm II* in Knokke.

Little photos are known of war booty taken by submarines. Here is part of a 7.2 cm gun taken of a Q-ship off Lowestoft by *UC-63* (TT)

Propaganda poster for the donation to help the U-boat weapon (TT) ▶

THE REVERSE OF THE COIN: THE SINKING OF A U-BOAT

Propaganda and fame surrounding the U-boat service was huge. Just like service in the airforce it was portrayed as something heroic, adventurous and elitist. At the outbreak of war there was no shortage in the rows of volunteers who came forward to report to recruiting offices. As the war progressed most seamen were never given any choice and were just assigned to a certain unit of the navy. Life on board a U-boat was not only claustrophobic, uncomfortable and unhealthy, but death was omnipresent. There was the danger of asphixiation due to chlorine gas from leaking batteries. This could be caused by seepage of seawater within the pressure hull. A U-boat could be rammed, torpedoed, bombed or machine-gunned. The chances of surviving a mine or torpedo explosion on a vessel of 30 to 50 m in length were usually non-existent. If one had the luck of surviving, it usually concerned crewmen who had been on watch in the conning tower or on deck and had been thrown free from the wreck. Then they had to have the luck of being spotted by the enemy ship and picked up. Chances of survival in the cold waters of the North Sea were minimal. Weighted down by all kinds of clothing and equipment, stunned by the explosion, covered in oil, thrown into a state of shock and numbed by the cold, survival was usually limited to several minutes. Those who were situated next to the place of impact could be seen as the 'lucky ones', when they were killed outright. Crewmen who were

The Miller family from Erfurt lost two sons in the spring of 1918: Karl, NCO with the army, and Kurt, NCO-engineer with the U-boats (TT)

One of the only known graves of a U-boatman in Flanders. This is for Gustav Reinhardt, who lies interned in the cemetery of the Sint-Donaaschurch in Zeebrugge (TT)

in other compartments could survive an explosion due to the different watertight doors if they had been shut. But it would not necessarily mean survival. They would be dragged down with the sinking wreck until they hit the bottom. When ballast tanks could not be pumped with air, they were condemned to a cruel death of slow suffocation, drowning and even suicide. The top secret diving unit created by the Royal Navy, known as the 'Tin Openers', were assigned to diving and investigating newly sunken U-boats to retrieve secret documents and other pieces which could reveal valuable information. Dusty Miller, one of the pioneers amongst the divers, was usually confronted by numerous bodies when he had to enter a wreck. The bodies of drowned seamen were crammed together in certain compartments. His first traumatic experience had been when he found all the victims of the sunken *UC-2* in the stern compartment of the wreck. *UC-2* had been accidentally rammed and cut in two by the cargoship *SS Cottingham* on 2 July 1915. Somehow, part of the crew had been able to make it to the engine room. Witnesses on the British ships spoke of a secondary explosion some hours later. This had meant that a mine from its own cargo had detonated. The second explosion probably breached and flooded the stern section which drowned the survivors.

Being stuck in a sunken U-boat must have been one of the worst nightmares for a U-boatman. *Oberleutnant z. S.* Neuerburg survived the attack of the destroyer *HMS Garry* on his *U-18*. After the lookouts on *HMS Garry* had spotted *U-18's* periscope, the destroyer turned and was able to ram the conning tower and break off one of its periscopes. After that the hunt was opened on the unfortunate German.

Neuerburg:

'Now commenced an hour which neither I, nor anyone else on board the boat, will forget to our dying day: a struggle for existence - to escape one of the most horrible deaths that one can picture to oneself. The hydroplane motor gave out, for no apparent reason, suddenly jamming at 15° down. Only by dint of great efforts could we succeed in connecting up and moving the hand-gear. No. 2 was dripping with perspiration, huge strong man as he was, he groaned and moaned. He did his duty to the uttermost and I can still see the stoker at the after hydroplanes nervously chewing and gazing first at me and then at him with vacant eyes. Then again we all of us stared at the depth gauge. The boat rose and sank constantly at steep angles up to 30°. The men were ordered to run forward, then to run aft; tanks were blown and again flooded; for a short time the motors whirred, then again they stopped, and above all sounded the clear matter-of fact orders of the captain (...) Then twice in quick succession a big bump. We had touched bottom. Someone shouted 'We are aground'. No, our bows tilted downwards, we were going still deeper! Now we were pumping out the tanks for all we were worth, we were rising higher still. 'We shall break surface, Sir' shouted Sprenger from below. 'Not under any circumstances' was the reply. No. 2 made a last effort. Hydroplanes hard down; and then there was a crash above the engine-room which made us realise that we had again been rammed, by a trawler this time. Thank Heaven no water came in. The same terrifying business we had just been through re-commenced. The boat shot upward and downward. The men rushed forward and then aft (...) Everything was rattling about. In the forepart of the boat was a fearful mess. We stumbled over loaves of bread, kettles and cooking pots from the galley. In the captain's and officers' cabins everything lay strewn about, boots, clothes, cigars, boxes and bottles (...). We sank again. Then bump! We had struck forward and then I felt the boat sliding downwards, deeper and deeper. Man the pumps! Man the pumps!! Ballast pumps broken down! (...) From the conning tower came the report 'Steering gear jammed. Man the hand wheel' and then from the engine room 'the motors have broken down'. We stared at each other in despair. This was the end.'[85]

At last by means of compressed air the crippled boat came to the surface and surrendered to *HMS Garry* which was close by. Before leaving the submarine, the captain opened the valves so as to sink her.

Dusty Miller had found evidence in the wreck of a large UB-III class submarine, sunk off Dover, that the crew had been alive after their U-boat had been sunk. Some of them had even committed suicide. When he opened the conning tower hatch he was confronted by the corpse of the captain who showed gunshot wounds to the head and stomach. More than 30 crew members had been trapped in the small confines. Several bodies had evidence of bullet wounds and he found a pistol at the foot of the ladder running up to the tower. Several letters and envelopes were drifting around in the area where he had entered. Hastily scribbled notes had been made by the survivors addressed to their loved ones. Miller said he would never forget the expressions of horror on the faces of those who had drowned or committed suicide. '*A most terrible scene.*'(86)

Most of the crew of *UB-55* would be fated to end in the same way as the previous U-boat, on 2 April 1918. *UB-55* had attempted to cross the Dover Barrage, but near the Varne buoy her hull scraped the net or the cable of an anchored mine. At a depth of 12 metres a mine detonated near the stern and the sea started to pour in. The aft ballast tanks could not be blown and *UB-55* sank to the bottom at 25 metres. Shortly after hitting the seabed, water started seeping into the control room and chlorine gas started to leak from the submerged batteries. When the pressure started to rise a number of seamen committed suicide by stuffing their mouths and nostrils with wads of cotton and diving below the surface. Others tried to shoot themselves in the head, but the damp cartridges refused to fire. In the end two men managed to escape through the conning tower hatch and 20 others through the hatch above the forward torpedo room. The ascent killed most of the survivors and only a handful reached the surface alive. 90 minutes later, a drifter, which had been searching for oil and wreckage, appeared and managed to rescue her commander, *Oberleutnant z. S.* Ralph Wenninger and seven others.

Captivity and the manner in which survivors were treated at sea varied from situation to situation. German propaganda had convinced most of the U-boatmen that they should not fall into British hands. Survivors from the sunken *UB-72*, which had been picked up by the British, were surprised by their decent treatment and one even asked their rescuers why they had saved them. He told them that all U-boat crews had been informed that there was no point in surrendering as the British considered them pirates. And pirates would be treated accordingly: they would be hanged immediately when landed. A similar declaration was made by survivors from *U-103*.(87) Generally survivors were treated well, but there are cases known of utmost brutality. The British submarine *HMS E-34* had managed to stalk and torpedo *UB-16* on 10 May 1918 off Harwich. *UB-16*, which had been cruising on the surface, was struck amidships, below the tower, and sank immediately. Her captain, *Oberleutnant z. S.* Vicco von der Lühe, who had been on the tower was flung into the sea and came off as the only survivor. He was picked up by *HMS E-34* and interrogated. After von der Lühe refused to tell his captors his U-boat number, the first officer put a pistol to his head and threatened to shoot him. In the end the British removed his socks and put his feet against an electric heater in order to torture him to make him speak up. In the end von der Lühe was imprisoned ashore and died later in the war.(88) British sources do not mention this incident and the facts prove it as a war crime. The crew of *HMS E-34* would never be able to testify about this incident as the submarine was lost with all hands two months later off Terschelling.

An account by *Obermaschinistenmaat* Arthur Enigk gives us an idea of the treatment which the British gave to certain U-boat crews. The 23-year old Enigk was rescued on 27 April 1916 by the torpedo boat *HMS Firedrake* and taken as prisoner-of-war. His U-boat, *UC-5*, under command of *Oberleutnant z. S.* Ulrich Mohrbutter had stranded on the Shipwash and was subsequently scuttled by its crew. However, the Royal Navy managed to save the U-boat and tow it to Harwich where it was investigated. When *UC-5* had been scuttled, Enigk ended up in the sea and spent 50 minutes treading water which led to temporary paralysis of his lower body. Once on board *HMS Firedrake*, his comrades had to massage him to enable his circulation to flow and get his body temperature up. The prisoners were locked up in Harwich naval base and there treatment was quite brutal. Enigk suffered several days from hypothermia which resulted in abdominal cramps. All the survivors from *UC-5* were locked up in cells and only after three days received dry clothing. The single cells only measured 2 x 2 m and only little light came through a small window. About ten days after their incarceration they were marched to a fort near Harwich where they were imprisoned in a damp cellar. They had to sleep on a hard earthen floor and only got a thin blanket with which they could cover themselves. During the day they received a hard piece of bread and water and in the evening they warmed themselves with a cup of tea. The maltreatment would not end right there and two days later they were transferred to Shrewsbury prisoner-of-war camp. British soldiers guarding the compound told them this was a special camp to house pirates and war criminals. It had been the former workshop for locomotive engines and was so unkempt that several holes had appeared in the walls. Rainwater penetrated the roofs and wetted the straw bags which had to be used as mattresses. The prisoners were forbidden to close up any holes. There were no possibilities to dry their clothes or bedding and they had to live in a constantly damp and cold atmosphere. During the winter there was hardly any heating available. Lunch consisted of large beans which let off an obnoxious smell when boiled. They received hardly any meat and when they were lucky enough to get a portion, it was usually rotten. Due to the maltreatment Enigk still suffered from stomach pains and had to be treated by a doctor from the Swiss Red Cross. By the end of 1917 the prisoners of *UC-5* were transfered to Stobs POW camp in Scotland and later to Brockton camp. Circumstances were poor and they were supposed to survive on a daily serving of soup, a single potato and a small quantity of vegetables or oats and very little meat. Further there was a mixture of 112 gr of old and 112 gr of fresh bread. Occasionally there was a spoonful of margarine available and two cups of coffee at a daily rate. Finally Enigk and some of his comrades were exchanged for British prisoners on 1st April 1918 and ended up in Holland. Once back on the continent he fell sick again and had to undergo treatment. Enigk's story was actual proof that the British had developed an early form of concentration camp and had thought of a psychological style of warfare.

THE BASES

The general plan of organisation of the German naval units in Flanders made Bruges the headquarters of the navy. It was also the location for the main wharf for maintenance and repairs to the U-boat fleet. There were numerous docks available for U-boats and smaller jobs, without the need for docks, could be carried out on torpedo boats. From Bruges, canals ran to Zeebrugge and Ostend where there was a connection to the sea. As a rule U-boats and surface craft were based in Bruges Harbour and only left the inland safety to the harbours on the coast when they were ordered on immediate patrol. Ostend was also equipped for maintenance and repair works and the dry docks were only used when there was no more available space at Bruges. The importance of Ghent and Antwerp was generally low throughout the war, due to the fact that they were far away from the battlefront of the sea. By 1917 this was slowly changing and the importance of the Ghent docks rose due to the continuous bombardments on Ostend and Zeebrugge. Antwerp was only used for lenghty repairs to small vessels.

An aerial view of the Mole and harbour of Zeebrugge. To the west of the foot of the Mole stands the Palace Hotel (TT)

The entire organisation of dockyards in Flanders was called the *Kaiserliche Werfte* or Imperial Yards. They would not only be responsible for repairs to ships, but also delivered more than 150 armoured shelters, pedestals for anti-aircraft guns, pontoons for naval units and the construction of huge floating docks. By the end of 1918 more than 5,000 men were at work on these wharves.

ZEEBRUGGE

The then modern harbour of Zeebrugge had only been in use for seven years when the Germans marched in in 1914. The harbour had been built after a proposition by Baron de Maere in 1875 to dig a canal which would link Bruges to the sea. The name 'Bruges-seaport' was created. It was only in 1890, 15 years later, that theory would be put into practice after the lobbying of the Ghent parlementarian de Smet de Naeyer. In Parliament he was a staunch supporter for a harbour for fast ferries which would rival those of Ostend and Antwerp. Even King Leopold II supported the ambitious plan to make Bruges more prosperous through the port of Zeebrugge. After approval, excavation work was started in 1896 on a huge canal, an immense seawall, lockgates and a fishing port in Zeebrugge. The finished harbour of Zeebrugge was inaugurated by the King on 23 July 1907. To the north of Bruges two docks were dug, as well as quaywalls and installations constructed. Later on this would become Bruges' inner harbour.

The harbour of Zeebrugge consisted of two areas: on the seaside the port area with the harbour wall (or Mole), the inner harbour with lockgates and fishing port and on the landside the canal which stretched toward Bruges.

The harbour wall had a total length of nearly 2.5 km and created a sheltered bay with safe depths where merchant ships could anchor and take on or unload cargoes. The wall consisted of four sections. The first part was a concrete pier of 232 m in length which stretched from the dunes up to the low water mark of the beach. The second was a jetty style pier which measured 300 m. This pier was constructed of a solid wood flooring, supported by steel beams which had

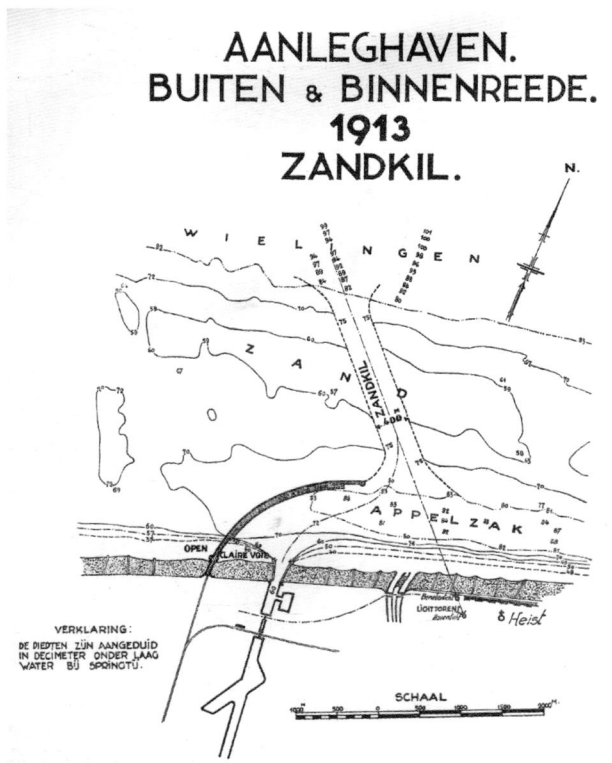

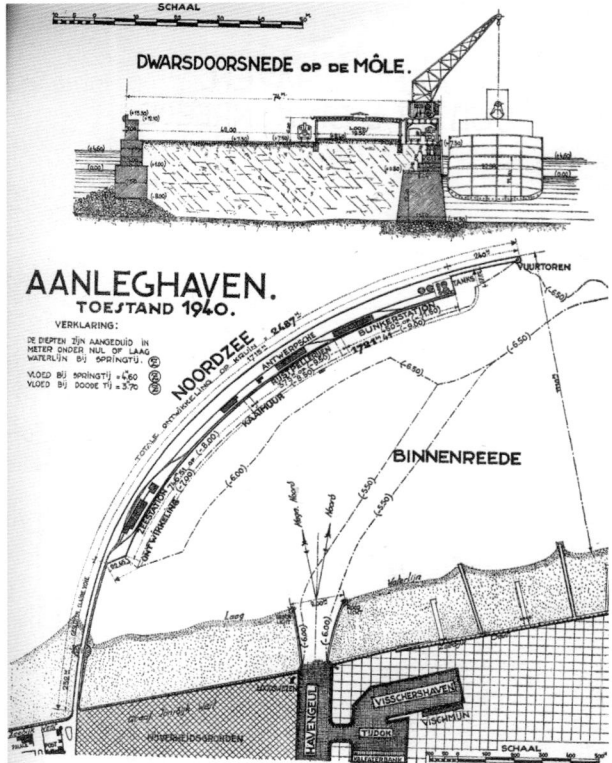

Pre-war views of Zeebrugge Harbour and her entrance passages (Vandamme)

A photo taken of the 282 m long sea lock, connecting the Bruges Canal to the sea (TT)

A closer view of the Zeebrugge Mole: at the inside lie several A-class Torpedo boats, armed trawlers and a dredger (TT)

A UB-I boat navigates cruises through the Zeebrugge locks (TT)

been rammed into the mud and strengthened with concrete. Theoretically, the prevailing current had to serve as a cheap dredging system which would keep the harbour free of silt. During the famous Zeebrugge Raid in April 1918, the British submarine *HMS C-3* was rammed deep between these metal girders. The bow of *HMS C-3* had been loaded with 5 tons of explosives which were detonated to prevent German reinforcements reaching the battle on the Mole. In the postwar period of reconstructions of the harbour facilities, the engineers realised that the constant flow through the pier could in no way stop the silting up of the harbour. After this period a full concrete harbour wall would replace this section.

The third and longest part of the wall measured 1.715 m and had a breadth of 70 m. It was a massive wall which had a protective fortification and parapet built on the western side. This gave the western side of the harbour wall a total height of 35 m above the surface of the sea. This wall gave protection to the anchorage against the predominant northerly and westerly winds. In peacetime two dozen ships could easily find shelter in the bay during stormy weather.

The last section of the wall had a length of 240 m, on a breadth of 9 m and ende with a 14 m broad lighthouse on the point. A general depth of 8 m was created in the immediate vicinity of the inner part of the harbour wall. Between high and low water there was a tidal drop of 4.5 m.

On the broadest part of the wall, a quay-area was created with three large hangars where the sea station was also located. Ten electric and two steam-driven cranes were sited on the edge of the quay to help unload docked ships. Cargoes could be laden on traintrucks which could head inland immediately by railroad track.[89]

During the war the hangers were reused by the Germans as a base for their seaplanes and baptised *Seeflugstation Zeebrügge*. Pilots and aircrews would be housed in the nearby railway trucks.

Just to the north of the dam a large shipping lane was created which connected the harbour of Zeebrugge to the Wielingen channel and the North Sea. It would be known as ''t Pas van het Zand' and stretched over 3,000 m and had a breadth of 400 m and a general depth of 7 m.

U-12, under command of *Kapitänleutnant* Walter Forstman, entered Zeebrugge as first German U-boat

A view of the Zeebrugge inner harbour with the two piers (TT)

Just before leaving for open sea, the crew of a UB-II boat talks to the men of a returning UB-I submarine. In the distance are the piers of the inner harbour and the distant Mole (TT)

in October 1914. Forstmann, who would earn the *Pour le Mérite* or Blue Max, wrote to the German Admiralty that his U-boat could moor without any problems on the inner part of the seawall, in the vicinity of the sea station. Due to the deck being almost level with the surface of the sea, a number of pontoons had to be arranged to serve as a docking area. But even in relatively bad weather, such as a northwesterly gale force 7 or 8, U-boats could enter and leave the inner harbour, preferably at high tide.

Power facilities for the U-boats were also present and this was provided by a large cable which ran from the mainland from the electricity works sited on the seawall to a converter near the sea station. In peacetime this would provide power to the tram and harbour facilities, but now it proved ideal to load the batteries for the electric engines of the U-boats.[90] A disguarded Belgian dredger was used throughout the war to prevent the harbour from silting up. Numerous workshops on the seawall served as repair facilities to the dredgers. Tools, hydraulic presses, a smithy and cranes were present and useful to care for lightly damaged U-boats and surface craft. Steam, necessary to heat installations on board U-boats, was generated in the disused railway engines which were parked along the seawall. Maintenance and technical crews to care for the docked U-boats were housed in the buildings of the sea station which also housed toilet and wash facilities.

The large outer harbour also had as important function the protection of the two pierheads and lockgates of the inner harbour. The inner harbour consisted of a large sealock which had a length of 282 m, a breadth of 20 m and a depth of 9 m. Access was possible by means of a 750-m long dug canal in the inner harbour. This canal was protected by two, large wooden piers, each provided with a lightbeacon at the end.

The inner harbour was shaped on the northern end by the canal which originated in Bruges. This ended in a basin and dock area. To the east of the harbour mouth there was the fisheries port which had more than 600 m of quayside. This had been built in 1906 and consisted of two shallow docks with a depth of about 4 m. The fisheries port gave protection to shallow draught warships and was ideal for U-boats and *Vorpostenboote*.

The harbour, the anchorage and its installations were protected by clusters of artillery implacements which had to ward off possible attacks and bombardments from the sea. To the east of the seawall three 10.5 cm calibre guns were sited. On the seawall or Mole, six 8.8 cm artillery pieces had been erected behind the parapet and faced west. To the west of the Mole stood four 15 cm and two 28 cm calibre canon in the area of dunes behind the beach. The arc of fire of these canon covered the area around the anchorage as well as that of the Mole. Batteries of large calibre canon, sited in Blankenberge and Knokke, could reach further out to sea.

In May 1915 the Imperial Dockyard ordered 2,000 m of steel nets and 1,000 m of woven steel thread

A view of the end of the Mole with the lighthouse, taken in 2014. This part of the old harbour has now been totally swallowed up by the modern containerport (TT)

The furthest part of the Mole, with a battery of 8.8 cm guns pointing out to sea (TT)

Zeebrugge village in 1914. In the foreground is the pilotstation (TT)

which would serve to protect and partly block the harbour. The nets were suspended from 60 to 80 m long barges which were connected and hung up to a depth of 9 m.[91] The barges, which were sited in the anchorage toward the end of the Mole, with their nets had to stop or obstruct possible torpedo attacks on the ships moored alongside the wall. To the eastern side of the anchorage was a 300 m long barrage of nets of various lengths, suspended from moored buoys which served to hinder fast-moving enemy ships. Between both areas of obstructions a gap of 100 m breadth was kept open for friendly ships entering and leaving the harbour.

At the foot of the seawall there were hardly any pathed roads or installations around the village of Zeebrugge. Up to 1910 there had not even been a connecting road to Blankenberge and there was no habitation in the harbour area. There was only a large building were a government service was housed. Pre-war travellers found themselves stranded in a real desert without any roads, lighting, houses or hotels. In Zeebrugge's hayday, before 1914, large shipping companies, such as the Hamburg-Amerika Line or the North Eastern Railway, found this situation unacceptable. Agreements made between the Hamburg-Amerika line forced the '*Maatschappij der Brugsche Zeevaartinrichtingen*' to deepen '*t Pas van het Zand* to 9 metres and start the construction of a luxury hotel, *the Palace Hotel*. In July 1914 the hotel was opened and German ships were welcomed by a Belgian parliamentarian. Not even a month later, in August, war was declared and large amounts of German warships entered the anchorage, but then without a welcoming comittee!

Zeebrugge was connected to the interior by a 10 km long sea canal which had a maximum depth of 8 m. In profile it tapered up, with a breadth of 22 m on the bottom and 70 m on the surface.[92] Along the banks there were numerous factories which handled and stocked lubricating oil, cokes, coal, sugar, petrol and diesel-oil.

U-boats which had to leave for sea would leave Bruges in group to facilitate movements through the locks at Zeebrugge. At their arrival in Zeebrugge they would be docked along the seawall, hidden and protected beneath concrete shelters or would leave immediately on patrol. Normally U-boat crews would stay aboard their U-boat at Zeebrugge as their were little facilities in the village. From January 1915

The only surviving structure near the Mole pre-dating 1914 (TT)

the amount of U-boats which entered Zeebrugge increased and it pressed the need housing for these crews. In the spring of 1915 the impressive Palace Hotel was arranged to house the fleet commander, the fleet doctor, the halfflottilla commander, a flotilla engineer and a halfflottilla engineer. All received private accommodation and adjoining work areas. A communal room served as an office. Private rooms were alocated to house 16 captains, four first officers and four chief engineers. Lower grade officers, who before had a lodging to themselves, had to make room for a senior rank and share a room with a colleague. Crewmen were given rooms in the former Hotel Becassine and surrounding houses. The *Werft Division* extended the houses with quickly constructed huts. Besides parts of the Palace Hotel there were also spaces in the former pilot station converted to office areas. In March 1915 another area of Zeebrugge was prepared to house six officers and 80 crewmen from the U-boats.

The use of the lodgings at Zeebrugge would be short-lived and the nerve-center was moved to the harbour of Bruges in April 1915. This was because the Palace Hotel and the surrounding buildings proved to be an excellent target for bombarding British monitors. Command of the flotilla was moved to the house once owned by Catulle at Fort Lapin, situated to the north of Bruges. The flotilla leader of the *U-Flottille Flandern* became the armed trawler or *Vorpostenboot Frigg*, known as *Fischdampfer B*, which was berthed along the Zeebrugge seawall. Choosing the *Frigg* as headquarters vessel had been a specific choice. A former trawler was less conspicuous as a target then a torpedo boat or destroyer.

Overall control of the harbour fell to the command of *Kapitänleutnant d. R.* Menzell.

During the month of June 1916, the British merchant ship *SS Brussels*, owned by the North Eastern Railway company, was boarded at sea by crewmen from the *Torpedoboat G-102* and brought into Zeebrugge. At a later stage *SS Brussels* was moored alongside the seawall, near to the seaplane base and served as an accommodation ship for torpedo boat crews.

After the Zeebrugge Raid, on 23 April 1918, it looked as if the sunken blockships *HMS Intrepid* and *HMS Iphigenia* would obstruct the passage for middle to large U-boats. This changed a few weeks later as the Germans removed two wooden piers on the western bank of the entrance to the canal. This was just beside the sunken ships and with dredgers they managed to create a 15 m wide passage. After these works the blockships proved to be no more hinderance to entering and exiting ships no matter the state of the tide.

A view on the Zeebrugge Mole and Roads. Torpedo boats, and trawlers are berthed against the inner wall (Heiko Hermans)

The wreck of the *SS Brussels*, sunk in Zeebrugge Harbour after the St. George's Day attack in 1918 (TT) ▶

BRUGES

In Bruges the Germans took over the docks, renamed it *Kaiserliche Werft Brügge*.[93] and used it as berthing area for their U-boats. *Oberleutnant z. See d. R.* Bauer was given the task of harbour captain and *Kapitänleutnant* Timmermann was responsible for the *Minenwerkstatt Brügge* or mine depot and repair shop.

The *Kaiserliche Werft Brügge* became the most central of all German wharves in occupied Flanders. *Oberwerftdirektor* was *Kapitän z. S.* Pohl who was aided by *Fregattenkapitän* Schütte. Technically, the area was divided in the zone Bruges and the zone Ostend, but both stood under overall command of *Marine-Oberbaurat* Buschberg.

Hafenbau and *Kanalwesen* were assigned to *Marine-Baurat* Hedde. His task was the design and construction of yard buildings, the upkeep of the harbour and canals, etc. *Marine-Baumeister* Frede was responsible for the *Hafenbauabteilung I Brügge-Nordhafen* and made the planning and construction for all shelters and bunkers for the U-boats as well as the protective infrastructure in and around the harbour. He was supported by *Hafenbauabteilungen II en VI*.

In Ostend, the *Hafenbauabteilung III* (*Marine-Baumeister* Hacker) en *IV, Maschinenwesen* (*Marine-Baurat* Ruthe) were responsible for solving any technical problems in the harbour.

Bruges Harbour seemed to be ideal to let U-boats have a refit, overhoal or repair due to its large lengths of quayside and numerous workshops. The sea canal entered the harbour at its northern end in two recently dug docks and basins. This was the Nijverheidsdock and Janssendock. The Germans renamed them the northern and southern torpedoboat-harbour. The sea canal ended in the Groot Handelsdock with on its eastern side a branch leading to a smaller dock known as the Klein Handelsdock. This area would become known as the north basin with western and eastern arms. After the Second World War the Janssendock was filled in and the Nijverheidsdock was dug out and lengthened.

In 1914 Bruges had a total of 1,350 m in quaylength with all kinds of facilities. Four large hangers would be reconstructed as workshops and a number of steam-powered cranes could be used for loading torpedoes and mines. The inner harbour was connected to the Flemish interior by a network of canals. The

This drawing shows an imaginary view of a UB-boat cruising on the Bruges canals. At the back is one of the famous ancient gates of the city (Willy Stöwer)

164

A UC-II boat leaves Bruges to head along the canal to Zeebrugge (TT)

The small merchant dock was a bustle of activity, mid-war, with several U-boats lying side-by-side, waiting to be supplied with torpedoes and mines (Jörn Jensen)

A huddle of military vessels lie near the U-boat shelter in Bruges (TT)

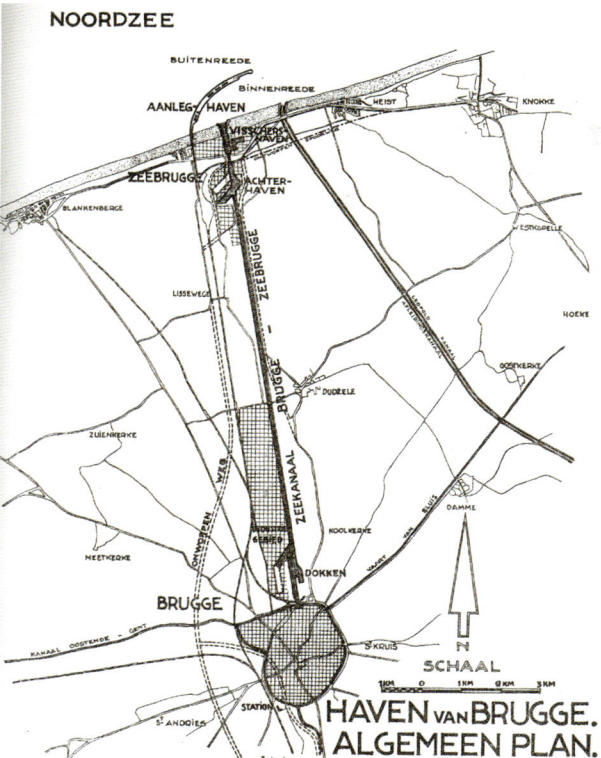
Bruges' docks are connected to the sea by a 12 km long canal (Vandamme)

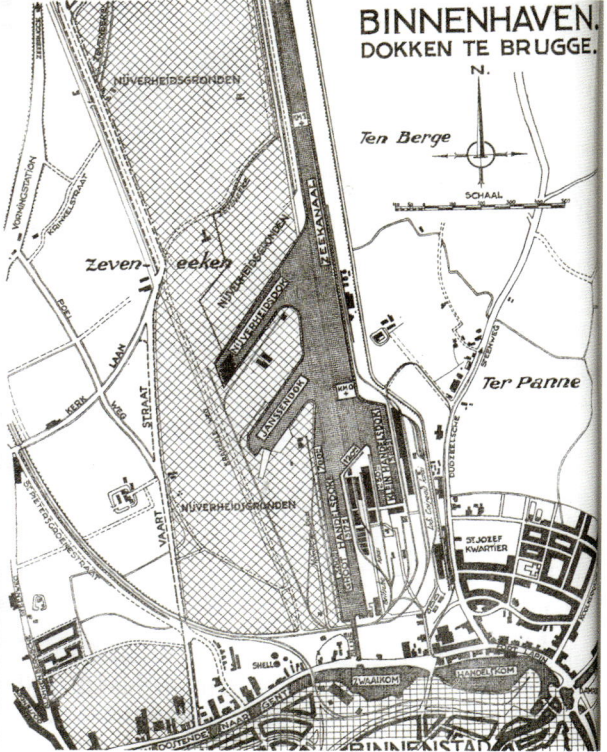
Bruges Harbour consisted of four docks: the large and small merchant docks, the Janssensdock and the Nijverheidsdock (Vandamme)

A proportionally incorrect, but interesting drawing of a Bruges half shelter, probably the small merchant dock (TT)

Hangars under construction in the Kaiserliche Werft, Bruges. The Bruges skyline is visible in the background (BArch)

Interior view of a dockyard building under construction (BArch)

Schipdonk Canal connected it to Ghent and the Lys, and there were canals leading to Ostend and Plasschendale-Veurne. A lock was situated between the docks and the canal Ostend-Bruges-Ghent. It had a length of 172 m, a breadth of 12 m and a depth of 4 m. Near to the town of Bruges, on the ring, lies the old merchant dock area which dates to the 17th century. Facilities here were fairly primitive and there were only 400 m of quayside available. The canal Ostend-Ghent proved to be perfect to ship U-boats and surface craft, as it had been made for a capacity of ships up to 2.000 BRT.

By 1918 the *Kaiserliche Werft* consisted of seven floating docks of varying sizes. Workshops were situated in a large building on the eastern dock. On the western side of the same dock there were workshops for hullplates and engines. On both sides of the main dock concrete shelters were built, partly hanging over the water. These constructions were meant to protect U-boats against possible air-attacks. All buildings, except those of the engine- and steelworks, were bombproof. Even though some buildings were not fortified against air attack, they were provided with concrete-lined trenches. Of all buildings, the supply dumps for mines and torpedoes were the most heavily constructed with ceiling thicknesses ranging from 1 to 2 m.

A torpedo boat passes a half shelter with U-boats in the Bruges docks (TT)

The most typifying sight of Bruges as a U-boat nest were the long half-shelters built along the banks of the west and east basins of the north harbour and the eight large U-boat bunkers situated on the northern side of the Groot Handelsdock. Locally, these massive bunkers were known as the 'Acht Zaligheden'[94] and from the inside the rows of supporting columns gave the construction the look of a gigantic Egyptian temple.

A British postwar analysis of the harbours and coastal defences in Flanders indicated that the British were impressed by the general sturdiness and the meticulous way everything had been planned, engineered and executed in this dockyard area. It

During a British bombardment of the dockyard in 1917, several buildings were hit and partly destroyed (TT)

The covered *UB-13* lies beneath a half shelter in the north part of the small merchant dock (TT)

Washing hangs on the jumping wire of a U-boat, sheltering with two others beneath a half shelter in Bruges docks. The photo was taken during Easter 1917 (TT)

In the first two years of the war, a fair amount of prize vessels were brought into Zeebrugge. This drawing shows us the Dutch *SS Zaanstroom* being led by a Flanders U-boat towards the locks (Willy Stöwer)

Several buildings sited on the Bruges ringroad were used to accommodate U-boat crews (TT)

The same location in 2014 (Luc Commeine)

was obvious that the Germans were expecting to be remaining permanently in Flanders. If the war had lasted a few more years, then the dockyard would have come to a capacity where it would be able to build its own ships. The dockyard was so big and well equipped that U-boats could be repaired almost immediately and they did not have to wait for vessels still up in dry dock. It was estimated that the total network of facilities at Bruges and Ostend could maintain the entire British fleet of 133 submarines. In British ports, many minor problems on submarines had to be solved by their own crews. On the German side there was a special unit, the *Werft Division*, or Dockyard Division, which immediately took care of the needs of a returning U-boat.

From January 1915 onwards, decent lodging for officers and men of the Bruges based U-boats were sought. Initially only private housing was used near the harbour. From 1917 up to the end of the war the large seminary located on the Potterierei was used partly as accommodation for U-boat crews.

But the greater part of the crews were housed in accommodation ships. By the middle of 1915 housing on land had been created for 30 officers, 30 engine-room candidates and 350 petty-officers and crew. Flotilla staff was partly housed on the leading flotilla ship (usually an armed trawler or merchant ship) and later partly on shore. The amount of staff was quite extensive and consisted of the captain, his aide, two or three engineers, a surgeon, two paymasters, a senior petty-officer and 18 petty-officers and men. A building near the dockside would be converted

Many prize ships ended up in Bruges Harbour as depot ships, such as the *SS Zaanstroom* (TT)

On 5 July 1916, the British ship *SS Lestris* was escorted into Zeebrugge (TT)

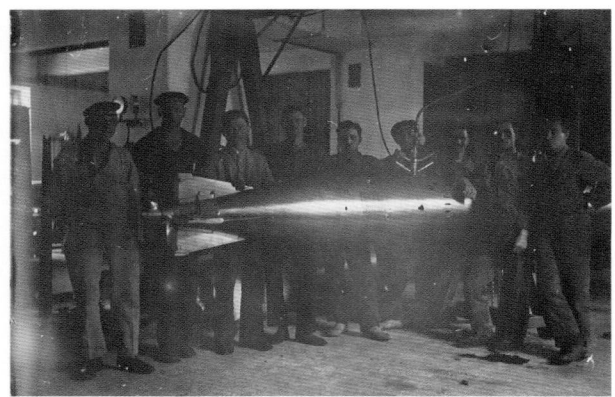

Seamen and mechanics gather around a hoisted torpedo engine in the Torpedo-Reparaturwerkstatt (TT)

for office functions and occupied by a *Feldwebel* (senior petty-officer), three petty-officers and 30 men. Besides having berths and storage space, there was also an area for a mess as well as bathing and washroom facilities for officers, cadets and enlisted men.

In the early years of the war a number of neutral and enemy shipping would be stopped and boarded at sea by boarding parties from U-boats or torpedo boats. It was normal practice to check the cargo manifest as well as inspect the holds. When neutral ships would have been heading towards an enemy port with a cargo which would be useful to the enemy, then these ships would either be sunk or taken as a prize to a port in German hands. It would be of course more advantageous if a ship could be brought in where a cargo could be used by the Germans. In 1916 a total of 20 ships, mainly Dutch, but also some British, Belgian, Norwegian and a Brazilian ship were escorted to Zeebrugge. In the last two years of the war it only amounted to four ships being captured and not sunk. This was because the manner of the U-boat war had changed drastically. Fewer ships could be stopped on the surface and just sunk at a distance. The months of September and November 1916 proved to be the most successful for the capture of useful ships. A total of 11 vessels would enter Zeebrugge and three of them were the Dutch *SS Niobe* (by *UB-12*), *SS Zeemeeuw* (by *UB-37*) and *SS Batavier II* (by *UB-6*). November saw the capture of seven ships and four of these were the Dutch *RSS Koningin Regentes* (by *UB*-19), *SS Batavier VI* (by *UB-29*), *SS Midsland* (also by *UB-29*) and the Norwegian *SS Birgit* (by *UB-17*). The other ships had been stopped and escorted to Zeebrugge by torpedo boats. Two of these were the British steamships *SS Brussels* (North Eastern Railway Company) and *SS Lestris* (Cork Steamship Company) which were captured respectively in June and July 1916 by *G-102* and *G-104*.[95] Some ships were allowed to sail away after further investigation, but most stayed behind in Bruges or Zeebrugge or were escorted to ports in Germany.

Captured ships were usually put to use in occupied ports. *SS Niobe* was turned into the mothership for the fast *Motorboots Division* in May 1917. The holds were adapted by the *Kaiserliche Werft Brügge* to hold berths and living spaces for petty officers and men. Closets and cupboards for personal items, tables, trunks and benches were created by employed carpenters. The carpentry of the *Kaiserliche Werft* was housed in the Delhaize furniture works on the Blankenberge bridge near the canal for Ostend. Hammocks could be hung almost anywhere and bathroom facilities were created. Showers mainly were for the engineers of the U- and T-boats whose ships would be moored close to the accommodation vessels. Steam was always kept up on board so as the ship could be easily moved at short notice. *SS Lestris* and *SS Niobe* were berthed in the northern torpedo boat harbor, whilst *SS Zaanstroom* lay at the entrance of the northern basin, on the western side.

The former Catulle Brewery, near the merchant port of Bruges, housed a large technical workshop. The buildings were well protected and lay close to the quaysides which made the transport and storage of the numerous batteries for the electric engines possible. Fine mechanical work was also done in this building, besides being a repairshop for battery units.

The periscope and optics workshop had its own building on the torpedo boat peninsula. Towards the end of the war, in July 1918, the former spinnery near the Gentpoort room was fitted with lathes and turned into a torpedo repair works. Torpedo-bodies and engines were stored in the former furniture hangar on the Nieuwe Meers 1 and in the former soap factory on the Dominikanenrei 11*, as well as in the brewery on the Wollestraat 23. The candidate-priests residing in the Nieuwe Meers were evicted to make room for U-boat crews.

From the day the *U-Flottille Flandern* was created on 29 March 1915, the officers occupied the house which belonged to René Fraeys in the Sint Jorisstraat

---

* The Nieuwe Meers is now known as Zonneke Meers and the Dominikanenrei is now the Predikherenrei.

Across the mess building stood the headquarters of Korvettenkapitän Bartenbach. He (8) is gathered with the German Emperor Kaiser Wilhelm II (6), commanding Admiral von Schröder (7) and a number of U-boat officers, some of them are Otto Steinbrinck (10), Werner Dollmann (killed in action only four days after this photo was taken, with the sinking of UB-55) (11), Erwin Wassner (14), Ralph Wenninger (15) (captured when UB-55 was sunk), Hans Walther (16), Johannes Ries (22) (KIA as commander of UC-71), Kiesewetter (26) (arrested as war criminal after the war for the sinking of a hospital ship) (TT)

in Bruges. This lay just across the flotilla commander's residence, Karl Bartenbach, who was quartered at number 20. This impressive building still stands and is now the headquarters of the local newspaper, the *Brugsch Handelsblad*. The officers' mess in the Sint Jorisstraat was depicted as a beautiful private palace with large, high-ceilinged rooms illuminated by crystal chandeliers. The rooms were arranged with tasteful furniture and the tables were bedecked with expensive silverware and porcelain. The location of the command centre of the *U-Flottille Flandern* is not known for sure, but it was most probably in the Vlamingenstraat 82, next to the Jesuit church. It was described by the Germans as a house built by the Jesuits. With its angular structure and ancient charm it looked the part too. From 'kleinkarierten Fenster'.[96] one could look upon a narrow alley. The actual plans of attack for the *U-Flottille Flandern* were devised from this location.[97] A relaxation place, or casino, was housed in the neo-gothic mansion belonging to Jules Catulle, at Fort Lapin on the Bruges town suburbs.

An unidentified Belgian restaurant in Bruges centre was a magnet for U-boat officers as it served fresh oysters almost on a daily basis. But the did not only come to enjoy the oysters as they also enjoyed flirting with the landlady's stunning daughter.

Not only in Bruges did life prove to be good. Just outside the city there was an old manor house which served as a retreat for officers.

The U-boat base, dockyards and facilities in Bruges harbour proved to be a constant annoyance to the British. Due to its sheer scale and large number of U-boats which could be docked there at one time, it was a prime target for the Allies. But Bruges lay at 12 km distance from the sea, connected by the sea canal to Zeebrugge, and could not be touched by ship based batteries. Its infrastructure could only be bombed from the air. Several bombing raids were undertaken, with a concentrated intensity during 1917.

One of these attacks took place in the early hours of 3rd February. It was freezing cold and at a height of 2 km the temperature was -22°C. Several aircraft of the attacking British squadron were forced to return

A view of the house which belonged to René Fraeys, in the Sint Jorisstraat 20, Bruges, which was used throughout the war as the U-boat officers' mess (TT)

Entrance steps leading up to Bartenbach's headquarters, a view taken in 2014. The house is now the property of the local newspaper *Brugsch Handelsblad* (TT)

Main entrance to Bartenbach's command, on the Sint-Joris-street (TT)

In a neogothic building, sited next to the Jesuit church in the Vlamingstraat, attack for the U-boats were devised (TT)

or simply crashed due to the problems of the cooling water freezing. The docks of Bruges were covered by large drifting icefloes. In the end, six Sopwiths of n° 5 Squadron were able to unleash 23 Le Pecq and six 112-pound bombs on the area. Around midnight of the same day three short distance bombers from n°4 Squadron were able to make a sortie whereby 18 112-pound bombs were dropped on the docks and the airfield of Koolkerke. Several hangars were hit, but no ships or aircraft were damaged. Repeated attacks were carried out on 7 and 9 of February with ten Sopwiths releasing nearly 100 112-pound bombs on the docks. Most of them exploded in the basins, but on 7th February a large fire was started which was visible up to Allied-held territory at Petit Synthe. During these bombardments a record of 3.5 tons of bombs had been dropped on Bruges Harbour. The material damage was significant. A German report stated the loss or damage of three wooden hangars, an accommodation building for U-boat crews, the roof and gate of a *Minenlager* or mine-depot, several railtracks, an ammunition dump for 8.8 cm shrapnel shells and a storage for detonators. Despite the heavy bombardment and resultant fires, the Germans suffered no casualties. A number of bombs missed their targets and ended up in a civilian neighbourhood. A row of 13 houses was completely destroyed and besides 14 civilian dead, there were a large number of wounded.[98]

One of the very few photos known of the fabulous U-boat casino in the house of Jules Catulle, Fort Lapin (TT)

THE FABULOUS U-BOAT CASINO

'*Es gab da einen alten Ratskeller, einen Keller mit gotischen Bogen, dessen Mauern einen Meter dick waren. Das war der nächtliche Versammlungsort für die kühne Schar, die die Meere unter ihrer Oberfläche durchfurchten.*'[99]

The casino and part-accommodation for the officers of the U-boat fleet was situated in a large manor house in Fort Lapin, the Sint-Pieters area of Bruges. Before the war it had been the property of the industrialist, Jules Catulle. It had been built in French neo-Baroque style by the Brussels architect G. Martin in 1906. Due to the proximity to the docks, and the comfort and facilities of the building, it was immediately used as a retreat for officers returning from their patrols. The spacious cellars were adapted as a sort of festive hall and with their robust construction gave enough protection against possible air raids. In the cellar was a supply of 4,000 bottles of wine which the overjoyed Germans drank within a couple of weeks.* The entrance towards the cellar was situated just next to the house's main stairwell. The walls along the steps and the cellar itself were abundantly decorated with a large array of frescoes. In the building there was little furniture present which would fit in the cellar. Tables, benches and chairs were especially made by carpenters in Bruges to fit in the basement. The cellar was further adorned with dozens of objects taken from enemy ships, such as bells, telegraphs, navigationlights and liferings.

Even after the Germans had abandoned the building in 1918, a large number of bells, which had been taken from British merchant and fishing vessels, were still present on the wall along the stairs. Sadly enough nothing is known of the fate of these interesting pieces of history.

The frescoes, to say the least, were impressive, and ran throughout all the rooms of the cellar and can be considered as an artwork in their own right. They depicted charicatures of mines and torpedoes which danced, embraced

---

* The Catulle family was not present during the German invasion, but their servant stayed on in the building throughout the war. Her testimony spoke of the consumption of the entire supply in just a couple of weeks time, but this, of course, has to be taken with the necessary scepticism.

The former U-boat casino in Fort Lapin, now converted into an Apero-bar (TT)

A view of the rear of the U-boat casino during construction works in 2004 (TT)

Von Schröder and Bartenbach, surrounded by officers on the same steps of the U-boat casino in 1917 (TT)

and kissed each other. The mines had British peaked caps and other Allied trade marks, whilst the torpedoes were painted with faces of deceased U-boat officers. Monkeys lavishly drinking champagne, the torpedoing of 'John Bull', the personification of England, different U-boat types in wreaths and slogans such as '*Das Leben froh geniessen, weil man ja lebt nur so kurze Zeit*'[100] decorated the walls. There were also historical occasions depicted, such as the escorting of the captured merchant ship *SS Brussels* and her captain, Charles Fryatt.[101] The frescoes wove a story of risk, adventure, from victories to morbid excitement and certain death which hung above the head of each U-boatman. A report of the British Admiralty commission of 1920 also mentioned the fact that the captured Captain Fryatt had been invited to dine with the U-boat officers in the building. They told him that he was a gentleman and they were on friendly terms up to the moment he saw fit to show off his watch. The watch had been given to him by the British as a reward for his attempt to ram the German U-boat *U-33* in the North Sea during the previous year. The atmosphere took a 180° turn and he was immediately apprehended and imprisoned. Not long after he faced a military tribunal and was found guilty of espionage and executed by firing squad in Bruges. After the war, the casino went back into the hands of its owner and the frescoes disappeared beneath a layer of whitewash. But not before the artist Maurice Sieron took the opportunity to copy the paintings on canvas. There are two sets of paintings surviving, one held by the Bruges' Archives and Museums, the other at Atlantikwall Museum Raversijde. The paintings were used in a temporary reconstruction of a number of rooms of the casino at the Zeebrugge museum. It was only in 2004 that we realised that the original frescoes still survived on the walls of the cellar of the building in Fort Lapin. In the then derelict and empty building, beneath the original whitewash, parts of the fabulous frescoes could be retraced. The building has now been totally restored and renovated and is run as an apero bar 'Salon Lapin'. Sadly enough, the new owner had been ignorant of the important history of the building and many of the frescoes and walls disappeared when the rooms were enlarged. The delicate whitewash has been replaced by a depressing, thick brown paint, which surely has done no good to the 100-year old paintings.

Photos taken in the former Zeebrugge Museum (with the reconstruction of the cellar of the U-boat casino) and its frescoes, which were copied on to cloth after the war (TT)

Part of the cellar, photographed in 2004. This was the original gathering place and these very walls were richly decorated with frescoes (TT)

When part of the whitewash was removed, fragments of the frescoes came to light (TT)

An armed trawler escorts a UC-I type boat in the harbour of Ostend (TT)

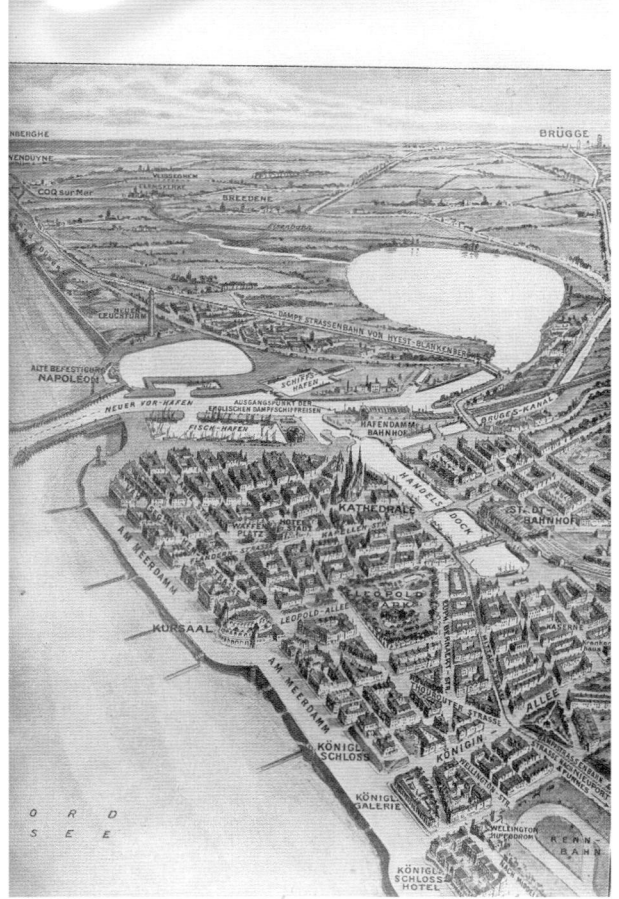

A drawing of the town and port of Ostend in 1914 (Illustrierte Zeitung)

OSTEND

In 1914 it looked as if Ostend would be designated as the main base for the U-boat fleet. Actually there were enough mooring places, hangars, accommodation, dry docks, yards and workshops spread out over the western, but mainly eastern port areas. Facilities were available to tend to damaged U-boats and also give them an overhaul. The dockyard was ready for use and in the buildings of the Ostend Electric Works there were loading facilities for the batteries of the electric engines.

But not only is a good infrastructure is necessary for a well-functioning U-boat base. A large number of natural elements, such as current, tidal drop, depths and location, made Ostend less desirable than Zeebrugge.

For 200 years Ostend had a harbour which was protected by two wooden piers which stretched half a mile out to see in west-northwesterly direction. The angle of the piers offered relatively good protection to the inner harbour during prevailing northerly and northeasterly winds. The construction of the piers on wooden columns was meant to give a constant flow of the currents during the tidal drop.

During the night of 15 November 1915, the high-seas U-boat *U-8* entered the harbour of Ostend. At that moment there was a northwesterly storm force

After a shelling of the Ostend Harbour and docks by British monitors, an armed trawler and a U-boat were hit. To the left is a dry dock with a docked U-boat. (TT)

7 and *U-8* had great difficulty entering the sanctity of the inner harbour without suffering damage. She entered during low tide and in the harbour the heavy groundseas beat just above the conning tower. The unrestricted flow of the tide between the columns of the piers gave the U-boat more problems with which to contend.

The German officers conning the U-boat were not familiar with the current which pulled and sucked at low- and high tide far into the harbour. The helmsmen had a hard job to keep her steady and dock her safely to the quayside. There was also a relatively high drop of roughly 3 m between high- and low tide and only the area around the docks on the eastern side had been dredged sufficiently. *U-8* had to moor in the undredged area near the present Demey-lock, at the station. At low tide her keel touched bottom.

A U-boat lies partially hidden beneath a half shelter in the Ostend merchant dock (TT)

A UC-II type submarine comes alongside a trawler in Ostend. In the background, the powder magazine and quarantine building are recognisable (TT).

The sea station was hit and severely damaged during the same attack (TT) ▶

Ostend had to also contend with the problem of regular attacks by enemy aircraft. Repairs and refits of U-boats could only be done during the night or in the early hours of the morning. During the day the U-boats had difficulty in finding refuge beneath the surface as there was not enough depth to hide the entire vessel. The moored U-boats were usually camouflaged by adding fake wooden bow and stern sections. Seen from the air, they would take on the appearance of barges.

Safety would improve much more once concrete half shelters were erected along the quaysides. The area on the eastern side of the harbour entrance was also totally cordoned off with wirefence to keep unwelcome visitors out.

The quays on the side of the docks were well equipped and even when there was a tide running, the loading of petrol and diesel progressed fluently. At a later stage, most of the necessities such as diesel fuel, coal, boiler water and pottable water were available in moored barges. A dredger would also be at work 24 hours a day to maintain a minimum depth of 2.5 m in the basin and a larger depth in the harbour mouth and other parts of the port.

In January 1915 a naval doctor made an investigation of the Ostend fresh water supply and did not find it sufficient enough fort he U- and T-boats which would be bunkering there. Some time after his findings a distillation plant was constructed with a holding tank for 40 tons of fresh water.

U-boats would leave the safety of Bruges Harbour in a group even when just heading to Ostend. This would ease their movements through the locks. This usually happened during the night, at 1 am, to be able to head to open sea in secrecy. If they had to wait at Ostend, they would be moored beneath concrete half shelters until orders were issued for them to head out on patrol. In contrast with the situation at Zeebrugge, U-boat crews would be housed in facilities throughout the city.

When the Allies had retreated they had left Ostend relatively empty, only leaving a number of obsolete, unwanted vessels. These were the cross-channel ferries *La Flandre, Leopold I* and *Princesse Joséphine*, as well as a lightship, a steamer belonging to the Zeebrugge pilotage, the schoolship *Ville de Bruges* and fisheries patrol vessel *Ville d'Ostende*. These would never be brought to working order by the Germans but converted and used as accommodation vessels for the crews of torpedo and U-boats. One of the first to be ready to serve in this role was the 358 ton pilotcutter *Ville d'Ostende*, which had been readied in the docks and anchored in front of the station on 13 March 1915.

Kapitänleutnant d. S. I. Kleeberg received command and organisation of Ostend Harbour and *Marinebaumeister* Linde would be responsible for the *Hafenbau Ostende*.[102] By the middle of 1917 a total of 1,200 men were at work at the *Kaiserliche Werft*, Ostend division. These personnel mainly consisted of officials and workmen. Nine different cellars located in the city were allotted to them in case the wharf came under attack from air or sea.

The fisheries patrol vessel Ville d'Ostende and the training ship Ville de Bruges lie side-by-side in the second dock at Ostend. Both ships were used as accommodation ships for U-boat crews. The tower of the St-Jozefs church is visible (TT).

The Ostend docks: the merchant dock housed several U-boats. At the right hand corner of the photo is the RYCO yacht club building and the beginning of the Spuikom (TT)

In May 1918 a 230 pound bomb hit the end of a half shelter on the Zeebrugge Mole (TT)

This photo shows the function of a heavy concrete roof: a U-boat bunker in Bruges is heavily damaged, but the bomb did not penetrate further (BArch)

IN THE HARBOUR: ALARMS AGAINST AIR ATTACKS AND CAMOUFLAGE

The harbours of Ostend and Zeebrugge had to contend with regular visits by British and French observation aircraft and bombers. Before and even after the construction of the concrete half shelters, a number of precautions had to be taken during an aerial attack. During the night the crews had to remove the firing pistols from the torpedoes, stow the flag and flag staff and let down the radio masts and smokestack. The U-boat had to be totally covered with sailcloth which was hung like a curtain over the hull and superstructure. Or partly hung when she lay beneath a half shelter. Day and night an officer and skeleton crew would be on watch, a machinegun set up on the quayside. 24-hour patrols on land had to keep an eye on the U-boat and warn the crew in time for an upcoming attack. When enemy aircraft had flown over the harbour at dusk it was usually for observation purposes and after their passing the U-boat would be repositioned. This was so that she did not run the risk of a planned night-time attack. If it was technically possible, a U-boat also had to be ready to sail at a moment's notice, with closed vents and mains. At high tide it was possible for a U-boat to duck beneath the surface and hide during a raid. At Zeebrugge this was possible throughout the whole day as there was sufficient waterdepth in the Roads. Radio contact would also be maintained with the surrounding units, such as the *Fliegerabteilung, Signalstation, Kommandatur, Ballonabwehrbatterie* and *Hafencompagnie*.[103] This was possible by making morse signals through the optics of the raised periscope of the submerged U-boat. This was also a necessary measure to call the U-boat back to the surface so as not to let the crew waste any time on the bottom. It was feared that the softness and suction power of the muddy bottom would create problems for the U-boat when she wanted to return to the surface.

In January 1915 there was quite an ambitious plan to build a gigantic covered area in the middle on one of the Bruges docks. Barges or lighters would be anchored to both quaysides and a hall would be created by erecting wooden pillars, covered by a large surface of hard canvas. In principle, a large, square, floating circus tent. The engineers responsible for its planning realised by March of the same year that it was not feasible to make the tent surface bombproof.[104] The construction would be discovered fast enough by the Allies and seen as a prime target to bomb. The consequences for a small fleet of sheltered U-boats would be catastrophic.

ATRAPPEN

Two of the three Atrappen or decoy U-boats in Ostend Harbour can be seen in the bottom right hand corner of the photo. They served to confuse aircraft and spies (TT)

Atrappen or dummy U-boats were placed in 1915 in a number of locations in Ostend Harbour and on the canal leading towards Bruges to mislead Allied aircraft. They consisted of lightly made wooden constructions which had been locally constructed, were of the same size as the normal U-boats and were conveniently placed in obvious locations. At Ostend there were two *Atrappen* which measured 65 m on a width of 6 m and had to imitate the large Ocean-going U-boats. A few months later the workshop turned out a 1/1 size small UB-Class submarine. One large and one smaller dummy U-boat lay hull to hull to the north of the bridge over which the de Smet de Naeyer laan lay. After the burning of the airship *L-12*, her surviving gondola was put near the 2 U-boat dummies. The other large U-boat dummy was moored on the east side, near the docks. At Zeebrugge there were also two large dummy U-boats which had been moored in the harbour.[105] It has not been proven if these wooden constructions had an impact on Allied observations and bombardments on both harbours. It could have been that the extensive espionage network provided enough information for the British to neglect the *Atrappen*.

A dummy U-boat on the Bruges Canal (TT)

An Attrapp in Ostend Harbour. The Gondola of the burnt out L-12 lies beside her (Jörn Jensen)

U-BOAT BUNKERS, CONCRETE HALF SHELTERS AND OTHER PROTECTIVE INFRASTRUCTURE

The German Admiralty wanted from the start of its occupation a permanent solution for the protection of the fleet of U-boats which stood under constant threat of bombardment from air and sea. The regular movement to different berths and the submerging of the craft proved to be virtually impossible to maintain, mainly due to the arrival of more and more U-boats from Germany. Dry docking of U-boats undergoing maintenance had to also be possible in relatively protected environments for the U-boat as well as for the workforce employed. The solution was to build concrete awnings or half shelters under which the U-boat could find protection. At a later stage completely covered shelters or 'stables' would be built and the construction activities would end in the building of eight titanic bunkers.

Responsibility for the design and building of these structures came in hands of German engineers who stood under command of *Marinebaurat* Nübling, who was followed up by *Oberbaurat* Peter Hedde in March 1916.

KRAGUNTERSTANDEN

In Ostend harbour there were two types of half shelters. On the eastern bank of the floating dock (merchant port) a concrete shelter measuring 71 m in length and with an overhang of 6 m in width was constructed. It could harbour either one large U-boat or two small UB-types. In fact the half shelter was more of a construction to hide submarines from the view of spying planes as it was not totally bombproof. Due to the height between the surface of the water at high tide (4 m) and the top of the quayside a simple construction could serve as an overhang. This was built of 20 cm thick steal girders (I-profiles) measuring 9 m in length with an in between distance of 0,5 m. They were connected to each other by iron slats which were arranged diagonally across the girders. On this rested a layer of wooden beams which had a thickness of 5 cm each. Above the beams, in the intermediate part, sacks filled with clay were placed and above this was the final roofing consisting of a similar row of wooden beams. At the side of the quay the construction was weighted down by a wooden caisson filled with earth to keep the heavy roof in position. The roof lay almost horizontally across the dock. The construction cost the German Admiralty 20,000 Marks.

A typical photo illustrating the U-boat war: A UB-III boat lies sheltered in the enormous U-boat bunker in Bruges Harbour. Left stands her creator, Marine-Baumeister Trede (BArch)

To protect the roof, the minimum impact weight of 20 kg bombs, eight nets were hung on the top as well as the bottom of the half shelter at a distance of 0,5 m between each. Theoretically the top net would slow down the speed of the falling bomb, whilst the bottom one would be able to stop the largest bits of debris dropping on to a sheltering U-boat. There was even a proposition made to stack empty shell cases on top of the roof, just under the netting, so as to act as a cushioning function. It is not necessary to add that this last proposal was classified as unpractical and too wasteful in terms of indispensable brass.

Close to the Ostend dockyard area, near the eastern side of the harbour, a similar half shelter with a horizontal roof was built, but of more robust construction. Beams (I-profiles) with a thickness of 25 cm were placed on nearly 2 m high concrete pedestals on the quayside. The pedestals were interspaced at 2 m intervals and most rear ones were anchored almost to a depth of 2 m into the quayside. The beams had lengths of 10 m and were placed at every 0.5 m. The profiles were held together by diagonally fitted iron slats which were covered by a 15 cm thick layer of reinforced concrete. This gave a height beneath the shelter of more than 5 m at high tide.

Besides placing nets, there were also wiremesh nets, wooden framework with earthen filling and plating constructed around and on top of the half shelters. Most of the construction work had started in March 1915 and was fullfilled by the Belgian contractor Smis-Valcke (later changed to Beliard).

Early 1915, in the north of Bruges Harbour, a similar construction as that of Ostend was built in the western basin at a cost of 100,000 Marks. Here the shelter had to be heightened because between the surface of the water and the top of the quayside

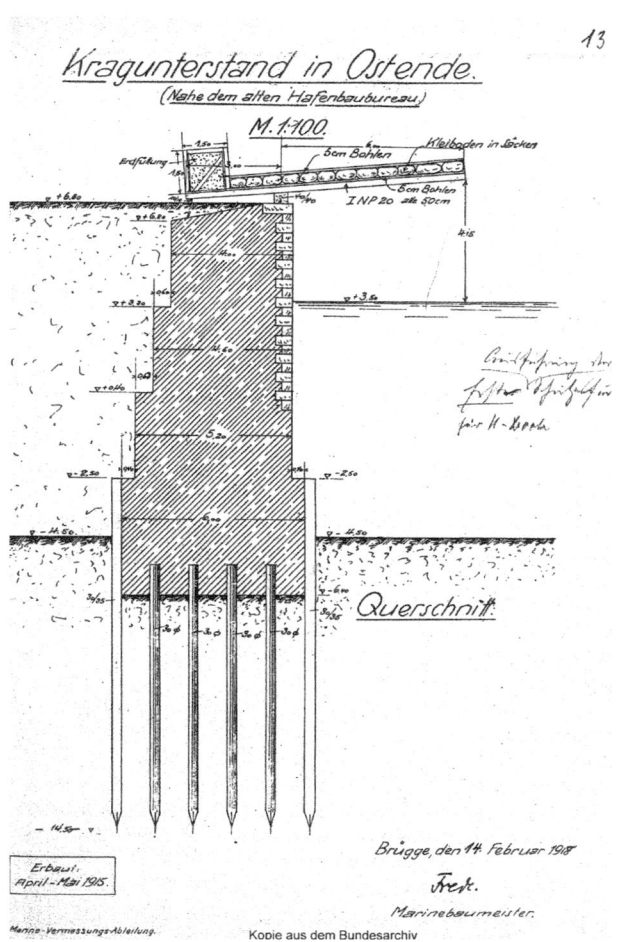

Technical drawing of a half shelter at Ostend (BArch)

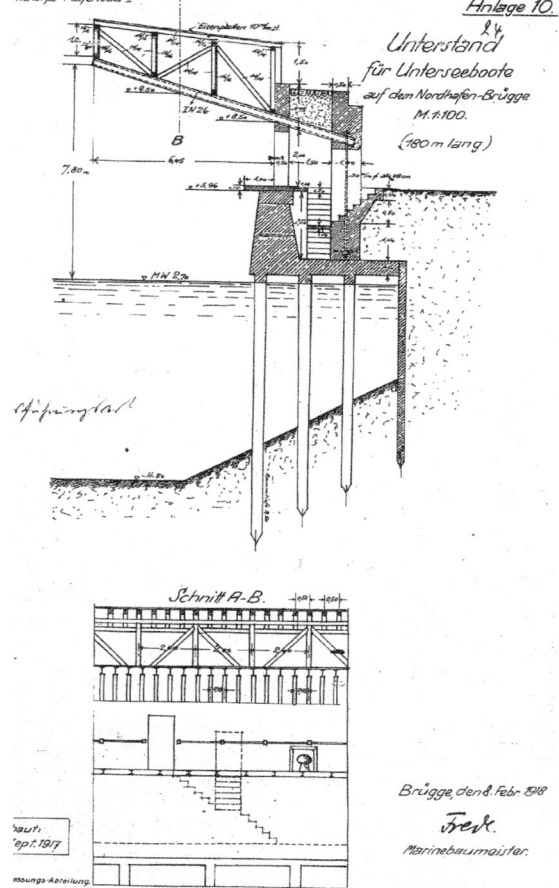

Technical drawing for a half shelter at Bruges (BArch)

A half shelter in the northern section of the small merchant dock (BArch)

A half shelter has just been completed in the western basin of the Bruges docks in 1915 (BArch)

there was only 3 m of free space. A slanting roof with a 30° angle was anchored by double rows of thick, concrete pillars. The pillars nearest to the quayside had a height of 1.5 m, those to the landside 1.2 m. The roof consisted of 7 m long I-profile beams with a thickness of 20 cm, placed at 0.5 m intervals from each other. The beams were held together by overlapping lengths of steel plate. This system gave much more rigidity than diagonal slats. The horizontal beam rested upon a 1.5 m high vertical beam and it was further held by concrete to a second, 70 cm high, vertical support which formed the rear anchoring system. On the top of the area, where the beams had been secured to the pole, there was a concrete caisson filled with sand. This maintained the necessary pressure to keep the roof in position. The roof had a total length of 70 m and it created a shelter with a width of 4.5 m and a height of nearly 6 m. For extra protection against direct impacts of bombs, the top of the caisson was connected to the edge of the roof by means of 1 cm thick corrugated iron sheets which rested on iron beams. Between the corrugated iron sheets and the steel structure of the underlying shelter there was a hollow area. The function of this double-roof construction was simple: the lighter iron sheets would detonate an aircraft bomb and the steel sub-roof would protect the U-boat against fragments of the explosion. The half shelter offered protection to one large or two small U-boats. Heavy wooden beams were placed horizontally against the quayside and served as fendering between the masonry wall and the hull of the U-boat. With the arrival of larger U-boats and the heavier airraids on Bruges (in 1917 alone more than 1,200 aerial bombs had been dropped on Bruges) there was an urgent demand for stronger and larger shelters.

In the spring of 1917 a 180 m long half shelter was constructed on the quayside of the western basin, in the Bruges north harbour. This was almost similar to the one in the eastern basin save a few important changes. The concrete pillars now had a height of more than 2 m and inside the heightened area there was room for a shelter for men (between the two pillars). The heightened roof now gave 7.8 m space beneath it for U-boats to shelter under. The top of

A half shelter located at the entrance to the canal, in the direction of Zeebrugge (BArch)

An enormous half shelter gives a UC-II boat protection in the western dock basin (BArch)

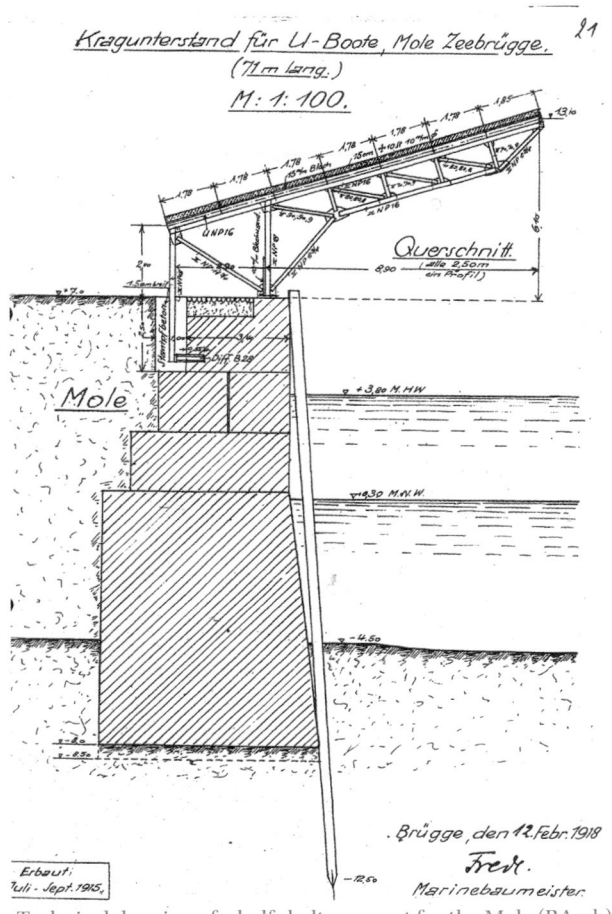

Technical drawing of a half shelter meant for the Mole (BArch)

the roof was constructed of corrugated iron and the subroof was heightened to 1.2 m above the ends of the I-profile beams and 1.5 m above the caisson on the rear side. The larger inner area would have to catch the impact of an explosion if it failed to detonate on the outside and penetrated deeper down.

A half shelter was also built on Zeebrugge mole and it measured 70 m in the length. The height above the top of the quayside and the surface of the sea did not seem sufficient enough, like in Ostend, to build a construction from the ground up. There was only 3 m space at high tide between the surface of the sea and the top of the quayside. Engineers had to build a half shelter which consisted totally of iron profiles in latice work. The roof consisted of 13 m long I-profiles with a thickness of 16 cm. They were bolted to each other every 0.5 m by diagonally placed iron latice work. The whole was finished by covering the top with a layer of reinforced concrete with a thickness of 15 cm. Beneath this the half shelter was supported by a steel framework with a double row of steel pillars on the harbour side of the Mole. The front pillar, which stood the closest to the water had a height of 2.8 m and the inner one was 2.2 m and anchored up to 2.5 m deep within the concrete base of the Mole by means of a concrete block. The shelter looked like half a roof which had an angle of 30°. Due to its construction there was now almost 10 m height beneath it at high tide and within there was a protected width of 8.9 m.

A completed half shelter on the Zeebrugge Mole (TT)

U-BOAT PENS

At the same time in 1915, when the half shelters were being constructed along the quaysides, the construction of four U-boat pens were being completed. Two were located in the north basin of the Bruges docks whilst the others lay in the Zeebrugge inner harbour. The construction was almost identical with all four, except the roof of the pens at Zeebrugge. The coverage had to be high enough so as a small floating dock with a U-boat could pass beneath it.

At Zeebrugge, both pens had a cofferdam which consisted of long iron plates which were driven up to a depth of 15 m in the ground. The layout of the steel plates of the cofferdam formed a rectangular area which measured 70 m in length and 8.5 m in width. A mechanical digger would dig out as much ground as possible from between the plates up to a depth of 10 m. A connecting part of soil would be dug away by a bucket dredger in the harbour. The surrounding soil would come up to the top of the cofferdam which created a depth of 4 m at high tide. On top of the cofferdam a vertical construction was built, consisting of wooden pillars which had a diameter of 30 cm and were placed at an equal distance of 3 m. On the exterior the pillars were strengthened and anchored by steel cables set in concrete bedding. The wooden pillars were connected on the top by steel beams which carried steel I-profiles in their breadth. The I-profiles which ran in the breadth of the dock and had a thickness of 38 cm, had to support the roof. At 0.4 m intervals such a profile was inserted and

A fresco in the former U-boat casino gives an idea of the Bruges docks. To the right a U-boat pen is visible (TT)

A U-boat pen in Bruges, now non-existent (TT)

Baumeister Trede and Oberbaurat Hedde pose for the photo near a completed U-boat pen in Bruges (BArch)

Interior view of a U-boatpen (BArch)

supported an 8 mm thick iron covering plate which ran over its entire length. Above the plate there was a 0.4 m thick layer of sand which had to provide the necessary elasticity in case a bomb would impact. Above the layer of sand a layer of 15 cm thick reinforced concrete was poured on, after which the roof was crowned by a layer of earth of 0.3 m thickness. After a couple of weeks the earthen mound would have grass and weeds growing on it, which then would serve as ideal camouflage and make the stable blend in with the surrounding landscape. At high tide it was possible to manoeuver a floating dock with U-boat measuring 5 m in height in this kind of shelter. Between the surface of the water and the bottom of the roof there was about 8 m headroom. Construction of the pens was started by Smis-Valcke in May 1915 and completed in October of the same year.

The constructions in Bruges were similar to those of Zeebrugge with the only difference that the roofs were supported by slanting wood pillars. This was because no anchoring system was provided on the sides. The roof also consisted of I-profile beams which were laid out in their width and had a thickness of 0.3 m. On top of the 8 mm thick iron plating there was also an elastic layer of sand of 0.4 m thickness which was filled in a wooden cofferdam. This would also be covered by a concrete layer with a thickness of 15 cm. The top was covered by a mound of earth 30 cm thick. In April 1915 work was started and five months laters, in August, they were ready for service.[106]

Here we also can observe the typical 'phase-system' of bunker construction in the naval dockyard. A layer of earth, overgrown by vegetation, would serve as camouflage, a layer of concrete which would make the bomb detonate, an elastic layer of sand which would cushion the explosion and the underlying iron construction to prohibit further penetration of a heavy bomb.

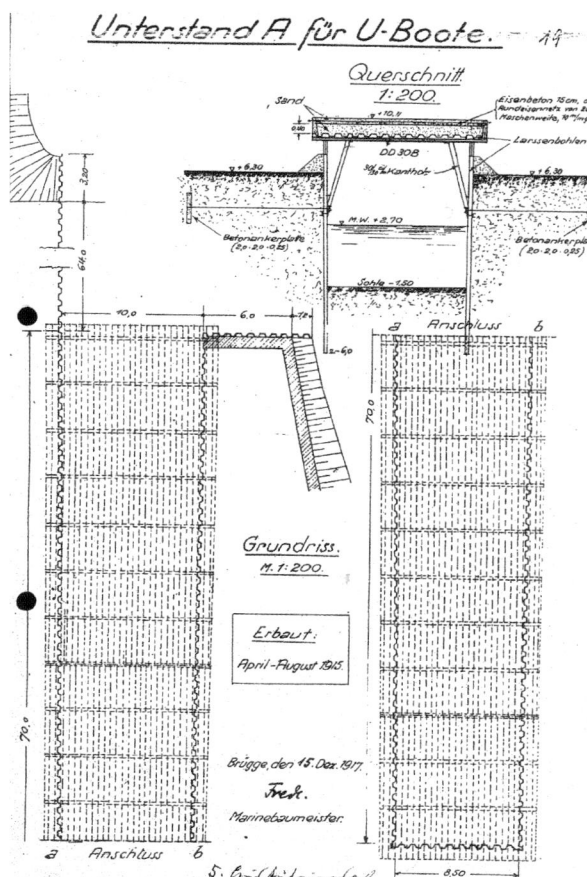

Technical drawing of a U-boat pen (BArch)

The crew of *UC-64* stand assembled in front of the U-boat pen where there U-boat has been berthed (TT)

Under the summer sun, the crew find time for some football (TT)

U-BOAT BUNKERS

August 1917 saw the *Hafenbau Division* starting the construction of a collosal bunker for multiple U-boats in Bruges Harbour. The idea was to create a gigantic pen on the surface of the water where U-boats could lie protected next to each other. Eight separate, covered berths were created within. One pen had a depth of 62 m on a breadth of 8.8 m. Small and middle-sized U-boats could completely fit in the space, but the larger *UB-III* U-boats would have part of their stern protruding from the shelter. The construction of the U-boat bunkers was carried out at the end of the northwestern basin and would take seven months of work. To save on digging labour, the Germans picked up on the pre-war excavations of the uncompleted dock.

The bunker was built on a construction of wooden pilings which lay beneath the surface of the water.

In August 1917 construction was started on an enormous group shelter for U-boats in the northwestern basin (now Nijverheidsdock) (BArch)

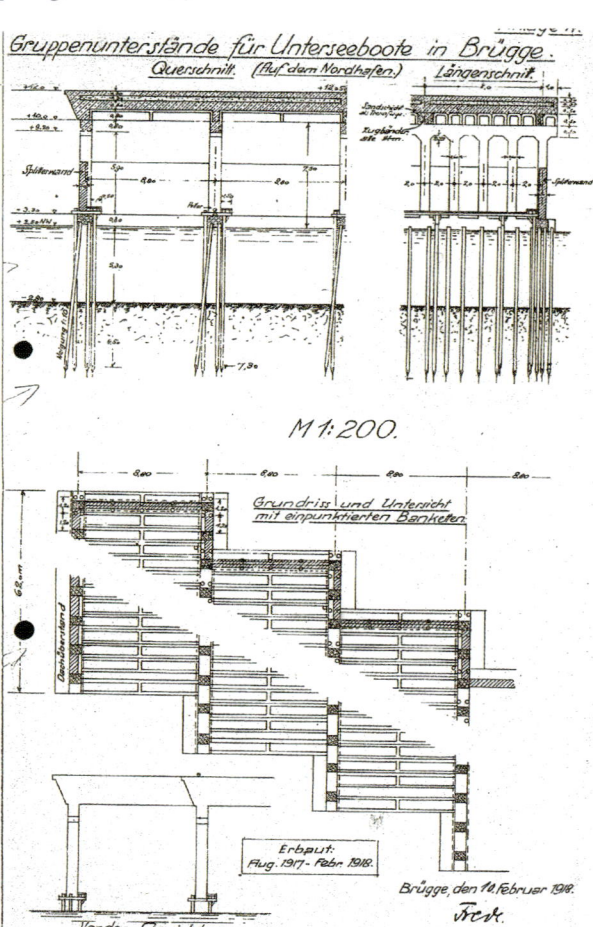

Technical drawing of the group shelter in the northwestern basin (BArch)

The U-boat bunker, photographed by the American author Robert Grant in 1938 (Grant)

When Bruges was captured in 1940, the condition of the U-boat bunker had not really changed. This photo, from the photo-album of a Wehrmacht soldier, shows the concrete openings shut with iron gates (Gunther Deweerdt).

The groupshelter was taken in use for the first time in the spring of 1918. The local populace baptised the construction "the eight blisses" (BArch)

A full frontal view of the U-boat bunker in the northwestern basin, situation mid-1918 (TT)

Interior view into one of the shelters (TT)

The 10 m long pilings had been driven up to 5 m deep in the bottom of the dock and guaranteed a stable construction. The pilings which protruded from the surface had to carry horizontally arranged, concrete beams. On top of the beams stood rows of concrete pillars which served as the supports for the roof. The pillars had a thickness of 0.6 x 0.8 m, with a height of 7.5 m. They stood at 2 m intervals and on their tops were connected by horizontal buttresses made of reinforced concrete. The buttresses were connected in width by inverted U-shaped beams with a thickness of 0.1 x 0.8 x 9 m in length. The idea was that these inverted beams would be able to better divide the weight of the roof. These beams made the bottom layer of this thick roof. On these supports lay the actual roof, which consisted at the bottom of a 0.6 m thick layer of concrete, in the middle lay a 0.3 m spread of gravel, and it was finished on the top with a 0.3 m thick layer of double reinforced concrete. Total thickness of the roof came to 2 m. The last layer was known as the detonating layer and served to force detonation of a bomb on impact. The elastic movement of the inserted layer of gravel served to dampen the power of the explosion and let the ensuing pressure dissipate on the last thick layer of concrete. This phase-system of detonating-, elastic- and support layers was found to be of sound design and from then onwards carried out by the harbour division on the construction of all large bunkers and shelters.[107]

DRY DOCK

By the end of 1914 the German navy had asked for bids from several Belgian construction firms for the expansion of the Ostend dry dock located in the *Bassin d'Evolution*. German constructors seemed to demand more time in finishing certain jobs. The local firm Smis-Valcke claimed that it would be able to complete the necessary work in five weeks for the sum of 45.000 BEF. This was quite a low sum in comparisson with the work which had to be carried out: 10.000 cbm of ground had to be dug, 390 large wooden pilings had to be driven into the soil and 1.500 cbm of concrete had to be produced and poored. The costs which some German firms had to charge for the building of coastal batteries all along the coast were much higher. To be able to obtain the contract, Smis was also prepared to pay a bond of 10,000 Marks. Apparently the firm had 3% of Belgian government rent and requisition bonds at its disposal. If the job would not be finished

Dry dock for U-boats in Ostend (Jörn Jensen)

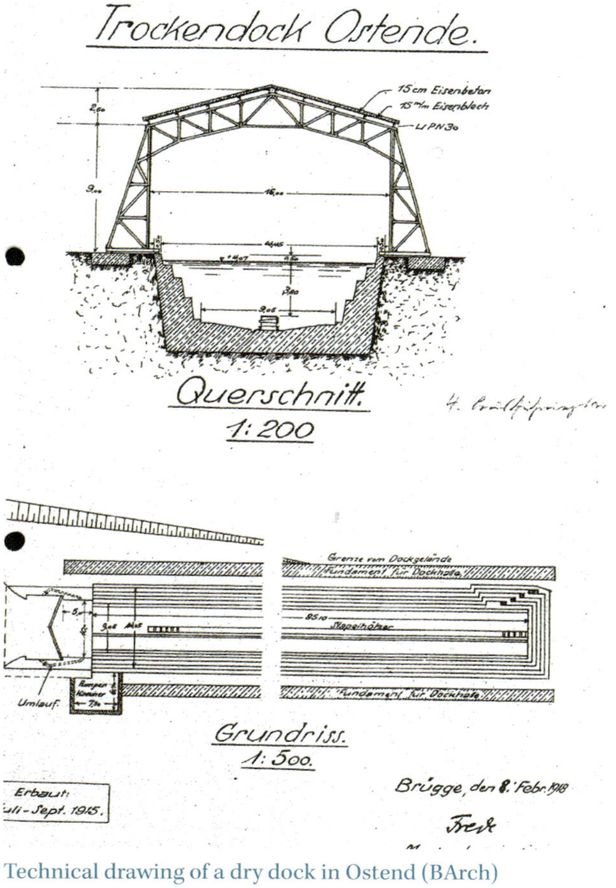

Technical drawing of a dry dock in Ostend (BArch)

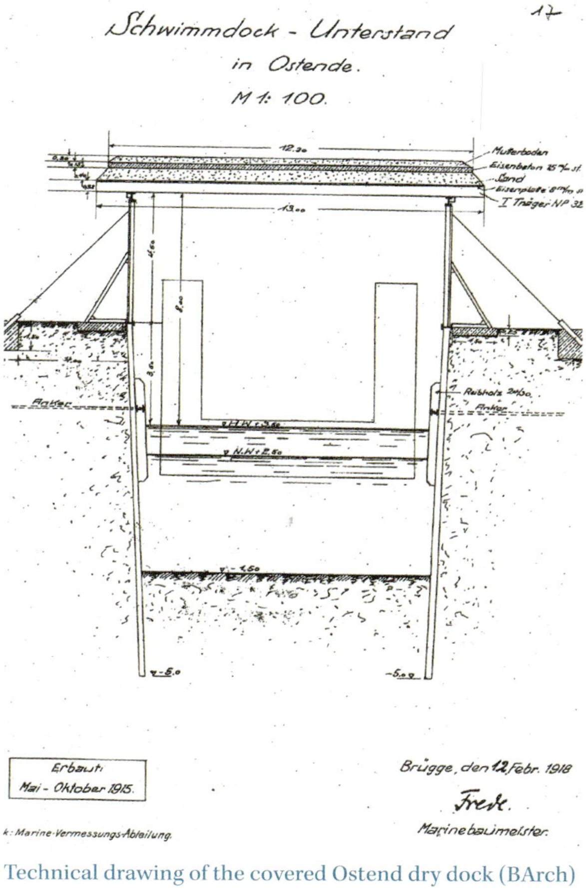

Technical drawing of the covered Ostend dry dock (BArch)

A U-boat of the UC-II type stands in dry dock in Ostend (BArch)

The crew of a UC-II boat pose for the camera. Their U-boat has just been launched from the dry dock in Ostend (TT)

punctually, the company Smis could count on an oversight fine of 5.000 BEF deducted from its final sum. In the end, Smis was asigned the contract and in February 1915 was able to start with excavation and pile-driving works. All other works, such as the further excavation and concreting of the pit, interior construction with pitprops and the building of the pump house and pump rooms were only finished in June of the same year.[108] This was about two months later then Smis-Valcke had originally promised! The quoted prices and dates from the German firms probably would have been much more realistic. Besides losing the bond and being fined, it turned out to be a costly undertaking for the firm. The delays could have also been caused by the acceptance of too many construction works in three harbours.

The pumps for the pumping room were delivered by the *Bauwerft*. Even when the dock had been finished, the case was not finished for the German navy. The whole construction had to bombproof and provide enough room for U-boats as well as torpedo boats. The iron construction work of the superstructure and the concreting of the roof was consigned to the German firm Hein. Lehmann & Co. of Düsseldorf.

The important dry dock at Ostend was given a roofing which could be compared to the shelters along the Zeebrugge Mole. The dry dock had a length of 85 m, on a width of 15 m, a depth of 3 m and a ceiling space of 9 m above the surface of the water up to the roof. The sides and roof were built of a lattice work of iron girders, covered by corrugated iron plates. On the mushroom-shaped roof stood I-profile beams with a thickness of 16 cm. Its whole was covered by corrugated iron plates with a thickness of 15 mm and on

the upper part was a layer of 15 cm thick reinforced concrete. The finishing touch was made in August 1915. To provide more light in the dim interior of the dock area, the inner walls were painted with white oil-based paint. The top was treated with tar and was to attract less attention to the construction. Along the insides of the dock about 20 bollards were fitted so the docked vessel could be secured.[109]

The pens as well as the dry dock have totally disappeared when the Ostend fishing dock was built in the years following the end of the Second World War. The location of the pens and the dry dock have to be situated somewhere beneath the present-day Hendrik Baelskaai on the eastern side of Ostend.

UB-13 is pulled into dry dock for an inspection of her hull (TT)

OTHER BUILDINGS

It was not only necessary to protect the U-boat fleet against bombing raids. The crews, the dockyard workers, munitions and supplies also had a necessity to be protected.[110]

Several primitive bunkers and shelters were built in the port of Bruges in 1915. These had the appearance of a half-excavated mineshaft and were intended to house torpedoes and detonators. Rectangular ditches were dug up to 2 m in the ground with an access stairwell. All four sides were strengthened with logs and covered with planks. In the centre stood three wooden supporting pillars and the room created an interior area of 10 m in length, on a width of 4 m and a height of 2.4 m. On top of this space a strengthened roof was built which protruded only about 0.5 m from the surrounding ground. Supporting beams carried 50 mm thick, iron plates strengthened with iron rails and side-irons. The iron was covered over with roofing material. The whole construction was covered up with a hill-shaped mound of sand which had a height of 1.8 m. In the sandy hill was also a corrugated iron plate with a thickness of 15 mm to provide greater protection against possible impacts. The construction was built with the same principle as the concrete bunkers. The first iron plate detonated the bomb, the sandy layers caught the pressure of the impact and the remaining power would be diffused on the iron

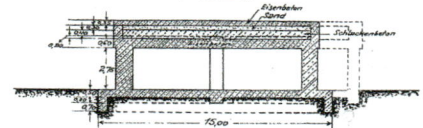

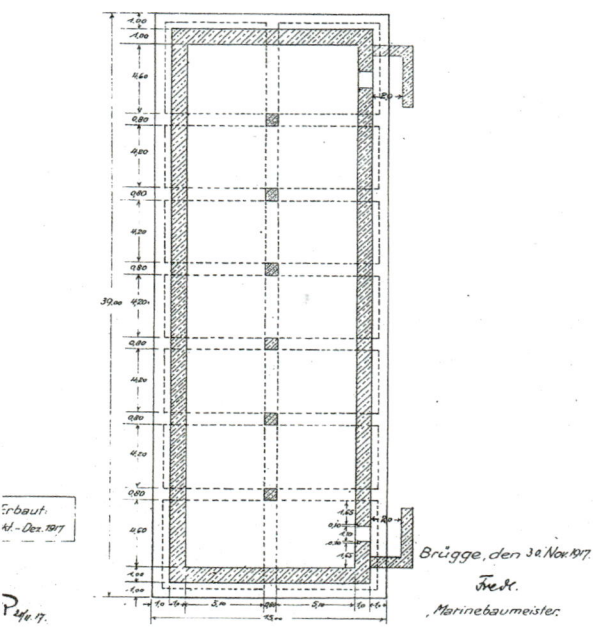

Technical drawing of the interior of the storage area for torpedo warheads (BArch)

Concrete sheltered magazine for storage of torpedo warhead at the Bruges dockyard (BArch)

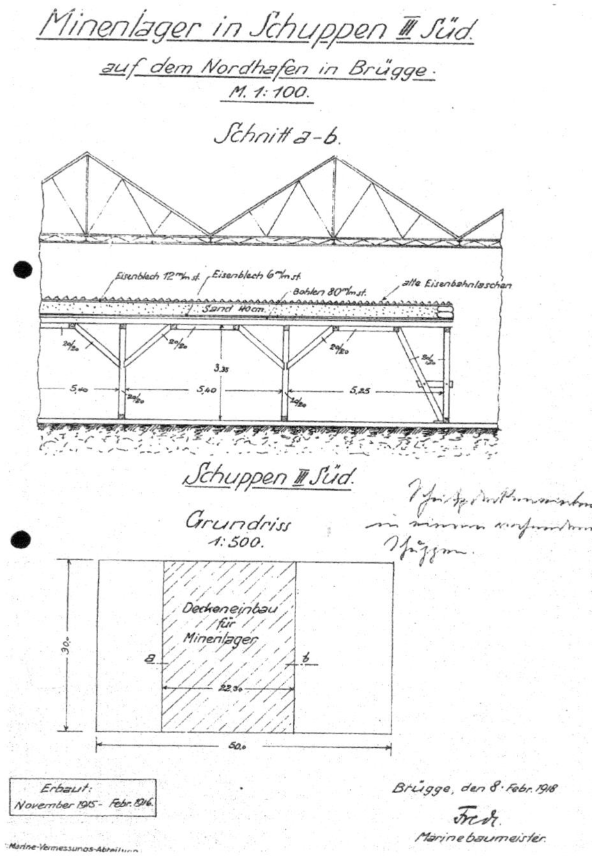

Technical drawing of the mine depot, first model (BArch)

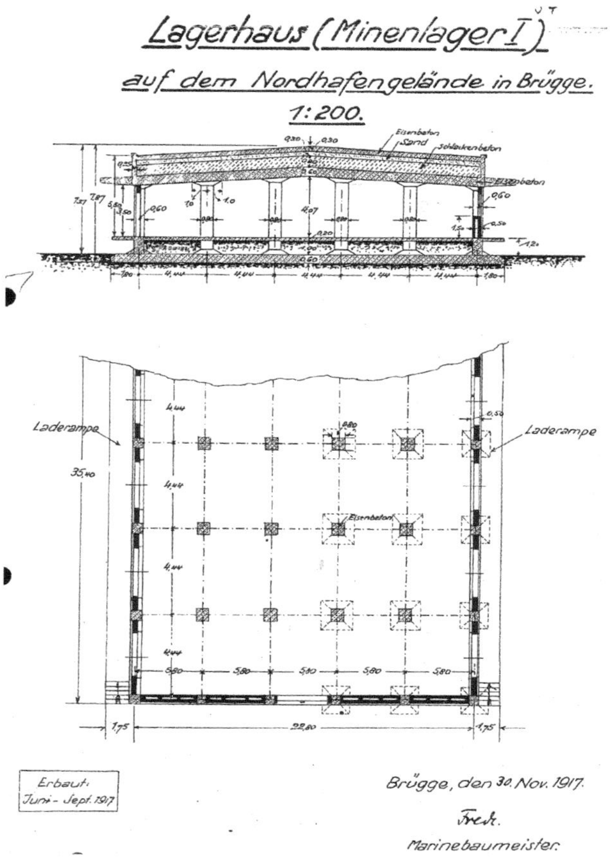

Technical drawing of the mine depot, second model (BArch)

roof construction. Although the construction was logically and strongly built, there was the realisation that a direct hit would make the shelter collapse.

To improve the provided shelters at Bruges, newly designed bunkers for housing torpedo ammunition were constructed between October and November 1916. The space lay as deep as possible beneath the surface, with only the top of the roof protruding from the soil. A space measuring 10 m in length on a width of 8.2 m and a height of 2.2 m was dug. The sides now consisted of 0.5 m thick concrete with a double row of masonry cemented to the inside. In the middle stood four concrete pillars. The walls and pillars supported a 0.5 m thick platform of reinforced concrete. A sandy hill covered the platform and in the middle of it were 10 mm thick iron plates. Access to the underground space was possible via two sets of stairs. By the end of 1917 these storage bunkers evolved to entirely above ground constructions with heavy concrete walls and roofs.

Besides torpedoes, mines also were a delicate part of the armament of U-boats. Because mines, with their anchoring and sinking systems, proved to be quite sizeable objects, these were kept above ground in strenghtened spaces. Between November 1915 and February 1916 the mines were stored in hangars which had been part of the pre-war harbour complex. Within the hangars was a wooden construction with a height of 3.3 m. Sides and ceiling consisted of wooden beams and the roof was built of an underplate of sheet-iron, a layer of sand, and above this another layer of sheet-iron. This type of construction would not be long in use and changes were sought in December 1916 for a number of reasons. As with the first type of subterranean buildings for torpedo munitions it was presumed that a direct impact would destroy and collapse the shelter. Secondly, the *Kaiserliche Werft* was looking towards expanding the existing hangars as workshops for the construction and repair of U-boats were necessary. Larger

ALLIED COUNTERMEASURES.

INTERCEPTION OF RADIO MESSAGES, ESPIONAGE AND PRISONER INTERROGATION

Radio-and wireless telegraphy was used for the first time in history on an extensive basis during the First World War. U-boats would try to transmit as little as possible and mainly used the radio to listen to Allied shipping communication. At sporadic intervals short, coded messages were sent to Bruges to report the location of the U-boat, the progress of the patrol, possible damages it had sustained and the day of return. These messages were sent in code, but could also be intercepted by the enemy. At the start of the war the Allies had two choices. At first they could disrupt and hinder the messages or else they could let them communicate undisturbed, intercept and analyse the messages to gain information.

The British would concentrate their efforts on the second choice after the Admiralty had received a remarkable and generous gift. The Russian navy had presented them with a codebook on 13 October 1914, which their naval units had found on the body of a German sailor in the Gulf of Finland. The sailor had been a radio operator on the stranded German cruiser *SMS Magdeburg*. He had been killed in action by a Russian shell and with him were found the codebooks of the German navy.

With the codebooks, messages could be deciphered, but were not legible. After a long search and with logical thinking, *Fleet Paymaster* Rotter, who was employed on the task, found the key to the codes. Rotter was seen as the main expert and codebreaker within British Intelligence. Whilst employing simple logic he came upon replacement tables (a=r, b=h … etc), which was kept in place for three months. Later in the war the tables were changed weekly by the Germans and by 1917 even every 24 hours.[112]

When a message was deciphered, it could be compared to similar messages transmitted by U-boats. The location of a patrolling U-boat could be traced on gridcharts which had fallen into the hands of British Intelligence via espionage or after divers had recovered them out of recently sunk U-boat wrecks. Identification of a U-boat was simplified after U-boats were assigned call numbers. The numbers were changed regularly but were systematically divided amongst different flotilla. Also via documents found on board sunken U-boats, combined with a logical analysis, the British gained quite a fast lead on the identity of a detected U-boat.

Interception of radio messages was not the only way to trace the paths of U-boats. Via Allied and neutral sailors many reports came in concerning observations and intricately detailed descriptions of U-boats. All this information was connected and it was possible to get an idea of what different U-boats had done on a patrol. Attempts were also made to keep files on the abilities and achievements of various U-boat commanders. In the case of captains of minelayers, an insight could be made in their operating mode and how and where a future minefield would be sown.

Spies and deserters also gave much information on U-boat construction, personal information about officers and crews, dates of departure and return, and the operations of a certain flotilla. In neutral countries, observations were made and reported on the movements and passage of U-boats.

One of these spies was 41-year old, mother of three, Anne De Beir, a Bruges native. At the outbreak of the war she was living in Dunkirk, as she had been married to a French national. Her son enlisted in the army and Anne gave help to Belgian refugees and wounded soldiers. Via an acquaintance she was put into contact with the French Secret Service (the *Deuxième Bureau*) and received a military passport for movements in the cities around Dunkirk as well as across the Channel in Folkestone. In Folkestone she received basic military training and became agent 8F30. In early 1915 she made her way via Holland to Bruges where she was housed by her sister who owned a hotel in the Sint-Annarei. Intelligence was gathered through a friend who eavesdropped on Germans in his inn as well as conversations held in her sister's hotel. Anne was responsible for smuggling information across the border to Holland where carrier pigeons were sent to England. She mainly obtained information concerning the Bruges U-boat base, the location of ammunition dumps and the German coastal defence system. Anne De Beir's network started to blossom and from her

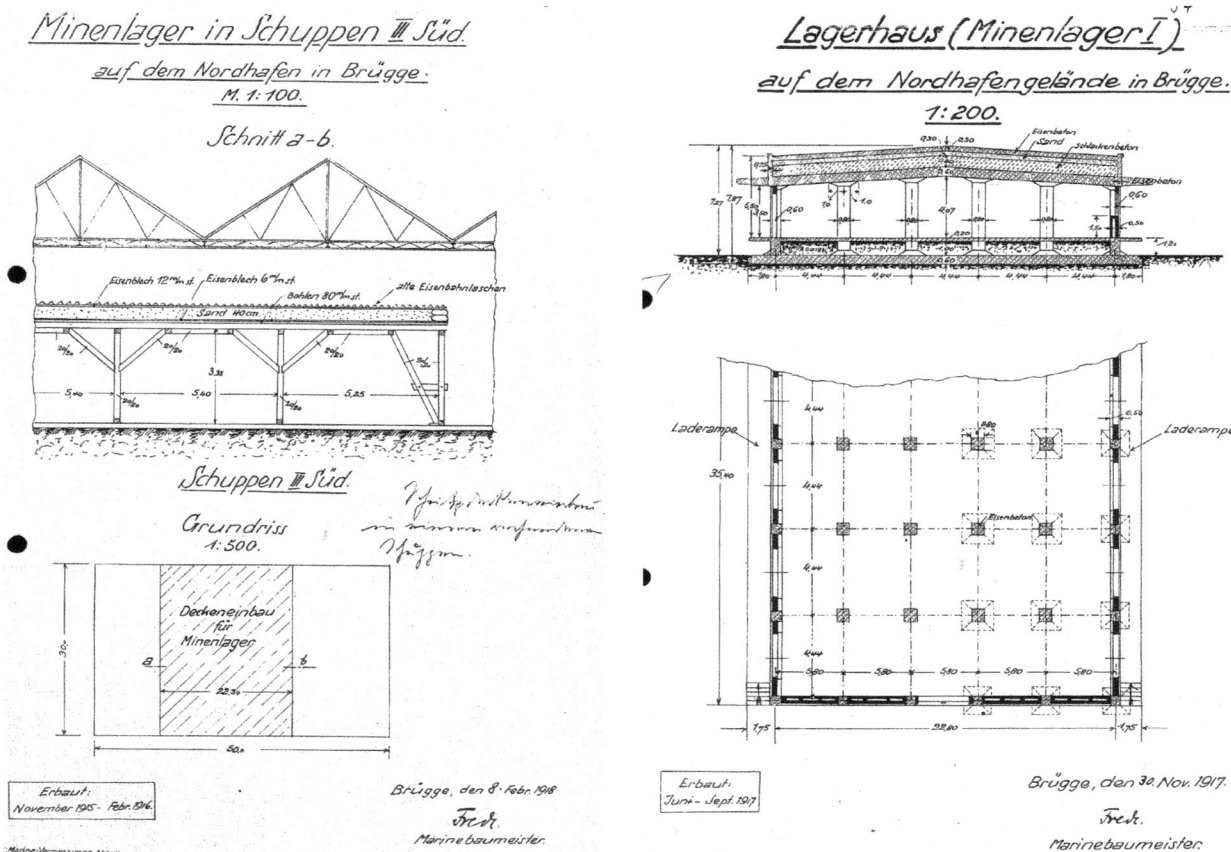

Technical drawing of the mine depot, first model (BArch)

Technical drawing of the mine depot, second model (BArch)

roof construction. Although the construction was logically and strongly built, there was the realisation that a direct hit would make the shelter collapse.

To improve the provided shelters at Bruges, newly designed bunkers for housing torpedo ammunition were constructed between October and November 1916. The space lay as deep as possible beneath the surface, with only the top of the roof protruding from the soil. A space measuring 10 m in length on a width of 8.2 m and a height of 2.2 m was dug. The sides now consisted of 0.5 m thick concrete with a double row of masonry cemented to the inside. In the middle stood four concrete pillars. The walls and pillars supported a 0.5 m thick platform of reinforced concrete. A sandy hill covered the platform and in the middle of it were 10 mm thick iron plates. Access to the underground space was possible via two sets of stairs. By the end of 1917 these storage bunkers evolved to entirely above ground constructions with heavy concrete walls and roofs.

Besides torpedoes, mines also were a delicate part of the armament of U-boats. Because mines, with their anchoring and sinking systems, proved to be quite sizeable objects, these were kept above ground in strenghtened spaces. Between November 1915 and February 1916 the mines were stored in hangars which had been part of the pre-war harbour complex. Within the hangars was a wooden construction with a height of 3.3 m. Sides and ceiling consisted of wooden beams and the roof was built of an underplate of sheet-iron, a layer of sand, and above this another layer of sheet-iron. This type of construction would not be long in use and changes were sought in December 1916 for a number of reasons. As with the first type of subterranean buildings for torpedo munitions it was presumed that a direct impact would destroy and collapse the shelter. Secondly, the *Kaiserliche Werft* was looking towards expanding the existing hangars as workshops for the construction and repair of U-boats were necessary. Larger numbers of mines were being delivered almost at a daily rate and had to be stored in larger, protected areas. Quite late in the war, in June 1917, work was started in the northern part of the port area on two *Lagerhäuser* or *Minenlager*.[111] The newly constructed shelter had a surface of 35 m in length on a width of 23 m and was built entirely above ground. The bottom of the building consisted of 0.6 m thick loose concrete. On this floor stood rows of square concrete pillars with a thickness of 0.8 m and a height of 5 m. On the floor a layer of soil with a thickness of 1 m was added between the pillars. Above the ground a concrete floor plate was poured and served as actual flooring for the mine room. Loose ground and concrete bits in the bottom served as its elasticity function: the impact of an explosion would bury itself in the ground and so restrict damage to the more important pillar structures. The areas between the pillars and the outer walls were sealed using 0.5 m thick masonrywork of bricks. Avoiding the use of full concrete walls served to protect the roof and its carriers against an impact: the power of an explosion would blow the masonry outwards and let the force dissipate sideways. It was obvious that the contents was highly dangerous as the roof had a thickness of more than 2 m. The roof was mushroom-shaped and consisted of four different layers. The bottom layer, which rested on the tops of the pillars, had a thickness of 0.6 m and was made of reinforced concrete. On this lay a 0.8 m thick layer of normal concrete, a third layer of sand and after this another 0.3 m thick layer of reinforced concrete. Access to the hangar was made through several loading ramps which were protected by thick concrete roofs. The construction took four months and was only finished in September 1917.

Just after its completion, work was started on a new *lagerhaus* for torpedo munition and was of similar design to that of the *minenlager*. The only difference was that the roof was of a flat construction, had a height of 2.75 m and was longitudinal in design. This was completed in December 1917.

In the same area a sheltered engine room was built for the Bruges broadcasting and signal station, as well as a loading station for U-boats. The loading station or compressor house was built in August 1917 and served to charge the batteries of the electro-engines

The storage depot for mines (*minenlager*) at the Imperial Dockyard Bruges (BArch)

of the U-boats. It measured 12.5 m in length, on a width of 8.5 m and had a height of 4 m. It was shaped by concrete pillars which made up the side walls. The interior walls were made up of masonry and brick and the roof was built of a metre-thick slab of reinforced concrete.

A number of shelters and bunkers in the harbour area were built to give shelter to the labour force of the *Werft Division*, the guards and the crews of moored U-boats and other vessels. In the spring of 1917 work was started on the construction of two large shelters where room was provided for 100 men in one and 275 men in the other. The 100-man shelter only had an interior space with a length of 6.6 m on a breadth of 5 m and a height of 2 m. The building was above ground, divided in three passable areas and had a roof with a 1 m thick concrete and a 0.35 m layer of sand. The sides were made of masonry around a core of sand. The second bunker, built in January 1918 was of the same design, just larger and more robust. The bunker was half-concealed beneath the soil and had a length of 13 m on a width of 6.8 m and a height of 2 m. The walls were completely made up of reinforced concrete and the roof had a thicker concrete layer of 1.5 m.

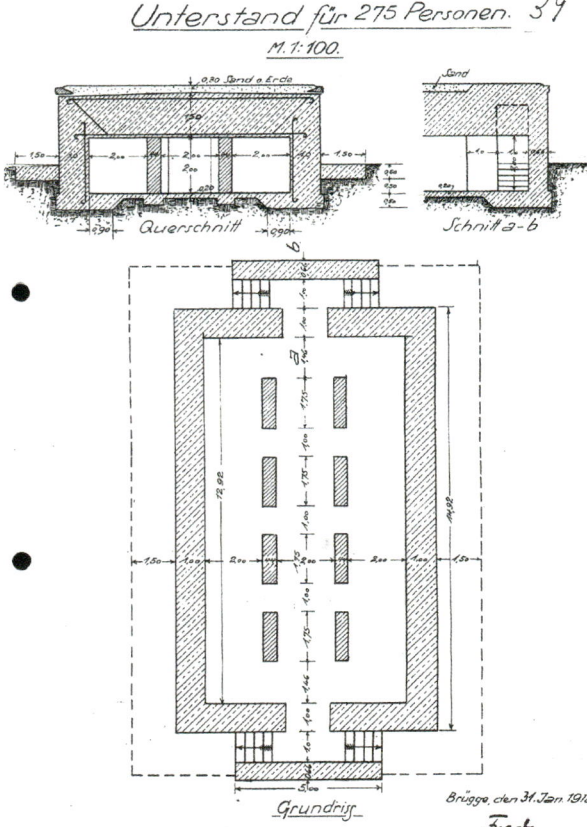

Technical drawing of a personnel bunker (BArch)

A large bunker which housed the engine room for the sending and signal station in Bruges (BArch)

201

ALLIED COUNTERMEASURES.

INTERCEPTION OF RADIO MESSAGES, ESPIONAGE AND PRISONER INTERROGATION

Radio-and wireless telegraphy was used for the first time in history on an extensive basis during the First World War. U-boats would try to transmit as little as possible and mainly used the radio to listen to Allied shipping communication. At sporadic intervals short, coded messages were sent to Bruges to report the location of the U-boat, the progress of the patrol, possible damages it had sustained and the day of return. These messages were sent in code, but could also be intercepted by the enemy. At the start of the war the Allies had two choices. At first they could disrupt and hinder the messages or else they could let them communicate undisturbed, intercept and analyse the messages to gain information.

The British would concentrate their efforts on the second choice after the Admiralty had received a remarkable and generous gift. The Russian navy had presented them with a codebook on 13 October 1914, which their naval units had found on the body of a German sailor in the Gulf of Finland. The sailor had been a radio operator on the stranded German cruiser *SMS Magdeburg*. He had been killed in action by a Russian shell and with him were found the codebooks of the German navy.

With the codebooks, messages could be deciphered, but were not legible. After a long search and with logical thinking, *Fleet Paymaster* Rotter, who was employed on the task, found the key to the codes. Rotter was seen as the main expert and codebreaker within British Intelligence. Whilst employing simple logic he came upon replacement tables (a=r, b=h ... etc), which was kept in place for three months. Later in the war the tables were changed weekly by the Germans and by 1917 even every 24 hours.[112]

When a message was deciphered, it could be compared to similar messages transmitted by U-boats. The location of a patrolling U-boat could be traced on gridcharts which had fallen into the hands of British Intelligence via espionage or after divers had recovered them out of recently sunk U-boat wrecks. Identification of a U-boat was simplified after U-boats were assigned call numbers. The numbers were changed regularly but were systematically divided amongst different flotilla. Also via documents found on board sunken U-boats, combined with a logical analysis, the British gained quite a fast lead on the identity of a detected U-boat.

Interception of radio messages was not the only way to trace the paths of U-boats. Via Allied and neutral sailors many reports came in concerning observations and intricately detailed descriptions of U-boats. All this information was connected and it was possible to get an idea of what different U-boats had done on a patrol. Attempts were also made to keep files on the abilities and achievements of various U-boat commanders. In the case of captains of minelayers, an insight could be made in their operating mode and how and where a future minefield would be sown.

Spies and deserters also gave much information on U-boat construction, personal information about officers and crews, dates of departure and return, and the operations of a certain flotilla. In neutral countries, observations were made and reported on the movements and passage of U-boats.

One of these spies was 41-year old, mother of three, Anne De Beir, a Bruges native. At the outbreak of the war she was living in Dunkirk, as she had been married to a French national. Her son enlisted in the army and Anne gave help to Belgian refugees and wounded soldiers. Via an acquaintance she was put into contact with the French Secret Service (the *Deuxième Bureau*) and received a military passport for movements in the cities around Dunkirk as well as across the Channel in Folkestone. In Folkestone she received basic military training and became agent 8F30. In early 1915 she made her way via Holland to Bruges where she was housed by her sister who owned a hotel in the Sint-Annarei. Intelligence was gathered through a friend who eavesdropped on Germans in his inn as well as conversations held in her sister's hotel. Anne was responsible for smuggling information across the border to Holland where carrier pigeons were sent to England. She mainly obtained information concerning the Bruges U-boat base, the location of ammunition dumps and the German coastal defence system. Anne De Beir's network started to blossom and from her seamstress, milkman and a good friend at a jewellers on the Bruges market more information poured in. She become quite brazen and sometimes crossed the border with two caged pigeons beneath her skirts!

But her repeated excursions did not go unnoticed and on 18 October 1915 she was arrested in Bruges by the *Feldpolizei*. They discovered on her person two letters which had to be smuggled for two Belgian soldiers fighting on the front line. Her daughter managed to destroy all communications which were left in the hotel before the Germans were able to investigate. Anne was sentenced a month later to death for aiding deserters and the smuggling of post. The then mayor of Bruges, Visart de Bocarmé, pleaded to Admiral von Schröder to lend her clemency. He pledged to tend to all the graves of the German sailors and soldiers in the Bruges cemetery for eternity. Anne was given a stay of execution and her death penalty was converted to a prison sentence. After that she was transferred to Germany where she spent 33 months in various prisons. On 10 November 1918, near to death, she was released and made her way back home. She would continue her resistance work in the Second World War and eventually passed away in 1971 at the age of 97.[113]

The destruction of a U-boat could deliver enormous amounts of information. Some prisoners were more talkative than others and spoke about their previous patrols and assignments as well as those of other U-boats. During the interrogation of five prisoners taken from *UC-65*, the British obtained much knowledge on how the U-boats managed to slip through the Dover Barrage. It was mainly her captain, Oberleutnant z. S. Claus Lafrenz (nicknamed Lala) who had a loose tongue and was able to reveal much to his British interrogators. *UC-65* had been torpedoed off Beachy Head by the British submarine *HMS C-15*. Lafrenz and four others were on watch on the conning tower when the explosion catapulted them away. They were the only survivors of its 26-man crew. Secrecy about intelligence gathering and prisoner interrogation by the British was maintained at such a high level that German high command knew nothing of the loss of *UC-65*. Her sinking, at the end of 1917, happened at a time when many of the old hands of the *Flandern Flottille* were being killed in action. When Oberleutnant z. S. Werner Fürbringer (nicknamed Fips) survived the sinking of his U-boat, *UB-110*, in July 1918, and ended up in British captivity,

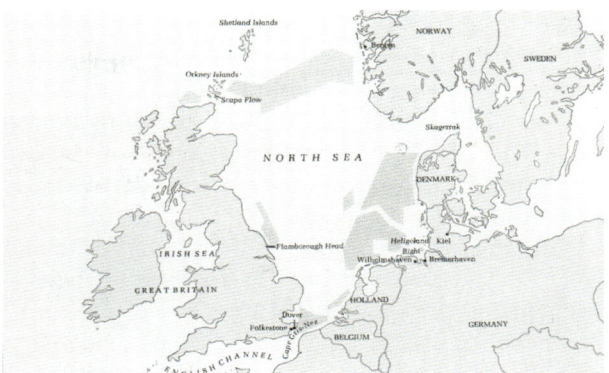

A map showing a general view of the Allied mine fields in the southern North Sea, German Bight and northern passage (Gibson and Prendergast)

he was surprised to hear from his interrogators that Lafrenz was still alive. But what astounded him more was the detailed knowledge that the British Admiralty possessed concerning operational aspects of the Flanders Flotilla. The Germans thought that British knowledge was due to the network of spies.

In the end it would be the Intelligence Service which won the war on the U-boats. By the end of the war they knew exactly where every U-boat was, what it had achieved on a patrol and if it was already on its way back home. German codebooks had come quite early on in the hands of the British and the codebreakers were able to decipher all German codes. After deciphering, this information was immediately passed on to the surface and air units for them to ambush and destroy an unsuspecting U-boat. If it was known that a U-boat was returning home, then mines would be strewn all along its return path. German prisoners were astounded to know how much information the British had gathered, even with details such as the nicknames of U-boat captains.

NETS, MINES AND FIELDS

For centuries the English Channel has been the main shipping route between Great Britain and the continent. Besides finding many possible targets to sink in this area, the Channel was also the shortest route to the main shipping lanes of the Western Approaches and the Irish Sea.

Lord Admiral Sir Roger Keyes had seen this at the beginning of the first year of the war: '*To render an area immune from submarines it is necessary to protect its boundaries below water. For this reason a zareba of mines, dangerous to submarines, must be laid out. As the submarine moves in a vertical as well as a horizontal plane, the defence must be of the nature of a wall, and minenets appear to be the most suitable means of effecting this protection'.*

In 1915 the Dover Patrol received orders to built a barrier of steel nets which ran in the narrows of Folkestone to Cape Griz Nez. The North Sea, with its storms and heavy swells, proved to be an impossible area to link a continuous net. It was made of linked sections of 100 m length, which hung at depths between 10 m and 40 m. The nets were made of lightly galvanised steel-wire with meshes which measured 3.5 to 4 m across. 150 glass floaters at regular intervals were supposed to keep the nets suspended. On the bottom there was no anchoring system, but separate nets were linked by means of steel clamps. The whole had to be sturdy enough so as not to break due to currents and storms, but still retain a certain amount of suppleness to wrap itself around a U-boat which had become entangled in it. In daring night-time actions, torpedo boats and motorboats would also lay lengths of nets off the heavily defended Belgian coast. The areas between the Thornton-, Rabs- and Ruytingen Banks were covered with parallel rows of nets. A steel net had the principal intention to entangle a U-boat whereas it would be forced to surface to free itself from its precarious situation. Once on the surface it would be attacked by surface craft which could destroy it. As the war progressed it was seen as useful to attach two contact mines on each net which would detonate upon touch. This extensive net system was finished by the end of 1916, but had two setbacks. The connecting clamps between each net had to rupture at the right moment and not during a heavy tidal flow or storm. In the Channel, depths vary from 50 to 60 metres. If the nets reached the sandy bottom, the pressure, which came on it every six hours with ebb and flood, would be too much for it. After three weeks, large amounts of the steel links had been chafed through due to the effects of the tides. Miles of net drifted away or simply sank to the bottom and was lost. Regular raiding sorties made by the torpedo boats and destroyers of the *Zerstörer Flottille Flandern* in the Dover and Ruytingenbank area were meant to destroy or capture large lengths of these steel nets. British buoys, nets and glass floats can be seen on numerous photos when they were being offloaded on to the Mole at Zeebrugge. By 1917, the Royal Navy classified the net system as unsuccessful.

The success of the mine led the British to replace the net barrier by fields sown with anchored mines. The British mine was quite simple and consisted of a cylinder which held an explosive charge. The mine would explode when the side of a ship bumped into the mine. Within the mine, metal plates would make contact and generate an electric current which detonated the explosives. The British mine was, like its German counterpart, mounted on an anchoring system or steel chair. By means of rails on the stern of a minelayer, rows of mines would slide off the ship and into the sea. Once the mine had reached the bottom, held in place by the weighted sinker, it would loosen and head toward the surface whilst being held in check by a connecting cable. The drum on the sinker would let the cable unroll up to the set depth. The British mine was of a lesser quality and had two major flaws. After a certain time seawater would leak through the seams and corrode the metal detonators making the mine unreliable. Without meaning to, the British mine would defuse itself after a certain lapse in time. A second setback was that the mine, after it had been laid, almost immediately shot up to the surface, making it a hazard to the minelayer.

In February 1917 the Royal Navy had started creating a deep minefield in the Dover Barrage. It was meant to seal the entrance of the Channel in the area between Folkestone and Cap Griz Nez. The area was littered with mines which had been set out in eight parallel lines at two to three different depths, each with

A comical drawing depicting the lethal mine nets in the Dover Barrage (An Flanderns Küste)

a between distance of 50 m between. The whole surface contained 4,000 mines which had been anchored to the bottom. To prohibit nightly crossings of U-boats on the surface, the whole area would be lit up by powerful arc lights, mounted on monitors or light vessels. Torpedo boats made constant patrols to force a U-boat to submerge. In three areas, just off Cap Griz Nez, in the middle of the Varne bank and off Folkestone, exits were left for the patrol vessels. This titanic undertaking was finished in December 1917. By the spring of 1918 this field had been given the sinister nickname of 'U-boat Cemetery' as 12 U-boats and their crews had been sunk in just a few months. The last ever U-boat which managed to pass unscathed through the Barrage was *UB-88* on 11th August 1918. We may assume that the Royal Navy had found the precise technique in sealing off an area of sea by the end of the war. *UB-109* had the unpleasant honour of being the last U-boat to be sunk in the Dover Barrage on 29 August 1918.

Even though the Dover Barrage consisted of countless mines, nets and was patrolled day and night by a fleet of all kinds of vessels, a large number of U-boats still managed to pass through on the outward as well as the homeward bound voyages. Usually they would not submerge as then they would be totally blind, but cruise slowly on the surface. A U-boat captain would seek out the less well guarded points of the coast on the French or British sides and then head towards the middle, over the Varne Sandbank, to the other side. The illumination of the entire area by heavy arc lights did not make this task any easier. *Oberleutnant z. S.* Karl Stöter, captain of *UB-35*, wrote in his journal on 24 December 1917: '*Spotlights sited on the Varne up to the Colbart (sandbank) made the whole area very bright, also because light was reflected off the white cliffs. I approach close to the enemy coastline where my boat comes in total illumination several times. Sailing under the very noses of the guardvessels is an unpleasant experience, but usually we manage to slip through*'.[114]

Through researching the wrecks and the discovery of lost U-boats we can assertain the effects of the minefields. Just at the entrance to the notorious Dover Barrage, in the area between the Westhinder and the Varne, the British had laid two smaller minefields in 1917 and 1918. These smaller, lesser known fields managed to inflict more losses on U-boats leaving on patrols than any other field, besides that of the Dover Barrage. The effects that these fields had was unknown to the British and the Germans and it is only nearly a

British sinkers, buoys and nets taken from the Dover Barrage lie in Zeebrugge dockyard (Heiko Hermans).

century later that we can get an idea of its impact. Near the Fairy Bank are three UB-III class wrecks, two UB-II class and three UC-II class submarines which have all been given up as missing on patrol. *Oberleutnant z. S.* Hans Galster, captain of *UC-51*, made a note in his journal about large concentrations of mines just an hour sailing from the entrance of the Dover Barrage. On 4 August 1917 *UC-51* was on an outward bound journey towards the Western Approaches. When she had reached the Westhinder, dozens of mines were visible on the surface.[115] He mentioned that it concerned a field which the British had sown on 7 June, so there was some knowledge by the Germans of British activities in this area.

When systematically researching this area for its targets I was baffled to find so many previously unknown U-boats sunk in just a small area. Most of them showed visible evidence of having been sunk by mines, with sections of bows or sterns blown off. The U-boat wrecks showed no evidence of having been penetrated or opened by the Royal Navy during the time for further inspection. This area must have been a blank spot to the Allies concerning its success or was too close to the enemy coastline to undergo salvage or diving operations.

By the middle of 1918 the Channel crossing had become so precarious that some U-boats changed their normal route and chose the northerly route, via Scotland, to reach the western hunting grounds. This was a more time and fuel-consuming route, which was also being taken by the U-boats leaving from German ports. The Americans came up with the grandiose plan to also block or hinder their passage by constructing the Northern Barrage, a larger counterpart to the Dover Barrage. This meant the mining of a 250 mile long stretch which spanned from the Orkneys up to the southern part of Norway. The unrealistic number of 200,000 mines had to be laid in the same way. The construction of the Northern Barrage was started in March 1918 and by October 'only' 70,000 mines had been laid. Three different sectors were assigned as safe passages: sectors A, B and C. In the middle was sector A which ran in a northeasterly direction. Sector B concerned the Fair Isle passage between the Orkneys and the Shetlands. In the east lay Sector C, in Norwegian waters, near Utsire. The destruction of five U-boats, of which *UB-104* and *UB-113* were part of the Flanders Flotilla, could not be counted as a large succes for the Allies in comparison with the cost for its construction and maintenance. It was an area which often proved to be more dangerous for British and American ships. Antenna mines were more sensitive mines and could detonate when they were being placed. Mines often exploded due to the activities of storm and swell.

PATROL VESSELS

Several units of the Allied navies were specifically employed for combating the U-boats. These mainly concerned well manoeuvrable and fast ships, such as torpedo boats and destroyers. Building a naval vessel from scratch was lengthy and time-consuming and with monthly sinkings of their merchant fleets on an all time high, there was a pressing demand for more patrol vessels to be brought into service. For this function, the Royal Navy looked towards fishing vessels, yachts and motorboats. Great Britain was a huge seafaring nation and every harbour housed up to hundreds of wooden and iron ships. After pressing large numbers of them into naval service, they underwent changes in the dockyards. They were equipped with minesweeping or laying apparatus, armament and extra berths. They were usually crewed by men who knew their own vessels, fishermen and local seamen who had been recruited by the navy and were commanded by a naval reserve officer.

By the end of 1917 a total of 726 ships had been adapted as minesweepers, of these 412 were former fishing vessels. In 1916 they could clear about 180 mines at a monthly rate, which would nearly be doubled at 355 mines in 1917. Minesweepers stood on the frontline and had a dangerous and difficult task to fulfil. By the second half of 1916 a total of 35 minesweeper were lost and in the beginning of 1917 this went up to 84. Despite losing many vessels, they were able to lessen the losses with the merchant fleet. In the first half of 1917, 90 merchant ships were lost due to mines. By the end of the same year this had been reduced to 'only' 50 losses.

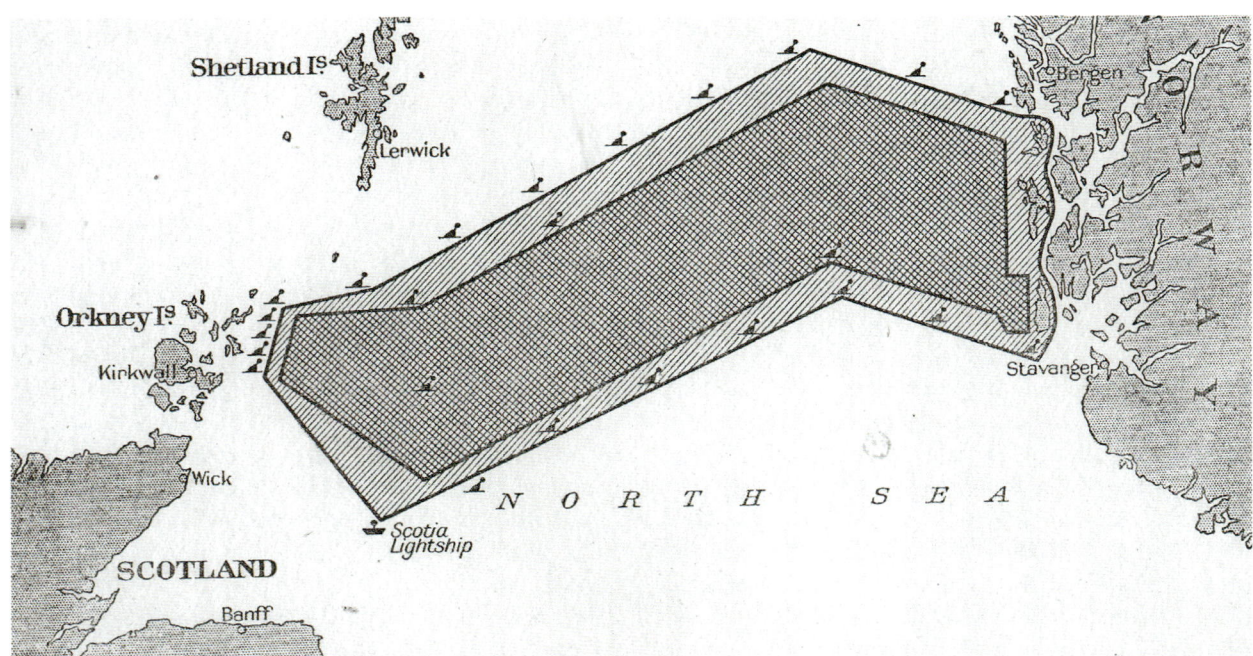

The Anglo-American mine field of the Northern Barrage, situation 1918 (Gibson & Prendergast)

DEPTH CHARGES

The invention of the depth charge meant the end of the safety for a U-boat once it had submerged. A depth charge was actually a simple weapon consisting of a metal drum which was filled with an explosive charge. It was fired from the deck of a ship or rolled from the stern into the sea and exploded automatically when it reached the set depth.

By January 1916 the British had developed two types of depth charge. The first was the so-called D-type depth charge with a charge of 150 kg, meant for use on board fast moving ships such as torpedo boats. The other was also of the D-type, but displaced 60 kg, and was used on board slower vessels such as trawlers or drifters. Up to June 1917 there was an accute shortage of depth charges and only two were given to every naval vessel. Production and availability increased exponentially after this, mainly because of the entry of the United States in the war.

When a depth charge detonated at a distance of less than 9 m, the hull of a U-boat would suffer heavy damage and force it to the surface. At less than 4.5 m from the hull, the explosion would prove to be fatal to the U-boat and her crew.

A counterpart of the U-boats: a British submarine of the E-class (Chatterton)

BRITISH SUBMARINES

Reports of direct successes of U-boats against British submarines were sparse. During the war U-boats were only able to torpedo and sink four British, only one by a U-boat of the Flanders Flotilla. This was *HMS E-22*, which was torpedoed by *UB-18*, commanded by *Oberleutnant z. S.* Otto Steinbrinck, on 25 April 1916 near the Brown Ridge off the Dutch coast.

After divers of the Royal Navy were able to study and document the wreck of the German *UC-2* off the British east coast, construction work was started on a small fleet of minelayers. Six submarines of the E-class were adapted in 1915 to carry mines in two rows of ten shafts: *E-24, E-34, E-41, E-45, E-46* and *E-51*.

They were supplied with anchorline contact mines of the S-MK IV type. They were smaller and lighter than their German counterparts and had a weight of 250 kg with a diameter of 0.53 m. Their charge consisted of 95 kg of Amatol and they could withstand a maximal depth of 50 m. As with the UC-I type boats the depth setting of the mines had to be done in harbour as during the patrol there was no access possible to the shafts.

The minelayers of the E-class were assigned to the 9th Submarine Flotilla and were based in Harwich. Up to the spring of 1918 they had to mainly combat the U-boats in northerly waters by laying mines in the German exit routes. This area was the German Bight with Heligoland, Horns Riff and the northern Dutch coast. During three years of war six submarines were able to lay a total of 2,469 mines. The E-class were able to destroy many merchant vessels, patrol ships and several U-boats such as *UB-61* and *U-75* and put a lot of pressure on German minesweepers. Their effect was so big that the U-boats of the northern ports were forced to take the more time-consuming easterly route, via the *Kaiser-Wilhelm-Kanal* (now Kiel Kanal) and via the Kattegat to reach the North Sea.

AIRCRAFT

In 1915 the British and French airfleets could only spare a handful of aircraft which were assigned to anti-submarine patrols. Their armament consisted only of a machinegun and the scarce radio-apparatus on board would often be unreliable. By the end of the second year of the war they were technically much more advanced and a load of bombs weighing between 30 and 50 kg could be carried. They booked little success as aircraft were slow and could be seen miles away by a good lookout on a U-boat. Their contribution mainly consisted in disrupting the routines of U-boat crews. Every time an enemy plane was spotted, the crew had to clear the deck and submerge the submarine for safety reasons.

EXPLOSIVE PARAVANE

The explosive paravane was a torpedo-shaped device, a sort of underwater 'glider' which was developed between 1914 and 1916 by Commander Usborne and Lieutenant Burney, funded by Sir George White, founder of the Bristol Aeroplane Company. Initially developed to destroy naval mines, the paravane would be strung out and streamed alongside the towing ship, normally from the bow. The wings of the paravane would tend to force the body away from the towing ship, placing a lateral tension on the towing wire. If the tow snagged the cable anchoring a mine then the anchoring cable would be cut, allowing the mine, to float to the surface where it could be destroyed by gunfire.

Lieutenant Burney developed explosive paravanes as an anti-submarine weapon, as a 'high speed sweep'. It was a paravane, containing 36 kg of the explosive TNT towed by an armoured electric cable. The warhead was fired automatically as soon as the submarine touched the paravane or towing cable or by hand from the ship's bridge. It could be quickly deployed into the water, could be towed up to 25 knots and recovery if unsuccessful was reasonably simple. The paravane was more economic than the depth charge as it only exploded when it would touch the U-boat hull.

HYDROPHONE

The hydrophone was the forerunner of the ASDIC, the system to detect U-boats during the Second World War. It consisted of a submerged microphone which could pick up the sound of the propellors of a U-boat. The pinpointing only worked in theory, as in practice it was impossible to give any indication of the direction of the noise source.

On 23 April 1916 there was a remarkable incident between a U-boat and two drifters which had been converted into Q-ships. The drifters *Hobbyhawk* and *Cheero* were patrolling about 10 miles to the northeast of Smith's Knoll. They had been equipped with specially designed nets to which mines had been attached. The nets were being dragged about 600 m behind the ships which still were able to move at a speed of 3 miles. Batteries had been linked to the netmines to be able to detonate them when a U-boat got caught in one of them. Both ships were also fitted with hydrophones to pick up the specific sound of a U-boat. By evening, *Cheero* picked up the signature sound of the electric engines of a U-boat which was fast approaching them. About 45 minutes after contact had been made, the cable dragging the nets went taut. The tension lessened somewhat and tensed again whereafter an explosion occurred in the nets. The sound cut off immediately and was followed by a shockwave which shot out of the water to a height of 4 m. The surface went flat and there followed an explosion at larger depth, followed by large amounts of oil which came to the surface. The crew was ordered to haul in the nets, but these proved to be under great tension. six crewmen managed to pull in one net after great effort and in it was a large fragment of steel plate. In a third net more, smaller fragments of steel were discovered, possible that of a mine or a U-boat. The British assumed that *UC-3*[116] had been sunk here, but *UC-3* would be sunk closer to home, in the *Vlakte van de Raan*, off Zeebrugge. It is possible that a different U-boat had been hit and sunk or that it concerned a cluster of mines which had been detonated. The sounds picked up by the hydrophone could possibly have come from a U-boat which happened to be close by. As mentioned before, hydrophones were not known for being accurate instruments.

DECOY VESSELS AND Q-SHIPS

Early on in the war, the Royal Navy was looking for an effective method to combat the U-boats on the high seas. U-boats were very vulnerable on the surface and would never intentionally come into the range of the guns of a torpedo boat or any other enemy naval vessel. At that period of time depth charges had not been invented and the British wanted to find a way to lure a U-boat as close as possible within the range of the guns. Only innocent looking targets such as schooners, drifters and slow-moving merchant ships could entice a U-boat captain to surface his boat and sink the ship by gunfire instead of wasting an expensive torpedo.

SS Vittoria was converted and taken into Royal Naval service on 29 November 1914 as their first Q-ship or decoy vessel. *SS Vittoria* looked like a normal merchant ship but was armed with concealed quick firing guns. Even though she patrolled an area where U-boats had been sighted, she had no luck and was not able to confront any U-boats and was taken out of service in January 1915. But *SS Vittoria* meant the beginning of a new kind of warfare for which the Royal Navy was assigning more drifters, sailing craft and merchant ships with concealed armament.

Usually they were given fake names and home ports and sometimes markings of neutral countries were painted on funnels or hulls. Behind deck cargoes, added superstructure, concealments and cut-in-half sloops hid artillery pieces behind which skilled Royal naval gun crews waited in anticipation.

U-boat captains were usually thrifty with their supply of torpedoes and would prefer to sink an enemy ship with the deck gun or explosive charges. Before unrestricted U-boat warfare had been introduced it was normal practice for a U-boat crew to inspect a captured ship. If it was an Allied or neutral ship with a cargo destined for an enemy port then it was a legitimate target for destruction. When an unsuspecting U-boat would venture closer to the target, the White Ensign would be hoisted, the camouflage dropped and the guns would swing out and open fire. The simple action of flying the navy's battle flag at the right moment indicated that it was a legitimate naval vessel which existed under International Law. The attacking ship and its crew could then not be accused of piracy or espionage when military personnel were on board a merchant vessel. When the distance to the target was short and the fire of the guncrew accurate, then only a few well-placed shells could cripple a U-boat by damaging the pressure hull. For both ships the battle was one of life and death as a Q-ship ran the risk of being torpedoed, when the U-boat did have the opportunity to submerge.

The British went as far as pressing into service small ships such as sailing smacks. This was begun in the fishing port of Lowestoft in August 1915. The *UB-I* type U-boats were very active along the British east coast and managed to sink dozens of trawlers and drifters on a weekly basis. Four smacks were converted and their crews of fishermen thickened by Royal Navy men who could man the single gun. The Q-ship would then hide amongst a fleet of fishing vessels and wait for a U-boat to come to the surface. The decoy trawler *Inverlyon* managed to sink *UB-4* with all hands on 15 August on the Smiths' Knoll. The ships *Q & E* and *Pet* also were able to engage U-boats but those managed to escape unscathed. There were only a few Q-ships which were able to attack, damage and sink U-boats but for most of the volunteer crews it meant monotonous patrols at sea, with very little action. Q-ships did have a profound impact on the way the war was being waged. U-boat captains had become very weary and would study a target much more closely before attacking it. The development of the Q-ship was such a success that by October 1916 already 47 were in operation around the British Isles.[117]

UB-18, one of the first UB-II U-boats which would operate from the Flemish ports in the western part of the English Channel, would have the misfortune of several encounters with Q-ships. Between September 1916 and October 1918 *UB-18* fought no less than seven battles with Q-ships. They mainly concerned sailing ships and a number of merchant vessels. The Q-ships were usually deployed on the shipping lanes of the western part of the Channel, the Irish Sea, the Shetlands and along the British east coast.

By the beginning of 1917, the U-boat campaign was at its height and thus also the activities of the Q-ships. By then there were 180 ships employed of all sizes and armament with tonnages that varied between 200 and 4.000 BRT. The organisation of the decoy vessels was assigned a special department within the Admiralty. The importance of combatting the U-boats was at its height now as food supplies were dramatically low, with only a couple more weeks remaining before Great Britain would have to surrender and discuss terms with Germany.

Out of total U-boat losses in the war, 11 were sunk by Q-ships. There were more than 80 cases were a U-boat had been damaged during a confrontation.

Two stacked up British submarine mines (TT)

THE Q-SHIP *PENSHURST* MAKES THE U-BOOT FLOTTILLE FLANDERN INCUR TWO LOSSES

One of the most successful Q-ships was *SS Penshurst*, captained by Commander Grenfell, RN. It was also the only Q-ship which had battled with the same U-boat during two consecutive days.

SS Penshurst had the profile of an oil tanker, with three masts, a funnel abaft and bridge amidships. The 1,191 ton *SS Penshurst* had been brought into service on 9 November 1915 and patrolled the area to the north of Scotland, Ireland and the western Channel area. For a long year the ship did not have any success. This changed on 29 November 1916 when she was patrolling off the Lizard. At a distance of 7 miles she noticed the merchant ship *SS Wileyside* which had stopped. As they approached, a small object to her port was seen. This object fired a warning shot at a distance of 5 miles and proved to be a U-boat. It was *UB-19*, which had stopped and boarded the Q-ship *Behrend* and sunk it with explosive charges. The U-boat ignored *Penshurst* and was approaching *SS Wileyside*. Grenfell wanted to lure the U-boat away from *SS Wileyside*, ordered stop engines and ordered part of the crew to carry out a mock evacuation with the lifeboats. The U-boat was 3,000 m from *SS Penshurst* and continued on a parallel course. Grenfell observed three men on the tower who gave orders to the gun crew on deck. When it became clear that he would not be able to approach any closer, he let his three guns open fire on the U-boat. The shots missed their target and the U-boat, now known as *UB-19,* submerged panic stricken. This took some time as some crewmen were still on deck and had to get below. Grenfell let two depth charges drop on the area where *UB-19* had dived, but without result. He and his crew were deeply disappointed because now that the true function of *SS Penshurst* was known, it would certainly be broadcast to other U-boats. But Grenfell did not give up so easily and immediately changed the look of his ship by painting it a different colour and shortening the foremast. At dawn, on 30 November it seemed that *SS Penshurst* had been baptised into another ship. Shortly afterwards Grenfell picked up a wireless signal from the cargoship *SS Ibex* which had spotted a U-boat about 20 miles northwest of the Casquets. Grenfell immediately ordered full speed ahead towards the area and around 13h50 the conning tower of a submarine was observed 5 miles to the south of *SS Penshurst*. Some time later a float plane arrived on the scene and dropped a bomb on the position of the U-boat. The U-boat submerged and Grenfell signalled the plane to approach him. He asked the pilot to work together with him to locate the U-boat. The

plan failed when the plane crashed into the sea and *SS Penshurst* had to come to its rescue. All hope o catching the U-boat seemed to have gone, when at 15h14 everyone was surprised by a shell which crashed into the sea about 200 m in front of the ship. The U-boat had surfaced and was 6,000 m behind *SS Penshurst*! At 16h12, when the U-boat had approached to 1,000 m, Grenfell ordered full stop and let part of the crew carry out a mock evacuation. It seemed to work and *UB-19* approached the port side with the intention of demanding the ship's papers to the captain. When *UB-19* had come to within 250 m from *SS Penshurst*, the guns opened fire. The Germans had been taken totally by surprise. Its gun crews had been eyeing the lifeboats from the mock evacuation and had been put at ease. Shells from the starboard 6-pounder gun penetrated the hull in the area of the engine room and rendered *UB-19* unable to dive. Both 12-pounder guns fired roughly 80 rounds at point blank range. Large parts of the tower

In a cut-out liefboat a gun is hidden on board the British Q-ship *Penshurst* (Chatterton)

and plating from the hull were ripped away. *UB-19* sank bow first after only 10 minutes into the engagement. Lifeboats from *SS Penshurst* managed to save *Oberleutnant z. S. Erich* Noodt, *Leutnant* Karl Bartel, Ingenieur-Aspirant Eigler and 13 crewmen. Seven Germans perished in the attack. After interrogation, one of the survivors of *UB-19* said that they had become stuck in the nets of the Dover Barrage several times. When they were questioned about the disguise of *SS Penshurst*, one of the U-boatmen gave a reply which typified the *U-Flottille Flandern*: 'We take so many risks, after which we become lax'. For his perseverance and skill, Grenfell was awarded the Distinguished Service Order by the King. A Distinguished Service Cross and a Distinguished Service Medal were awarded to two of his crew as well as £1,000 in prize money. This would not be the end of the adventure for *SS Penshurst*.

On 14 January 1917, she was on patrol between the Isle of Wight and Alderney. In the afternoon, at 15h50, one of the lookouts observed a U-boat approaching them on the surface. When the U-boat had come to 3,000 m it opened fire. Grenfell ordered engine stop and went on to the mock evacuation. The U-boat, identified as *UB-37*, approached on the starboard side of the bow and its guns kept on firing on *SS Penshurst*. When *UB-37* was at a distance of 700 m, she changed course, stopped and showed her full profile. The German gunners increased their rate of fire and hit the Q-ship twice in the bridge. The telegraph connection to the engine room was severed and the hydraulic release mechanism of the depth charges on the stern were hit and cut. A shell had also killed a gunner, gunlayer and wounded two others, one of which was the signals rating who had to hoist the battle flag before they could go into action. The crew kept their heads cool and at 16h24 Grenfell ordered their guns to open fire. The first shot of the 12-pounder hit the foot of the tower which set off an explosion amongst the ready-use ammunition. Large fragments of steel from the tower were flung into the sea, amidst billowing black smoke. A second shell hit the hull behind the tower and the starboard 6-pounder hit the tower at least four times. *UB-37* sank stern first below the surface. *SS Penshurst* did not lose any time and sailed across the location and dropped several depth charges. This time there were no survivors from the stricken U-boat.

A month later in the western part of the Channel, *SS Penshurst* was again involved in a battle with a U-boat, now of a larger class, *U-84*. After receiving several hits in the tower *U-84* managed to submerge and escape, but not before leaving a deep impression on its crew. In the following months there were four more encounters between U-boats and *SS Penshurst*.

On Christmas Eve 1917 *SS Penshurst* was on patrol in the southern part of the Irish Sea. A U-boat was spotted about 5 miles in the distance and was heading straight for the Q-ship. Shortly afterwards the U-boat dived and at 300 m distance fired a torpedo. The Q-ship was hit between the boilers and the engine room. Although the ship was sinking, part of the crew remained behind their guns and managed to fire six rounds at the U-boat. One hit the target and the U-boat dived and disappeared. *SS Penshurst* sank the next day, on 24 December.[118]

The Q-ship *SS Penshurst* (Chatterton)

Convoy sighted! (Claus Bergen)

Dive! Dive! Dive! (Claus Bergen)

CONVOYS

The fate of the U-boats had more or less been decided by the middle of 1917, when the Allies organised their merchant fleet in groups or flocks which could easily be protected. By mid-July the convoy system was applied for the most hazardous stretches between Great Britain and France. A month later this was also used for the crossing of the Atlantic. Convoys would be protected by torpedo boats, destroyers and armed trawlers. The amount and the positioning of the protection depended on the size and importance of the ships. The disadvantage for a U-boat captain was that too many targets presented themselves in too short a time and there was a large chance for heavy retaliation after his action. Due to the presence of observation balloons above a convoy, a periscope or conning tower would be readily visible and the escorts promptly warned.

Convoy protection for ships, leaving the British Isles, ceased at 15° longitude west, roughly 450 miles from the Irish coast. The warships left the merchant ships to their fate and returned to their own ports to escort another convoy. By the end of 1917 two convoy routes had been designated, coming from the United States, across the Atlantic, to western Europe. The northerly route would proceed along the 49° latitude and arrive at the British west coast. The southern route swung towards the Bay of Biscay and ended up in Brest, St.-Nazaire and Bordeaux. With the increasing amount of escorted merchant ships, their monthly losses fell rapidly. In the end, the U-boats left the area around the Irish Sea because of the danger of attack and concentrated more on Channel shipping. Here there was still enough choice of single, unprotected ships.

ROYAL NAVAL DIVERS

Not only was it important for the Allies to destroy the U-boats by all means possible, but also to gather information on their activities and modi operandi. '*For the acquisition of information of inestimable value to the successful prosecution of the war*'. After the sinking of *UC-2* off Lowestoft on 2 July 1915 and the buoying of the site, began the career of a small top secret unit of the Royal Navy. This was a war of intelligence against the U-boats and the activities and successes of the unit remained secret for 50 years after the end of the First World War. What was known before that was left

British hard hat divers are let down from a salvage ship to investigate a sunken U-boat (The Sphere)

to rumour and hearsay. The divers who decended on the wrecks of the recently sunk U-boats did it only for the possible recovery of information. This came up in the form of documents, codebooks, charts, diaries, technical manuals and personal items.

The Admiralty Salvage Section was formed at the end of 1915 as a branch of DNE (Director of Naval Equipment) and stood under control of Commodore Fred Young, RNR. The Salvage Section was created for the clearance of all kinds of wrecks strewn around the British Isles, which the war had brought with it. U-boats were far from its sole purpose and largely separate to its main function. By 1918 the Salvage Section had taken over all salvage operations and forced commercial firms aside which also had been involved in wreck recovery. It had grown to own and operate 15 salvage craft and its headquarter staff was manned by ten officers and 22 civilians. It is credited to have been involved in the salvage of 450 ships, which were returned to service. At least seven of the salvage ships have been known to have been employed for U-boat salvage work. These were the recovery barge *YC-10*, *Anchorite*, *Ranger*, *Melita*, *Racer*, *Corycia* and *Moonfleet*. During four years they were able to locate and dive a total of 22 U-boatwrecks. Of these,

three were salvaged intact: *UC-5*, *UC-44* and *UB-110*. The salvage officers who were specialised on U-boat wrecks were Commanders Young, Davis, Malet, Kay, George, Wheeler, Vine, McGuffie and Damant.

On 29 March 1918 a special section dedicated to salvage work on U-boats was created and led by two officers and four divers.[119] Commander Guybon Chesney Castell Damant, OBE (M) was to head it and would take control over many operations. U-boat diving reached its peak in the summer of 1918 when more of them had been sunk closer inshore. Besides officers, salvage masters, seamen and engineers there were a few dozen well-trained divers who would become known as 'The Tin Openers'*. These divers often had to risk life and limb to enter freshly sunken U-boat wrecks to recover as much information as possible. With their cumbersome suit, weights, hose and helmet they had to squeeze through hatchways and work in unimaginably difficult conditions often choking down fear and the wish to flee to the surface after encountering dozens of bloated corpses, flotsam and oil, in claustrophobic conditions where visibility

---

* This was a reference to what the British called the U-boats: the Kaiser's tin-coffins.

was sometimes down to only a hand-breadth away. There was also the danger that their airhose would snag on jagged edges of the wreck or cut their suit.

One of these 'characters' was chief diver Ernest Charles 'Dusty' Miller, a former shipwright, who was serving with the Royal Navy. Using their knowledge of ships and after a while knowing what a U-boat felt like, they would aim for recovering navigational and other instruments, secret codebooks, charts, personal possessions and letters from the crew. Miller would be awarded the DSC in 1919 for 'distinguished services in connection with dangerous and important salvage work'.

Mostly the salvage ship had to work in a dangerous zone where U-boats were operating and where depth charges and mines would be exploding at short distances away. In 1918 they were diving almost daily in the active minefield between Dover and Cap Griz Nez. They knew very well that the explosion of a mine within a mile of the operations would be fatal to a diver.

When descending onto the wreck of *UB-56*, Miller noticed that a steel net and cable with an unexploded mine was wrapped around the propeller shaft of the mangled stern part of the U-boat. *UB-56* had been sunk with all hands three days before, on 19 December 1917, by one of the mines of the Dover Barrage. When Miller had reached the conning tower he was startled by a second mine which also hung from its cable and lightly swayed to and fro with the current. It was precariously close to the steel hull of the U-boat! He managed to stay calm and pulled the mine away from the hull with one had and with the other he removed the detonator. He was even able to remember the painted serial number on the shell of the mine and indicate it later on on the location plans of the minefields.[120] On the same wreck he was able to penetrate the U-boat through the damaged stern section. He had to satisfy himself with the search for intelligence in the after torpedo room as the control room was unattainable. Here he found a small wooden chest. Its contents would prove to have a large impact on the construction of British torpedoes. It contained the magnetic firing mechanism for a *Schwarzkopf*-torpedo. This mechanism allowed the detonation of the explosive charge when it was close to or under the steel hull of a ship. It was the forerunner of the magnetic installations which were used extensively in mines and torpedoes of the Second World War.

Having nerves of steel proved to be a crucial attribute for the Tin Openers when penetrating an unknown wreck. Being a wreck diver myself, I know very well what dangers these early diving pioneers had to undergo. They usually had to descend in any kind of circumstance, with or without visibility or current. The freshly sunken U-boats would still be full of corpses and this would weigh psychologically hard on even the toughest sailor. This proved to be so for Dusty Miller when he descended on the wreck of *UB-4* on 19 August 1915. Visibility was moderate and even outside the wreck his torch only gave him limited sight. After he had removed the tower hatch with explosives, he was surprised by a German who met him at the tower ladder. Miller was taken aback when the corpse drifted past him and gazed at him with open eyes. He was known for his cool-headedness and after a few moments his panic subsided and he concentrated on the job. The corpse had been caught in the remains of an airpocket and forced it upwards. He grabbed the corpse by the collar and let it sink away in the depth next to the wreck. The worst was still to follow. After he had descended the tower ladder and entered the pitch dark interior of the control room he had to squeeze himself through the packed bodies of the other drowned crewmen. He felt his panic rising again and had difficulty keeping it under control. When Miller had controlled his anxiety he tied the corpses to the bulkhead and only then could he start the search for ship's documents. In those early days of diving there was also little known about decompression and the effects which pressure and nitrogen had on the human body. To avoid decompression accidents as best as possible a set pattern was applied. During the ascent Miller would make a stop at 10 m for 5 minutes, following a stop at 6 metres for 10 minutes and a final one at 3 m for 15 minutes. On his way up to the surface he would make up-and-down movements with his limbs. This exercise movement was taught to him during his training and was said to increase the blood circulation and shorten the decompression time.[121]

Towards the end of the war Miller had to investigate an unknown *UB-III* class U-boat which had been sunk off Dover. At first he had trouble getting through the hatch on the tower due to the heavy swell on the surface. Close to the inside hatch he came upon the body of the captain which had got stuck with its clothes on a locking pin. The body showed gunshot wounds to the head and abdomen. Miller still fought with terrible nightmares and memories of this incident long after the war. In this specific wreck he had encountered 30 corpses of which half had indications of suicide and gunshot wounds. Because a shell had entered the engine room and the U-boat was not able to surface anymore the crew was sentenced to an agonising death of slow suffocation. Some of the survivors had written letters to their loved ones and letters and envelopes floated around. Miller managed to gather several letters together with rings, watches, crucifixes and a few Iron Crosses.

For a long time after the end of the First World War the exploits of the Royal Naval divers remained top secret. Official archived documents were only officially open to the public in the late 1960s and Miller had been allowed to give his first interview to the press in 1926 about his wartime accomplishments,[122] albeit with considerations of the Secrecy Act. The information recovered by the diving teams proved to be indispensible to the war effort indirectly and to combatting the U-boats directly.

BRITISH INVASION PLANS AND BLOCKADES

Already in the autumn of 1915 the British were devising concrete invasion plans. It was the brainchild of Admiral Sir Reginald Bacon, who wanted to seize the port and town of Ostend by landing 9,000 troops on the beach with pontoon barges. This did not materialise as the Germans were extending the coastal defences by three lines of batteries and fortifications in 1916. In the middle of 1917 the plans were taken out of the closet as the British now wanted to make a landing on the beaches between Middelkerke and Westende. At sea, the U-boat war waged on relentlessly and the situation for the Allies started looking bleaker. There was the urgent necessity to neutralise the activities of the U-boats by shutting down Bruges. This could only be done by capturing the ports of Ostend and Zeebrugge and so barring them access to the North Sea. It was to have a landing from the sea coincide with a thrust from the army from the south of west Flanders. The land assault finally materialised at the end of July 1917, known as the 3rd Battle of Ypres, but its motion slowed and became stuck in the mud of Passchendaele. What should have been an operation lasting just three weeks, turned into a battle of attrition lasting three months.[123] On 15 October 1917 all further landing plans were shelved.

Still, the British needed to call an urgent stop to the activities of the U-boats. This necessity materialised on 23 April 1918 with the dual attacks on the ports of Zeebrugge and Ostend with an immense fleet of ships. The main body consisted of the obsolete cruisers *HMS Vindictive, HMS Thetis, HMS Intredid, HMS Iphigenia*, the former Mersey ferries *Daffodil and Iris*, torpedo boats, destroyers, *Motor Launches* and *Coastal Motor Boats*. A smaller fleet consisting of the cruisers *HMS Sirius* and *Brilliant* headed for Ostend.

A few days after the Zeebrugge Raid: a UC-II type boat and a torpedo boat pass through the sealock to sail past the block ships and reach open sea (TT)

The attack on Ostend failed: block ships *HMS Sirius* and *HMS Briljant* missed the harbour mouth and ended up on the beach of Bredene (TT) ▶

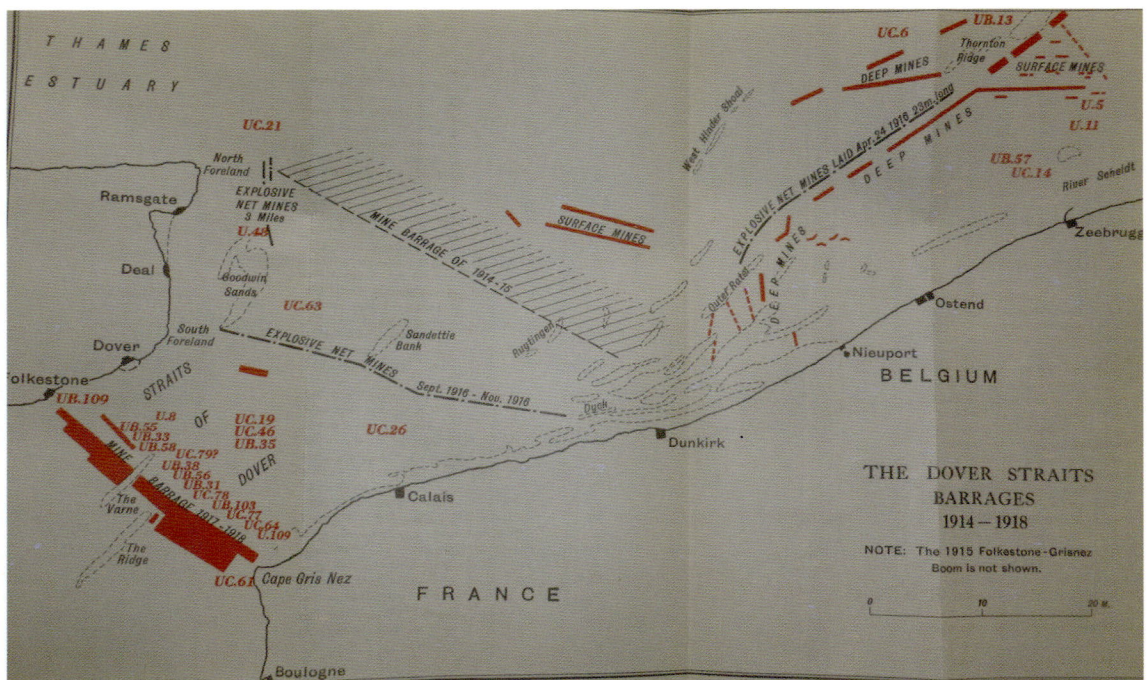

A: Chart showing losses of German U-boats between the Dover Barrage and the Dutch coast (Gibson and Prendergast)

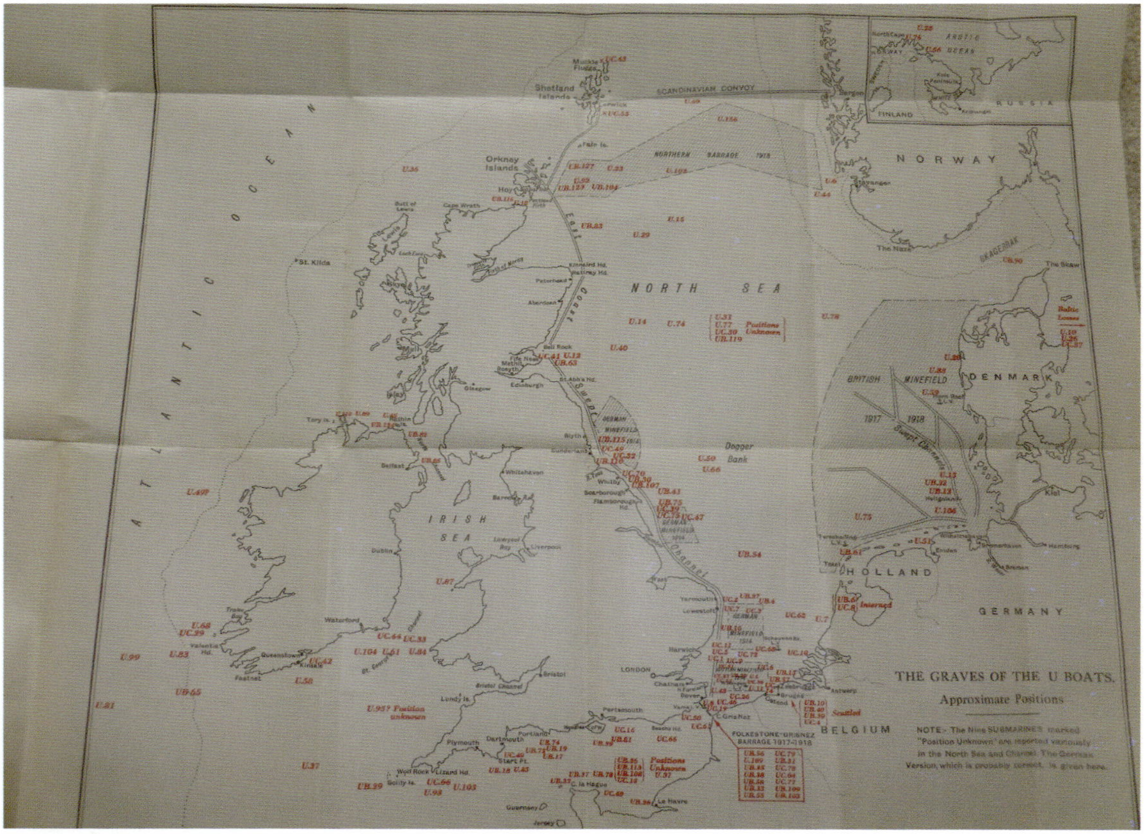

Chart showing U-boat losses around the British Isles (Gibson and Prendergast)

At Zeebrugge, three blockships were intended to be sunk and obstruct the canal going towards Bruges. *HMS Vindictive*, supported by the two ferries, would be positioned on the seaward side of the Mole to unleash a detachment of Royal Marines. This was meant to cause a diversion from the main purpose of the attack: the three blockships entering Zeebrugge Roads. The blockships *Thetis, Intrepid* and *Iphigenia* completed their mission of sinking themselves in or near the entrance to the canal. It had been an enormous endeavour by the British, but still the blockships did not totally obstruct the passage of the U-boats. On 25 April, *UB-16* managed to slip past the wrecks of the blockships at high tide as the first German U-boat. A few weeks later, the Germans removed the western pierhead making passage for middle to large sized U-boats possible. For the Royal Navy it rather symbolised a moral victory, proving that the German-occupied ports were not totally impregnable.

At Ostend, *Sirius* and *Brilliant* missed the entrance to the harbour through confusion and navigational error and ended up stranded at Bredene.

A second attempt at blocking Ostend was made on 10 May, this time using *HMS Vindictive*. The Arrogant-class cruiser, which now had been transformed into a blockship, failed to be sunk across the harbour mouth. She ended up almost parallel to the eastern pier and did not obstruct the passage of the German ships.

OPERATIONS OF THE U-BOATS OF THE *U-FLOTTILLE FLANDERN*

In an extensive work it is only befitting to include the exploits and losses of the main players. Delivering an all inclusive documentation on every detail of every one of the 93 U-boats which once were housed in the Flemish ports is not an easy task. The most reliable sources of historical information were found in daily reports, *Tagesmitteilungen*, and war diaries, *Kriegstagebücher*, kept at the *Militärarchiv* in Freiburg im Breisgau. This was combined with the work carried out by Bendert in his research on the UB- and UC-boats of the Imperial Navy. Where necessary, facts were confirmed or refuted by the works of Grant and Gibson & Prendergast. For investigative work in situ and the identification of the wrecks we find on the seabed at present, I was mainly reliant on my own dive investigations. This was combined with information gained by other Belgian, English, French, Dutch, German and American divers. References concerned the extensive work of Dr. Innes McCartney, mainly concerning wrecks rediscovered on the southwest coast of the UK and the western part of the Channel; Alain Richard, with wrecks of the northern French coast and Ron Young and Pamela Armstrong with references to wrecks between Dover, the Thames going over the east coast, of the UK. U-boat wrecks discovered in the area stretching from the French border, across the Thames Estuary with the numerous sandbanks, the Belgian territorial sea, the Scheldt Estuary up to the North Hinder and the east coast of the UK were mainly researched by Dirk Termote and the author.

NAUTICAL ARCHAEOLOGY AS A MEANS TO DISCOVERING LOST U-BOATS

When we take a closer look at the present day chart of the Flemish Banks, the D11, one cannot but notice the countless depth markings, sandbanks, traffic routes and buoys. The most obvious and perhaps also the most intriguing are the obstructions, foul grounds and wrecks which are indicated as a navigational warning to shipping. In the Belgian territorial sea alone there are the known remains of 277 wrecks, most of which have been identified. 32% of these remains, almost a third, concern military remnants dating to two World Wars. They mainly concern small coastal units such as *Vorpostenboten* (armed trawlers), *Sperrbrecher* (sacrificial ships for minefields), *Kriegsfischkutter* (armed drifters), motor launches, harbour tugs, torpedo boats, destroyers and of course U-boats. Almost 3% of the wrecks, a total of 11 wrecks, concern those of lost U-boats.

WRECKS AND THEIR LIFESPAN

Artificial obstructions on the bottom of the sea, such as sunken ships, disintegrate under the influence of fauna

The researchers Tomas and Dirk Termote

and flora, tides, electrolyses, storm and corrosion. We humans have also managed to leave a legacy on the wrecks with all kinds of activities such as the deepening of shipping lanes, commercial and navigational salvage, heavy trawling and dredging. All this will expose many wrecks and make them corrode faster.

Each type of wreck has its own lifespan, whereafter it will collapse and the remains will get buried by sand. The remains of wooden ships and aircraft will have suffered the most, mainly in the period after the Second World War when we see a rapid change in more destructive fishing methods such as the trawl net. Light remains protruding from the seabed do not form a great obstacle for a system of nets which act like a plough on the seabed.

The lifespan of a steel ship, such as a 20th century merchant ship, is about 50 years. This varies in how much a wreck is protected by sand and at what depth it is sunk. The deeper it lies, the more protection it gets against the actions of swell and storm. The author's father, Dirk Termote, was witness to the destructive process when comparing his earlier diving experiences on different wrecks on the Flemish Banks. The wreck of the cross-channel ferry, *MV Queen of the Channel*, sunk in 1940 during Operation Dynamo on the Middelkerke Bank, was relatively intact when discovered in 1987. The bow stood proud, with stowed anchors, anchorwinch and foot of the mast as recognisable structures. The author could bear witness in his own diving career, after not even 20 years, of the sides of the bow collapsing outwards, leaving parts of the superstructure strewn around and buried under the seabed.

U-boats, with their robust construction, mainly consisting of double hulls, can be classed as wrecks which are the sturdiest against the power of nature. Usually a lifespan of 100 years can be given to these kinds of wrecks. As wrecks they are also some of the most recognisable structures which can be identified even by a non-diving public. Sidescan and multibeam images indicate the obvious differences of a U-boat wreck and that of other obstructions. The prominent 'cigar shape' and the centrally placed tower are their most obvious characteristics. Although nature does give these wrecks some respite, human destructive influences carry on remorsesely. During the summer of 2005 a Dutch trawler happened to snag the wreck of a UC-II class submarine near the Fairybank (see wreck descriptions under *UC-66*). One of the nets was obviously deeply stuck in the wreck, but with lots of tugging and pulling it broke free after eight hours. With this knowledge the author was able to witness the influence of 3000 HP on a wreck. The net had snagged the stern, on the upper deck part of the engine room. As there were no large pieces of wreck protruding here, the net and its chains had been stuck on the aft torpedo-loading hatch. The oval, steel hatch had been totally dislocated and together with a large fragment of net, deposited behind the stern, in a scour near the propellers. Such a hatch has a weight of 300 kg, with a length of 2 m on a breadth of 1 m. It has two large hinges and eight double locking nuts, each measuring 4 cm in diameter, which had to ensure a watertight seal to the U-boat. With the forced removal of the hatch, the author was able to catch a glimpse of the interior, two diesel engines, a stowed torpedo and a workbench with all kinds of tools. But nature did its work fast and not even three months later the engine room was covered up to the rim where the former hatch used to be.

IDENTIFICATION

When attempting to identify the wreck of a U-boat one must look for different features and recognition points. First and foremost a date and nationality must be uncovered. Although the amount of Second World War U-boats sunk in the southern North Sea is relatively small, one has to also take in mind that there were post-war sinkings. This was the case in 1998, when a relatively modern, Russian submarine was being towed across the North Sea to a breakers' yard. The towline had parted during bad weather and the submarine was lost near the Brown Ridge.

U-boat numbers were most often painted or welded on to the hull and tower, but have disappeared when the outer skin disintegrated. A type or boat number can be found on the hub of a propeller. Information found here must always be handled with necessary scepticism as it was not uncommon for available propellors to be taken to a dockyard and used on a submarine of the same class.

Wrecks of submarines usually end up on their keels, upright or either with inclinations towards the port or starboard sides. The amount of deterioration can give and idea of age and place it in the first or middle years of the 20th century. Typological identification is possible by taking measurements of the hull, size of the tower, the presence of torpedo tubes, armament on deck or mineshutes in the bow.

After a typological identification, a more specific identity of a site can be made after studying damages on the wreck. Was the U-boat mined, torpedoed, bombed or was it lost through internal explosion? The location of a wreck can be compared to historical sources to come to a positive identification.

Making a combination with underwater research and studying many archival documents has managed to confirm certain theories, but also disproved and/or amended some. Nautical archaeology gives us the opportunity to solve mysteries concerning disappeared U-boats. The gathered information has mainly been achieved by private initiatives from divers, sometimes in cooperation with governmental institutions such as the Hydrographic Department.

THE U-BOATS OF THE *U-FLOTTILLE FLANDERN*, CAREERS AND FATES

It is not my intention to just sum up all the U-boats which served in the Flanders Flotilla between 1915 and 1918, their successes and fates. This, of course, is a large part of the story, but it mainly serves as an illustration to the planning and execution which German high command hoped to bring Great Britain to its knees. The fate of most U-boats is known and a great number of wrecks have been located, shortly after their sinkings or either in the years which followed. But still, a large amount are still unaccounted for and simply vanished whilst on patrol, many owing to the effects of British minefields. As technical diving has evolved rapidly more and more of the unsolved disappearances have been uncovered and we have been able to assign identifications to newly discovered wrecksites. Careers of different U-boats have been researched as best as possible, combined with source material from the war diaries or *Kriegstagebücher* at the Militärarchiv in Freiburg and the excellent work of Bendert concerning the UB- and UC-boats. Information concerning the wrecks was gathered by the author's findings as well as information from other divers.

UB-BOATS

UB-2

UB-2 was launched on 18 February 1915 and was brought into service by *Oberleutnant z. S.* Werner Fürbringer. *UB-2* would be the first UB-boat to reach the Flemish front. *UB-2* had left Germany on 8 May 1915 and would reach Zeebrugge, after having difficulties in stormy weather, three days later. *UB-2* would carry out a total of 25 patrols in the North Sea between 18 May 1915 and 7 March 1916, but only managed to sink ten ships. She was plagued by many engine problems, failing torpedoes and attacks by enemy Q-ships. The fact that she stopped many neutral ships at the North Hinder and Maas junctions also made up for a low score for *UB-2*.

Early on in July 1915 *UB-2* nearly failed to return from her patrol. At the beginning of the patrol she managed to slip through the Dover Straits without any problems. At Cap Antifer Fürbringer noticed a merchant vessel which he tried to sink with two torpedoes. Both misfired and with a sinking heart he had to watch his prey disappear over the horizon. Without any results it was decided to commence the return trip. Shortly afterwards the clutch between the diesel and electric engine broke. It was only possible to continue the return on the electric engine. Fürbringer and his crew found themselves in a dire situation as the closest friendly harbour was Ostend, which lay 120 miles east of their position. The batteries would allow them to cover a distance of another 12 miles before they would be drained. Fürbringer let all his faith and patience fall upon the tide which would carry them through the net barriers between Dover and Griz Nez. On the flood *UB-2* stayed on the surface drifting with a speed of 3 miles per hour eastwards. When the tired crew turned, they had to let the boat down to the seabed and remain there so as not to be pulled westwards again by the ebb. This system was repeated twice a day for four days running. When flowing with the tide Fürbringer let the crew come up and row with planks and even rig a small sail on top of the tower. These actions had more the purpose to keep up morale than give any forward propulsion. They were also becalmed and it became furiously hot. The rigging of a sail made *UB-2* look more like a small drifter than a surfaced U-boat. The limited provisions and water had to be rationed amongst the 13 crewmen, but soon the situation started to look critical. With every stay on the bottom the air became sparser and everyone started to gasp for lack of oxygen.

During their time on the seabed, the four engine room ratings worked nonstop on the clutch, but despite their hard efforts they did not manage to get it working again. Off Boulogne *UB-2* went to a depth of 63 m, but the U-boat proved to be of a sturdy construction and did not show any problems. On the fourth day they had managed to drift pass Calais and the Dover Barrage and tried to come into wireless contact with the *Marinekorps*. No messages reached them and now there loomed the threat that they would start drifting in a northeasterly direction, towards the Dutch coast and the British minefields. By the evening of 6 July a sudden panic struck the watch as they had seen a submerging submarine at 4 miles distance. Just before Fürbringer called to let *UB-2* dive, another U-boat popped up in front of them in short range. He managed to abort the dive on time when he saw the characteristic 'eyes' on its bow and recognised her as *UB-16*. *Oberleutnant z. S.* Hans Valentiner had been ordered by high command to undertake a search for the missing *UB-2*. A tow was handed over, but wonder above wonder, the engineer had managed to repair the clutch at that very moment. In the end, *UB-2* managed to reach Ostend on its own power on 7 July.

On her eighth mission, at the end of August 1915, *UB-2* would again escape from death's jaws. After two days of sailing, the Yarmouth Roads was reached and they managed to torpedo the patrol vessel *Miura*. The following day *UB-2* approached an innocent looking trawler. When the crew of the trawler spotted the U-boat they left their ship and *UB-2* was able to approach her to about 300 m. Suddenly fire from a hidden machinegun was opened up, forcing *UB-2* to dive. Fürbringer fired his second torpedo, but it ran towards the seabed where it exploded. After the explosion, *UB-2* surfaced, thinking that the enemy had been hit, but was greeted by more gunfire. She dived again and stealthily crept away from the danger zone. Her attacker was the Q-ship *Pet (LT 560)*.

After the case with the Q-ship *UB-2* made 16 more unsuccessful patrols and on 15 March 1916 command was handed over to *Oberleutnant z. S.* Karl Neumann. Neumann transferred *UB-2* from Zeebrugge to Libau where she joined the 5th *U-Halbflottille*.

After seeing some action in the Baltic, *UB-2* was transferred to the U-boat school at the end of 1916. Her career ended in a German breakers' yard after the war.

UB-4

UB-4 was transported to Antwerp in several sections and reached the port of Bruges on 23 March 1915 where she went into service under the command of *Oberleutnant z. S.* Karl Gross. Gross was able to carry out 14 patrols in the North Hinder, Maas and British east coast areas but could only torpedo three ships. From 9 until 12 April 1915, *UB-4* found herself on patrol in the North Hinder area. *UB-4* was the first U-boat to arrive in Flanders and then torpedo and sink the British merchant ship *SS Harpalyce* (5.940 BRT).

A UB-I type U-boat enters the harbour of Ostend (TT)

Rare photos showing five UB-I type U-boats ready to leave for sea within the Zeebrugge locks. It concerns *UB-4* (Gross), *UB-5* (Smiths), *UB-12* (Wieland), *UB-16* (Valentiner) and *UB-17* (Wenninger) (U-Boot-Archiv Cuxhaven)

On a second patrol in that same month *UB-4* torpedoed another merchant ship, without visible flag or recognition marks. In the end it proved to be the Greek *SS Ellispontos* (2.988 BRT), and Germany had to pay reparations to its owner.

The 13th patrol, from 13 to 15 August 1915, would prove to be fatal for Gross and his crew. It had been his intention to take *UB-4* to the Yarmouth area for finding ships to sink, but the exact details of his plan remain unknown. On 15 August, at 20h15, *UB-4* ordered a British trawler to stop in the area of Smith's Knoll. Little did Gross know that it concerned the Q-ship *Inverlyon* which stood under command of Gunner Ernest Jehan, three reservists and its peacetime skipper. The non-suspecting *UB-4* surfaced and approached the trawler from its starboard side. Jehan took position next to the hidden 3-pounder gun and two other crewmen armed and concealed themselves. Gross stood on his own on the tower, next to the hatch, whilst giving commands to steer *UB-4* closer. Gross called out to the British, probably hailing them to stop. When *UB-4* had approached to about 25 m distance, Jehan ordered the Ensign to be run up and everybody to be prepared around the gun. Then he shot at Gross with his pistol, which also was the sign for his gun crew to open fire. The first and third rounds hit the centre of the tower and exploded inside. The second round tore off the back part of the tower. Gross was killed by the impact of the explosions and his body fell into the sea to starboard. Parts of the tower as well as the German ensign, flew away. *UB-4* started to sink and now two men were visible and part of a man in the tower hatch. *Inverlyon* kept on firing on *UB-4*, now at a distance of only 8 m. The gunners managed to hit the tower four and the hull three times. *UB-4* finally sank bow first whereafter three survivors came to the surface. One still seemed to be alive and skipper Phillips took his clothes off and jumped into the water with a lifebelt. It was a brave but futile attempt as none of the crew survived the sinking of *UB-4*. *Inverlyon* had put a net out and was able to hook the wreck and take a position. At 5 am two messenger pigeons were let out to notify about the sinking.[124]

Almost immediately after the sinking of *UB-4* the Royal Naval dive team was called in. Three days of bad weather followed and it would only be on the fourth day that Commander Damant wanted to take the risk of sending diver Dusty Miller onto the wreck. Miller descended along the tow cable left by *Inverlyon* on the site. *UB-4* lay at a depth of 33 m and Miller came on the hull, near the tower. The U-boat lay on its port side amongs masses of high kelp. Despite the very graphic report of the impacts of *Inverlyon*'s gun, Miller could only find one hole in the hull. This was too small to let him gain access to the accommodation. The tower had been damaged but the hatch was shut and Miller wanted to blast it off. He placed an explosive charge on the hatch and ascended back to the surface. After he made it safely back on board the ship they detonated the charge which had been connected with electric wiring. With his second dive Miller saw that the charge had neatly blown the hatch open. When he wrenched the hatch free he was met by a corpse which had been freed by the explosion. He pulled it up and let it sink into the depths beside the wreck. After keeping his fright under control he descended down the tower ladder with the intention of searching for secret documents. Miller had to keep his nerves under control as he was crowded by floating corpses in the control room. Before he could search the area he had to tie the bodies to the ceiling to give him some space. It only took a few seconds after which he discovered a strongbox, which he manoeuvred through the narrow tower. Once outside he attached a rope to it and signalled to the crew to pull him and the box to the surface. With his second U-boat wreck, Miller has once again scored the jackpot. In the box lay soaked but legible codebooks, a blueprint of the plan of *UB-4* and two charts where the freshly laid German minefields in the North Sea had been marked.[125]

The wreck was re-discovered by British divers and is known to be in position 52° 43' 027 N 02° 17' 885 E, near the Smith's Knoll Spar buoy. Overall depth on the wreck is 30 m. *UB-4* is heavily damaged and broken and it looks like some heavy salvage work was carried out on the wreck. Due to the sandy bottom, part of the wreck has sunken in the seabed.

UB-5

UB-5 was transported in segments by rail to Belgium in March 1915 and re-assembled at the Hoboken wharf. On 25 March 1915 she was commissioned and came under command of *Oberleutnant z. S.* Wilhelm Smith. During the period between 14 April and 18 September 1915 *UB-5* would carry out a total of 17 patrols and sink a total of six enemy vessels. One of her first victims was the British merchant ship *SS Ptarmigan* which was torpedoed at the North Hinder. The other

The crew of *UB-6* poses for the photo, gathered on the tower in the small merchant dock in Bruges. The rear has a message from seaman E. Prigge to Fraulein Luise Lorentzen (U-Boot-Archiv Cuxhaven).

UB-6 lies in Zeebrugge Roads alongside the captured Dutch merchant ship *SS Batavier II* (Jörn Jensen)

ships concerned four drifters which were stopped near Cromer and sunk using explosive charges.

On 20 July 1915 Smith made an unsuccessful attack on the British *SS Brussels* near the southern part of the Inner Gabbard and had to return home. *SS Brussels*, commanded by Captain Charles Fryatt, would later in the war be stopped by the torpedo boats and brought to Zeebrugge as a prize of war.

Her last five patrols concerned unsuccessful patrolling actions in the arear around the Middelkerke bank. This would be the last mission for *UB-5* in Flemish waters as she was transferred to Libau in the Baltic on 6 October 1915. *UB-5* seemed to suffer constantly from technical problems and in September 1916 served as school ship in the U-boat school for the remainder of the war. After the Armistice, *UB-5* was scrapped in Germany.

UB-6

UB-6 was commissioned on 8 April 1915 after being assembled and tested at Antwerp. Her first captain was *Oberleutnant z. S.* Erich Haeker. Between 30 April 1915 and 11 March 1917 *UB-6* was able to carry out 60 patrols and sink 15 ships.

During her first trip she managed to sink the torpedo boat *HMS Recruit* (335 BRT) 30 miles southwest from the Galloper light vessel. Due to bad ballasting after the loss in weight of the fired torpedo, *UB-6* shot out of the water and dived immediately to the seabed at 37 m. *HMS Brazen*, companion of the sinking *HMS Recruit*, searched in vain for *UB-6* which already was on its return route to Zeebrugge.

On 21 June 1915 *UB-6* had the honour to be the first Flanders U-boat to cross the Dover Straits. Her mission was to gather intelligence on minefields and enemy shipping movements. In the Boulogne Roads two small merchant ships and a hospital ship, accompanied by dozens of patrol vessels, were spotted. No torpedoes were expended and Haeker decided to return home.

In the following month *UB-6* was able to stop five drifters off Southwold in which explosive charges were placed. *Purple Heather, Merlin, Speedwell* and *Woodbine* sank, but the fifth, even with the suffered damages was saved by its crew.

During its tenth trip, from 10 to 14 August 1915, the trawler *Leander* was sunk off Yarmouth. Soon after *UB-6* managed to escape death by a hair's breath when the next trawler they had stopped, *LT 649*, proved to be a Q-ship. The captain forced her to stop by firing off several carbine rounds in front of her bow, but shortly afterwards a two-pounder gun was uncovered and at 150 m distance the Q-ship fired on *UB-6*. Haecker acted quickly and immediately ordered his U-boat to dive.

Functions of a *UB-I* class U-boat were diverse. During a patrol in the Westhinder area, *UB-6* managed to save the crew of *Seaplane 209*. On its way home, north of Ostend, a floating observation platform which served as fire directory for British monitors against the coastal batteries, was destroyed.

On 24 September, *UB-6* had to make an emergency dive after being attacked by enemy aircraft. She was hit by a bomb and water gushed in through ruptures in the tower hatch. Water short-circuited electrical contacts in the control room and created a fire. *UB-6* crashed onto the seabed at 21 m depth. The impact of the bomb had also damaged the supports of the diesel engine, but after a few hours the engineer managed to repair the

damage and *UB-6* was able to get back to Zeebrugge. On its way to Bruges via the sea canal the engine totally gave up and *UB-6* had to be towed to dry dock.

After Haecker came two other captains, but *UB-6* proved to be an unlucky vessel for them and they did not manage to book any results. In the end *UB-6* came under the command of *Oberleutnant z. S.* Karsten von Heydebreck on 22 July 1916. It was only after his sixth patrol that he booked his first success in September 1916. It concerned the Norwegian steamship *Linborg* (400 BRT) which he sunk off the Maas Light Vessel.

On the 42nd mission, on 22 September, *UB-6* was able to sink the Belgian barges *Germaine, Maria De Jonghe, Lichtevreden II* and *Rosalie* in the same area. The next day, 23 September, Heydebreck stopped the Dutch merchant ship *SS Batavier II* (1.328 BRT) and ordered it to sail to Zeebrugge, due to the presence of goods destined for Great Britain.

UB-6 seemed up to now to be a safe, but quite unsuccessful U-boat as the next ten patrols were without result. On 10 January 1917 a new captain, *Oberleutnant z. S.* Oskar Steckelberg, took over her helm. After a few unproductive months, *UB-6* left Zeebrugge on 10 March 1917 on her final patrol. This would be its 60th patrol and it was carried out in the Maas area. During the night of the 12th, *UB-6* hit a sandbank due to a navigational error and was towed to Hellevoetsluis by Dutch naval vessels. *UB-6* was then interned and in 1919 handed over to France where it was broken up at Brest.

UB-10

This *UB-I* type submarine was launched on 20 February 1915, disassembled and transported in segments to Antwerp where it was reassembled. It would become famous as one of the most successful U-boats of the Flanders Flotilla, under the command of *Oberleutnant z. S.* Otto Steinbrinck. On 27 March, *UB-10* was pulled into Bruges docks by a coaster and would be the first U-boat to join the newly created *U-Flottille Flandern*. *UB-10* would survive the entire war and sink a total of 36 ships.

On his first patrol, Steinbrinck was able to track down his first victim near the North Hinder light vessel. By the evening of 14 April 1915, the Dutch *SS Katwijk* had been torpedoed and sunk. The Dutch ship had made the fatal mistake of sailing with doused lights, but still, the German Empire paid compensation to the company for its loss.

The area known as the Hoofden proved to be quite frustrating for many U-boat captains. Steinbrinck experienced this in four consecutive patrols. *UB-10* had to let 20 neutral ships sail by without being able to take any action.

On 28 June 1915, *UB-10* became the second U-boat to pass successfully on the surface through the obstructions of the Dover Straits. But even then Steinbrinck did not have any luck in finding shipping on the British side of the Channel and had to return via the same route.

Steinbrinck's luck changed on 30 July and he managed to bag eight trawlers off Lowestoft. It concerned *Coriander, Fitzgerald, Quest, Achieve, Strive, Athena, Prospector* and *Venture*, which were sunk with explosive charges. Two days later he could torpedo and sink the British merchant ship *SS Fulgens* near the Haisborough Light Vessel. The patrol ended for *UB-10* with the stopping and sinking of the drifter *Alert*.

Steinbrinck described the crews of trawlers as usually friendly and willing (probably out of fear!). Usually they were manned by four or five men and offered him and his crew fish and other supplies. Mostly they would point out smoke on the horizon which meant the approach of a possible warship. One

UB-10 has left the lock and heads on the canal towards Bruges (TT)

◄ *UB-10* awaits to enter the canal towards Bruges after a successful patrol. On the extended periscope hang several flags of sunken ships (TT)

UB-10 on manoeuvers in Zeebrugge Roads (Heiko Hermans)

227

of the fishermen had also been crewing a vessel which had been sunk by *UB-12* in the same week.(126)

It was obvious that Steinbrinck wanted to thin out the British trawler fleet and managed to sink the drifters *Xmas Rose* and *Arbor Vitae* off Lowestoft and torpedo the merchant ship *SS Rosalie* (4.243 BRT). Steinbrinck often felt sympathy for the friendly crews who offered them flowers and fish. He towed their lifeboat with

A U-boat would often surface amidst a fleet of trawlers and 'ask' for fresh fish from the fishermen (TT)

UB-10 to the nearest Dutch merchant ship who took them aboard. By the evening ten August, *UB-10* would end its patrol with the sinking of 10 more drifters off Cromer. These concerned *Esperance, Trevear, Young Admiral, Palm, George Crabbe, Illustrious, Welcome, George Borrow, Oceans Gift* and *Humphrey*.

From 23 to 27 August 1915, *UB-10* was used as a defensive weapon against British monitors bombarding Zeebrugge. Together with *UB-5* and *UB-17* she went in for the attack, but Steinbrinck missed his chance at attacking the British as they had were long gone when they arrived on the scene. But her patrol was not in vain and that same day *UB-10* spotted and saved two survivors from the recently sunk torpedo boat *A-15*. *A-15* had been engaged and sunk by two Royal Naval torpedo boats on the Middelkerke bank.

It would be a few months later, in December 1915, that *UB-10* would have anymore successes. In the early hours of the 19th she left Zeebrugge to arrive at Boulogne Roads around midnight. It was a clear night, with a full moon and a becalmed sea. Seven anchored merchant ships were spotted, but *UB-10* could not attack on the surface in such circumstances. Steinbrinck therefore ordered to submerge *UB-10* to a depth of 8 m and proceed. The ships were grouped behind Boulogne light vessel. As *UB-10* carried only two torpedoes, Steinbrinck had to make the decision which ships to aim at and sink with his load. At a distance of 450 m he fired on the furthest ship, which was hit and sank after four minutes. Two smaller ships tried to escape him and he fired on the fourth one at a distance of 800 m. At 01h00 *UB-10* sailed past the light vessel and after seven minutes there was nothing to be seen of the torpedoed ships, the *SS Belford* and *SS Huntly*. After a 35-hour patrol *UB-10* returned back to base and she would be the first small UB-boat to successfully use torpedoes in the Dover-Calais area.

On 13 January 1916 *UB-10* was transferred to her new captain: *Oberleutnant z. S. Reinhold Saltzwedel*. *UB-10* had known her most successes under Steinbrinck, who managed to sink a total of 27 ships (13.379 BRT). Fourteen other captains succeeded him, but none of them came close to the same numbers.

It would only be on its 35th patrol, on 19 March 1916, that *UB-10* managed to gain a result. In the area near to the Kentish Knock light vessel Saltzwedel managed to hit the British *SS Port Dalhousie* with an underwater shot.

The successes which *UB-10* had known before seemed to have passed and she was plagued by problems on her 36th patrol. Saltzwedel was not able to locate any targets near the Kentish Knock due to the large presence of enemy torpedo boats. After this, damage was observed to the regulators of the hydroplanes. On the second day of her patrol, on 21 March, just before *UB-10* wanted to engage a merchant ship, the hydroplanes refused to respond and the U-boat dived uncontrollably to the seabed. The helmsmen managed to bring *UB-10* back up to depth but she hit a submerged wreck which damaged her slightly. *UB-10* made it safely back to port, but had to undergo a week of repairs in Bruges.

During the 41st mission, on 1 May 1916, the crew of *UB-10* was able to down a British seaplane with their machinegun. Saltzwedel did not gain any further successes on the five following patrols and he had to relent his command to *Oberleutnant z. S.* Gustav Buch. Buch had even less success on 11 missions and was only able to torpedo the British torpedoboat *HMS Lassoo* about 8 miles west of the Maas light vessel on 13 August. Command of *UB-10* changed four times between 12 September and 3 March 1917, and a total of 14 unsuccessful patrols were carried out.

It would only be on its 73rd patrol, from 20 to 23 March 1917, that *UB-10*, under her new captain, *Oberleutnant z. S.* Erich von Rohrscheidt, that another success would be gained. *UB-10* came upon the heavily damaged Dutch steamship *SS Amstelstroom* on 23 March to the northeast of the North Hinder. She had been abandoned by her crew after she had been heavily damaged by German torpedo boats the night before. Von Rohrscheidt decided to torpedo and sink the ship.

One month later UB-10 torpedoed and sunk the Dutch *SS Minister Tak van Poortvliet* and on the same day managed to cheat death. At 10h20 the bridge watch spotted an enemy periscope and at the same time saw the tracks of two torpedoes heading for her! It had been too late to take evasive action. The first torpedo just missed her stern and the second one hit *UB-10* amidships, but failed to explode! A third fired torpedo failed to miss *UB-10* as well due to malfunction of the depth setting and ran beneath her hull. *UB-10* immediately submerged and was able to escape the British submarine. The next day *UB-10*

During the summer of 1980, the wreck of *UB-10* was discovered and salvaged by the Tijdelijke Vereniging voor Bergingswerken and re-buried on the outside of the Zeebrugge Mole (Piet Lagast)

was able to sink the Dutch sailing ship *Elizabeth* with explosive charges.

Thirteen unsuccessful patrols followed, with two new commanders.

It would only be on 20 August, 1917, on its 92nd patrol, that *UB-10* managed to sink another ship. This was the British *SS Edernian*, which was torpedoed 6 miles southwest of Southwold. Her new captain, *Oberleutnant z. S.* Fritz Gregor was able to sink a further three drifters off the east coast. These were the British *Unity* and *Rosary* and the Belgian *Jeannot*.

His career on *UB-10* was shortlived and between 8 September 1917 and 12 September 1918 followed only seven patrols, which were all without result. *UB-10's* luck seemed to have run out and there were no more results although it carried out another 23 patrols before the war ended.

On 5 October 1918, *UB-10* came to an inglorious end when she was sunk on purpose off the coast of Heist so as she would not fall into enemy hands. This was about half a mile out to sea, off Heist, where she was hit by gunfire from the *Braunschweig* battery (also known at the 'Zoute' battery).

The remains of UB-10 were re-discovered in the summer of 1980 by the Tijdelijke Vereniging van Bergingswerken[127] and lifted off the seabed by the salvage vessel *Norma*. Divers Piet Lagast and Johan de Vent, then employed by the company, witnessed a relatively intact wreck which only missed the outer hull and conning tower. It could be that the tower had been hit by a shell fired from the Braunschweig battery or just had been lost due to the regular trawling activities after the Second World War. During the salvage *UB-10* hung in the slings of the gigantic crane, but at that very moment no one knew what was to be done with the wreck. The naval bomb disposal unit forbade any access to the wreck and there was no interest to make an investigation to remove possible ordnance. In the end it was decided not to scrap *UB-10* but to have it re-buried on the outside of the former Zeebrugge Mole. The wreck was covered up with sand and lies now at a depth of 15 m beneath the modern container port.

UB-12

On 2 March 1915 *UB-12* was launched and, just like her sistership, was transported by rail to Antwerp. She was commissioned on 29 March 1915 and came under command of *Kapitänleutnant* Hans Nieland. *UB-12* would sink a total of 18 ships during her career.

On the 8th mission, on 23 July 1915, the crew of *UB-12* experienced some terrifying moments when their U-boat became entangled in a net, when cruising on the surface. Luckily for them it was a 'normal' lost net from a trawler and not one of the steel nets which the British had been depositing in many locations against the U-boats. After some tugging, *UB-12* was able to free the propeller and surfaced about 30 miles off Lowestoft. In a kind of revenge *UB-12* attacked four drifters in the same area. They were the *Kathleen, Henry Charles, Prosper* and *Activity* which were sent to the bottom. In the next two patrols another five drifters were sunk in the same area with explosive charges. After a few weeks of patrols in the same area, *Oberleutnant z. S.* Wilhelm Kiel took over command of *UB-12* on 21 November 1915. Initially Kiel had difficulty booking any successes until he was able to sink three drifters to the southeast of Lowestoft on 21 February 1916. These were the British *W.E. Brown* and

Oleander and the Belgian *La Petitte Henriette*. Almost two months later, on 10 April, *UB-12* torpedoed the British *SS Silksworth Hall*. Kiel's command ended during the middle of June 1916 after he had rescued the crew of a crashed French aircraft.

Oberleutnant z. S. Georg Gerth took over command of *UB-12* on 26 June 1916, but initially failed to book any successes. On 5 July Gerth had been the last person to see the returning *UC-7*. *UC-7* would be lost with all hands due to mine explosion.

On 6 September the Norwegian merchant ship *SS Rilda* was sunk in the Hoofden and the next day the Dutch *SS Niobe* was forced by *UB-12* to head to Zeebrugge. *Niobe* would spend the rest of the war in Bruges as an accommodation ship. On his last trip Gerth managed to sink the drifter *Marjorie* at Smith's Knoll.

Command of *UB-12* was given to *Oberleutnant z. S.* Fritz Moecke on 4 November 1916. Between December 1916 and January 1917 he was responsible for the type change of his U-boat. The bow section of *UB-12* was totally reconstructed to carry four mineshafts with a storage capacity of eight mines.

From the beginning of 1917, the newly constructed *UB-12* left on her first patrol to the Calais area. She now had a new commander, *Oberleutnant z. S.* Ernst Steindorff, but did not know any successes. It was only by 23 March that one of her mines was able to sink the destroyer *HMS Laforey* 5 miles to the northwest of Cap Griz Nez. Patrols 50 to 54 consisted of mine-laying operations in the area of the Dyck light vessel, between Gravelines and Calais. On 20 April, the minesweeper *Nepaulin* and six days later the *SS Alhama* sank in the fields of *UB-12* to the north of Calais.

UB-12 carried out another 11 patrols until 10 July 1917, mainly in the same area, but also on the British east coast off Aldeburgh. Near Aldeburgh the British *SS Dulwich* and off Calais the minesweeper *Jupiter I*, were sunk.

Her last captain was *Oberleutnant z. S.* Ernst Schöller who took over command on 10 May 1918. His only success was the sinking of the British drifter *Calceolaria* near the Elbow buoy. *UB-12* never returned from her 98th mission. She had left Zeebrugge on 19 August 1918 to lay mines in the area of the Goodwins. Nothing was ever heard again of *UB-12* or her 19 crew. It was thought that she had been mined in the North Sea.

For more information on the wreck of *UB-12*, see the wreck description of *UC-10*.

UB-13

UB-13 was a typical, small coastal submarine which had been built on the Weser Werft Bremen and launched as builder number 222 on 8 March 1915. She too was disassembled and transported by rail from

The crew of an armed trawler take on lines from *UB-10*, to help her berth off the Mole (BArch)

231

UB-13 undergoing diving trials in the small merchant dock in Bruges, 1915 (TT)

Four seamen on the lookout for the enemy on board *UB-13* (TT)

UB-13 lies alongside a tug boat in Ostend harbour. In the background lies the packetboat *Princesse Joséphine* (TT)

In the Zeebrugge locks: *UB-13* lies alongside a UC-I and a UB-I type boat (TT)

At the end of July 1915, *UB-13* returns from a successful patrol on the British east coast. From the extended periscope hang the flags of the sunken trawlers *Salacia*, *Iceni* and *Young Percy* (TT)

Germany to Antwerp and rebuilt on the Hoboken wharf. She went into service on 6 April 1915 and stood under command of *Oberleutnant z. S.* Walther Becker. Between her commissioning and sinking *UB-13* was able to carry out 35 missions, which resulted in the sinking of 11 ships. Her area of operations was the North Hinder, the Thames Estuary and the British east coast.

UB-13 would only gain her first success on her sixth patrol, when, in June 1915 she managed to torpedo *SS Dulcie* off Aldebrugh. This was followed by the drifters *Salacia, Iceni* and *Young Percy* on 27 and 28 July. But *UB-13* proved not to be such a lucky boat for Becker due to all kinds of problems. The following patrol had to be cancelled due to the compass failing. On the tenth patrol, when she reached the Shipwash light vessel, her bow became entangled by a steel net. *UB-13* was not able to break free and even with the threat of enemy surface, craft Becker had to surface her so as to free the bow with wirecutters and chizels. The crew were able to free her on time and submerge just before a torpedo boat came on a ramming course towards her. This would not be the last incident for *UB-13*.

On 20 February 1916, the Belgian smack *Z-10*, *David Marie*, was stopped by *UB-13* and ordered to Zeebrugge. It was suspected by the Germans that the crew were involved in espionage (TT)

The crew of *Z 10*, obviously not looking very happy, have been ordered alongside *UB-13* to explain their activities... (TT)

In the middle of August 1915, when off Cromer, a malfunction in the firing mechanism of the torpedo tubes occurred. This major problem forced them to break off the patrol and return home. After the problem had been solved in Zeebrugge, *UB-13* returned to the Cromer area a week later, but now the tower hatch was not able to be shut watertight and the patrol had to be cancelled once more. A frustrated Becker carried out another e unsuccessful missions in the Middelkerke-Thornton area whereafter he was relieved of the command of *UB-13*.

Oberleutnant z. S. Karl Neumann was appointed as her new captain on 15th December 1915. Neumann managed to take *UB-12* on 12 patrols, but all without any success. It would only be on the 13th trip that something happened. On 20 February 1916 the Belgian drifter *Z 10*, *David Marie*, was brought into Zeebrugge as a prize. Shortly after the British drifters *Reliance*, *Try On*, *Harold* and *Trevose*, were sunk to the northeast of Lowestoft.

On 12 March 1916, her third and final captain, *Oberleutnant z. S.* Arthur Metz, took over command of the unfortunate *UB-13*. His first trip, the 33rd for *UB-13*, would seem to give him his first success. To the northeast of the North Hinder light vessel a large ship at anchor loomed out of the thick fog which had

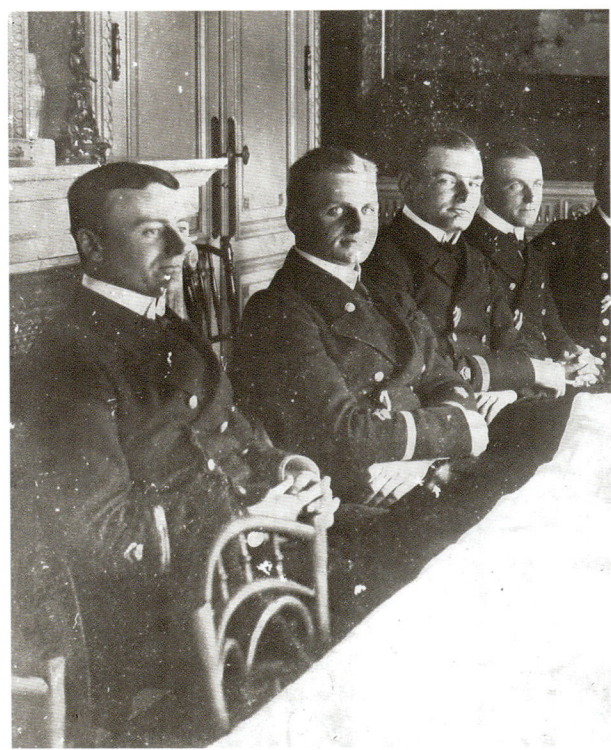

Officers of the U-boat *Flottille Flandern* sit together for a meeting in Bartenbach's residence. *Oberleutnant z. S.* Arthur Metz, captain of *UB-13* is the third from left (Heiko Hermans)

engulfed the area. Metz thought it concerned a British cruiser or aircraft carrier and fired a torpedo at her. In the end it proved to be the Dutch liner *SS Tubantia*, a neutral vessel. *SS Tubantia* was sunk, but all passengers and crew were saved by a Dutch torpedo boat. This incident caused international outrage and protest from Holland against German 'aggression' on the high seas. Metz was severely reprimanded by the German Admiralty for his mistake.

In the middle of April 1916 UB-13 returned to British territory, this time near the Kentish Knock. Again Metz managed to pick a wrong target and torpedoed a Danish schooner laden with salt destined for neutral Sweden. The German Empire had to pay compensation to its owners.

UB-13 left Zeebrugge on 23 April 1916 for its 36th and final patrol. She was accompanied by *UB-6*, *UB-10* and *UB-12*. Metz had received orders to attack shipping in the Southwold area. After her departure the German Admiralty lost all trace of *UB-13*. It was suspected that the day after her departure from Zeebrugge she had foundered in a British minefield.[(128)]

After returning from a successful patrol, the crew of *UB-13* are ready for a spot of leave on land (TT)

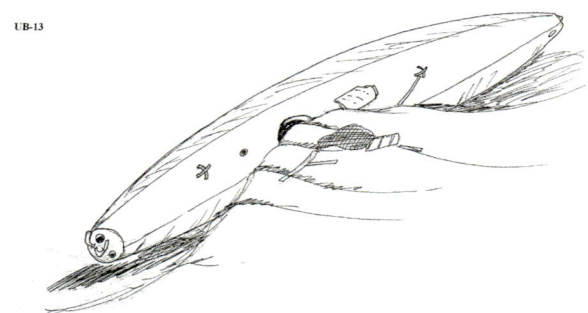

Drawing of the wreck of *UB-13*, which lies in the deep end of the Thornton Bank. She is intact, but misses the conning tower (TT)

British reports confirmed German suspicions. The British had started the laying of a large minefield about 18 miles to the north of the Flemish coastline. The intention was to make a tight cordon around the Belgian sea against sortying and returning U-boats. Four minelayers, with speeds up to 14 knots, were able to lay a total of 1,421 mines. They were accompanied by six drifters which each carried an additional 24 mines. On the Thornton Ridge a double line of deep mines 15 miles long were laid, together with 13 miles of mined steel nets and 14 light beacons. When the deep mines had been laid out, a number of explosive nets were sown on the seaward side of the field. Nets were also laid in the Westhinder area, 30 miles to the northwest of Ostend. On that day several explosions were heard from the direction of the nets. It concerned *UB-10* which had become entangled and attempted to free itself. In trying to break free she had detonated several mines, but without doing any damage to the U-boat. After eight hours of struggling, *UB-10* managed to get out and reach port safely. *UB-13* would not be as lucky. She managed to hit the anchor cable of the drifter *Gleaner of the Sea*, near the Thornton Ridge. Because of its maneuvering to break free, it hit and detonated a mine which had been in tow by the convoy. A patrolling aircraft noticed what was happening and dropped a bomb on the spot where wreckage and oil was welling up to the surface. *HMS Afridi* also came on the scene and swept the area with an explosive paravane where *UB-13* had been sunk.[129] No survivors were found and the wreck remained unexplored until it was discovered in the early 1990s.

The wreck of this UB-I class U-boat was first found by Dirk Termote in 1992 in position 51° 33' 142 N 02° 51' 653 E. The wreck is marked on the chart with the wreck-marking 28,0 WK and lies in deeper water to the north of the Thornton Ridge. *UB-13* reclines to port and has a maximum depth of 35 m. The remains consist of the pressure hull, minus tower and superstructure. In the bow, two closed bronze torpedo tube lids are visible. Beneath the hull is a scour where the depth is 35 m. On this part, beneath the hull, there is visible damage. The outer skin of the vessel is seen to be pressed inwards. There are several holes between the steel reinforcements making it possible to get a glance within the pressure hull. To the bottom of the bow a stowed anchor is also visible. The midships' section is heavily sanded up on both sides and parts of superstructure are spread around. On the deck a small lifting hook is visible and the oval opening of where the tower used to stand is filled to the brim with sand. Tower and superstructure are not present anymore and were probably destroyed by the explosions caused by the paravane. Behind the opening of the tower there is a triangular construction on deck with a closed hatch. This is the former torpedo-loading hatch.

UB-16

UB-16 was launched on 26 April 1915 and was transported in sections by rail to Antwerp. She was commissioned on 1 June 1915 and came under the command of *Oberleutnant z. S. Hans Valentiner*.

The career of *UB-16* would span a period of nearly three years in which she would fulfill a total of 86 patrols, resulting in the sinking of only 25 enemy ships. Valentiner was able to destroy the trawlers *E&C*, *Boy Horace* and *Economy* to the southeast of Lowestoft with explosive charges during his first voyage, from 1 to 6 June 1915.

A U-boat on the canal cruises in the direction of Bruges (TT)

A not so common occurrence: this drawing illustrates the collision between *UB-16* and a British submarine in the area known as the Hoofden on 27 February 1917 (Carl Engelien)

Oberleutnant z. S. Vicco von der Lühe, captain of *UB-16* (WZ-Bilddienst)

A month later, *UB-16* found herself in the area off Calais where not a single enemy target could be found. The patrol after this was however more successful when Valentiner managed to discover the damaged *UB-2* and tow it to Ostend.

On 8 August *UB-16* proved that mistakes at sea were not uncommon, when she was bombed by three German airships. Luckily for *UB-16* all bombs missed their target and she was able to return back to base unscathed.

At the beginning of September 1915 Valentiner had received orders to attack British trawlers in the Lowestoft area together with *UB-2*. The Q-ship *Inverlyon* was spotted on 7 September and taken under carbine fire by the crew of *UB-16*. The schooner did not react and Valentiner had the machinegun open fire on her. Two crewmen on *Inverlyon* were hit and wounded, the ship stopped and turned. When *UB-16* got within half a mile of *Inverlyon*, camouflage dropped from the 3-pounder gun and the Ensign was run up. The bridge watch of *UB-16* reacted swiftly, submerged and fired a torpedo at *Inverlyon* which

A-B-C: Underwater photos of the wreck of *UB-16*, sunk by *HMS E-34* on the North Hinder. The photos show massive destruction of the bow as well as the keel and conning tower (Nicolas Mouchart)

missed its mark. Some time later *UB-16* was again accompanied by *UB-2* and they both managed to destroy the drifters *Victorious*, *Emblem*, *Boy Ernie* and *Nimrod*. *UB-16* proved to be a nice target from the air and on 8 September she was yet again unsuccessfully bombed by a German airship.

In the following months there followed a number of unsuccessful patrols in the North Hinder area. During her 30th patrol, the Belgian drifter *Z.20* was spotted and stopped. *Z.20* was sailing under a Dutch flag and was put under suspicion of espionage and escorted into Zeebrugge on 23 June 1916.

During the following patrol, on 24 July, the body of *Oberleutnant z. S.* Georg Haag, captain of the missing *UC-7*, was found floating near the Schouwen bank. Haag was retrieved but later on given a burial at sea.

In the morning of 27 February 1917, *UB-16* just managed to escape death. In the area of the Hoofden she collided with the British submarine *HMS E-16*. *UB-16* was on the surface when it suddenly beached itself on the foredeck of submerged *E-16*! There was a moment of shock, whereafter her captain, *Oberleutnant z. S.* Niemer, immediately ordered full astern and he then had a torpedo fired at his British adversary at a distance of 700 m. The torpedo missed its target and both submarines sought the comfort of the depths to escape.

In January 1918, *UB-16* had another encounter with a British submarine. The periscope of *HMS C-16* suddenly emerged to the starboard of the surfaced *UB-16*. The watchkeepers on *UB-16* signalled to the periscope and after a while realised that it belonged to the enemy. Her captain ordered full ahead to escape. A torpedo fired from *C-16* narrowly missed the fleeing *UB-16*.

On 22 April 1918 *Oberleutnant z. S.* Vicco von der Lühe took over command of *UB-16* as her last captain. On 25 April *UB-16* had the honour as first U-boat to navigate past the blocked Zeebrugge harbour. During the night of 22 to 23 April, the Royal Navy had sunk three blockships in the entrance to the Zeebrugge Canal. But at high tide it was still possible for U-boats to slip past the obstacles. This would be her 85th patrol which she carried out without any success off Lowestoft.

The career of *UB-16* came to its end on the 86th patrol, which ran from 6 to 10 May 1918. According to British sources *UB-16* was attacked in the evening of 10 May off Harwich, in position 52° 06' 630 N 02° 01' 290 E, by the British submarine *HMS E-34*. *HMS E-34*,

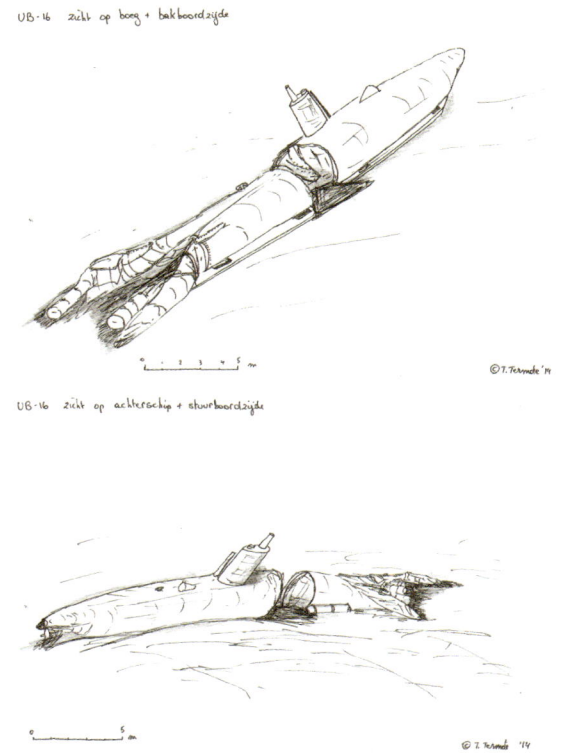

Drawings of the wreck of *UB-16*, sunk on the North Hinder (TT)

under command of Lt. Richard Pulleyne, was on a return trip to Harwich when he observed the submarine. As it was an area where many British submarines were patrolling, Pulleyne took the time to carefully study the silhouette of his adversary. In the end he was certain of its identity and ordered two torpedoes to be fired at *UB-16*, which now had changed course towards them.[130] The first torpedo hit the bow, but failed to explode. The second hit the hull just forward of the tower, exploded after which *UB-16* immediately disappeared. As by miracle *HMS E-34* managed to pick von der Lühe as sole survivor from the sea. The British brought him down to the control room where they demanded to know his U-boat number. He refused to speak, but the barrel of a pistol was pushed against his head. Electrical connections from a heater were attached to his feet so as he could be tortured to make him confess. After surviving the torpedoing and torture, *Oberleutnant z. S.* Vicco von der Lühe would finally die in a British POW camp a year later.

After the action, Commander Damant and his dive team were called to the area to try and locate the wreck. *HMS Moonfleet*, a salvage tug displacing

A UB-I boat manoeuvers to enter the lock (TT)

145 tons, searched a large area to the north of the Gabbard sandbank. An anomaly was discovered and divers descended in circumstances of nil visibility. According to the dive reports, only sections of steel plate were felt and it was assumed that the U-boat had disintegrated after impact.

The Royal Naval dive team most probably had discovered other wreckage as *UB-16* lies for the most part intact at a depth of 27 m. Its present day position is 52° 06' 075 N 01° 58' 658 E, only just over a mile from the original position which was given by Lieutenant Pulleyne after the sinking. First discovered and dived by wreckhunter Bob Hickson, she was later identified by the author as being *UB-16*. The wreck lies at a 45° angle to port in an area with large sandwaves. From bow just up to the engine room bulkhead, the submarine is intact. The tower still stands proud and there is a periscope standard with retracted periscope. Heavy damage is visible in the former engine room compartment and stern area. Here the starboard side is crumpled and torn, and many of the plates of the pressure hull have caved inwards. The wreck abruptly ends and the propeller shaft, which is sheared off, is visible. About 20 m from the wreck lie the remains of the tip of the stern as well as the rest of the shaft and the propeller. It is clear that the captain of *HMS E-34* had mistaken the location of the impact of his second torpedo on *UB-16*. It had struck the engine room and not the forward area. The explosion had devastating results, which had even ripped off 3 m of the stern area and deposited it away from the main body of the wreck.

UB-17

After *UB-17* had been assembled on the Hoboken dockyard, she went into service on 4 May 1915 under the capable command of Oberleutnant z. S. Ralph Wenninger.

UB-17 would mainly patrol in the areas of the North Hinder, Galloper and east coast areas of England. Its maiden voyage went without result, but on the second patrol, from 29 May until 2 June 1915, *UB-17* was nearly sunk twice. First by enemy aircraft and next by British destroyers which were towing acoustic devices in their wakes. Wenninger managed to take quick, evasive action by diving rapidly to the seabed. Ill luck seemed to pursue *UB-17* as on her third patrol only neutral shipping was observed and on her fourth mission she got tangled in a U-boat net off Orfordness. Wenninger managed to rip through the net by ordering full ahead. The fifth patrol did not fare much better when the compass refused to respond and *UB-17* was forced to head back to base.

The first success was made on his following patrol, from 18 to 20 July 1915, in the area near the Shipwash light vessel. Wenninger torpedoed the British tanker *Batoum*, but she was able to ground herself in a depth of 12 m. The day after the torpedoing of *Batoum*, *UB-17* got stuck in a net towed by patrol craft. Wenninger ordered her to descend to the bottom at 26 m. It was only after an hour, after making the U-boat do horizontal and vertical movements that they were able to tear the net.

The seventh patrol, running from 27 to 31 July 1915, did not give any results due to stormy weather and it was only on 6 August that *UB-17* managed to destroy the drifters *C.E.S.*, *Ivan*, *Fisherman* and *Hesperus*. Technical difficulties seemed to hound *UB-17* and the patrol had to be cut short due to leakage of the torpedo tube. It seemed that the German Admiralty had lots of patience with Wenninger as for his ninth patrol he was ordered to attack enemy monitors shelling Zeebrugge port. The loading of her torpedoes went much too slow and before *UB-17* even managed to put to sea, the bombarding fleet had long gone. As consolation price, *UB-17* ordered the Belgian schooner *Leon Mathilde* in to Oostende. The following patrols were carried out off the Flemish coast. Near the Dyck light vessel, *UB-17* managed to torpedo the French patrol vessel *Saint Pierre I* on 22 September 1915. It would be two months later before its next victim fell: the French netlayer *Jesus Maria* on the Bergues Bank.

For Wenninger, his last action with *UB-17* came on 30 January 1916. Off Lowestoft, the Belgian trawler *Marguerite* and the British drifters *Artur William*, *Radium* and *Hilda* were sunk.

Between 7 February and 8 July 1916 *UB-17* changed command six times, but no successes were made. Patrols were mostly carried out off the Flemish coast and in the area of the Hoofden. On 4 December 1916 command was taken over by *Oberleutnant z. S.* Ulrich Meier and he was only able to stop one ship. This was on 15 December when the Norwegian *SS Birgit* was stopped carrying food and victuals for Great Britain. As she was heading to the enemy, *UB-17* had the right to seize her and ordered her to sail to Zeebrugge. Meier carried out 20 unsuccessful patrols with *UB-17*. In the fall of 1917 command went to its penultimate captain, *Oberleutnant z. S.* Johannes Ries, who only managed to sink the trawler *Forward* off Southwold.

The last captain of *UB-17* would be *Oberleutnant z. S.* Albert Branscheid. He carried out five patrols (voyages 86 to 90) near the British east coast, all without results.

The 91st mission, after 11 March 1918, would prove to be fatal to *UB-17* and her crew. Grant mentions an attack by a Coastal Motor Boat, *CMB-20* on 18 March in the southern North Sea, which possibly could concern *UB-17*.[131] But it could also concern a different submarine as seven days was long for a patrol for a UB-I boat, unless it had suffered damage and was struggling to make its way home.

The heavily damaged wreck of *UB-17* was discovered in the late 1990s by Dirk Termote in the Belgian part of the North Hinder area. She lies at a depth of 41 m, in position 51° 40' 820 N 02° 25' 100 E and is almost upright with a slight inclination to port. Stern and midships areas, with tower are intact. The tower hatch is shut and the periscope is present, but retracted. About 4 m to the front of the tower, the U-boat is reduced to flattened wreckage. A heavy tear runs over this part and various hull plating has been forced inwards. Large amounts of molten battery parts lie strewn over the wreck and on the seabed. Some steel compressed airtanks are visible through the wreckage. The torpedo room of *UB-17* has been severely damaged and partly compressed. The damages on the wreck point in the direction that *UB-17* could have been hit by a torpedo from *CMB-20*.

UB-18

UB-18 was the first *UB-II* class U-boat to enter Zeebrugge on 16 February 1916. It would prove to be one of the most successful U-boats of the Flanders Flotilla and in only two years time she managed to sink 128 ships, a total amount of more than 130.000 BRT. This was possible due to the daring of two of her captains: Steinbrinck and Lafrenz.

The first commander of *UB-18* was Steinbrinck and during 24 February to 29 March 1916 he managed to sink seven enemy ships. At his return on 29 March, a year after the creation of the *Flandern Flottille*, he was awarded the order *Pour le Mérite* for his successes with *UB-10* and *UB-18*.

On his fifth patrol Steinbrinck returned to the Le Havre area. When he looked through the optics of the periscope on the evening of 4 April, he was disappointed. The anchorage was empty and he had to content himself with the sinking of the Norwegian *SS Baus* near Cap de la Heve. The patrol ended with the sinking of a further three ships.

Later that month, *UB-18* found herself in company with *UB-29* off Lowestoft. They had been ordered to lay in wait, as in the early hours of 24 April, the German High Seas Fleet made a sortie to attack the British coast. During the attack, Steinbrinck observed two British submarines which approached them. They were E-class submarines and he fired two torpedoes at them, both failing to hit the target or explode. After the failed attack *UB-18* surfaced and kept watch on the surface. Just after noon the watchkeepers again noticed two British submarines which were righting their radio masts as they lay on the surface. *UB-18* went in for the attack and yet again two fired torpedoes failed to explode. One of the British submarines, *HMS E-26*, noticed *UB-18* and went full ahead in an attempt to ram her adversary. *HMS E-26* managed to hit the netcutter on the bow of *UB-18* and submerged. At 17h40, Steinbrinck finally managed to hit the other submarine, *HMS E-22*, with a single torpedo. Even with the presence of the second submarine Steinbrinck

A UC-I boat in the Zeebrugge lock (TT)

had *UB-18* come to the surface to approach the sinking area and managed to pick up two survivors. These were signalman Harrod and 2nd engineer Buckingham. Both had been saved after floating around for an hour.[132]

The tenth patrol brought *UB-18* higher in the North Sea, in Scottish waters, where she would operate for two weeks. Around the end of the patrol, on 15 July, the crew of *UB-18* managed to board the Dutch schooner *Dina* and the Norwegian brig *Bertha* and fire both ships. Both had cargoes of pitprops destined for the tunneling companies on the Western front. On the route home *UB-18* managed to up its tally with the sinking of the drifters *V.M.G.*, *Gertrude*, *Waverley*, *Glance*, *Loch Tay* and *Loch Nevis* to the south of the Haisborough Sands.

Once out again on patrol, *UB-18* found herself in the Channel where she hunted for larger targets. On the British side, *UB-18* was able to sink ten ships and five off Le Harve. In the following patrol Steinbrinck decided to return to the same area as success had been good and off Beachy Head he stopped the merchant ships *SS Teesborough* and *SS Netta* (370 BRT). The ship's papers were examined after which both ships were sunk with explosive charges. On 5 September, followed the British *SS City of Ghent* and the Belgian *SS Marcel* which were en route from Hull to Cherbourg with cargoes of coal.

On 7 September, when *UB-18* found herself 10 miles to the south of the Lizard, she stopped a schooner with a shot in front of the bow. The innocent looking sailing ship immediately returned fire with two concealed guns. *UB-18* fired and hit the sailing ship several times, but broke off the battle as the enemy shells fell too close to the U-boat. Once submerged, Steinbrinck tried to intercept the schooner with a torpedo, but dense fog appeared and he let her escape. It had been the Q-ship *Q 17*, *Helgoland* (182 BRT), which was armed with four 12-pounder guns and a Maxim. *UB-18* continued on her mission and in the following days was able to sink four ships of varying nationalities off the Scillies. By the evening of 9 September, three steamships hove into view. When *UB-18* was spotted, the crews of the Norwegian ships immediately abandoned their vessels. The third ship, which was painted totally black, had a distinctive high bridge and two radio masts. It stopped for a short while, but continued on her way. The gunners of *UB-18* managed to hit the mysterious vessel six times which then caught fire. The ship stopped and let down its lifeboats halfway. Nothing further happened and Steinbrinck was apprehensive of the situation and ordered further firing on the target. Some time later the ensign was raised and fire on *UB-18* opened. It concerned another Q-ship, *Q-4*, *Carrigan Head* (4.201 BRT) which was armed with a 4-inch and two 12 pounder guns. *UB-18* dived and immediately commenced the attack. Steinbrinck fired a torpedo at the now fleeing *Q-4*, but it missed its target. At the helm of *Q-4* stood Lieutenant-Commander Herbert, formerly captain of the Q-ship *Baralong*. He had made quite a furore after he had sunk *U-27* with *Baralong* and then ordered to fire on the survivors.

Q-4 was lucky and managed to escape, but Steinbrinck did not stop there and the next day he sank 11 ships. His last victim on the 13th patrol was the Norwegian *SS Ethel*. Near the Cascets, *UB-18* had ordered *SS Ethel* to stop. On board there was a cargo of British coal destined for France. Steinbrinck ordered the crew to abandon ship in the lifeboats and fired his last torpedo at the ship. The torpedo ran beneath its hull and failed to explode. In the end the deck gun had to be used and with the last shells they fired into the *Ethel*. A few punctures were created, but the Norwegian refused to sink. In the meantime the supply of shells had run out and *Maschinenmaat* Müller decided to swim over to the ship. Once on board he opened the seacocks which made *SS Ethel* finally sink.

In October 1916, Steinbrinck would expand his horizons and bring *UB-18* to the western part of the Channel. He proved to have a nose to track down the enemy and on the second day of the patrol three ships were sunk off Le Havre after he had taken the risk of checking the ship's papers.

On 21 October *UB-18* reached the Cascets where she sank the Norwegian steamships *SS Fulvio* and *SS Rabbi* and the French sailing vessels *Condor* and *Brizeux*. On the morning of the next day they fired a warning shot at a merchant vessel which was sailing without a flag. As the ship did not react and just continued on its way, *UB-18* fired directly into its superstructure and hull. After the third shot the ensign appeared in the mast and the merchantman answered fire with two concealed guns. Steinbrinck had *UB-18* dive and tried to torpedo the Q-ship, but without result. It was the third time in his career that he had escaped from a Q-ship.

The third Q-ship seemed to be a sign for Steinbrinck to relent command of *UB-18* on 28 October to *Oberleutnant z. S.* Claus Lafrenz. Lafrenz had no success on his first patrol, the 15th for *UB-18*, and only encountered neutral ships. On the 16th patrol, which ran from 22 November to 5 December 1916, *UB-18* entered the Bristol Channel. During this patrol, in the western area of the Channel, Lafrenz managed to sink 17 ships with gunfire and/or explosive charges.

On his way back, when *UB-18* was south of Wolf Rock, Lafrenz wanted to halt a three-masted bark. After firing two warning shots, there came no reaction from the sailing ship. Lafrenz thought the superstructure and aft part of the ship suspicious and ordered the bridge and gunplatform cleared so as *UB-18* would ready to dive in an emergency. His suspicion was valid, because before even the last man had descended down the hatch, the bark dropped its camouflage and opened fire with two guns. It concerned the Q-ship *Mary B. Mitchell* (227 BRT) which had been armed with a 12-pounder and two 6-pounder guns. The shells flew wide and *UB-18* submerged. Again, *UB-18* was not able to sink the Q-ship and both vessels went on their respective courses. On 3 December, three ships were stopped and sunk to the southeast of the Eddystone.

In the Dover Straits, when *UB-18* was on the return leg of the patrol, the destroyer *HMS Llewellyn* spotted the U-boat and attacked. In the pursuit *UB-18* got entangled in a U-boat net, but was able to free itself later. The British wrongly indicated that *UB-18* had been sunk by *HMS Llewellyn*.

Between the end of December 1916 and 12 February 1917 two patrols were completed which resulted in the sinking of 11 ships. One was the Russian *SS Cerera* which was laden with 5,000 tons of coal destined for the French navy.

UB-18 saw a successful following two months under Lafrenz and 14 ships were added to its kills. On 15 May, luck would follow Lafrenz once more when they were to the north of Cap de la Hague and met a British Q-ship. When *UB-18* surfaced she lay 200 m away from the British vessel, later identified as the Q-ship *Glen* (113 BRT). This Q-ship proved to be much more aggressive and did not want to play the waiting game of helpless merchantman. From the moment the U-boat came into sight she opened fire with her two guns and it was only due to the quick reactions of the crew of *UB-18* that they were saved. At a distance of 4000 m *UB-18* surfaced again and opened fire on *Glen*. The action was shortlived and had to be broken off because of the pending darkness.

Leutnant z. S. Erich Dürr was first officer on board *UB-18* and was killed when she sunk in January 1918 (TT)

On 8 July, *Oberleutnant z. S.* Ulrich Meier took over command. Ulrich's first mission would be *UB-18's* 25th. Meier chose a total different area of operations than his predecessors and concentrated his actions on the North Hinder. On 22 July he was able to sink the Dutch sailing ship *Nereus* with gunfire and torpedo the steamship *SS Breda*. The unfortunate Breda had been shelled by *UB-35* some days before, but managed to escape. Two days later the tug *Oostzee* and its tow, the floating crane *Montevideo 488* cover went to the bottom. Both were on their way from Rotterdam to Uruguay. At the end of the patrol the sailing ships *Janna* and *Spes Mea* were also sunk. Three of the ships which had been sunk by *UB-18* in the North Hinder area have recently been rediscovered and dived upon.

On 22 September 1917 *UB-18* changed captains for the last time, now command went to *Oberleutnant z. S.* Georg Niemeyer. On her 29th patrol, from 6 to 15 October 1917 he managed to torpedo the British coal laden *SS Peebles* off Flamborough Head. During the following mission, on 31 October, *UB-18* got caught up in a battle with the Q-ship *Dargle* (176 BRT). This time *UB-18* had run out of her customary luck and was hit twice by the 6-pounder guns. Lucky for *UB-18* Niemeyer still managed to submerge his U-boat and escape death. Niemeyer would not have any further chance to prove his skills as *UB-18* would be lost on her 31st patrol. On 1 December 1917 *UB-18* left Zeebrugge to patrol the western area of the Channel. On 4 December, around 13h, she was 35 miles to the south of Start Point and exchanged signals with *U-84*. After this brief encounter all trace of *UB-18* vanished. According to British sources *UB-18* was rammed by the British trawler *Ben Lawer* just abaft the tower and was supposedly sunk with all hands in position 49° 17' N 05° 47' W. *Ben Lawer* was escorting a convoy of coalships on 9 December and had to brought into safety after the damage she had received from the ramming.[133]

We may accept that *UB-18* had probably been sunk in the western area of the Channel in the given position. Up to now, nothing is known about any discovered *UB-II* class U-boatwreck, mainly due to the large depths and the remoteness of the location.

UB-19

UB-19 was launched on 2 September 1915 and went into service on 17 December under the command of *Oberleutnant z. S.* Walter Becker. She arrived in Zeebrugge on 1 March 1916 and was added to the *Flandern Flottille*. Becker undertook 13 patrols between 9 March and 3 November 1916. He was not very successful and in eight months could only sink five drifters, two sailing ships and a steamship.

On 25 October, *UB-19* torpedoed the Belgian *SS Comtesse de Flandre* near the Casquets. After this trip, Becker was transferred to the U-boat school in Germany and *Oberleutnant z. S.* Erich Noodt took over command. On his first trip, the 14th for *UB-19*, the Dutch mailboat *RSS Koningin Regentes* was stopped and checked. The crew had acted suspiciously, by throwing packages over the side, when *UB-19* had hove into view. In the end the ship was let go. Noodt would not make any career with the *U-Flottille* because on his 15th mission, on 30 November 1916, *UB-19* met her end. A week before her sinking, *UB-19* had managed to sink four steamships off Beachy Head and Start Point. Finally *UB-19* would be sunk by gunfire from the Q-ship *Penshurst* in position 49° 56' N 02° 45' W.[134] The complete story of the battle can be read under the chapter concerning Q-ships.

The wreck of *UB-19* has not been located yet. Diver Innes McCartney has spent much research time in the area north of Hurd Deep in 1999 in an attempt to try to locate the wreck. It is surmised that *UB-19* was sunk mid-Channel somewhere between one of the Channel Islands and Start Point.

UB-20

UB-20 was launched on 26 September 1915 as construction number 250 with Blohm & Voss at Hamburg. After completion of trials she went into service on 10 February 1916 with the *Unterseeboots Flottille Kurland* in Libau and had *Oberleutnant z. S.* Max Viebeg as captain. In the Gulf of Finland *UB-20* was able to attack several Swedish, Finnish and Russian ships during eight patrols. Her ninth patrol meant a transfer to the *Unterseeboots Flottille Flandern*, arriving in Flanders on 26 March 1917. *UB-20* was assigned to Ostend and *Oberleutnant z. S.* Hermann Glimpf stood now at her helm. His first task was to intercept Allied shipping in the area of the Hoofden, North Hinder and the western part of the Channel. In 4 patrols Glimpf was able to sink 9 Dutch and British ships. At the end of her trip she was brought via the canal Ostend-Bruges to the *Kaiserliche Werft* for maintenance. Glimpf had been experiencing problems with the compass and periscope since early April 1917, after they had been dephtcharged. *UB-20* also seemed to have construction problems as the water pressure had forced fasteningbolts near the bow to blow, making the deck- and torpedo hatches difficult to shut. *UB-20* seemed to be plagued by bad luck and when lying in Bruges

A rare interior shot: three engineers pose between the diesel engines on board *UB-20* (Jörn Jensen)

UB-20

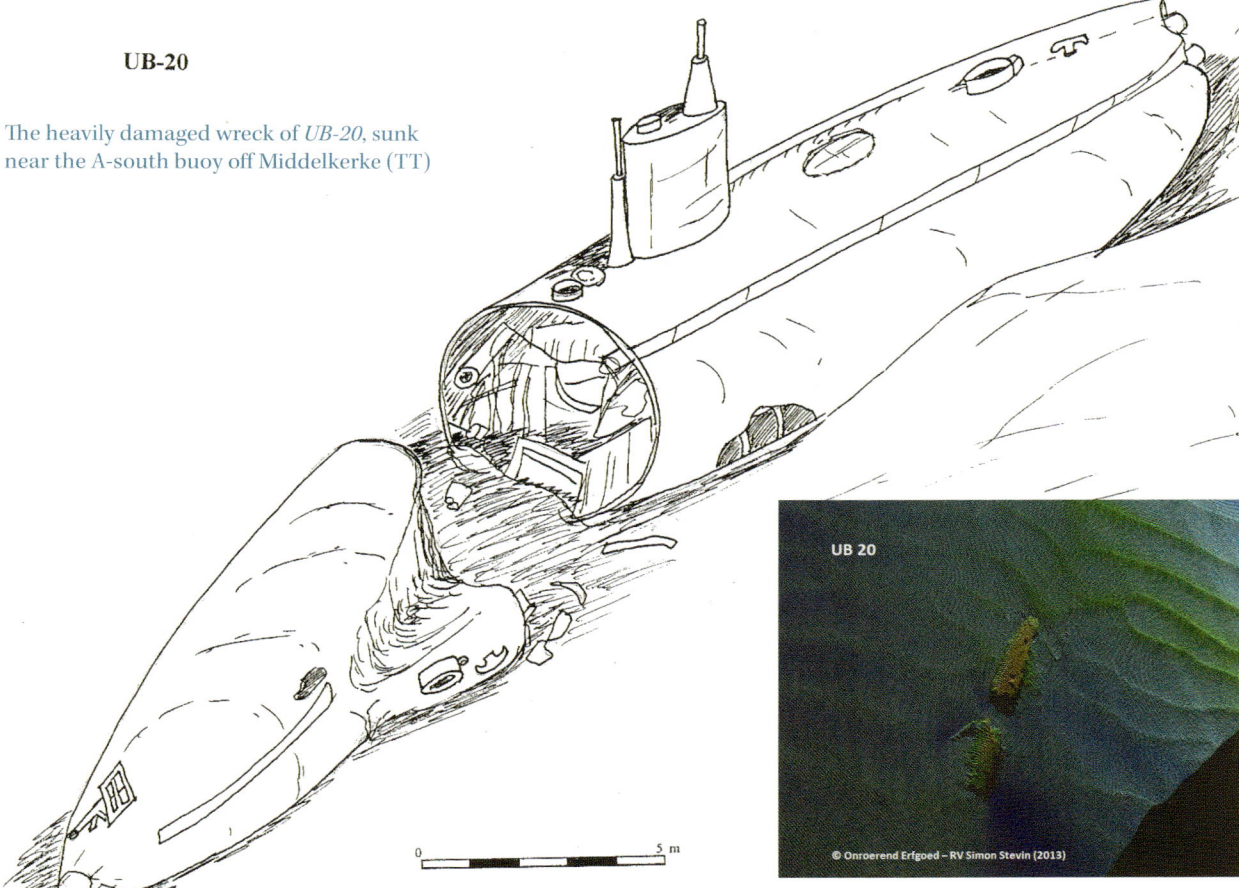

The heavily damaged wreck of *UB-20*, sunk near the A-south buoy off Middelkerke (TT)

Multibeam image of the wreck of *UB-20* (VIOE)

harbor she was bombed and damaged by British aircraft, forcing her to undergo five weeks of repairs.[135] On 28 July 1917, at 11h40, *UB-20* left Ostend harbor for a four-hour trial run to test the repairs done to the pressure hull. On board was only part of the crew, 13 men, as well as two men from the yard and two army officers. A large part of the crew had been taken ill from influenza and were being treated in hospital. British sources mistakenly suggest that Glimpf had embarked with *UB-20* on an unsanctioned pleasure trip, taking only half the crew and a large number of army officers and their girlfriends. Because there were only 12 trained men on board she would not have been able to handle and fell victim to an aerial attack.[136] After undergoing important repairs on the pressure hull, Glimpf would most certainly not take *UB-20* on a pleasure cruise. Before leaving Ostend harbour she had undergone several dive tests to make sure that a replaced hullplate would hold up, but now it was necessary to test her at a greater depth. Only the most necessary crewmen were kept on board as well as technical personnel to trace possible faults. The trial run would be undertaken in a 'safe area' and last only a couple of hours, but *UB-20* did not return and was given up as lost.

On the day of her disappearance two U-boats were engaged by British seaplanes. The situation of the wreck of *UB-20*, near the A-zuid, can write her off as one of the possible targets. The pilots mention in their report that it possibly concerned *UC*-type U-boats. This suspicion was later confirmed by the German Admiralty as being *UC-16* and *UC-65*.[137] From the coast also no incidents were observed in the air or on the surface of the sea in the area were *UB-20* was discovered. Damage on the wreck definitely points in the direction of a double mine explosion at the bow

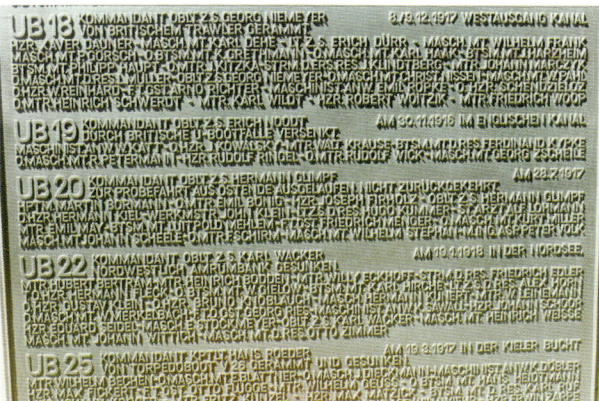

On the U-boat memorial at Möltenort, Kiel, names on plaques commemorate all the U-boats and crews lost during two World Wars (TT)

The grave of *Oberleutnant z. S.* Hermann Glimpf, wrongly written as Karl Glimpf, lies near the church of Loddenbjerg, Jutland (Gert Normann Andersen)

and near the engine room. The British Admiralty later confirmed that *UB-20* could have been lost in a newly laid British minefield. This field had been laid in secret on 25 July,[138] between the Westhinder and Akkaert banks. All 17 crewmen and passengers perished when *UB-20* was sunk. The body of Hermann Glimpf washed ashore in Jutland, on the Danish coast, on 3 September 1917. He was later buried near the church of Loddenbjerg under the wrong name Karl Glimpf.

The wreck of this *UB-II* class coastal patrol submarine is located near the Kwinte Bank, in position 51° 21' 190 N 02° 38' 326 E. It was discovered in 1988 by divers Dirk Termote and Piet Lagast and is indicated on the chart with the wreckmark 16,4 WK. *UB-20* lies broken in two parts at a maximum depth of 28 m. The bottom consists of hard sand with here and there clusters of small stones, not much larger than a fist. She is completely split at the engine room compartment, but both parts lie in a straight line to each other with a space of about 4 m between them. The aft section lies on its starboard side showing one of her propeller shafts and a depth rudder. At the front of the break, on the aft section, a glimpse inside the engine room is possible, but it is difficult to recognise anything due to the destruction and covering of marine growth. The hull, on the port side, which faces upwards to the surface, is heavily dented and pushed inwards as a result of the mine explosion.

The main part of the wreck consists of the bow and midship section. This part stands upright and at the section that has been split off, a good view is given of the cross-cut of the U-boat. Copper and lead cables hang from the former deckhead and a wedged watertight door are visible. On the deckhead itself is the after hatch which no longer has a hatch cover. Two metres from the hatch to the bow is an oval opening which gives entry to the control room. The former tower stood proud with two periscope standards until it was ripped from its footing and disappeared in 2014. This was probably the result of a large ship hooking its anchor and chain on the wreck and ripping the tower off. *UB-20* lies close to the large anchorage and pilot station of the Wandelaar. About 4 m in front of the section where the tower stood, is a circular construction on deck which stood the emplacement for the 8,8 cm deckgun. 3 m from here is the forward, slanting torpedo hatch and crew access. Both hatches are open. It is possible to look inside the forward torpedo room where the closed doors of both torpedo tubes are visible. The bow has been blown off to halfway along the torpedo tubes, which are in empty condition. *UB-20* probably hit her first mine here, destroying the bow, the second mine was responsible for ripping the U-boat in half near the engine room.

UB-23

UB-23 was completed on 9 October 1915 and went, five months later, into service on 13 March 1916. *Oberleutnant z. S.* Hans Voigt became her captain and brought her to Flanders. The first six patrols were spent in the area off Terschelling and near the mouth of the Tyne. Voigt was able to sink 17 drifters and three sailing ships near the Tyne by gunfire and explosive charge during the month of July 1916. On the seventh patrol, he headed to the Channel area, where he would also find good hunting grounds. Between the area of Beachy Head and Alderney he sunk four French trawlers, One British and three French sailings ships and a Spanish and French freighter. On the eighth patrol, at the end of October 1916, *UB-23* fought a battle with two British armed merchant ships, *SS Glenmay* and *SS Glenmorag*. There was a heavy swell and foul weather and the fight had to cease. Voigt proved to be a humane commander. This came to light after he had stopped a Norwegian ship with a cargo of coal. Due to the lifeboats not being seaworthy, he let the ship carry on its voyage. The next day he sunk *SS Snestad* and the schooner *Julia* and took on the crews as the weather had deteriorated. Later, he dropped them off on a neutral vessel. The patrol ended successfully for *UB-23* after sinking another six ships.

On 10 November 1916, command of *UB-23* was taken over by *Oberleutnant z. S.* Heinz Ziemer who continued patrols in the southern part of the Irish Sea and Channel area. At the end of November he managed to sink three ships, but missed the armed merchant cruiser *HMS Dyckland*. At the end of his patrol *UB-23* was able to torpedo and sink the British tanker *MT Conch* southwest of Anvil Point. The ship was en route from Rangoon to London with a cargo of petrol. *MT Conch* exploded and resulted in the loss of 28 lives. During her 11th patrol, early January 1917, *UB-23* was off the Casquets. Ziemer noticed a Danish cargo ship, named '*Kai*' and ordered her to stop so he could check the documents. The ship lessened its speed, but did not lower a lifeboat. It was only after firing her third warning shot, when *UB-23* was at 2,500 m distance, a lifeboat was lowered. Ziemer was being watchful and prepared to dive at any minute. When *UB-23* had approached to 500 m from the 'Dane', fake superstructure fell apart on the aft section and several concealed guns opened fire. It was a Q-ship, but the British had even left the Danish flag in the mast. Two shells hit the fuel and ballast tanks, but *UB-23* was still able to submerge to 50 m and escape. The Q-ship could not be identified, but it surely was not the *SS Kai* as it lay in Sunderland until 13 January. Ziemer decided to return to base, but the ordeal for the crew of *UB-23* was far from over. During the night of 14 January, *UB-23* came fast on the southern part of the Goodwins whereby half of the submarine was visible to the enemy. The crew had to wait one and a half painstaking hours for the flood to take them off the sandbank. When they had nearly reached Zeebrugge, they came upon thick fog. Ziemer missed the Zeebrugge Mole and entered the Dutch part of the Westerschelde. Dutch warships forced him to enter Flushing, where *UB-23* was searched. Luckily for Ziemer they seemed to be satisfied and released the U-boat which arrived in Zeebrugge on 15 January.

During 1917 *UB-23* changed command thrice. Her last captain was *Oberleutnant z. S.* Hans Ewald Niemer who took over on 20 March 1917. During five patrols he was able to sink seven ships. These were the Belgian tug *Marcel* and two towed pontoons *Pelagie* and *Florence* in the North Hinder area. On 23 July 1917 *UB-23* left on her final patrol, which would be in the western part of the Channel. Off the Lizard Niemer brought *UB-23* up to periscope depth in order to shadow a merchant ship. But a sharp lookout on the British patrolboat *HMS P-60* observed her periscope. *HMS P-60* immediately rushed to the location and dropped two depth charges. She was joined by the destroyers *HMS Narwhal* and *HMS Peyton* which also dropped a number of depth charges. The explosions caused heavy damage to the batteries and the diving capabilities of *UB-23*. Niemer let *UB-23* sink to the bottom where they waited for night to fall. Once back on the surface, they realised that their U-boat was so heavily damaged that they would not be able to dive anymore. Niemer decided to sail *UB-23* 360 miles further to La Coruna where he would have her interned. They reached the neutral Spanish port on 29 July 1917 and remained there for the rest of the war. The Spanish did not have much trust in the Germans and had the radio installations, all weapons, deck gun, explosives and important machine parts disassembled or confiscated. Both propellers were even taken off to impair possible escape attempts. Her captain, chief engineer and 15 crewmen were taken under guard to the barracks of Alcala de Henares in Madrid. The first officer and six crewmen were allowed to remain on board to work on the damaged diving gear.

On 22 March 1919, *UB-23* came into the hands of the French as war reparation, but eventually she was scrapped in 1921 in Brest. Her crew remained interned until the same time she was handed over and they were repatriated via the Dutch ships *SS Frisia* and *SS Gelria* back to Germany.[139]

UB-26

UB-26 was completed on 14 December 1915 and went into service one month later under the command of *Oberleutnant z. S.* Wilhelm Smiths. Smiths would only have a short career and his submarine would be captured on his first patrol. On 29 March *UB-26* left Zeebrugge with a mission to carry out attacks on troop ships off Le Havre. Smiths was disappointed when he arrived in an empty anchorage. In the end Smiths wanted to attack an exiting merchant ship, but was spotted and attacked by the French torpedo boat *Trombe*. Six British trawlers also joined in the hunt. In the panic to escape her seven assailants, *UB-26* rose to a depth of 11 m and bumped with the extended periscope against the rudder of one of the enemy vessels. *UB-26* was blinded in an instant and was caught in the steel nets which the trawlers had dropped. The *Trombe* dropped three depth charges on her location. The explosions were so close to *UB-26* that they damaged the pressure hull. In the meantime, the propellers got entangled in the nets and the overheated batteries caught fire. *UB-26* was forced to surface, whereafter the 21 crew members were able to

UB-26 was captured by the French navy, after she had been damaged and sunk off Le Havre (TT)

escape and were picked up by the attacking trawlers. The U-boat sank after the seacocks had been opened, but eight days later she was located and dived by divers of the French navy and ultimately salvaged intact. On board, documents were discovered relating to the sinking of the cross-channel packet *SS Sussex* due to the actions of a U-boat.[140] Other finds included the locations of German minefields off the Flemish coast and possible Allied minefields in the Dover Straits. After being repaired, *UB-26*, entered service of the French navy on 14 August 1917 as *Roland Morillot* and remained there for 14 years. She was finally scrapped in 1931 in Cherbourg.

UB-27

UB-27 was completed on 10 February 1916 and went into service two weeks later under the command of *Oberleutnant z. S.* Viktor Dieckmann. Only one and a half years later, on 19 July 1917, would she be added to the *U-Flottille Flandern*. The first part of her life *UB-27* spent with the *I. U-Halbflottille* in Helgoland. During this period she was able to sink two trawlers, three schooners, two barges and eight merchant ships on the east coast of Scotland. *UB-27* was transferred to the *II. U-Flottille* on 1 February 1917 and patrolled the area between Rotterdam and Harwich. On the North Hinder area *UB-27* was able to sink two Norwegian merchant ships. It seemed that *UB-27* would not remain in a permanent port for long time and for a third time she was transferred, this time to the *U-Flottille Kurland* in the Baltic. She now stood under command of *Oberleutnant z. S.* Heinz Freiherr von Stein zu Lausnitz and was based in Libau (now Lipaia). After having no successes in the Baltic and Gulf of Riga, *UB-27* was finally transferred to Flanders on 19 July 1917. For the first patrol, the 17th for *UB-27*, she headed for the area of the Hoofden three days after her arrival at Zeebrugge. This proved to be unsuccessful and on 29 July, when off the Smith's Knoll Spar buoy, her periscope was spotted by a lookout on the gun boat *HMS Halcyon*. The captain did not hesitate and had his ship ram *UB-27* at full speed and dropped two depth charges on her location. *UB-27* was sunk with all hands[141] in position 52° 47' N 02° 24'. Shortly after she had been rammed and sunk, air bubbles and oil surfaced and on the same day Royal Navy vessels sweeping the bottom with cables located a large object. Divers were sent down, but the poor visibility did not allow them to locate anything. Up to this day it is not sure whether this concerns the wreck of *UB-27*.

UB-29

UB-29 was launched on the last day of 1915 and was added to the *U-Flottille Flandern* on 8 March 1916. During the first 15 patrols of her career she stood under the command of *Oberleutnant z. S.* Herbert Pustkuchen. He decided to operate off the British east coast, near the Lowestoft area and in the middle of the western Channel area. Between March and November 1916 Pustkuchen was able to sink 30 ships. On 23 October *UB-29* got caught up in a battle with the Q-ship *Helgoland*. The 182 ton converted schooner was heavily armed with four 12-pounder guns, but Pustkuchen managed to steer his U-boat to safety. *UB-29* would become notorious for its attack on the French cross-Channel packet *SS Sussex* in the Boulogne Roads. During the night of 23 and 24 March a darkened vessel was spotted, with a black painted flag. The mystery ship found itself on the British shipping line and the shape of the stern resembled that of a minelayer. These elements made Pustkuchen take the decision to torpedo her. *SS Sussex* was hit in the bow area, which tore off. Hurried rescue attempts were able to salvage the rest of the ship and bring

A half-open torpedo door on the wreck of an unidentified UB-II type U-boat sunk on the Sandettiebank, possibly the wreck of *UB-29* (TT)

A view on the twin torpedo tubes of the blown up bow of a UB-II type boat sunk on the Sandettiebank. In both tubes, the torpedoes are still present, yellow blocks of TNT show where the the head was severed from the explosion (TT)

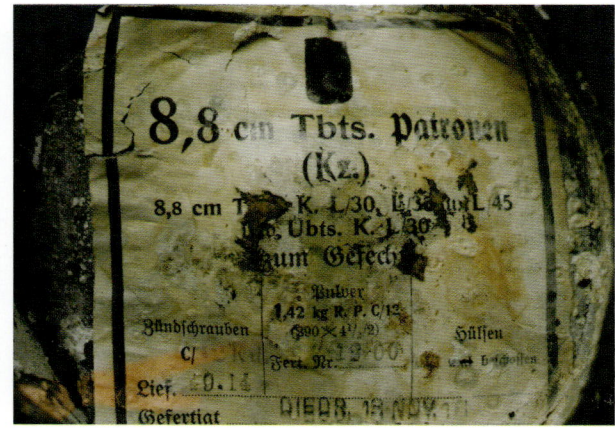

The wreck of the UB-II boat could possibly be identified by the discovery of a label on the inside of a watertight shell container. The date, 18 November 1916, can give us a *postquem* date (TT)

Open torpedo tube door from part of the severed bow section of the wreck of possibly UB-29 on the Sandettiebank (TT)

Open forward hatch on the UB-II type U-boat on the Sandettiebank (TT)

her in to Boulogne. However, there were 50 casualties, of which one was an American citizen. After this incident a large fuss was made around the 'barbaric' actions of U-boats and this would be one of the decisive reasons which would pull the US in the war. Oddly enough, Pustkuchen was not added to the list of war criminals by the Allies. He would also become one of the most successful captains which the *Flandern Flottille* had produced.

On 3 November 1916 *Oberleutnant z. S.* Erich Platsch took over command of *UB-29*. During his first mission he was able to capture the Dutch ships *SS Batavier VI* and *Midsland* and have them brought into Zeebrugge. They had been stopped on the North Hinder and were carrying cargoes destined for Great Britain.

Platsch did not get much opportunity to prove his worth when *UB-29* left Zeebrugge on her 17th and last patrol. Together with *UC-19* they left the base on 27 November and headed towards the Channel area. Fate would have it that both U-boats would be lost, with all hands. The exact location of the sinking of *UB-29* is not known, but through eyewitness accounts we can place her last action to the southwest of the Scilly Islands. Rescued crewmen from the Belgian merchant ship *SS Keltier* said they had been stopped by a small U-boat with the number '29' painted on the tower. On 13 December, *UB-29* was on her return voyage when she was noticed by the destroyer *HMS Landrail* in the Dover Straits. Lookouts on *HMS Landrail* had spotted the tower of a submerging U-boat shortly after midnight in the area southeast of the Goodwins, in position 51° 09' N 01° 46° E. This was 300 m from her position and two depth charges were dropped on the location. Immediately after the explosions large amounts of oil and wreckage came to the surface. The captain of *HMS Landrail* stopped to have some of the wreckage recovered as evidence. Two days later, large patches of oil were still visible on the location.[142] It is almost certain that a U-boat had been hit, but it is not 100% certain that it concerns *UB-29*.

No vital evidence had been found for the identification as *UB-29*. A likely candidate for the wreck site has been found to the north of the Sandettiebank, in position 51° 20' 910 N 02° 06' 430 E. This differs about 15 miles from the position given by *HMS Landrail* on 13 December 1916 and is located on the southern point of the Sandettiebank. It is also possible that *UB-29* was damaged and had been able to sail further until the moment she finally sank near the northern end of the Sandettie. The wreck in question was first discovered and dived by Dirk Termote in 1993. It concerns a *UB-II* class U-boat which lies on its port side with an intact tower and hull, intact just up to halfway up the torpedo tubes. The torpedo tubes bear witness to a heavy explosion which severed them partly. Inside the tubes the remains of the torpedoes and the explosive charges are clearly visible. All visible hatches are in open condition and there is a 8,8 cm gun in front of the tower. It was not possible to retrieve an identification number from the propellers as this part is totally buried by lost trawls and covered by a sand dune. An interesting label was retrieved on the inside of a ready-use ammunition container: '18 november 1916'. This is remarkable evidence which points to *UB-29*, as *UB-29* left for her final voyage on 27 November 1916.

UB-30

UB-30 was completed on 16 November 1915 and went into service with the *V. U-Halfbflottille* about six months later. Up to the end of 1916 she saw action in the Baltic and had Libau as base. Results were poor and during seven patrols *UB-30* was only able to sink six ships in the Gulf of Bothnia. It was decided that *UB-30* would be of more use in the North Sea and on 21 January 1917, she was sailed to Flanders via the *Kaiser-Wilhelm Kanal* (now Kielkanal). On 16 February *UB-30* experienced difficulties with her compass. In combination with thick fog it made the U-boat veer off course and beached in Walcheren, which was Dutch territory. *UB-30* was forced to enter Flushing under guard of Dutch torpedo boats where she was searched. In the end the Dutch decided to intern her and it was only after long diplomatic negotiations that she was finally released on 8 August 1917. Two weeks later, *UB-30* was able to carry out her very first mission from Flanders and she stood under command of *Oberleutnant z. S.* Wilhelm Rhein. Rhein proved to be moderately successful and in his career he managed to sink ten ships and damage a further two. On 24 March 1918, the U-boat shelters at Zeebrugge were bombed, resulting in damage to the stern of *UB-30*. The U-boat had to go for repairs in Bruges and after these were completed, command was taken over by *Oberleutnant z. S.* Rudolf Stier on 24 April. Stier carried out three patrols on the British east coast, between 20 May and 24 July 1918. He was not very lucky and managed to sink just one ship. The fact that shipping had been organised more and more in convoys did not make the task for a U-boat captain any easier.

On 6 August, *UB-30* left on her 19th and final patrol. Off Scarborough she sank the steamship *SS Madam Renee*, laden with copper pyrite. After this action her presence was signalled to a fleet of eager patrol vessels. A sharp lookout on the trawler *John Gillman* spotted the reflection of the periscope prism, at a distance of 300 m. The trawler immediately went in for the kill, rammed and damaged *UB-30*. *UB-30* dived and the trawler released four depth charges. Oil and air bubbles came to the surface and other trawlers dropped marker buoys on the location. Two hours later *UB-30* attempted to surface again, but was seen by the trawlers *John Brooker* and *Viola*. These opened fire on the surfaced U-boat, which was forced to dive again. Both trawlers dropped five depth charges. Ten minutes later Stier again attempted to surface his boat, but this time *UB-30* was heavily damaged and leaked much more oil and air. *John Gillman* and *Florio* forced him to dive again and deposited six depth charges over the area. A further total of 15 depth charges sealed the fate of *UB-30* and her 26 crewmen. Minesweepers snagged an obstruction by the evening of the same day, buoyed the spot and four days later Royal Naval divers managed to confirm that it was the wreck of *UB-30*.[143] *UB-30* had foundered in 27 fathoms of water, but the divers were not able to find any identifying number. Salvage of the wreck was cancelled as the Admiralty found it more important to salvage

UB-110 which had sunk off the north Yorkshire coast on 9 July.

The wreck of *UB-30* lies off the harbour of Whitby in a depth of 50 m. She was rediscovered in 1993 by British divers Carl Racey and Andy Jackson of the Scarborough Sub Aqua Club. The tower with both periscopes is intact, but the hatch has been blown off the wreck. This was found to port and was probably the handiwork o the Royal Navy divers who wanted access to the site. The wreck was positively identified by markings found on the propellers. The wreck stands upright, with visible damage to the bow, where it seems the depth charges blew away a section. This is evident by the scattered blocks of TNT which originate from her own torpedoes. In front of the tower is an 8.8 cm gun and one of the periscopes protrudes from its tube and is heavily bent over.[144] This is possibly the result of the ramming attempt made by the trawler *John Gillman*. The aft hatch is also open, but could have been made by the divers entering the wreck for intelligence gathering.

UB-31

After her completion, *UB-31* was added to the *U-Flottille Kurland* by the early part of 1916. She carried out seven unsuccessful patrols and only once did she come into contact with the enemy. This was on 4 October 1916 when *UB-31* nearly came into collision with the British submarine *HMS E*-19 off Farö. It was decided to transfer *UB-31* to the North Sea to reach better results and on 24 February 1917 she entered Zeebrugge. For most of her short career she stood under command of *Oberleutant z. S.* Thomas Bieber. During 14 patrols between 5 April 1917 and 27 January 1918 Bieber was able to sink 31 ships in the western part of the Channel. One of his greatest successes was the torpedoing of the P&O liner *SS Medina* three miles off Start Point. Bieber proved to be a cautious captain too as he managed to escape three incidents involving Q-ships. Although Bieber had proven his worth with *UB-31*, he was relieved on 1 February 1918 by *Oberleutnant z. S. d. Res*. Wilhelm Braun. Braun did not experience the same successes and was only able to sink three ships during three patrols. This was probably due to the fact that there were less single targets after the Allies had organised ships in convoys. On her 25th patrol, the 3rd for Braun, *UB-31* would end her career in the Dover Straits. *UB-31* had left Zeebrugge on 16 April 1918 and had crossed the Dover Barrage successfully. She was active in the Channel, up to her return on 2 May, when her periscope was observed by a lookout on the drifter *Lord Leitrim*. He saw a slow moving periscope between Folkestone and the Varne bank, right in the middle of the minefield. *Lord Leitrim* rushed to the spot and dropped a depth charge which resulted in oil and airbubbles rushing to the surface. The airships *SSZ-29* and *VZ-2* stayed above the position to keep an eye on a possible escape and led the drifters *Loyal Friend* and *Ocean Roamer* towards it. Once on the location, both drifters also let off depth charges, which detonated a nearby mine. This meant the end for *UB-31* and her crew.[145] Two U-boats disappeared that same night in the area. The other was a UC-II class minelayer, *UC-78*, but was sunk to the east of the barrage.

UB-32 was able to torpedo and sink the British *SS Southpoint* on 12 June 1917 in the Channel (TT)

250

The wreck of *UB-31* was found and dived by Royal Naval divers in 1918. Then it was given as located in position 51° 01' N 01° 16' E. The wreck was rediscovered by British divers in the early 1990s and positively identified on the numbering 'UB-31' which was stamped on both propellors. The wreck lies at a depth of 24 m, in position 51° 02' 06 N 01° 10' 22 E. She has an inclination to port, an intact tower and a large hole in the bow.

UB-32

Just like with her predecessors, *UB-32* was employed in the Baltic up to the end of 1916. She did not book any results and was brought over to join the *U-Flottille Flandern* in February 1917. Under command of *Oberleutnant z. S.* Max Viebeg, *UB-32* was able to sink 23 ships in five months' time. They mainly concerned many drifters and schooners, but also larger merchant ships. On 30 March, *UB-32* came across what seemed to be a suspicious looking steamship off Beachy Head. Viebeg ordered to open fire at a distance of 3000 m on what he suspected to be a Q-ship. He proved to be right as it concerned the Q-ship *Penshurst*, which was hit in the engine room and just below the bridge. But the British vessel fought back and opened fire on *UB-32* with its four deckguns. In the end *UB-32* submerged after spotting an approaching destroyer. The next day *UB-32* torpedoed the hospital ship *Gloucester Castle* near the Isle of Wight. As the ship sank quite slowly most of the crew, medical staff and wounded troops could be evacuated. The largest vessel which Viebeg managed to sink was the troopship *SS Ballarat*. She had a displacement of 11.120 BRT and was owned by the P&O and carried 1,750 troops of the 2nd and 4th Australian brigades. *SS Ballarat* sank 24 miles to the southwest of Wolf Rock, but all troops could be saved by the escorting ships. In early June 1917 *UB-32* engaged several convoys where she was able to torpedo *SS Vinaes* and *SS Mar Cor*. The takings were meagre and the costs high. After every attack on a convoy there followed the inevitable rain of depth charges as reward. Also the presence of aircraft and airships forced Viebeg to carry out many attacks during the night. On 12 June he was able to sink the 4,258 ton British steamship *SS Southpoint* about 30 miles to the southwest of Bishop Rock.

On 6 August 1917 *Oberleutnant z. S.* Benno Ditfurth took over command and in his short career was only able to sink one ship. He would leave Zeebrugge with *UB-32* on his final mission towards the Channel. Not much is known about the loss of *UB-32*. It was said never to have been able to pass through the Dover Barrage and already sunk the following day by depth charges from *MTB 358*. British sources talk of its destruction on 22 September by seaplane 8695. In the eastern part of the Dover Straits, the pilot observed a slow-moving U-boat, which submerged when the aircraft was spotted. Two bombs were released on her location and it was seen that the U-boat broached, fell to one side and sank amidst large bubbles of air, wreckage and oil. The position which was given after the supposed sinking was 51° 45' N 02° 05' E.[(146)] It is possible that an unidentified *UB-II* class U-boat to the east of the Sandettie concerns *UB-32* (described under *UB-29*) Up to now it has not been possible to identify the wreck in question.

UB-33

After its completion at the end of 1915, *UB-33* was sent to the Baltic where it only knew a moderate success. Patrols proved to be frustrating for the captain as most ships which they stopped and checked proved to be neutrals. By later 1917 the Admiralty decided to post *UB-33* in Flanders, together with a number of her sister-ships. On 22 December 1917, *UB-33* left for her first patrol in the western part of the Channel. In the coming four months, her captain, *Oberleutnant z. S.*

Oberleutnant z. S. Benno von Ditfurth poses on the tower of *UB-32*. In September 1917 he and his entire crew would be killed in action (TT).

251

Fritz Gregor, was able to sink 13 ships, most of which were sailings ships and trawlers. *UB-33* left for her final voyage on 6 April 1918. The German Admiralty never knew of her fate, which was confirmed by the interrogaters of the captain of *UC-75*. He swore to know nothing about the fate of *UB-33*, but the British knew all. On 11 April the drifter *Ocean Roamer* detected a heavy underwater explosion to the southwest of the Varne bank. This was accompanied by a thick cloud of smoke and a large fountain of water. When the drifter came to position 50° 56' N 01° 17' E, it found wreckage and oil. The wreck was dredged, found and securely buoyed, allowing the Special Diving unit which arrived two days later to dive the site. The wreck was heavily damaged having been mined aft and lay on its starboard side. Roughly 16 m² had been ripped away by the mine-explosion. A British mine, numbered 832, still drifted from its cable against the side of the U-boat. On the bow of the U-boat there was the painted 'eye' typical for the Flanders Flotilla. Gregor's body was recovered from the conning tower, inspected by Cooper of the Intelligence Division and after several items had been retrieved it was buried at sea. It was later stated that the body had gunshot wounds to the stomach and head. It was presumed that this happened to prevent him from opening the conning tower hatch to escape the sunken U-boat. The divers examining the compartments noted that some of the crew probably had been alive on the bottom after the U-boat had sunk. One body at least had its throat cut. Commander Damant cancelled any ideas of fully recovering the wreck. It was decided to blow the tower from the hull with 45 lbs of TNT. The following day the bridge helm and compass were recovered and the lower hatch blasted open, allowing further access to the divers. It was noticed that the explosion had set one of the torpedoes running and it was found hanging half way out of its tube! On 29 May, diver Dusty Miller was rewarded with his search by the discovery of a steel strongbox in the control room. This was said to have contained codebooks and charts.[147]

The wreck of *UB-33* lies in position 50° 56' 034 N 01° 17' 98 E. It was rediscovered almost 80 years later by divers Dave Batchelor and Bob Peacock. The remains of *UB-33* are partly buried under the sand of the Varne bank at a depth of 27 m. The wreck shows heavy damages near the stern and lies on its starboard side. The severed tower lies also over starboard and parts of the hull are crushed and torn.[148]

UB-34

This UB-II class submarine saw service with the *I.*, *II.* and *V. U-Flottille* before being transferred to the Flanders front at the last month of the war on 9 September 1918. Between August 1916 and September 1918 *UB-34* managed to carry out a total of 20 patrols in the area between the east coast and Scotland, and sink a total of 34 ships. *UB-34* knew of little success when she was part of the Flanders Flotilla due to the fact that in the late part of the war there were very few single targets to be had. *UB-34* left on her 21st voyage from Zeebrugge on 9 September 1918 and was commanded by *Leutnant z. S. d. Res.* Hans Illing. On 15 September *UB-34* narrowly escaped a torpedo fired from a British submarine. The next day her crew had to undergo an attack with 27 depth charges after Illing had sunk the trawler *Elise* off Blyth. When darkness fell, *UB-34* managed to sneak away to safety. Ill luck seemed to plague *UB-34* and the torpedoes which she fired at enemy ships in the following days missed their targets. When on the surface, the bridge watch had to be extra alert as there was a constant threat from the air. In the end Illing decided to return back home on 30 September as pickings were very meagre. At their return in Zeebrugge there was no good news: the base was being evacuated and *UB-34* was ordered to proceed to Helgoland. *UB-34* arrived in Wilhelmshaven on 4 October and it also meant the end of her career. She would be one of the few U-boats of the Flanders Flotilla which did not end up at the bottom of the sea.

Two days later *UB-34* was added to the U-Schule in Kiel, but had to be surrendered to the Allies on 26 November 1918. In 1922 she made her final voyage to Canning Town, where she was scrapped.

UB-35

Before arriving in Zeebrugge, *UB-35* had experienced a tumultuous career with the *I.* and *II. U-Flottille* and the *U-Flottille Kurland*. *UB-35* was launched on 28 December 1915 and operated out of Helgoland in the North Sea for the following 15 months. In total she carried out 15 patrols resulting in the sinking of 17 ships. After this she was moved to the Baltic, and based in Warnemünde, but pickings proved to be nil and she ended up back in the North Sea, this time with Zeebrugge as base. She stood under the skillfull command of *Oberleutnant z. S.* Karl Stöter who was

Oberleutnant z. S. Karl Stöter, captain of UB-35 (WZ-Bilddienst)

able to sink 15 ships in the next six months. On 17 January 1918, *UB-35* left on her final patrol. Off the Isle of Wight she was able to sink the *ships SS Mechanician, SS Molina* and *SS Serrana*. On 25 January she stopped the Greek freighter *SS Epstatios* off St. Catherine's Point. Stöter had two of his crew row out to the Greek vessel to place explosive charges in her hold. He was surprised by the patrol vessel *HMS P-34* and forced to crash dive. Both crewmen, who were still on the Greek ship, were captured. They were the lucky ones because the next day *UB-35* would be destroyed with all hands. After the incident with the Greek ship it is not sure what happened to *UB-35*. During the night of 26 January Stöter attempted the crossing of the Dover Barrage. Following normal procedure, he brought the U-boat to the surface and navigated amongst the lines of net buoys to the northeast of the minefield.* He was spotted by the destroyer *HMS Leven* which turned on *UB-35* at full speed. The destroyer managed to ram her, after which *UB-35* submerged. *HMS Leven* dropped a pattern of depth charges over the location. After the last depth charge had detonated, a lookout spotted seven survivors in the water. The British were only able to save one man, who died from his wounds on the journey back to port. Before he died he said he had been on *UB-35*. On the place of the sinking the British recovered a seaman's cap and some letters. Later on, the survivors of the *Epstatios*-incident confirmed that those were personal possesions of their comrades. The position of the sinking of *UB-35* was then given as 51° 03' N 01° 46'E.

UB-36

After spending the second half of 1916 in the Baltic, without gaining any successes, *UB-36* was transferred to Zeebrugge where she stood under the command of *Oberleutnant z. S.* Harald von Keyserlingk. His first success was the stopping of the Norwegian merchant ship *SS Avance* near the Maas Light Vessel. As she was laden with food destined for London, she was classed as war booty and ordered to sail to Zeebrugge. During its 11th patrol, *UB-36* was able to sink three ships off Cap Griz Nez, but was attacked by airships and destroyers which put up a long pursuit. In the end *UB-36* managed to escape, but on entering Zeebrugge was hit by a heavy groundswell. The sea crashed through the open hatches, flooded the engine room, and made both engines stop. A lookout on the bridge was sucked overboard and drowned. The port of Zeebrugge sent tugs to tow the helpless *UB-36* back.

UB-36 underwent repairs in the dockyard and a month later, on 9 May 1917, was able to leave on another mission, this time her last. Off the Channel Islands she sank four ships, one of which was the French *SS Ferdinand A*. *UB-36* attempted a second attack on the convoy, but her periscope was spotted by *SS Molière*. The French ship turned from the convoy and rammed *UB-36*. No sign of life was seen from the U-boat and the location was marked where large air bubbles welled up to the surface. *SS Molière* was later

---
* Grant, 1964, p. 81 states that UB-35 was at periscope depth. This is improbable as a periscope is very hard to spot during the night and it was also procedure to cross the minefield during the night on the surface.

examined in dry dock and a lot of damage was found near the bow, just below the waterline. The damage could only have resulted of her hitting *UB-36* as it was the only U-boat operating in that area at the time. Up to now the wreck of *UB-36* has not been discovered.[149]

UB-37

In contrast with the other *UB-II* class boats, *UB-37* did not see any service in the Baltic, but was immediately brought over to Flanders in May 1916. She stood under command of *Oberleutnant z. S.* Hans Valentiner who managed to carry out six patrols with *UB-37* in the area of Tyne Estuary and the western part of the Channel. He was able to sink a total of 15 ships and escort the Dutch motor vessel *Zeemeeuw* to Zeebrugge. *Zeemeeuw* had been checked near the Maas Light Vessel on 10 September 1916 and on board there was food destined for England.

For her last three patrols, between 12 November 1916 and 14 January 1917, *UB-37* changed hands to *Oberleutnant z. S.* Paul Günther. In the last two months of 1916 he sank seven drifters, four merchant ships and a bark. Twice *UB-37* came under fire, by an escort of the fishing fleet and by a tanker which it had fired upon. Times had become difficult for a U-boat. A few days after the incident with the tanker Günther tried and failed to penetrate a convoy which was too heavily guarded.

On 2 January 1917 *UB-37* left on her final patrol. During the first few days she was able to sink four ships, but on the 14th came in contact with the Q-ship *HMS Penshu*rst. After a gunbattle *UB-37* was mortally hit and sank with all hands in position 50° 07' N 01° 47' W*. The entire story of the battle is described in the chapter concerning the Q-ships.

The wreck of *UB-37* was discovered by divers in 1999 in position 50° 10' 20 N 01° 38' 40 W. Innes McCartney describes the U-boat as a very intact wreck, which lies on an even keel with an inclination over starboard. Maximum depth is 60 m, with a bottom consisting of hard sand and pebbles. Both doors of the torpedo tubes are open and on the deck in front of the tower is an 8.8 cm gun.

---

* the full story of this battle is to be found under the chapter of Q-ships, page 210

UB-38 reaches port after a patrol. Notice the typical Flanders' 'eye' on her bow (Herzog)

On 17 December 1916, *UB-38* took lifeboats in tow with survivors from the sunken Spanish *SS Ason* and brought them to the vicinity of land (Herzog)

UB-38

UB-38 was launched on 1 April 1916 and only five months later came into service under the command of *Kapitänleutnant* Erwin Wassner. He brought UB-38 over to Flanders and left on 15 September on his first patrol in the North Sea. Wassner was able to complete six missions, sinking a total of 17 ships. On 19 November 1916, *Oberleutnant z. S.* Wilhelm Amberger took over command and Wassner was appointed UC-69 as his next U-boat. During the following seven months Amberger managed to sink 18 ships, some of which proved to be very valuable to the Allies. Off Bishop Rock the Spanish steamship *SS Ason*, laden with copper ore bound for Great Britain, was boarded by men from UB-38 and sunk with explosive charges. On 1 May 1917 UB-38 sank the British SS *Ladywood* 15 miles to the southwest of Wolf Rock. On board was a cargo of 3,500 tons of copper. Three days later the Greek *SS Assos*, with 3,100 tons of corn, went down in the bay of the Seine, accompanied by the *SS Aghios Nikolaos*, laden with 3,500 tons of iron ore. During her 14th patrol UB-38 experienced engine trouble and had to return back to base. When she lay in dry dock at Ostend for repairs, the dockyard came under fire from monitors on 5 June 1917. Several shell fragments damaged the deck, taking the U-boat another two months out of commission. After final repairs were made, UB-38 made another four patrols with Amberger as captain. He was able to sink seven ships and when torpedoing the 8th vessel UB-38 suffered heavy damage. Off Start Point a steamship of about 4000 BRT was spotted and torpedoed. There ensued an enormous explosion with a huge fireball, probably created by the detonation of a cargo of ammunition. UB-38 found herself 500 m away from the explosion, but the shock wave damaged the electrical installations and shut down part of the batteries. Because of the incident the patrol had to be cancelled and returned to base to carry out repairs. After this patrol Amberger was issued with a larger UB-III boat to command and UB-38 would change commander twice more.

She left on her final trip on 29 January 1918 and stood under the command of *Oberleutnant z. S.* Günther Bachmann. After an unsuccessful patrol lasting ten days, UB-38 returned and on 8 February had started to run the gauntlet of the Dover Barrage. Around 21h25 the drifter *Gowan II* noticed a surfaced U-boat to the east of the northern end of the Le Colbart sandbank, at a distance of 3 miles. The lookouts on UB-38 had also noticed the drifter and dived immediately. UB-38 had sealed her own fate, because 20 minutes after she had dived a triple explosion resounded. An approaching destroyer and a number of trawlers were shaken by the underwater explosion. UB-38 had run blindly into the minefield. A reward of £ 1000 for her destruction was donated to the Dover fund for the families of the casualties of the Dover Patrol. The wreck was discovered in July 1918 by commander Damant's diving team. It was only described as a small UB-boat, with a painted eye on the bow, a deck gun and a single propeller. It had been sunk already a couple of months, which was confirmed by the growth on the wreck. Due to the wreck lying on its port side, the Royal Naval divers had mistakenly only seen one propeller. UB-I class U-boats, with single propulsion, have no deck guns.

The wreck of UB-38 was rediscovered in the 1990s by divers Dave Batchelor and Bob Peacock in position 50° 57' 838 N 01° 21' 632 E. The French Hydrographic department (SHOM) wrongly identified her as UC-78. The U-boat stands on its keel with an inclination to port. Maximum depth on the wreck is 33 m. The tower hatch is open and on the front the bow shows damage. In front of the tower is an 8.8 cm gun and on the bottom, in the sand lie several compressed air tanks. The stern section is totally wrecked, probably due to the triple mine explosions. Beneath the numerous lost trawls a damaged and bent, three-bladed propeller is visible.[150] The wreck of UB-38 was lifted from the seabed a few years back and deposited in deeper water. This was done to deepen the traffic lanes.

UB-39

UB-39 went into service on 29 April 1916 under the command of *Oberleutnant z. S.* Werner Fürbringer. Fürbringer, nicknamed 'Fips', would become one of the most successful commanders of the Flanders' boats. UB-39 would change captains once, which in one and a half years would sink the staggering total of 93 ships, 89.810 BRT.

During five patrols Fürbringer was able to sink a record number of 43 ships. Between 6 July and 30 October 1916 these were 23 drifters, 17 merchants vessels and three sailings ships. One of the drifters was *King James*, whose lifebelt was brought back

In the former Zeebrugge Museum were several trophies on display, one of which was the life ring of *SS King James*, a Grimsby trawler sunk by *UB-39*.

UB-39 was able to escape death by a hair's breadth after her periscope was rammed by the bow of *SS Pronto* (TT)

as souvenir and has been preserved in the Bruges archives. Besides sinking ships, *UB-39* also shelled the Seaham Iron Works with a symbolic 39 shells fired from her deckgun. Twice Fürbringer was able to escape from a battle with the enemy. On 9 September, when *UB-39* was about 13 miles northwest from Wissant, she stopped the Norwegian *SS Pronto*. Part of the crew boarded her to check the ship's documents. Suddenly a destroyer appeared out of nowhere and opened fire at 3,000 m range. Fürbringer immediately sheltered *UB-39* behind *SS Pronto*, but did not want to dive before rescuing his prize crew, which was still on board the ship. In the meantime, the destroyer had approached up to 1,200 metres and continued firing, even though *UB-39* had disappeared from view. In the end Fürbringer managed to rescue his crew and dive. Due to the haste to leave the surface, the tower of *UB-39* rammed the keel of *SS Pronto*, damaging the attack periscope and bridge heavily. On the same patrol *UB-39* pursued an unidentified merchant ship without flag. Fürbringer was suspicious and he was right to be: only minutes into the pursuit, the vessel changed course 180° and attempted to ram him. In the meantime, two camouflaged guns opened fire. *UB-39* was able to dive on time, but was bombarded with depth charges. After this patrol Fürbringer was assigned to the large minelayer *UC-70* and *UB-39* went to *Oberleutnant z. S.* Heinrich von Küstner on 8 November 1916. By the end of the war Fürbringer had commanded a total of six U-boats: *UB-2, UB-39, UC-70,*

UC-17, *UB-58* and *UB-110*. Von Küstner managed to keep the successes of *UB-39* up between 12 November 1916 and her final demise on 10 April 1917. During eight patrols she destroyed a total of 50 ships. On 3 January 1917 *UB-39* submerged amidst the French fishing fleet of La Rochelle. Von Küstner ordered all present ships to approach and in a couple of hours time he sank 15 drifters by explosive charge.

UB-39 failed to return to Zeebrugge from her 14th patrol. She left her base on 23 April 1917 and it was suspected that *UB-39* was mined on the return leg of her voyage, on 15 May. The only mention is that *UB-12* noted a heavy underwater explosion near buoy 3 in the Dover Barrage. This was in position 51° 07' N 01° 47' E. The explosion could have coincided with the loss of *UB-39* and all her crew.

The wreck of *UB-39* was first found and discovered by Dirk Termote and the author in 1995. This UB-II class U-boat lies at a depth of 34 m in position 51° 19' 995 N 02° 09' 382 E, to the east of the Bergues bank. She lies on her keel, inclined over starboard and is fairly intact. Her deck gun still stands in front of the tower and all hatches are shut. Information found on the label on the inside of an ammunition container eventually gave a post terminus date of the wreck: 'November 1916'. Positive identification was finally discovered after having cleard marine growth and incrustation from her port propeller which gave the number : 'UB-39 (II)'. The area of the explosion which was given in 1917 is a location to the southeast of the Sandettie bank. This is about 15 miles further south than the position which is known now, but here we have to take into account the circumstances and that sound underwater is very difficult to pinpoint exactly.

UB-40

After she was launched on 17 August 1916, *UB-40* would see two and a half years of war and have four different captains at her helm. *Oberleutnant z. S.* Hans Howaldt would be one of the most famous of these. By the end of the war, *UB-40* proved to be the most successful *UB-II* class submarine. Under Howaldt alone, 15 patrols were carried out, resulting in the sinking of 56 ships, a total of 89.654 BRT. For this feat Howaldt would receive the *Pour le Mérite* on 23 December 1917. In her total life *UB-40* would carry out 28 patrols and sink 99 ships (131.680 BRT).

One of the largest ships sunk was the hospital ship *SS Lanfranc*. In April 1917 she was struck by a torpedo

The barrel of an 8.8 cm deck gun, covered by lost trawls, looms out of the darkness on the wreck of *UB-39* (TT)

A closed deck hatch on the wreck of *UB-39* (TT)

Next to the wreck of *UB-39* lie several, unfired 8.8 cm shells, some still in their watertight containers (TT)

The wreck could be identified by the number 'UB-39', legible on her port propellor (TT)

and sunk 42 miles north of Le Havre. Howaldt had mistakenly identified *SS Lanfranc* as a troop ship because she was escorted by two Royal Navy vessels. Sadly 34 men were killed on the hospital ship, of which 15 were wounded German soldiers. Another was the British liner *SS Aparima* which had on board cadets for the New Zealand merchant navy. When she sank, on 17 November, 57 of them drowned. During the patrol preceding the award of his *Pour le Mérite*, the *UB-II* class submarine proved to have a very good diving speed. On the return leg of his patrol, when *UB-40* was southeast of the Westhinder light vessel, a speeding destroyer appeared from the shadows around midnight. The Englishman was on a ramming course for *UB-40* and Howaldt ordered just in time hard to port to put his U-boat in counter course. The three-funneled destroyer passed *UB-40* at 10 metres distance when she was already submerging. When only the tower still remained above the surface, the remaining bridge watch were able to dive into the tower and shut the hatch. Due to the excellent dive-capabilities of the U-boat she was able to dive in only 30 seconds and save them from a ramming. There followed the inevitable depth charging, but *UB-40* reached Zeebrugge without incurring any damage.

On her final patrol, on 30 July 1918, heavy damage was caused when *UB-40* was depth-charged by a destroyer. Water flooded inside through tears near the engine room, causing heavy damage to the batteries. *UB-40* managed to reach the safety of

The remains of the blown-up *UB-40* in dry dock in Ostend (TT)

These photos show damage to the bridge compass and periscope-optics of *UB-40*, after being hit by depth charges on 30 July 1918 (TT)

Bruges where she lay in dry dock for the remainder of the war. At the end of September *UB-40* was brought to Ostend, but on 2 October blown up and destroyed in dry dock.

UB-54

UB-54 was one of the first large *UB-III* type U-boats to join the *Flandern Flottille* in August 1917. On his first patrol, her captain, *Oberleutnant z. S.* Egon von Werner, had beginner's luck. On 20 August, about 120 miles from the Scilly Islands he torpedoed a small ship bearing no flag or recognition marks. After questioning the crew who had saved themselves in the lifeboats, they realised it was Q-8, *HMS Vala* which they had sunk. *UB-54* carried out another four patrols sinking a total of 13 ships. In one instance von Werner managed to sink an entire Belgian fleet of seven drifters with explosive charges in the Bay of the Seine. Von Werner's short career ended on 8 February 1918 when *UB-54* was handed over to her

A view on the starboard side of the tower of an unidentified UB-III type U-boat to the northeast of the Fairy Bank (TT)

Access to the tower is possible, as the hatch had been wrenched from her hinge (TT)

Leutnant z. S. Arved von Teichmann und Logischen, first officer, died in March 1918, when his U-boat, *UB-54*, failed to return from patrol (TT)

In front of the tower stands the foot of a 10.5 cm deck gun. The barrel was carried away by a trawler's snag and was deposited in the scour near the stern of the wreck (TT)

Around the tower are stacked 10.5 cm watertight containers for ready-use ammunition (TT)

Around the tower are stacked 10.5 cm watertight containers for ready-use ammunition (TT)

The bridge compass housing was pulled from the tower by a trawler and deposited next to the wreck (TT)

A tank with compressed air is built in the outer hull (TT)

Handwheel for a vent on deck (TT)

new captain: *Oberleutnant z. S.* Erich Hecht. *UB-54* left on 1 March for her 6th patrol in the Channel area, but what exactly happened to her remains a mystery. The sinking of a steamship off Portland on 7 March could possibly be tied to *UB-54*. A French radio message, intercepted by Bruges on 12 March, let the Germans suspect that *UB-54* might have got herself entangled in a net in position 50° 08' N 00° 16' W, about 30 miles northwest of Cap d'Antifer and was later destroyed by a French torpedo boat. According to British sources *UB-54* had been depth-charged and sunk by *HMS Thruster*, *HMS Retriever* and *HMS Sturgeon* in position 53° 15' N 00° 45' E.[151] This last boat proved to be *UB-78*, which, although heavily damaged, eventually managed to limp back to base. Also the location, in the southern North Sea, did not correspond with the area of operations of *UB-54*, which was the western part of the Channel. The French report was then already disguarded as being incorrect.

There are several different wrecks which can be linked to that of *UB-54*. McCartney talks of one large UB-III U-boat lying in position 50° 25' 00 N 00° 12' 30 W. It is in a good state of preservation with the bow showing four visible torpedo tubes and the stern two. Just in front of the tower is an 8.8 cm deck gun and around it are scattered several empty shellcases. All hatches are in closed condition.[152] A more likely candidate for *UB-54* is one of the three as yet unidentified UB-III class submarines sunk to the northeast of the Fairybank. This was an area of sea intensively dived and researched by Dirk Termote and the author in 1995, as it was the situation of a former British minefield during the last two years of the war. Its actual success was not even known in 1918 and a number of returning U-boats were lost and sunk in this area. In a rectangular area of 5 by 10 miles a total of seven UC- and UB-boats were discovered, some lying only a few hundred metres from each other. In position 51° 29' 333 N 02° 11' 361 E an intact UB-III class submarine lying upright with an inclination over port. The U-boat was fitted with a 10.5 cm deck gun and around its foot lie several, cased ready-use shells. On one of the locking rings there was a date, '1918'. Both deck hatches are in closed condition and there is no visible damage to the wreck. The tower hatch is gone and the twisted hinge could point to the fact that it was dislodged by a net snagging on the tower. The starboard propeller was found to be clear of nets and its hub was cleaned. Disappointingly enough, this only

A torpedo-loading hatch stands open (TT)

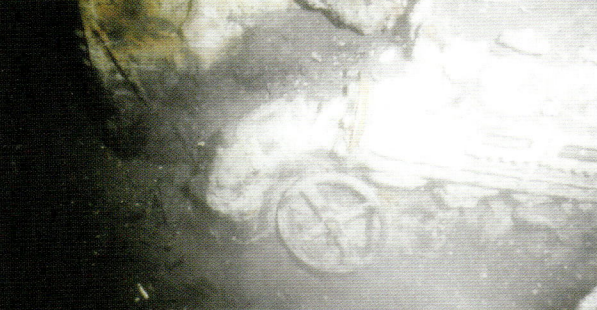

Rare inner view of the central control area with a handwheel and gauges (TT)

A view inside the forward torpedo room where the top two hatches of the tubes are visible (TT)

A view on the forward torpedo-loading hatch (TT)

A brass handle from a watertight shell container shows that the wreck dates from the last year of the war (TT)

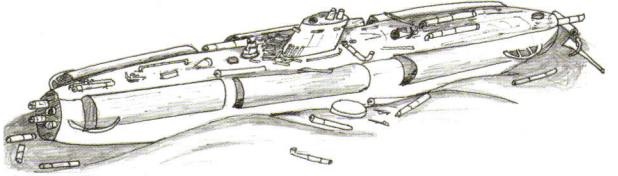

Drawing of the wreck of an unidentified UB-III type boat to the northeast of the Fairy Bank (TT)

261

showed a type number, 'UB-III' but no further specification as to what number of U-boat it concerned.

Another UB-III type submarine lies one mile to the east of the previous one, in position 51° 29' 170 N 02° 12' 917 E. Bottom depth for both wrecks is 43 m. This UB-III type is fairly intact, lying on an even keel with a slight inclination over port. There is damage on the point of its bow, most likely to have been caused by the explosion of a mine. The section of the top of the bow seems to have been ripped off and the inside of the four torpedo tubes are well visible. Just in front of the tower stands the foot of the 10.5 cm gun, but the barrel lies in the scour behind the wreck. Around the tower and in the sand lie several, full, zinc containers for ammunition for the gun. The stern also shows explosion damage, where the torpedo tubes are half visible. All hatches, the forward, the tower and both after hatches are open or are without a hatch cover. The disappearance of the hatches is mostly to have been caused by trawl snags rather than escape attempts made by the crew when the U-boat lay on the bottom.

A third, similar type, was found on the top of a sandbank only 2 miles north of the Fairybank. She lies in position 51° 26' 795 N 02° 19' 993 E at a depth of 22 m. She lies upright, but has been buried to three quarters deep

Retracted periscopes on the tower of a yet unidentified UB-III type boat on the Fairy Bank (TT)

A view of the forward part of the unidentified UB-III boat on the Fairy Bank. In the front is the foot for the deck gun (Harry Klerks)

Compressed air tanks fitted within the outer hull (Harry Klerks)

in sand dunes. Only the tower, the surrounding deck with two compressed airtanks, two hatches and the foot of the gun are visible. The tower hatch is open, but filled to the brim with sand.[153] In the late 1990s a fisherman's trawl snagged the gun and it was brought to the surface. This appeared to have been an 8.8 cm calibre gun.[154] The size of the wreck and the dimensions of the tower, as well as the quality of the materials used point to the direction of a UB-III submarine, built in the middle or later months of the war.

UB-55

UB-55 was launched on 9 May 1917 and went into service on 1 July under the command of Ralph Wenninger, nicknamed 'Seppl' by his colleagues. *UB-55* would be the third command of this veteran, as he had already commanded *UB-17* and *UC-17* before this. After *UB-55* was added to the *U-Flottille Flandern* in August 1917, Wenninger would carry out six patrols up to his eventual demise. During a time when *UB-55* had to contend with many convoys and their escorts, Wenninger was still able to sink 22 ships. One of his largest victims was the American SS *Chattachoochee*, displacing 8.007 BRT, which he torpedoed north of Wissant on 23 March 1918. It had been steaming in the centre of a convoy which was heading to Brest. Part of its cargo consisted of 120 army trucks. Wenninger had been forced to attack the convoy during the night as there was a large presence of escort ships and air cover. After two hours, and after firing three torpedoes, the leviathan SS *Chattahoochee* was finally sunk. To the southwest of Portland, *UB-55* was able to overcome a Q-ship. It was the 113 ton sailing ship *Danton* which had been converted to the Q-ship *HMS Wellholme*. The English ship did not stand a chance against the regular volleys fired from *UB-55*'s 10.5 cm gun, was hit several times, capsized and sank.

After returning from his sixth mission with *UB-55*, Wenninger was decorated with the coveted *Pour le Mérite* for his outstanding accomplishments with the U-boat division and his skill in planning an attack.

UB-55 left Zeebrugge on her final patrol on 21 April 1918. Besides having her normal crew of 28 on board, there were also seven extra men along who were being trained. During the early hours *UB-55* reached the Dover Barrage and dived when reaching a wall of searchlights. Shortly after leaving the surface an explosion occurred on starboard, between the engine room and stern. Two compartments flooded instantly

A diver explores the top of the conning tower of a UB-III boat on the Fairy Bank (Harry Klerks)

Oberleutnant z. S. Ralph Wenninger, captain of *UB-55*, survived the sinking of his U-boat in the Dover Barrage (TT)

and the U-boat ended up on the seabed at 30 m. Engineer Dietrich attempted to shut the watertight door between the engine room and the torpedo room, but it proved to be impossible. Everytime he nearly managed to close it, it was forced back by the flooding water. Water jetted inside and the men were thrown off their feet. As the starboard ballast tanks had been ruptured, Wenninger could not bring his U-boat back to the surface. The crews in the stern sections and engine room had all drowned and the survivors huddled near the hatches of the middle and foreship of *UB-55*. There were 12 of them in the foreward end and eight in the command centre. Lights went out and the survivors were forced to use handlamps. With the rising water, the internal pressure also increased, which lead to immense headaches. Breathing also became more difficult and painful. The penetration of seawater into the battery compartmens led to the leakage of chlorine gas. Panic started and two crewmen tried to commit suicide with a pistol, but did not succeed as the cartridges were damp. An hour and a half passed until the icy water had reached a height of 1 m. This made it possible to equalise the pressure and open the forward hatch and that of the tower. Wenninger knew that there were only four Dräger escape sets available. He divided the survivors in two groups: six men beneath the tower hatch and 12 men under the hatch in the torpedo room. When the hatches were opened, most of the crew was able to escape within an enormous air bubble. But of these most suffered embolisms and overexpansion of the lungs and were found dead on the surface. After one and a half hours there were still eight survivors floating on the surface, one of which was Wenninger. The were saved by the British trawler *Mate*, but one of them did not recover consciousness and died on the trip to Dover. Other ships had arrived on the scene and the British seamen were shocked to see the state of the German survivors. Two of them were vomiting blood and oil, whilst others did not stop screaming. During their later interrogation they seemed surprised by their good treatment by their British captors. The survivors were Wenninger, *Marine-Ingenieur* Friedrich Dietrich, *Oberbootsmannsmaat* Fritz Jahnke, *Torpedomaschinistenmaat* Alex Neumann, *Obermatrose* Ewald Kestner, *Aspirant* Roenspiess and *Heizer* Peter Hammel. After surviving the ordeal of *UB-55*, Roenspiess and Dietrich also would die. Roenspiess had suffered severe internal trauma, whilst Dietrich died seven months later from the Spanish Influenza in the officers' camp of Shipton.

Two days after Commander Damant's diving team discovered the wreck of *UB-56*, they found another U-boat with four torpedo tubes in the bow. As they wanted to enter the tower of this UB-III class submarine they placed a large amount of explosives around it. The resulting explosion detonated one of the torpedoes in the bow and destroyed it. When diving the wreck, divers found the body of a leather-clad sailor who had documents and keys in his pockets. The 8.8 cm gun was recovered from the wreck and it was only on 22 August that the wreck was finally identified as *UB-55*.

The wreck of *UB-55* lies between the Varne and Folkestone in position 51° 01' 324 N 01° 19' 796 E. It lies on its keel with an inclination to port and the general depth is 34 m. According to Alain Richard the bow shows heavy damage and certain parts are totally ripped to pieces and are covered by lost trawls and sand. The tower seems to

A smiling gun crew prepares to sink a schooner which has been ordered to hove to (TT)

be intact (even though in Damant's description charges had been placed around the tower) with both periscopes bent forward. There is no deck gun present and its footing is still visible. The stern is also damaged, but not as bad as the front. Two torpedo tubes, as well as the propellers are visible, but all show damages done by the mine explosion.[155]

UB-56

UB-56 was fated to have a very short career after she was launched on 6 June 1917. She went into service on 19 July with the *I. U-Flottille Flandern* and came under the command of *Oberleutnant z. S.* Hans Valentiner. *UB-56* was able to carry out three patrols in the Channel and sink four ships and damage one. On 13 November *UB-56* was lightly hit by the British *SS Aswell* which had turned to ram the surfaced U-boat. Valentiner was just able to avoid the attack, but *UB-56* was grazed on her superstructure. He then pursued *SS Aswell* below the surface and managed to torpedo and sink her eventually. On 18 December 1917, *UB-56* left Zeebrugge on her final patrol. During the night of 19 December, around 23h42, the destroyer *HMS Gipsy* picked up the sound of a heavy explosion somewhere between Cap Griz Nez and Folkestone, to the north of Le Colbart. At 00h10, the crew on board *HMS Gipsy* heard cries for help and with their search light could position two men in the water. They were able to save only one, in position 50° 56' 30 N 01° 22' E, but he died some time later. His clothing was marked with the name 'Bleeck', and later it proved to concern Max Bleeck, who was an engineer on board *UB-56*. *UB-56* proved to have been the first victim of a newly laid British minefield.

The wreck was located about six months later by Damant's diving team and on 12 August 1918 he made a report on board *HMS Moonfleet*. A U-boat had been discovered in position 50° 56' 45 N 01° 23' E with a damaged stern. After having lain for under a year on the seabed, the wreck had been totally filled up with sand. Although the divers did not find any direct proof, we may assume that it did concern the wreck of *UB-56*.[156]

The wreck of a UB-III class U-boat was rediscovered by Dave Batchelor in position 50° 56' 796 N 01° 23' 084 E at a depth of 28 m. The wreck is largely intact, but mainly covered by sand dunes. The tower has two retracted periscopes and the hatch stands open. In front of the tower stands a 8.8 cm deck gun. The current position more or less matches the position given in 1918 and we can assume with certainty that it is the wreck of *UB-56*.

Diver and researcher Alain Richard made calculations from the location where Bleeck was picked up *HMS Gipsy* and the tide which ran at the time. The tide was flowing in a southeasterly direction, which meant the explosion and sinking must have been to the northeast of the location. In just half an hour Bleeck would have drifted about 1 mile. This puts the mine explosion in position 50° 57' N 01° 23' 10 E, which almost corresponds perfectly with the location of the wreck.

UB-57

After being brought to Flanders on 20 September 1917, *UB-57* would see two captains during her short career: *Kapitänleutnant* Otto Steinbrinck and *Oberleutnant z. S.* Johannes Lohs. Steinbrinck was able to sink a total of 18 ships between 6 October and 29 December 1917. Command was given to Lohs on 2 January 1918 and in six months' time he was able to excel by sinking 28 ships and damaging three. The largest were *SS War Monarch* (7.887 BRT) and the armed merchant cruiser *SS Moldavia* (9.500 BRT). *SS Moldavia* was torpedoed off the Owers light vessel on 23 May whilst in convoy. On board was a detachement of American troops, of which 56 were drowned. Lohs proved to be very skilled and did not fear to carry out daring attacks. Near the Varne he pursued and torpedoed the steamship *SS Unity*, just before reaching the barrage of searchlights at the Dover Barrage. He

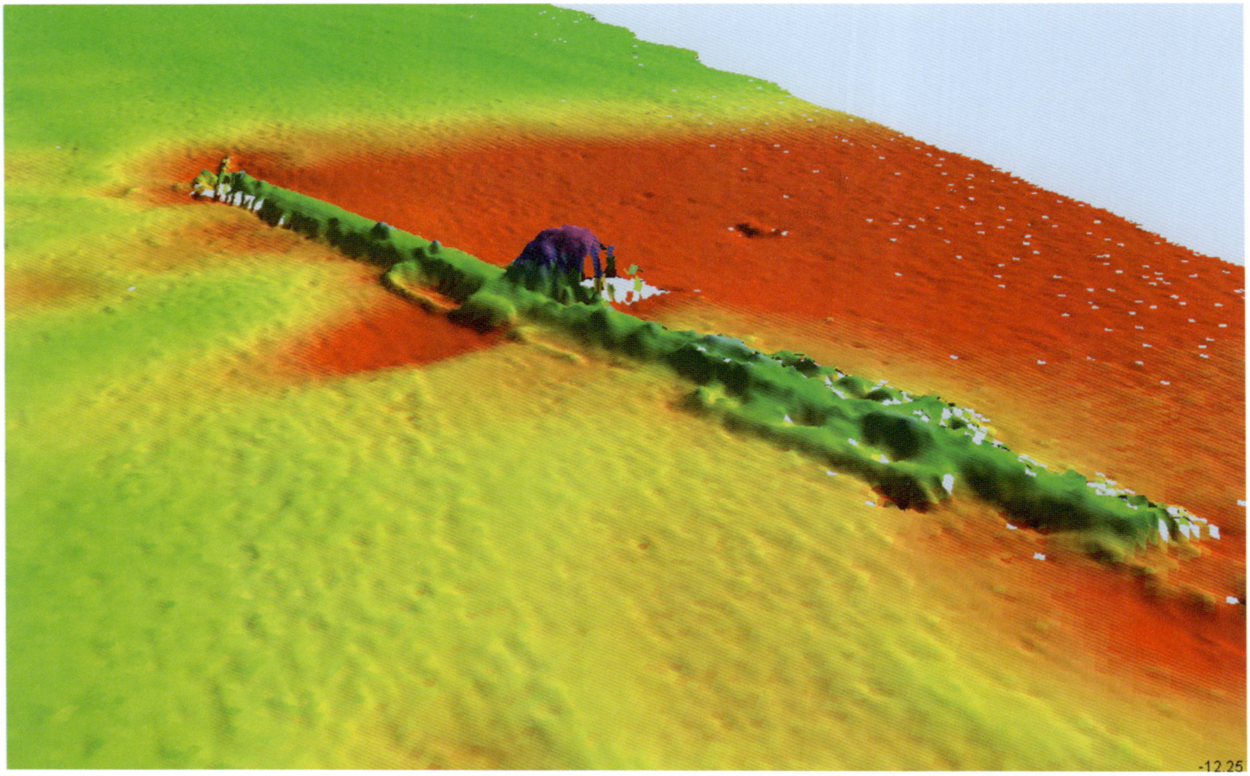

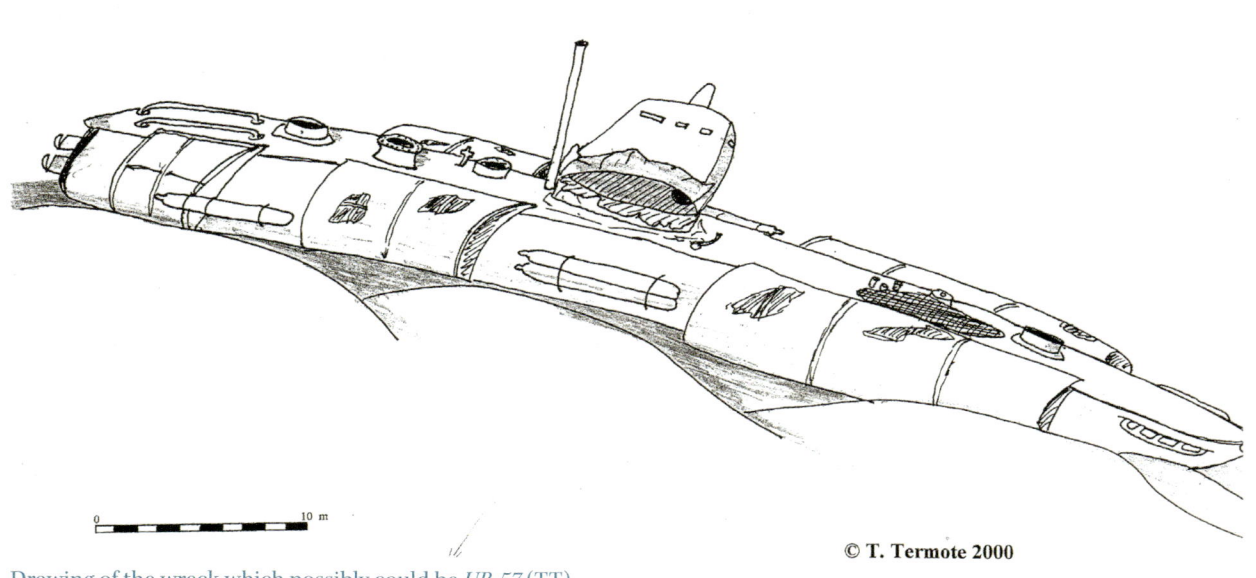

Multibeam image of the wreck of a UB-III boat off Zeebrugge. Possibly it concerns the wreck of *UB-57* (MDK-Vlaamse Hydrografie)

Drawing of the wreck which possibly could be *UB-57* (TT)

would also pursue ships on the surface and made them stop by firing at them with rifles.

But his luck would not last to the end and on 3 August 1918 *UB-57* left on her final journey. On 14 August, at 22h15, Lohs sent out a radio signal to Bruges to let them know that they were on their return and had sunk a total of three ships, totaling 15.000 BRT. This was the last sign of life of *UB-57* and was sent from the area of the Sandettie bank. An hour later Bruges wanted *UB-57* to signal again, but nothing more was heard. Also from the British side no news was picked up concerning the destruction of *UB-57*. It was then assumed that *UB-57* fell victim to a newly laid British minefield with magnetic mines which had been laid off the Flemish coast, about 8 miles to the north of Zeebrugge. The bodies of Lohs, his first officer Siegfried Fuchs and a couple of other crewmen washed ashore a week later at Flushing and Zeebrugge. The 26-year old Fuchs had only finished his course at the *U-Schule* in May 1918 and had entered service with the *I. U-Flottille Flandern* a week later. His body washed ashore near Zeebrugge on 2 September and three days later he was buried at the cemetery of Steenbrugge.

The search for the wreck of *UB-57* proved to be an interesting case study. A number of possible candidates present themselves as being that of the U-boat in question. It is possible that *UB-57* foundered in the area to the east of the Fairybank. If this is the case, then it would concern one of three unidentified UB-III wrecks described under *UB-54*. The most possible wreck would be that of the one lying in the shallows of the Fairybank, where the 8.8 cm deck gun was trawled up. The only fact that would give some doubt is that the bodies of Lohs and his bridge watch washed ashore only a week later in the Schelde. Experience with flotsam taught us that when in the area of the Fairybank or Westhinder, these would usually drift for months in the area between the Sandettie and the North Hinder without touching land. *UB-57* would actually have had to have been sunk closer to land to yield human remains at such an early stage. A more plausible candidate would be the wreck of a UB-III class submarine in position 51° 25' 439 N 03° 06' 27 E, situated about 6 miles to the north of Zeebrugge. It was first discovered and dived upon by Dirk Termote and the author in 1996. The wreck is seemingly intact and lies upright with a slight inclination over starboard. Maximum depth is 12 m and the wreck has sunk up to halfway up its hull into the sand.

The dimensions of the conning tower point to a large U- or UB-III class submarine. The tower has been ripped from its footing and lies over port at an angle of 60°, but is still partly connected by its base to the hull. The forward hatch is shut, but the tower hatch and one of the aft hatches are gone. The interior of the U-boat is almost completely filled with sand. Just in front of the tower, a foot for the gun was discovered, but the gun was not present. On the bow there are two of the four torpedo tubes visible, with both doors being partially open. The wreck was then wrongly identified as being *UB-59*. It could not concern this U-boat as she was blown up intentionally in her dry dock in Bruges in October 1918.

Damage to the tower and the disappearance of the gun can point to the use of underwater chains. This method of levelling wrecks was used in the main part of the 20th century to deepen the water column above shallow wrecks. It could also have been that the wreck was hit by a deep-hulled vessel and was damaged this way. In an official Belgian hydrographic report there was mention of the vessel *Sanderus* hitting an obstruction about 0.6 miles to the west of wreckbuoy 11 on 15 April 1985. It then concerned the wreck of the unidentified UB-III class

Oberleutnant z. S. Siegfried Fuchs, first officer of UB-57, was killed after his U-boat was sunk. His body washed ashore near Zeebrugge and was interned in the Steenbrugge cemetery (Boie)

submarine. The keelson of the *Sanderus* had been ripped open over 4 m. Diver Piet Lagast, inspecting the site for the company after the collision, was given the assignment to assess the height as the wreck was not marked on the chart. As there was no visibility at the moment of the dive, the type of wreck could not be determined, but a zinc-anode which had been ripped from the keel of *Sanderus* was recovered from the site.[157] It could have been that the *Sanderus* had hit the 2.5 m high tower at lowtide, which would only give it a free space of about 2.5 m.[158] The location and type of U-boat strongly points in the direction of *UB-57*. But a number of determining factors lack to identify it 100% as being this U-boat. The wreck of the UB-III class lies roughly 6 miles from the former Zeebrugge Mole. From German reports there was no mention of an explosion or a flash of light, which was the case with the destruction of *UC-14*, which was mined much further out from Zeebrugge. The wreck of this UB-III lies only a half a mile from the wreck of *UC-4*. As *UC-4* was intentionally scuttled in October 1918, this points also in the direction that this UB-III class submarine fell victim to scuttling. This theory can actually be ignored as German sources only mention four submarines which were left in Flanders. These were *UB-40* and *UB-59*, which lay in dry dock for repairs and were blown up and *UB-10* and *UC-4* which had been purposely sunk outside Zeebrugge harbour. But there is a large possibility that the UB-III, sunk in the area known as 't Scheur, is that of *UB-57*. Only better visibility on the location and the recovery of a part bearing a number can give us definitive proof.

UB-58

On 5 July 1917, *UB-58* was completed and in August came under the command of *Oberleutnant z. S.* Werner Fürbringer. During five patrols he was able to sink a total of eight ships, but *UB-58* seemed to be plagued by ill-fortune. On her first patrol there were many mechanical failures and on the second and third patrols several torpedoes refused to follow their courses. After being fired they would run to the bottom and explode on impact. It would only be the depth which saved *UB-58* from being destroyed by the explosion of her own torpedoes. The second, premature explosion brought some vital damage to *UB-58*, forcing Fürbringer to return and face the dangers of the Dover Barrage. It proved to be so frustrating and stressful that Fürbringer suffered a nervous breakdown and was ordered to recover at a field hospital. As temporary replacement, *Oberleutnant z. S.* Werner

Löwe took over command of *UB-58* and her crew. He left Zeebrugge on 9 March 1918 and was already lost on the next day with all 35 men in the Dover Barrage. At 04h15, to the north of the Varne light vessel, the watch on the patrolship *HMS P-24* heard three subsequent explosions and went to investigate the area. Two hours later the British discovered a large oilslick with pieces of wooden flotsam, cork insulation, some loaves of bread and documents drifting in position 50° 58' N 01° 14' E. The papers concerned a battery log and details of the trial run of *UB-58* at Bremen on 1 August. The location of the wreck suggested that the U-boat had snagged and dragged a couple of mines before these detonated. The wreck was soon located and divers from *HMS Moonfleet* were able to investigate the wreck on 9 August. The front of the U-boat had totally been blown off up to the 105 mm deck gun. The inside was totally wrecked and held a mixture of body parts, mattresses, clothes and cables. The deck gun was salvaged three days later and on the same day the wreck of another U-boat was discovered,[159] Fürbringer, whilst in hospital, had a premonition that his U-boat and loyal crew would not return from this patrol. Three weeks later he was told that *UB-58* had gone missing. He was deeply saddened by the news and said that part of him had died with them.

The wreck of *UB-58* was identified by diver Dave Batchelor by means of comparing the position of the oilslick from 1918 and the flow of the tide during the period of her sinking. The slick and objects would have drifted about 3 to 4 miles to the southwest from the location where they surfaced. When the location was put on the chart they arrived in the area where Commander Damant had indicated the position of two U-boat wrecks. Only one wreck was discovered in position 51° 00' 11 N 01° 18' 58 E, at a depth of 22 m. It could be positively identified as that of *UB-58* by the numbers which had been stamped on both propellers. There was no deck gun present on the wreck which corresponded with the historical information of the recovery. The wreck does show heavy damage to the forward part, as a result of the mine-impact, whilst the rest of the wreck is relatively intact.[160]

UB-59

UB-59 went into service with the *I. U-Flottille Flandern* in November 1917 under the capable command of *Kapitänleutnant* Erwin Wassner. Wassner was able to prove his worth and sink nine ships in the following

Scenes of utter destruction in Bruges Harbour in November 1918. With the retreat, *UB-59* was blown-up in dock. The explosion was so strong that the stern was totally severed and deposited a few hundred metres away (TT)

six months. After *UB-59* had torpedoed the French *SS Azemmour* on the morning of 20 March, in thick fog, they experienced an unbelievable occurrence. During the night, the crew of *UB-59* witnessed an immense explosion off St. Catherine's Point. There was still a heavy fog, but the crew was able to see the collision between the British *SS War Knight* and the American *SS O.B. Jennings*. The explosion had been caused by *SS War Knight* hitting a mine laid by *UC-17* near the Needles. *SS O.B. Jennings* was burning severely and had to be beached. 32 crewmen lost their lives. On 2 May 1918, *UB-59* departed on her final patrol. When she wanted to run the gauntlet of the Dover Barrage, during the night of 4/5 May, *UB-59* was heavily damaged by two mines after it was cruising at a depth of 15 m. After great effort the crew was able to blow the ballast tanks and bring *UB-59* to the surface. After carrying out basic repairs they returned with their heavily damaged U-boat to Ostend. *UB-59* was brought to Bruges and placed in dry dock, but was again damaged, this time by an aircraft bomb. By the evacuation of the Flemish ports in October 1918, *UB-59* was still in a state of repair and was blown up in dry dock to prevent falling into enemy hands.

UB-74

Before *UB-74* joined the *I. U-Flottille Flandern* on 25 January 1918, she would see service with the *V. U-Flottille*. On 21 February, *Oberleutnant z. S.* Ernst Steindorff took her on her first patrol. During three missions, *UB-74* was able to sink seven ships.

On 26 May 1918, the periscope of *UB-74* was spotted by an attentive lookout on the steam yacht *Lorna*, in Lyme Bay, off Portland. Her commander, Lt. C.L. Tottenham, steered her full speed towards the location and was able to surprise the diving *UB-74* and hit her tower lightly. After the ramming, *Lorna* let go a depth charge, followed by a second one at 50 m distance. The depth charges seemed to have hit their mark because soon afterwards a large air bubble erupted and four objects were found. Tottenham let another depth charge be dropped on the spot. Shortly afterwards the crew of the Lorna heard vague cries for help in German: '*Kamerad, Kamerad!*'. Four survivors could be seen in the water, but only one of whom was still alive by then. The British managed to save him after which he confirmed that it was *UB-74* and that they had sunk a total of three ships since leaving Zeebrugge. Three hours later he died from the symptoms of decompression sickness and the wounds which had been inflicted on his body by the force of the explosions. The last depth charge had probably also killed his three comrades and fatally wounded him. On the location, a cap was fished up with a captally which read: '*Unterseeboots Abteilung*'. Tottenham received the DSC for the destruction of *UB-74*.

In June, Royal Navy divers, under supervision of commander Davis on the recovery vessel *Corycia*, descended on the wreck in position 50° 32' N 02° 32' E. The wreck stood on an even keel at a depth of nearly 39 m. The tower hatch was open and on the port side of the stern there was a 12 m long gash, with a width of 7.5 cm over its length, through the pressure hull. This had been caused by the explosion of the depth charges. On 6 June, divers had to open the forward hatch by means of explosives, gaining them access to the officers' mess. They were confronted by numerous bodies, flare munition and two metal cans. A log book was also found but it contained no information on the three sinkings which the survivor had spoken about, but the log had also not been filled in since 16 May. It did mention that *UB-74* had survived the ramming attempt from a steamship off Beachy Head on 13 May. Nothing more of interest was discovered and by the end of the month the tower was destroyed. A periscope and some small objects were recovered and sent to London for further investigation. The deck gun was also recovered. One of the divers who had worked during three months on the wreck of *UB-74*, was Dusty Miller. Miller would receive the DSC[161] in July 1919 for his role in recovering information from the wreck amidst difficult circumstances.[162]

The wreck of *UB-74* was re-discovered by divers and lies in position 50° 31' 48 N 02° 33' 34 E. It lies on a bottom of hard sand and shell with a general depth of 32 m. Commercial salvage was carried out on the wreck in the 1970s, whereby propellers and torpedo tubes were removed. During these activities, a torpedo supposedly exploded and destroyed large parts of the wreck. In 1999, Innes McCartney describes the wreck as heavily destroyed, with the hull blown open up to the keel. Bow and stern sections do not seem to be present anymore. The tower does not stand on the wreck anymore, but lies some distance from the main part. This was blown off with explosives by the Royal Navy and dragged to the spot where she lies now. The deck gun is also missing, although a lot of munition is scattered near the former footing.

UB-78

Before joining the I. *U-Flottille Flandern* on 18 February 1918, *UB-78* had carried out some unsuccessful patrols when at Helgoland with the *V. U-Flottille*. From the Flanders bases *UB-78* was only able to carry out three patrols, sinking two ships and damaging one. 1918 proved to be a difficult year for the U-boats, mostly because they had to contend with convoys and their numerous escorts. After *UB-78* had torpedoed *SS Polleon* in the estuary of the Tyne, she was bombarded with 25 depth charges. She suffered damaged to the superstructure where a section of the conning tower had been dented and the jumping wires were damaged. A torpedo had to be wasted on the 86 ton trawler, *Border Lads*, due to the lack of single sailing targets and also because of the large presence of the enemy on the surface.

UB-78 left Zeebrugge on her final voyage on 18 April 1918, under the command of *Oberleutnant z. S.* Arthur Stossberg. Off Folkestone she was lying on the surface trying to detect troop transports, when lookouts on *HMS P-33* spotted the surfaced U-boat. *HMS P-33* set course to ram the U-boat, but would eventually collide with the escorted troopship *SS Queen Alexandra*. *HMS P-33* slowed down and enabled *SS Queen Alexandra* to increase speed and go on a ramming course for the U-boat. Captain Angus Smith had increased the speed of his ship to 20 knots and was able to hit *UB-78* in her stern compartment. *HMS P-33* appeared on the spot and dropped a depth charge, but *UB-78* had already sunk. The escort marked the location with a buoy in 51° 01' N 01° 17' E and accompanied the damaged troopship back to harbour. The next day *HMS P-33* came back to the location of the sinking and discovered a 7 mile long track of battery acid and oil on the surface.

The wreck was later relocated in position 51° 01' 03 N 01° 16' 48 E and positively identified by the markings '*UB-78*' in both propellers. She stands upright with a general depth of 23 m.

UB-80

UB-80 turned out to be a very successful U-boat under the command of *Kapitänleutnant* Max Viebeg. Between 19 November 1917 and 1 October 1918 she was able to sink 24 ships and damage two, during seven patrols. On 1 October 1918 Viebeg was ordered to leave Zeebrugge with *UB-80* and sail towards Germany. A week later she arrived at Wilhelmshaven and was added to the *II. U-Flottille*. At the end of the month *UB-80* partook in a protective fleet of U-boats which had to guard the German High Seas Fleet for their last great sortie against the British. This never materialised and on 26 November 1918 *UB-80* was delivered with the 5th *Staffel* to the United Kingdom and sailed to Harwich. Afterwards she was given to Italy and broken up in May 1919 at La Spezia.

UB-81

UB-81 became part of the *I. U-Flottille Flandern* on 11 November 1917, about three months after having been completed. She would not survive very long and already be sunk on her first mission by a British mine. With her sinking, Germany would also lose one of its greatest Aces: *Oberleutnant z. S.* Reinhold Saltzwedel. Saltzwedel was to become the 11th most successful U-boat captain of the First World War and for the destruction of 150.000 BRT in shipping he was awarded the coveted *Pour le Mérite*. Almost his entire success was accomplished with the minelayer *UC-71*.

On the evening of 30 November 1917, *UB-81* was about 12 miles west of Beachy Head where she was able to sink the *SS Molesey* out of a convoy. Pickings in this area were poor and in the days following the sinking *UB-81* sailed westward to track down solitary ships. On 2 December the weather turned stormy and to give his crew some rest, Saltzwedel ordered the U-boat to be submerged to 20 m depth. At 17h45, when they were off the Owers light vessel, a British mine exploded against the stern of *UB-81*. The aft torpedo room completely flooded and the crew was not able to blow the ballast tanks. *UB-81* rapidly sank to a depth of 30 m. Water started to seep into the dry compartments and a solution had to be sought for their precarious situation. Saltzwedel had the torpedoes from the forward tubes removed and the crew continuously manned the pumps to empty the forward compartment. After completing this task he had all the remaining compressed air blown into the forward tanks to make *UB-81* rise to the surface. This plan succeeded and the bow shot to the surface and hung there at an angle of 53°. One of the top torpedo tubes could be opened after which the crew started to climb outside. The weather worsened and the four crewmen who were on the outside held on to the hull for dear life. The others had to await their turn as it was freezing cold outside. The situation started to worsen because the mouth of the tube only protruded 1 m above the choppy surface. Saltzwedel ordered another three men to crawl out of the tube and let the others prepare themselves to escape. On the outside *Bootsmaat* Wagner ignited several flares which attracted the attention of *HMS P-32*. When *HMS P-32* came closer and started to pick off survivors from the bow, she hit *UB-81*, which caused her to go under and sink. The British speak of a sad accident which was caused by the worsening weather, the Germans accused them of intentional ramming. Whatever was the cause, 28 men, including Saltzwedel, still trapped in the forward torpedo room drowned when *UB-81* sank. The two surviving officers of *UB-81*, *Marine-Ingenieur* Denker and *Leutnant z. S. d. Res*. Freudendahl said that the survivors were well treated by their British captors. The British captain excused himself for hitting and sinking *UB-81* and offered them cakes and whiskey in the officers' mess.[163]

A rare view of the business end of a UB-III type boat (TT)

The wreck of *UB-81* was rediscovered by diver and historian Martin Woodward. The wreck lies in position 50° 29' 22 N 00° 58' 12 E at a depth of 30 m. Although she sank intact, the wreck did suffer from post-war commercial salvage activities. *UB-81* lies in two pieces with both halves some distance from each other. Bow and stern

A view on the conning tower of *UB-81* with retracted periscopes (Martin Woodward)

The 8.8 cm deck gun on the wreck of *UB-81* points upwards to a long-disappeared enemy (Martin Woodward)

have been totally blown open. The tower has also been blown from its footing by means of explosives and lies to starboard. The stern torpedo tubes are visible and it is possible to peer inside the wreck. Propellers and bow torpedo tubes have long gone and were probably recovered for their scrap metal. An 8.8 cm gun used to remain on its original footing for many years, but has recently fallen to the bottom after being corroded. A number of finds, such as lamps and a signal horn, are now on display at the Bembridge Shipwreck Museum, on the Isle of Wight. There was talk that *UB-81* had displaced itself 20 miles after its sinking in 1917 due to 'rolling' over the seabed. This would have been caused by pockets of air still present in the ballast tanks, helped by the influences of the swell and current.[164] This theory can most certainly be considered as absurd, as a 650 ton weighing submarine, which would be filled up to 90% with water and silt, would most certainly not be able to move anymore, even with the heaviest of swells. It is possible that the wreck was only discovered after lots of difficulty and its position lost again, by the non-existence in those days of the excellent and unmissable GPS positioning system.

UB-88

UB-88 was the last of the '80 class UB-boats which would operate out of the Flanders bases. When she was launched on 11 December 1917, none of her builders would suspect that she would end her career at the bottom of the Pacific Ocean. *UB-88* was transferred in June 1918 to the *I. U-Flottille Flandern* and was commanded by *Kapitänleutnant* Reinhardt von Rabenau.

During four patrols Rabenau managed to sink 14 ships and damage another. Besides mainly British and Swedish ships, the American steamships *SS Berwind* and *SS Lake Portage* were also sunk. *UB-88* mainly had to deal with convoy-bound vessels and the inevitable rain of depth charges which followed after an attack. Von Rabenau and his crew could count themselves the lucky ones as they survived the war and returned to Wilhelmshaven on 4 October 1918, where *UB-88* was added to the *II. U-Flottille*. As *UB-88* had suffered heavy damage to her electrical installation on the last patrol, she remained in maintenance up to the end of the war. On 22 November 1918, *UB-88* was handed over to Great Britain and sailed across to Harwich. After that she was assigned to the United States and on 4 April 1919 made the crossing of the Atlantic Ocean to New York. Here *UB-88* was added to the fleet of the United States Navy with a special commission. *UB-88* would sail around the entire United States coast, from the East Coast, around Florida, through the Gulf of Mexico as a propaganda- and curiosity object. Finally she went via the Panama Canal to the West Coast where she ended up in California in 1921. The navy wanted to get rid of her and on 3 January 1921, *UB-88* was deliberately sunk by gunfire from the destroyer *USS Wilkes* off San Pedro.

UB-88 arrives as war booty in Miami Florida (Gary Fabian)

Leutnant z. S. Erhard Tobye was for a while first officer on board *UB-88* and survived the war (Boie)

UB-88 in Brooklyn Navy Yard, New York (Gary Fabian)

American seamen taking a break amidst the diesel engines of *UB-88* (US Naval History & Heritage Command)

An American naval officer and seaman pose in front of the four forward torpedo tube hatches of *UB-88*. On the covers the slogan 'Gott mit uns' is still legible (US Naval History & Heritage Command)

UB-88, flying the American stars and stripes arrives in New York Harbour as US prize after crossing the Atlantic (Gary Fabian)

UB-88 in the Lake Union Lock. Her typical 'Flanders' eye' is recognisable (Gary Fabian)

UB-88 in Harwich, just before leaving to the US (Gary Fabian)

UB-88 lies alongside the US naval steam tug *USS Bittern* in the Panama Canal (Gary Fabian)

UB-88 photographed whilst making the crossing of the Panama Canal (Gary Fabian)

UB-88 at the end of her 'tour': the harbour of San Diego, California (Gary Fabian)

The sad end to *UB-88*: deliberately sunk off California (Fox Newsreel)

UB-103

UB-103 would remain under the command of *Kapitänleutnant* Paul Hundius from her launch up to her sinking, a year later. She was added to the *I. U-Flottille Flandern* on 8 March 1918, when finally brought into Zeebrugge. During six months, *UB-103* operated in the areas of the Irish Sea, Bristol Channel, off Cornwall and the Spanish north coast.

On 28 April 1918, off Falmouth, the unsuspecting *UB-103* came in contact with a Q-ship which altered course to her and opened fire. During the rapid dive, a shell bored through a tank in the stern, followed by a rain of depth charges. Hundius and his crew were lucky and managed to escape and continue their patrol. Hundius managed to fulfil a total of five patrols sinking a total of 13 ships. Two more ships could be placed under his name, if it had been *UB-103* which had torpedoed the British *SS Gibel Hamam* and *SS Kendal Castle* in Lyme Bay. On 14 August, *UB-103* left on her final patrol and headed out of Zeebrugge toward the west coast of France. Hundius would be attempting to seek out and destroy American trooptransports.

UB-103 probably never made it that far, because she was spotted by the airship *SSZ-1* near the Dover Barrage. It could have been that *UB-103* was damaged during her crossing as she left a long oilslick trailing behind her, which was visible from the air. The airship caught the attention of the drifters *Young Crow, East Holme, Fertility, Calceolaria* and *Pleasants* and guided them to the source of the oil spill. *UB-103* dived deep to escape from her pursuers. The airship dropped a number of bombs and the drifters started depth-charging the location. During the next half hour, three explosions were registered and nothing more was seen of the U-boat. It is not sure if the bombs of *SSZ-1* or the depth charges or the mines of the Dover Barrage ended the life of *UB-103*. *UB-103* would be the final U-boat to have been destroyed by the Dover Barrage.

Shortly after her sinking, the wreck was said to have been discovered and dived by Commander Damant's dive team, after which £ 1000 reward was paid out. This was said to have been in position 50° 52' 20 N 01° 26' 80 E. Up to now, no UB-III class submarine was found in this position between Le Colbart and Cap Griz Nez.

UB-104

Like most other UB-III U-boats, the lifespan of *UB-104* ended up being very short in 1918. She went into service with the *II. U-Flottille Flandern* on 24 July 1918. Her captain, *Oberleutnant z. S.* Thomas Bieber, was able to sink six ships on his first patrol. These were two Dutch sailing ships in the area of the Hoofden and five steamships off the British east coast. On his second patrol Bieber chose to round Scotland to arrive in the hunting grounds of the western Channel area. *UB-104* left Zeebrugge on 6 September and went missing after that with all hands. Her last sign of life was a mention in the KTB of *U-57*. This stated that *UB-104* had exchanged recognition signals with *U-57* at the entrance to the North Channel in the Irish Sea. There are two possible explanations for the loss of *UB-104*. According to British sources she was sunk in the western sector of the Northern Barrage, near Fair Island, by a mine on 19 September. Just after the war, US minesweepers *Heron* and *Sanderling* supposedly came upon the wreck of a unidentified U-boat when clearing mines in the Northern Barrage. A second possibility is that *UB-104* managed to completely navigate around

Leutnant z. S. Stephan Glaser, 1st officer of *UB-103*, killed when his U-boat was sunk in the Dover Barrage (Boie)

Leutnant z. S. Hermann Bremer, Thomas Bieber's 1st officer, was also killed when *UB-104* disappeared with all hands (Boie)

Multibeam sonar image (Gary Fabian)

A GERMAN FLANDERSBOAT OFF LONG BEACH, CALIFORNIA

A few years ago I came in touch with US diver and researcher Gary Fabian. He told me the story that when he was an angler in 1989 he bought a book on the wrecks of southern California. He was fascinated by the story of *UB-88*, a First World War U-boat which had been sunk only a short distance from Los Angeles! The existence of *UB-88* was common knowledge through reports made by the navy and through local newspapers which mentioned that it lay just in front of the Long Beach Harbour, California. The rumours remained but nobody had the actual coordinates of the sunken U-boat.

Finally Fabian set up a small group in 2002, together with Ray Arntz, to locate the wreck of *UB-88*. A year was spent searching intensively for the wreck and for Fabian it almost became an obsession. He went through naval archives looking for information, but the diaries of the ships present at the time of the sinking of *UB-88* were quite vague. The wreck was finally discovered after 14 months of search by means of sidescan and multibeam. *UB-88* had been sunk in the deep water of the Catalina Canal, to the southeast of the Los Angeles Harbour lighthouse. A team of technical divers was set up, with Kendall Raine and John Walker, later joined by Scott Brooks and Fred Colburn.

The tower of *UB-88*, crowded with fish (Kendall Raine)

Photographic mosaic of *UB-88*, seen from above (John Walker)

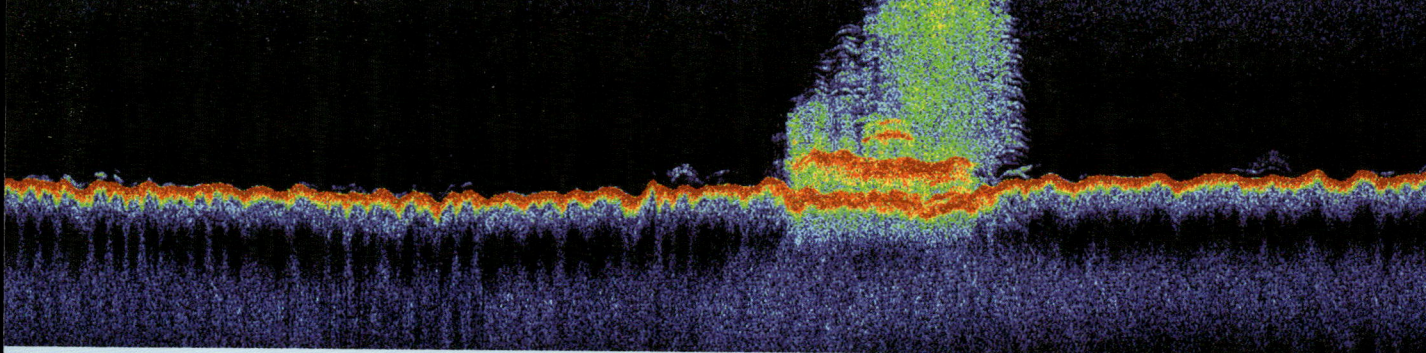

Sidescan-Sonarimage (Gary Fabian)

UB-88 lies upright at nearly 90 m depth and is quite intact. Part of the superstructure and outer skin have been corroded after having lain on the bottom for more than 90 years. The foot of the gun still stands in front of the tower, but the gun was already removed before she was sunk. Several hatches are open and the propellors are still present.

The protective casing for the periscopes situated on top of the conning tower (Kendall Raine)

The foot of the long-disappeared 8.8 cm deck gun (Kendall Raine)

An open hatch on deck (Kendall Raine)

the British Isles and was able to sink three ships in Lyme Bay on 16 and 17 September. Due to a shortage in fuel and the necessity to get back home, Bieber may have decided to take the shortest route back, through the Dover Barrage. If he had taken that route, *UB-104* possible could have been sunk in the minefield to the east of the Fairy Bank. If this is the case, *UB-104* could be one of the UB-III wrecks which were fitted with a 10.5 cm gun (described under *UB-54*).

UB-106

UB-106 was launched on 21 July 1917 and originally meant to join the *I. U-Flottille Flandern*, but this was cancelled after a deadly diving accident. On 15 March 1918, when she had been used by the U-boat school, she sank during manoeuvers off the Schlei Estuary. The cause was the failure to close the bow torpedo tube doors, which drowned the entire crew. Three days later the salvage vessel *SMS Vulcan* came to the location and was able to recover *UB-106*. She was put into dry dock, underwent repairs and added to the *U-Schule* Kiel. After the Armistice, *UB-106* was destined to be handed over to England but beached near Falmouth in 1921 together with *UB-86*, *UB-97* and *UB-112*. In the following years major parts of the four Falmouth U-boats were salvaged, but most parts remained and can still be dived now.

UB-107

UB-107 was launched on 21 July 1917 and five months later went into service under the command of *Kapitänleutnant* Hans Howaldt. Howaldt was ordered to bring *UB-107* over to Zeebrugge, but decided to attack shipping on the British east coast on his way down south. He managed to sink two ships and damage one when attacking a first convoy. On 14 May 1918 he attacked a second convoy, but disaster struck. All three fired torpedoes missed a merchant ship and another failed to explode on another. The convoy sailed passed and all *UB-107*'s torpedoes had been spent. Howaldt had the U-boat submerged to load the batteries and give his crew some rest. When he had *UB-107* surface again around midday, something went wrong with the ballasting of the U-boat which immediately forced her to dive, whilst Howaldt had just emerged from the hatch. He managed to jump clear, shut the hatch and hold on with one hand to the extended periscope. Luckily the U-boat was cruising slowly and he managed to hang on to the periscope. To make matters worse, a trawler had spotted the trouble and headed towards him whilst firing at the periscope at a distance of 2000 m. The shells threw up fountains of water around *UB-107* and it would not be long before they would get hit. Inside the U-boat the tanks were blown and a minute later tower and hatch were free of water. Howaldt jumped down from the periscope, opened the hatch, and disappeared below. Whilst still turning the handwheel, *UB-107* dived full speed below the surface and left the frustrated trawler behind. Two days later *UB-107* arrived at Zeebrugge and joined the *II. U-Flottille Flandern*.

On 17 May 1918, *Kapitänleutnant* Eberhard von Prittwitz und Gaffron took over command of *UB-107*. Born in 1889, von Prittwitz was a descendant from nobility, and had held the rank of *Kapitänleutnant* since 1917. At the outbreak of the war he had served as captain on six different torpedo boats. After following a course at the *U-Schule*, he joined the *U-Flottille Flandern*. Between May and July 1918 *UB-107* was able to sink seven ships off the British east coast. On 26 July 1917, *UB-107* left on her final patrol and would be lost with all hands. According to British sources she had been spotted by a motorlaunch off Scarborough. Around 21h00 on 27 July, the trawler *Calvis* and the destroyer *HMS Vanessa* discovered *UB-107* to the southeast of Whitby in position 54° 23' N 00° 24' E. She lay surfaced and both British ships set full speed towards her. *UB-107* managed to spot them and dive, but was attacked with a rain of depth charges. During the following two hours the hunt for *UB-107* was started with hydrophone and depth charges. Not much later oil and air bubbles came to the surface not far from the position where *UB-107* had been seen for the first time. The next morning a trawler recovered the headless corpse of a sailor. This was the version from the British Admiralty concerning the sinking of *UB-107*, but no UB-III class U-boat has been found in the area.

In 1985, the wreck of a UB-III class submarine was discovered by accident by divers who were going down to

◄ A UB-III type boat in the small Merchantdock, Bruges. In the background a torpedo boat and a large floating dry dock are visible (TT)

free some lobsterpots. Funnily enough they dived on the wreck of SS *Malvina*, which was sunk on 2 August 1918. It was not only SS *Malvina* which had been discovered by chance, but also that of *UB-107* which lay partly under the stern of the merchant ship! The wreck lies in position 54° 08′ 350 N 00° 04′ 742 W, about 1.2 miles to the north of Flamborough Head, a large distance from the original position. It could be that *UB-107* had torpedoed SS *Malvina* on 2 August or had hit a mine, whereby the sinking SS *Malvina* had ended up on top of the wreck of *UB-107*. Both wrecks lie on a hard, sandy bottom with a general depth of 26 m. The 1,244 ton *Malvina* is broken in two and part of the U-boat lies beneath the engine room segment of the merchant ship.[165]

UB-108

UB-108 joined the *I. U-Flottille Flandern* on 22 May 1918 and was commanded by *Oberleutnant z. S.* Wilhelm Amberger. Amberger was able to sink two British ships off the east coast in the following month. On 2 July 1918 *UB-108* left on her 2nd patrol, but did not return and has been missing with all hands. Grant mentions the possibility that *UB-108* had gone through the Dover Barrage. On 10 July the lookouts of two drifters noticed a trace of oil and air bubbles which proceeded in eastnortheasterly direction. This was in the area between Folkestone and the Varne bank. The patrol vessels dropped four depth charges, which resulted in three large explosions, followed by oil coming to the surface. It was also possible that they had bombarded an existing wreck. Up to now nothing is known about the location of the wreck of *UB-108*, but it is possible that she is one of the UB-III class U-boats to the east of the Fairybank (described under *UB-54*).

UB-109

Oberleutnant z. S. Kurt Ramien commanded *UB-109* after she had been launched on 7 July 1917. It was only seven months later that she would finally be added to the *I. U-Flottille Flandern*. Ramien decided

Oberleutnant z. S. Wilhelm Amberger poses for a photo in his digs in Bruges. Shortly after the photo was taken, on 10 July 1918, he would perish with *UB-108* and her entire crew in the Dover Straits (TT)

Leutnant z. S. Hans Hassel, Amberger's first officer, would also be killed when *UB-108* was sunk (Boie)

to be ambitious on his first patrol and left for the Irish Sea in April 1918. He managed to sink four ships and make two unsuccessful attacks on a US submarine and a Q-ship. On his second patrol, Ramien would venture to the furthest area for a Flandersboat: the Azores. *UB-109* left on 27 July and would remain at sea for nearly a month. The search for enemy ships proved to be frustrating and nothing was spotted for two weeks. In the end Ramien had to return home, as fuel and supplies were running low. On the way back he was able to torpedo three ships. But *UB-109's* luck ran out when trying to cross the Dover Barrage on 29 August. At 02h00 she had reached Dungeness and attempted a crossing as near to the coast as possible in a waterdepth of just 10 m. At 03h30, when *UB-109* was able to pass by two light vessels, the sound of her propellers was picked up by hydrophones. The guard vessels alerted the coastal stations which detonated a line of mines automatically. A heavy explosion followed and *UB-109* sank with a list and sank to the bottom at 20 m. The impact of the explosion was so intense that it ripped the pressure hull and sent heavy shockwaves throughout the U-boat. Water gushed in through enormous rents in the stern. When the lights went out, panic broke out and men were falling over each other. Ramien later told his interrogators that his crew was shouting loudly one moment and then the next all went quiet. The explosion had thrown him against the periscope housing and he tried to recover his wits. After recovering he crawled up to the conning tower where the helmsman and navigating officer were still conscious. He tried to talk to them but everywhere there was hissing of ruptured tubes releasing compressed air. *UB-109* was rapidly filling with water which was already rising up to the tower. Ramien had to stand on the top of the ladder with the navigating officer just below him. After some pushing and shoving the hatch blew open and both men were propelled through the opening by the release of pressure. They remained blocked for half a minute, but after some pulling managed to release themselves and ascend to the surface. Ramien said that he felt that his lungs were void of oxygen, but somehow air seemed to slowly keep on trickling naturally out of them. When he had reached the surface, one of his radio operators, a helmsman and the navigating officer appeared as well. By miracle another five men had been able to escape. Immediately after the explosion, the men from the forward torpedo room had been able to open the hatch, letting five men escape. One of the stokers had been forced through all the compartments of *UB-109* by the rush of incoming water whereafter he was forced through the forward hatch to the surface. Ramien shook off his leather jacket and boots so as he was able to float easier. After 45 minutes, eight survivors were picked up by the British trawler *D-10*. The ninth man had drowned.

The Royal Navy diving team had been well trained and used to locating and diving a sunken U-boat. Not even 12 hours had passed after the sinking of *UB-109* when *HMS Moonfleet* came on site. Explosives were not used on *UB-109* and divers Blackford and Clear gained access to the control room by entering the wreck through the forward hatch and passing out the bodies and other material recovered through the conning tower. Both divers had to work in unimaginably difficult conditions. During the following week, a detailed study of the wreck could be made and much valuable material was recovered. One of the finds was a map which detailed *UB-109*'s entire journey around Gibraltar, Spain and the Azores. The divers also stated that the interior of the U-boat was quite warm, this was from heat eminating from the batteries beneath the metal gratings. Six m abaft the tower, the damage was clearly visible and the rest of the stern was totally destroyed.[166]

The wreck of *UB-109* was rediscovered in position 51° 03' 73 N 01° 14' 13 E in a depth of 29 m. The wreck shows heavy damages and has been totally severed into two parts. Identity was confirmed by the number 'UB-109' which was stamped on one of the propellers. Oddly enough the other propeller was marked 'UB-104'. By studying the information from the Royal Navy diving team, we can be very sure that the wreck is that of *UB-109* and not of the still missing *UB-104*. Engine room and stern sections have been totally destroyed, but the wreck is fairly intact from tower up to bow. All hatches are open and a 10.5 cm gun still stands on its foot.

UB-110

It would be the loss of *UB-110* which would bring a stop to the career of the successful *Kapitänleutnant* Werner 'Fips' Fürbringer. *UB-110* was launched in September 1917 and was brought over to Flanders in the spring of 1918 to join the *II. U-Flottille Flandern*. During his trip down, Fürbringer wanted to attack shipping on the

The wreck of *UB-110* lies in dry dock in Newcastle-upon-Tyne, after Royal naval salvage vessels had salvaged her from the sea-bed on 7 October 1918 (Grant)

east coast, but had to relent due to bad weather. When *UB-110* had nearly reached Ostend on 27 June, she was attacked with bombs and machinegunned by British aircraft. The gun and bow were lightly damaged, putting *UB-110* for a week into dry dock.

Life of a UB-III class U-boat was fairly short in 1918. This would also be the case for *UB-110*, which would be sunk on her first patrol.

Fürbringer decided to head for the British east coast once more to attack the numerous convoys. Off Scarborough he managed to torpedo one steamship out of a convoy and on 19 July he attacked a second convoy, but was stalked and bombed by *ML 49* and *ML 263* with depth charges. *UB-110* suffered damage to her stern and water started to pour into the engine room. After this, one of the hydroplanes jammed, making *UB-110* shoot to the surface. In the port electric engine there was a short circuit and a fuel tank was badly damaged. In the meantime, the destroyer *HMS Garry* had come to the scene, opened fire and rammed *UB-110* near her tower. *HMS Garry* slid off the damaged *UB-110*, but the captain let his vessel ram her again full speed for a second time. *UB-110* was mortally damaged and Fürbringer ordered everyone on deck. The entire crew, other than the two radio operators, had managed to exit the U-boat. Despite *UB-110* being in a sinking condition, with a crew jumping overboard, the escorts kept up their fire. The survivors had a hard time at the hands of the British. Nearly the entire crew had managed to exit the sinking *UB-110*. They drifted helplessly in the sea and had no means to defend themselves. Forster, a *Maschinistenmaat*, was brutally beaten by a British petty officer when he tried crawling up the side of a torpedo boat. Some crewmen on the torpedo boat opened fire on the survivors whilst others threw lumps of coal at the heads of the floating Germans. Smaller vessels approached and opened fire with their machine guns. Fürbringer saw his aide looking at him desperately and so he swam towards him. The aide was hit by a large lump of coal and killed instantly. *Oberleutnant* Loebell, who had been shot through the thigh, was nearby but did not have a lifevest. He asked Fürbringer to let him die in peace, as he thought the British would butcher them all anyway.[167] Finally the captain and 12 crewmen were saved, whilst the others floated around dead in their lifejackets. Fürbringer was later on brought as prisoner on *HMS Satellite* at Yarrow. On the way to the train station he was given a hard time by local fishermen.

The wreck of *UB-110* was not difficult to locate as oil was constantly leaking to the surface. Commander Wheeler managed to find the wreck on 19 July 1918 in position 54° 39′ N 00° 55′ E, at about 4.5 miles to the northeast of Saltburn pier. Divers descended on the wreck and it was then decided to completely recover the wreck. This titanic job was completed on 4 October when she was lifted using the lifting pontoon *YC-10* and brought into dry dock and studied. On 9 October, important codebooks, documents and radio logbooks were found. The wreck was later towed to the Tyne for demolition, but beached on 18 May 1919.

UB-111

UB-111 was launched in September 1917 and was only ready for her first patrol in July 1918 when she had been added to the *II. U-Flottille Flandern*. *Oberleutnant z. S.* Egon von Werner took command and he headed for the Firth of Forth the next month. *UB-111* unsuccessfully engaged a convoy and on her way back von Werner was able to stop seven Dutch trawlers near the Hoofden and sink them with explosive charges. On her second and final patrol she left Zeebrugge on 14 September and headed for the western entrance to the Channel, via the North Sea and around the Shetlands. Due to stormy weather the patrol had to be cancelled and on 14 October *UB-111* headed for Wilhelmshaven where she was added to the *II. U-Flottille*. *UB-111's* career came to an end when she was handed over to England and scrapped in 1920.

UB-112

Like *UB-111*, *UB-112* was destined to have a short life, with only two patrols. She went into service with the *II. U-Flottille Flandern* on 21 July under the command of *Kapitänleutnant* Wilhelm Rhein. On the British east coast, Rhein had a bit more luck than *UB-111* when he chanced upon three unescorted ships. Two British and one Swedish ships were torpedoed on her first patrol. On 17 September *UB-112* left for her final patrol and headed to the western end of the Channel. Heading around the Shetlands she went to the Isles of Scilly and was able to torpedo eight ships. On 18 October she received a radio message that the Flanders bases had been evacuated. Rhein decided to head around the north of England towards Germany. On 24 November 1918, *UB-112* ended her career after being delivered to England. She was towed to Falmouth for scrapping in 1921, but due to stormy weather, the tow parted and *UB-112* ended up on the beach, together with a few other U-boats. The wreck was partly dismantled and scrapped.

UB-113

After arriving at Zeebrugge on 24 July 1918, *UB-113* joined the *II. U-Flottille Flandern* and came under the command of *Oberleutnant z. S.* Pilzecker. He was only able to carry out one patrol, from 6 to 20 August, during which he sank one ship off Scarborough. On 14 September, *UB-113* left for her final voyage, but nothing is known of her and the fate of her crew. She had left Zeebrugge together with *UB-111*, rounded Scotland to end up in the western part of the Channel.

The wreck of *UB-113* has not been found, or identified amongst the known UB-III type wrecks, but it is possible that she was sunk in the western part of the Channel. Grant and Gröner suggest that *UB-113* hit a mine off Boulogne on 9 October.[168] This is doubtfull as no U-boat commander wanted to risk the crossing of the Dover Barrage anymore.

UB-114

Historically this U-boat never actually operated in the North Sea, let alone was based in one of the Flemish harbours. But after her launch on 23 September 1917, she was assigned to the *I. U-Flottille Flandern* on 4 May 1918. When exercising her trim in Kiel Harbour, *UB-114* sank with the loss of seven lives. After she was recovered, the war was over and she was handed over to England on 26 November 1918. Hereafter she was handed to France and ended up in the Toulon scrapyard in July 1921.

Leutnant z. S. Helmuth Ohly, 1st officer on board *UB-113*, would not reach home after his U-boat was lost in the Northern Barrage (Boie)

UB-115

UB-115 was one of the last UB-III class U-boats to arrive in Zeebrugge in September 1918 and attached to the *I. U-Flottille Flandern*. On 18 September, under the command of *Oberleutnant z. S.* Reinhold Thomsen, she left for her first and only patrol towards the British east coast. Three days later Thomsen managed to sink the small steamship *SS Staithes* off Sunderland. Eight days later *UB-115* was sunk with all hands. In the afternoon of 29 September, the British airship *R-29* observed a large oilslick on the surface, to the southeast of Coquet Island. *HMS Ouse* and *HMS Star*, accompanied by numerous drifters, came on the location and released dozens of depth charges on the suspected U-boat. Some hours later, motorsounds were picked up by their hydrophones. The rain of depth charges continued until 18h25, after which the noise stopped. We can assume that it concerned *UB-115* which was operating in the area. Oil kept welling up during the night and the following days. Two days later two minesweepers arrived on the location and pinpointed an obstruction which was obviously still leaking oil.

The wreck of *UB-115* lies in position 55° 14' 468 N 01° 22' 440 W about 4.5 miles to the northeast of Beacon Point, Newbiggin-by-the Sea, at a depth of 49 m. The wreck had been dived on in 1973 and described as lying on an even keel, intact, with all hatches shut. Presently it has been described as broken in two halves.

UB-116

Like her sister ships, *UB-116* was fated to have a very brief career with the *U-Flottille Flandern* after she arrived in Zeebrugge on 15 August 1918. She made one patrol, but this went without any success. Finally she was sailed back to Wilhelmshaven after the Flemish ports were evacuated. At her arrival, on 4 October, *UB-116* was added tot he *III. U-Flottille*. On 25 October *UB-116* left Helgoland for Scapa Flow. Her captain, *Oberleutnant z. S.* Erich Stephan seemingly wanted to carry out a final attack on the British fleet. *UB-116* had bad luck and the sound of the electric engines was picked up by the patrol vessels. She ended up in the middle of a minefield which was detonated manually, at a distance, sinking *UB-116* and killing all her crew. Later that year the wreck was discovered by Commander Damant on *Corycia*. Diving commenced on 1 November and books and papers immediately began to be recovered as the divers edged their way through the usual debris towards the control room. On the day of the Armistice more intelligence was recovered, along with the deck gun. Salvage Section divers

A photo taken during training in Germany in 1916. Left: Kolbe (Captain of *UB-119*), second from left: Amberger (captain *UB-10* and *UB-38*), right: von Heydebreck (captain of *UB-6* and later *UC-63*) (U-Boot-Archiv Cuxhaven)

arrived and plans were made to lift the U-boat using *YC-10* after recovering *UB-110*. With the war now over, the Intelligence Division cancelled all further work on the wreck and the site was abandoned. This ended the wartime contribution of the Special Section.[169]

UB-117

UB-117 was completed in November 1917, but it would be nearly a year later when she was ready to be brought over to Zeebrugge. On 5 September 1918 *UB-117* underwent her first patrol and stood under the command of the veteran *Kapitänleutnant* Erwin Wassner. During the three-week long patrol Wassner was able to sink five ships around Cornwall. He did not want to risk his U-boat through the dangerous Dover Straits and both outward as well as inward bound patrols were made around the Shetlands. A second patrol never materialised because *UB-117* had to proceed to Wilhelmshaven on 30 September to join the *II. U-Flottille*. Finally she was handed over to England in November 1918 to end up in the Felixstowe breaker's yard in 1920.

UC-BOATS

UC-1

Even being one of the smallest U-boats of the Flanders Flotilla, *UC-1* was able to carry out a record number of 80 patrols in a lifespan of 25 months and sink or damage a total of 50 Allied ships by laying several minefields. This was accomplished between 28 June, 1915 and, up to her disappearance in July 1917. *UC-1* would operate close to home, in the Thames Estuary, the Kentish Knock, the Downs, the east coast, the North Hinder and the Calais area. Amongst her victims were numerous British naval trawlers which had been used as minesweepers.

UC-1 arrived in Zeebrugge on 25 June 1915 and left four days later on her first mission in the Thames. Under command of her first captain, *Oberleutnant z. S.* von Werner, she released 12 mines to the northwest of the Kentish Knock light vessel. *UC-1*'s first victim was the torpedo boat *HMS Lightning*, which hit a mine, severing the bow and sinking her.

On her 25th patrol, in March 1916, von Werner released 12 mines near the North Hinder light vessel. It would only be four months later that the Dutch ships *SS Maas* and *RSS Koningin Wilhelmina* would fall victim to the field and be sunk. Both shipwrecks were discovered in the 1990s by Dirk Termote and his diving group. *RSS Koningin Wilhelmina* was a paddlesteamer which had been on route from Flushing to Tilbury with passengers and mail.

The success of the small minelayer truly proved itself in July 1916 when *UC-1*, on her 36th patrol, laid two fields, each counting six mines, to the northeast of Southwold. On the same day the naval trawler *Astrologer* and the steamship *SS Tugela* were sunk. In the following days the dredger *Mercurius*, the trawler *Whooper* and the merchant vessels *SS Alto*, *SS Mopsa* and *SS Claudia* hit mines and sank in the same field which had been laid by *UC-1*.

A UC-I type boat enters Ostend Harbour (Jörn Jensen)

A UC-I type boat lies moored in the small Merchantdock in Bruges (TT)

UC-2 on the return from a patrol. She would later on hit a mine and sink with all hands (TT)

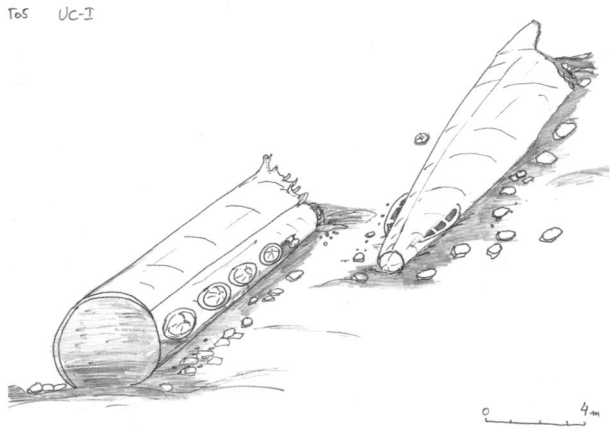

Drawing of the heavily damaged wreck of UC-1, sunk north of the Sandettiebank (TT)

The second officer from left is Christian Mildenstein, captain of the doomed UC-1 (U-Boot-Archiv Cuxhaven)

Even the fast destroyers were not spared from the ever present danger of invisible mines. On 8 November 1916 HMS Zulu ran on a mine which was laid by UC-1 near the Dyck light vessel. The explosion caused the stern to be severed, but the main part of the ship stayed afloat and was towed by the French torpedo boat Capitaine Mehl to Calais. At a later date, HMS Zulu was fitted with a new stern, which originated from her sister ship, HMS Nubian, which had been torpedoed and had lost her bows. With the coalescence of both parts the destroyer was baptised HMS Zubian.

The seventh and final captain of UC-1 was Oberleutnant z. S. Christian Mildenstein, which had taken command on 2 June 1917. He was able to carry out five patrols in which two minesweepers were mined and sunk. On 18 July 1917, UC-1 left Zeebrugge for her 79th and final patrol. She was heading for the Calais area and nothing since has been heard of her and her crew.

The British claim that *UC-1* was spotted on 24 July in the area of the Thames Estuary by five seaplanes. Each aircraft was able to fly over the target and drop their bombs successfully on *UC-1*.[170] This claim has to be treated with a certain amount of scepticism as 24 July was a week after *UC-1*'s departure from Zeebrugge. Patrols of UC-I class U-boats would not encompass more than three to four days in total. It could have been possible that *UC-1* had to contend with problems and was delayed on her return to base. Also, the area where the U-boat was supposedly spotted does not correspond with the area of operations for *UC-1*.

The wreck of *UC-1* was found and dived in the autumn of 1995 by veteran researcher Dirk Termote in position 51° 27' 220 N 02° 02' 990 E and is situated in the northbound shipping lane. The wreckage bears witness to a very heavy explosion. The wreck is totally severed in half and both parts lie on a hard bottom at 43 m depth. A heavy impact had struck *UC-1* amidships, beneath the tower, which flung the U-boat partially upwards. Both sections lie in a straight line, but the stern faces the rent in the bow. There is no conning tower present and it is assumed that this was totally destroyed by the explosion. The forward part of the U-boat is missing, as are two of her front shafts. The four remaining shafts still contain the load of mines.

The area where this UC-I class minelayer was discovered corresponds with the course that *UC-1* had taken in 1917 to reach the area of operation near Calais. The fact that the mines are still in their shafts proves that *UC-1* was sunk on 18 July, the day of her departure. The scale of the destruction could point towards the impact of a torpedo from a British submarine. Or else *UC-1* had unknowingly hit a British mine in a freshly laid field.

UC-2

UC-2 would never be able to prove her full worth as she was lost with all hands on her very first minelaying operation. *UC-2* was operational on 17 May 1915 and came under command of *Oberleutnant z. S. Karl Mey*. She left Zeebrugge on 29 June and headed towards the east coast to lay mines off Lowestoft. On 2 July, the British steamship *SS Cottingham* reported a collision with an object. Minesweepers were immediately sent out to search the area. By evening, a heavy underwater explosion was detected. Wreckage and oil came to the surface and the location was buoyed. Chatham dockyard divers came on site and observed that the U-boat was heavily damaged aft. It was then suspected that it concerned *UC-2* which had hit one of its own mines whilst laying a field in the Stanford Channel, Great Yarmouth. The discovery of a German submarine minelayer also meant a breakthrough for the British as they had been baffled by the mystery of minefields appearing in the most unlikely places. The local commander wanted to recover the forward section of the wreck for the purpose of gathering intelligence, but Admiral Oliver at the Admiralty ordered the wreck to be blown up. All that was learnt of what was there came from the sketches of the divers. For the entire story of *UC-2*, see UC-I type submarines.

UC-3

UC-3 went into service on 1 June 1915, under the command of *Kapitänleutnant* Erwin Weissbach. Her area of operations was similar to that of *UC-1*, mainly concentrating on Calais, Dover and the Thames Estuary. Weisbach managed to carry out nine patrols between 3 July and 26 September 1915, mining only five ships. One of his victims was the Belgian trawler *Nieuport* which snagged one of his mines in her trawl off Calais. When hauling in the 'catch', the mine exploded, destroying the wooden ship and killing her crew.

Oberleutnant z. S. Erwin Wassner took over command on 5 October 1915 and in seven months carried out 15 minelaying operations with *UC-3*, sinking or damaging a total of 15 Allied ships.

The third and final captain of *UC-3* was *Oberleutnant z. S.* Günther Kreysern. He managed to carry out two unsuccessful missions in May 1916 in the area between Gravelines and Calais. On 25 May, *UC-3* left for the east coast with the intention of mining the area around Aldeburgh Napes. Kreysern succeeded in his mission as *UC-3* was spotted returning home in the early hours of 26 May by the departing *UC-1* and *UC-6*. Some time later, around 11h00, *UC-3* signalled to another U-boat. This was *UB-6* which was on patrol near the North Hinder light vessel. This would be the last sign of life of *UC-3* and her crew. When on her way to Zeebrugge, she sailed into a newly laid British minefield, south of the Schouwenbank and was mined. The mines which *UC-3* had laid were effective and the British merchant ships *SS Denewood* and *SS Golconda* sank after hitting them.

British sources had obviously wrongly mentioned *UC-3* as sunk on 23 April 1916. According to them she had been caught in the mine nets of the Spar buoy (off Norfolk) and was blown up by the trawler *Cheero*.[171] This probably concerned another U-boat which had been able to escape.

The wreck of *UC-3* was found and dived by Dirk Termote in 1994 in position 51° 35' 551 N 03° 07' 947 E. She lies in a depth of 18 m, on the top of the Rabsbank, in the Dutch territorial waters. *UC-3* is quite intact, but misses the tower and her outer skin. The wreck lies on her portside at a 70° angle. At the time of her discovery, all mineshafts were totally free of sand. The shafts were empty and gave the diver the opportunity to swim completely through them. Midships, near the former foot of the tower, the wreck is gradually swallowed up by sand. To starboard, near the first mineshaft, a circular opening of 75 cm diameter was noticed. The steel plating has been forced roughly inwards, is torn and points to the impact of an explosion.

All proof on the site point towards identifying the wreck as that of *UC-3*. The empty shafts show that she was on her return to Zeebrugge and the location, on the Rabsbank, to the south of the Schouwenbank, indicates that she had unknowingly sailed into a newly laid British field, with the known consequences.

The described condition of the wreck was the situation up to 1999. From that date, the sandbank has shifted, covering the wreck totally. Every year a search of the position is made to find any trace of the wreck, but she has not appeared above ground for the last 15 years.

UC-4

UC-4 would be the only UC-I class minelayer to survive the entire war. After having served for about half a year in the Baltic, *UC-4* was brought over to Zeebrugge and joined the *U-Flottille Flandern* in February 1916. In that same month she laid a minefield off Aldeburgh, sinking the British *SS Cedarwood*, *SS Tergestea* and the Belgian *Aduatiek*. Mines were laid in March in the Downs, resulting in only one ship being damaged. The German Admiralty did not seem to know what to do with *UC-4* and after her ninth patrol was sent to Libau in the Baltic. Her next three missions were plagued by bad

UC-3 is lifted into the water at Kiel dockyard in 1915 (U-Boot-Archiv Cuxhaven)

UC-4 on patrol (Herzog)

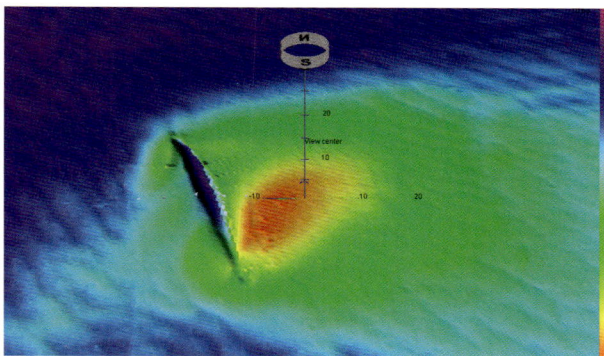

Multibeam image of the wreck of UC-4 in 't Scheur, near the Zeebrugge shipping lane (MDK-Vlaamse Hydrografie)

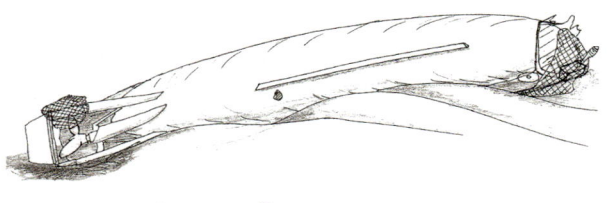

Drawing of the almost intact wreck of *UC-4*, minus tower (TT)

luck. On the 11th patrol the hydroplane jammed and stormy weather hampered navigation. The laid fields did not have any effect because the Russians were able to locate them in Moon Sund. On her 12th patrol, the captain fell badly ill and the helmsman had to take over control. Finally *UC-4* nearly met her end when aircraft bombs were dropped near to her off Filsand.

On 15 September 1916, *UC-4* was sent back to Flanders were she would also remain for the rest of her career. *UC-4* would know nine more different captains and carry out 60 patrols between 17 October 1916 and 17 July 1918. Her main areas of operation were the Thames Estuary, the Downs, Lowestoft, Great Yarmouth, Aldeburgh Napes and the Shipwash. In almost two years she would sink 28 ships. These mainly were armed trawlers attempting to clear freshly laid fields. On 17 September 1917, *UC-4* managed to save the crew of a French seaplane. Engine failure had forced them to land off the Flanders coast.

On 17 July 1918, *UC-4* ended up in the shipyard for a total revision of the engine, which took two months. It was not possible to finish the job, before the Flemish bases were evacuated and *UC-4* was towed out to sea on 2 October 1918 and scuttled in front of Zeebrugge Harbour.

The wreck of *UC-4* was dived and identified by the author in 2003. She lies in position 51° 25' 234 N 03° 06' 261 E on her portside in a depth of 12 m. The wreck is partially covered in a muddy bottom and, oddly enough, just as is the case with *UC-3*, the conning tower is also missing. The mineshafts are empty and only half visible. A hydroplane, a horizontal rudder and the top of the single propeller are visible near the stern.[172]

UC-5

UC-5 would become famous for being the first U-boat to be captured intact by the British after she had wedged herself on a sandbank in the Thames Estuary.

Before her capture, *UC-5* proved to be quite a successful U-boat for the *Flandern Flottille*. *Oberleutnant z. S.* Herbert Pustkuchen captained her and brought her to Zeebrugge on 27 July 1915. Not even a week later *UC-5* left on her first mission to lay mines at the Kentish Knock. Three days later the naval trawler *Leandros* was mined and sunk in Knock Deep. During 14 different minelaying operations, between early August and middle December 1915, *UC-5* was able to sink 22 ships. One of these was the converted paddle minesweeper *Brighton Queen* which had

UC-5 is brought into Harwich as British prize, after she was stranded in the Thames Estuary (The War Illustrated)

A British Royal naval cadet examines one of the mines extracted from *UC-5*'s shafts (The War Illustrated)

been mined off Middelkerke. A minefield laid off Dover was responsible for the sinking of the hospital ship *SS Anglia* on 17 November 1915. The 2,000 ton ship was on her way from France to Britain with 385 wounded soldiers. After hitting a mine, steerage was lost and she could not be stopped immediately. Neglecting her own danger, a destroyer managed to manoeuver herself alongside the stricken ship and save the largest amount of wounded. A total of 134 died when *SS Anglia* finally sank. A merchant ship, *SS Lusitania*, which had come closer to help with the rescue also struck a mine and was sunk. At present, these wrecks are very popular amongst the southern England diving community. Mines of the small *UC-5* would also sink the large British submarine *HMS E-6* with all hands, on her outward bound patrol from Harwich.

On 29 December 1915 *UC-5* left on her 15th patrol, this time under a new captain, *Oberleutnant z. S.*

Ulrich Mohrbutter. During the following four months he was able to sink eight ships during 18 missions.

On the 28th patrol things would go wrong for *UC-5* and her crew. On 26 April 1916, Mohrbutter had set a course from Zeebrugge to Harwich and arrived in the Thames Estuary around midnight. Due to a navigational fault *UC-5* ended up on a sandbank of the Shipwash. Stressful hours followed for her crew when the tide fell three hours later, totally exposing the U-boat. Because it was still fairly dark, they did not get noticed and by 6 am *UC-5* was able to float herself free at high tide and head on a northeasterly course. By dawn *UC-5* arrived in the area near the Sunk lightship but was not able to surface for taking a bearing as there was too much activity of enemy ships. Mohrbutter had *UC-5* descend to the bottom and decided to wait. At 09h15 *UC-5* surfaced so that the captain could take a bearing on the lightship which lay close by. The lightship did not bear any recognition marks and Mohrbutter steared clear of her. About an hour later *UC-5* got stuck in a shallows (it was going to ebb) in position 51° 59' N 01° 38' E. The increasing tide pushed the U-boat crosswise and she shallowed more and more. The situation started to look bleak and Mohrbutter decided to jettison any secret documents and ready *UC-5* for destruction. He also had a message sent out to Zeebrugge base, but his message was intercepted by the British. They immediately sent out the destroyer *HMS Firedrake* to her location. When the destroyer hove into view, Mohrbutter had *UC-5* evacuated and had the explosive charges detonated. The charges did not explode the mines and only minor damage was caused to the U-boat. It was fairly easy for the British to capture *UC-5* intact. The entire crew was saved and went into a prisoner of war camp for the duration of the war. The recovery of *UC-5* from the Shipwash bank was one of the first cases involving the Admiralty Salvage Section divers. By 16 May *UC-5* had been refloated and brought to the beach near Harwich pier. Some Intelligence was recovered, although much had been disposed of by the crew before they attempted to destroy their U-boat. After studying *UC-5*, she was paraded all around Great-Britain and later on even in the United States for the purpose of collecting warbonds. It gave the general public an idea how minelayers were put to use. By the end of the war *UC-5* was scrapped.

UC-6

UC-6 would see quite an intense career up to her loss in September 1917. From the moment she was launched on 24 June 1915, she carried out a total of 88 minelaying operations under six different captains. The most famous would be *Oberleutnant z. S.* Graf von Schmettow and Zerboni di Sposetti. In a period of 27 months *UC-6* was able to sink or damage 64 enemy ships. Von Schmettow held the lead with 43 sinkings during 28 missions. He proved his worth in choosing areas where he would be certain in mining several ships. At the end of February 1916 *UC-6* dropped mines in the area off Dover Harbour. *SS Maloja*, with her 21,431 tons, was the largest vessel of the P & O, struck a mine and started to sink. She was on route to Bombay with 456 passengers and crew. *SS Maloja* sank 2 miles to the southwest of Dover pier with the loss of 155 lives.[173] A Canadian merchant ship, *SS Empress of Fort Williams*, came to the rescue of the sinking ship but she in turn hit a mine and was sunk. In the following days the remaining mines of *UC-6* sank the naval trawlers *Angelus*, *Weigelia* and *Flicker*.

UC-6 under sail off Southwold, 1915. After the diesel engine had given up, making use of the tide and the wind in a rigged sail were the only options to be able to keep under way (TT)

293

A ship which played in the minds of many a fortune seeker was the *SS Batavier V*. The Dutch merchant ship was on route from London to Rotterdam when it hit a mine near the Inner Gabbard on 16 May 1916. This area had been mined by *UC-6* a week previously. Besides carrying a cargo of rice and coffee there was also an amount of gold bullion on board with a value of £210,000. Up to today it is not known if this cargo was totally salvaged...

It would not only be the crew of *UB-2* which would make use of logic to save their U-boat after the engine refused to start. *UC-6* ended up in a precarious situation after she had laid her 12 mines off Southwold on 25 July 1916. Her captain, *Oberleutnant z. S.* Otto Ehrentraut, put *UC-6* on a course to Zeebrugge, but shortly afterwards something in the diesel engine gave way, making them lose propulsion. The batteries could not suffice to get them on the electric engine. Ehrentraut did not let his crew sit idle and ordered them to immediately haul up the emergency sail. This had been made from sailcloth with the intention to shield the tower. Surprisingly enough a dominant northwesterly wind gave a speed of 2 to 3 knots to put enough distance between them and the east coast. Two days later, and after 'sailing' for 52 miles, *UC-6* came to the area near the Schouwenbank. They were sighted by *UB-19*, which threw out a cable and towed them to Zeebrugge.

UC-6 seemed to be plagued by technical difficulties. On 18 November 1916 she had dropped her 12 mines to the north of the Outer Gabbard bank. On the return route the clutch of the diesel engine broke, making the U-boat stop dead in the water. To make matters worse, a heavy storm picked up during the night. Radio signals and several pigeons were sent off to request help from the base. During the next night, her captain, *Oberleutnant z. S.* von Zerboni di Sposetti had *UC-6* settle on the bottom at 30 m. But even at this depth the violent surge of the storm was well felt. On 20 November they came to float precariously close to the new minefields which the British had laid on the Schouwenbank. *UC-6* was running very slowly on the electric engine to preserve energy for the batteries. All lighting, heating and also the gyrocompass were turned off to save as much electricity as possible. Finally Zeebrugge sent out a torpedo boat to aid them with a tow.

UC-6 would yet again request help for a tow after her propellor got damaged. On 10 July 1917, *UC-6* was moving slowly at a depth of 16 m, whilst dropping her mines in Queens Channel, in the Thames. Suddenly her propellor struck a wreck and became difficult to manoeuver. To make matters worse, *UC-6* came fast on the Kentish Knock but at high tide was able to float off again. It seemed to have become a tradition to rig up a sail on *UC-6* as the crew was obliged to yet again put up the emergency sail. In the end the torpedo boat *V-81* came to their aid and towed them to base.

UC-6 had escaped death several times. This was specially noticed by her crew on 29 June 1917 when making the outward bound patrol she became stuck on the surface in a steel net to the east of the Kentish Knock. At dawn the crew was able to cut the net to pieces and remove it. Frighteningly enough, it was not just an innocent bit of net, as there were several explosive charges attached to it at regular distances. It had been a miracle that none of the charges had exploded with all the movement. One of the mine-nets was taken on board *UC-6* and taken home for further investigation.

UC-6's long-lasting luck would finally come to an end when she left on her final patrol on 27 September 1917 to the Thames Estuary. She was commanded by *Oberleutnant z. S.* Gottfried Reichenbach and he intended to lay mines near the Kentish Knock. *UC-6* was never heard of again and it was suspected that she had run into the new mine nets laid out by the British. *UC-6* was said to have been mined in position 51° 30' N 01° 34' E. Another British source states that *UC-6* was spotted on the surface by seaplane 8676 on the southwestern corner of the Thornton Bank. The plane is said to have bombed and sunk the U-boat.[174] Most likely this concerns another U-boat, which also escaped the bombs, as in this area no wrecks of this type of U-boat have been discovered. It is almost certain that *UC-6* fell victim to a British ruse where a German minefield was cleared and replaced by mined nets. At 14h30, on 27 September, observers on the Kentish Knock light vessel picked up the sound of U-boat engines nearby. Two hours later, five underwater explosions were heard. After about an hour of silence, the engine sound was picked up again and at 17h55 again three explosions were heard. Four months later, the mine nets were brought to the surface and it proved to contain evidence of a mined U-boat. Three fragments of steel plate, a part marked '*Schmierröhre Anker Winde*'[175] and a mine sinker were taken on board.[176]

The wreck of *UC-6* was discovered by divers in 2005 between the North Foreland and the southern buoy of the Kentish Knock. This is at 8.8 miles to the northeast of the North Foreland in position 51° 30' 102 N 01° 34' 695 E. The position matches exactly with the position that *UC-6* would have struck a mine. The wreck is quite intact, sanded up and lies at a depth of 22 m. The first two shafts are empty, but shafts 3 and 4 still contain their cargoes. The conning tower is well visible as is part of her stern. Rudders and propellers are totally buried in the sand.[177]

UC-7

UC-7 was launched on 6 July 1915 and arrived the next month in Zeebrugge. As was the case with her sister ships, *UC-7* would prove to be a successful U-boat. In a nine-month career *UC-7* was able to complete 32 patrols, mainly in the area of the Kentish Knock and the Downs as well as the east coast. Between 21 August 1915 and 5 July 1916 she was able to sink a total of 31 ships. One of her largest victims was the British light cruiser *HMS Arethusa*, which sank just off Harwich.

On 3 July 1916, *UC-7*, under command of *Oberleutnant z. S.* Georg Haag, left Zeebrugge for the Downs and was never heard of again. The last sign of life was reported by *UB-12* which crossed the path of *UC-7* to the west of the Bligh Bank on 5 July. *UC-7* was coming from the North Hinder after completing a minelaying mission. Hereafter *UC-7* was lost with all hands in the area between the Bligh Bank and Zeebrugge, which had been freshly mined by the Royal Navy. On 19 and 22 July the bodies of Karl Stapel and Fritz Lange washed ashore on the Flemish coast. During the same period Dutch fishermen came upon the body of *Oberleutnant z. S.* Karl-Hanno Fischer off the Schouwenbank. Two days later the body of Haag was found by *UB-16*, recovered, and buried at sea. The report stated that the body showed obvious signs of an explosion, i.e. that the U-boat had been mined. There was now no doubt that *UC-7* had hit a mine on her return journey.

The wreck of *UC-7* was discovered and dived for the first time by Dirk Termote in 1993. The wreck of *UC-7* is heavily damaged and lies at a depth of 23 m in position 51° 31' 604 N 03° 08' 438 E. The wreck is totally severed in front of the tower, abaft the lifting hook and the first mineshaft. Both fragments lie paralel to each other at a distance of 4 m. The mineshafts are empty. The break shows the effects of a heavy explosion, bent hullplates and remains of melted and fused battery parts are strewn inside and outside the wreckage.

The empty shafts point out that *UC-7* had fullfilled her mission and was on the return voyage. The power of the explosion shows that a mine was detonated under or close to the hull of the U-boat. *UC-7* was most likely on the surface as the discovery of four bodies points in the direction of a watchkeeping crew on the tower.

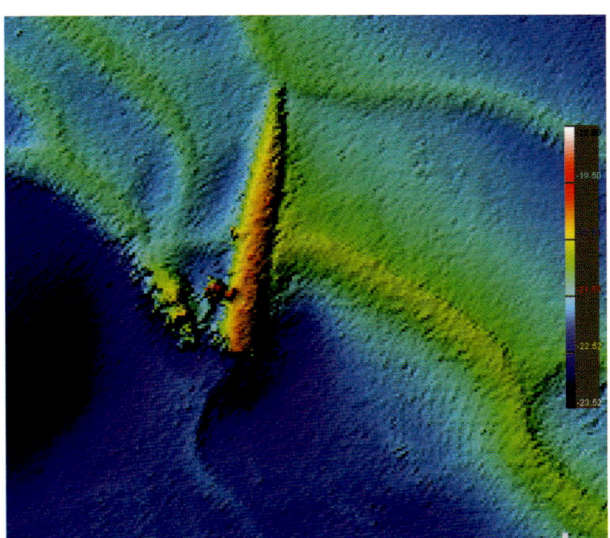

This multibeam shows the wreck of *UC-7* broken in two parts (Rijkswaterstaat)

Drawing of the wreck of *UC-7*, sunk in the Westpit (TT)

The wreck could be positively identified after diver Johan Devolder had recovered the propeller.

UC-8

UC-8 was launched in July 1915, but was not transferred to Flanders immediately. She served in the U-boat school at Kiel as a training boat until the late autumn. At the end of October, command was given to *Oberleutnant z. S.* Walter Schmidt and he was given the task to bring *UC-8* to Zeebrugge. *UC-8* actually served as a replacement for *UC-11*, which had been plagued by technical problems and was being overhauled in the dockyard. Pure technically, *UC-8* was added to the *U-Flottille Flandern*, but would never reach a Flemish base and not sink one enemy ship. On 3 November *UC-8* left the harbour of Emden towards the Dutch island of Terschelling. When reaching the Terschelling light vessel on the 4th, things went wrong. Due to miscalculation of the tides, Schmidt ended up getting stuck in the shallows in Dutch territorial waters. Several attempts were made to free the U-boat, but all in vain. Dutch tugs approached and managed to tow *UC-8* from the sandbank and brought her in to Geldern. U-boat and crew were immediately interned. The German Empire undertook long negotiations with the Dutch government to free its U-boat, but without result. In the end the German government gave *UC-8* in 1917 to the Dutch navy, where she was added and renamed as *M-1* on 13 March 1917. *M-1* would serve in the Dutch navy until 1932, after which she was scrapped. The German crew was only released in October 1916 out of Dutch captivity.

UC-9

Just as her sistership, *UC-8*, *UC-9* would also see service with the U-boat school at Kiel. But in comparison with *UC-8*, she would have an extremely short life. After serving two months in Kiel, she was brought to Flanders at the end of September 1915, captained by *Oberleutnant z. S.* Paul Schürmann. He took *UC-9* on her first and final patrol on 20 October to the northeastern part of the Thames to mine the area of the Long Sand. Since she had left Zeebrugge, nothing was ever heard of the U-boat and her crew. The reason for her loss is most likely due to a mine explosion. It could have been that *UC-9* had hit a British mine or hit one of its own mines whilst laying a field. The body of *Marine Ingenieur Aspirant* Karl Neuhaus was recovered near the Long Sand by the British about a month later, on 12 November 1915.

A UC-I type submarine was found by diver Bob Peacock in position 51° 10' 6 N 01° 43' 47 E.[178] The wreck lies to the south of the South Falls buoy, in the shipping channel. Up to now its identity still remains a mystery, but there is a big possibility that it concerns *UC-9*. Normally it would be more logical to look for the wreck closer to the Long Sand. The suspected position of her sinking was 51° 47' N 01° 37' E, but no minelayer has been found in this area.

Oberleutnant z. S. Paul Schürmann, captain of *UC-9*, in his lodging in Bruges, 1915 (TT)

UC-10

UC-10 arrived in Flanders mid-December 1915 and was prepared for her first patrol. She left on 28 December and headed to the eastern part of the Thames Estuary. Her captain, *Oberleutnant z. S.* Alfred Nitzsche dropped *UC-10's* mines to the south of the Galloper light vessel. A few days later these took effect and sank three Dutch ships: *SS Ellewoutsdijk, SS Leto, SS Apollo* and the Norwegian *SS Fridtjof Nansen.* Nitzsche would prove to quite a successful captain and in a further 19 missions with *UC-10* he managed to sink 11 ships.

On 17 August 1916 *UC-10*, now under a new captain, *Oberleutnant z. S.* Werner Albrecht, left Zeebrugge to mine the Humber Estuary. No one on board would suspect it to be their final mission. After *UC-10* had successfully released her cargo off the British east coast they started on their return to base. When they reached the North Hinder light vessel, they crossed paths with *UB-10*. Albrecht gave *Oberleutnant z. S.* Reinhold Saltzwedel, captain of *UB-10*, the news that they had had a successful patrol and also had sunk the trawler Dragoon. Saltzwedel would be the last person to see them alive. At 16h35, near the Schouwenbank, *UC-10* was struck by two torpedoes from the British submarine *HMS E-54*. She had been cruising on the surface, but after the impact the British were not able to find survivors.

The wreck of *UC-10* was discovered and dived for the first time by Dirk Termote and René Simons in 1995 in position 51° 39' 328 N 03° 17' 322 E. She lies at a maximum depth of 33 m and the wreckage clearly shows the tremendous damage caused by the explosions. The captain of *HMS E-54* was quite a good shot to be able to double hit a moving target of only 30 m length at a couple of hundred metres distance. The wreck lies in two parts: the tower and stern and the foreship. The midship section with the tower lie on their starboardside and the front of this part shows a heavy dent in the pressure hull and the entire front part with the shafts is missing. Between the engine room and the control room, the U-boat is totally severed, but both segments are only 3 m separated from each other. The front section lies about 30 m separated from the main body of the wreck, in a straight line. The mineshafts are well recognisable and empty.

Divers Arie Visser and Martin Bakker believe these remains are that of *UB-12*. *UB-12* was the only UB-boat which had been converted to a minelayer with four shafts. *UB-12* disappeared in 1918 when she was on a minelaying mission in the Thames Estuary. Because of the visible presence of only four shafts in the bow and the destruction of the wreck, they suspect it is the wreck of *UB-12*. But nothing discovered on the wreck has given an indication of a U-boat number. The destruction on the wreck is very intense and should rather be seen as the impact of a torpedo. The absence of two shafts can also be seen as a result of the explosion. Only further research which will be able to reveal the true identity of the wreck in question.

UC-11

Even though *UC-11* had a fairly high number in the UC-I class, she would have the honour of entering Zeebrugge Harbour as the first U-boat minelayer.

UC-11 would survive nearly three years of war, complete 81 successful patrols and sink 25 ships. She mainly operated between the Goodwins and Harwich, between 29 May 1915 and her sinking in June 1918. It was mainly in the centre of the Thames Estuary, near the Shipwash, Sunk, Long Sand, Queens Channel and Black Deep that her mines would sink several ships. Amongst her victims were several warships, such as the Torpedo boats *HMS Mayfly, HMS Greenfly, HMS Kale* and several minesweepers. Command of *UC-11* changed ten times.

On 24 June 1918 *UC-11* left on her 82nd patrol and was captained by *Oberleutnant z. S.* Kurt Utke. Utke

Oberleutnant z. S. Werner Albrecht, captain of *UC-10* (WZ-Bilddienst)

297

had only received command of the U-boat a week before, after his colleague *Oberleutnant z. s.* Werner Lange fell ill and had to be hospitalised. The 25-year old Utke had already had an extensive career before being assigned to *UC-11*. He had served on the heavy cruiser *SMS Yorck* which had carried out the bombardment raid on Yarmouth in 1914, but was transferred to the naval infantry in Flanders shortly afterwards. He saw action in the trenches around Nieuwpoort, but his superiors saw more potential in him in a shipboard command than at the head of an infantry detachment. In February 1915 he took on the role of gunnery officer on the battleship *SMS Von der Tann* and took part in the Battle of Jutland. A year later he volunteered for U-boats and after a six-week course for first officer, he ended up on *UC-71* in Flanders. By the middle of 1918 he had been well prepared to command a UC-II class boat. But he missed this chance and had to settle for the smaller UC-I class. Utke was actually unlucky that he had just replaced the sick Lange on *UC-11*. At 17h, on 24 June 1918, Utke left Zeebrugge for Harwich. The next day, at 9 am, *UC-11* surfaced near the Shipwash to let her captain study the shipping routes. Once they arrived near the Sunk light vessel he took a bearing through his periscope with the gyrocompass. At that moment they were 4 miles to the northeast of the lightship in position 51° 55' N 01° 41' E. From here he steered a westerly course at 3 knots, intending to pass along the southern side of the Shipwash. By 9h45 a heavy explosion hit *UC-11*'s stern. Utke, who was alone inside the conning tower, was flung from one side to the other by the force of the explosion and momentarily lost

UC-11 on trials on 13 May 1916. Petty officers stand around the tower of the U-boat (TT)

consciousness. Rising water quickly brought him back to his senses and he tried to open the tower hatch. The water in the submarine had compressed the remaining air enough to easily open the hatch. He shot out through the hatch and surfaced in an enormous air bubble. He swam as hard as he could with the tide trying to prevent himself from being dragged under by his soaked clothes. Finally he managed to grab hold on to a barrel-shaped buoy and in the distance he spotted the masts of the Sunk lightship. Utke proved to have luck on his side that day because the lifeboat *Patrick* came to his rescue half an hour later. He was exhausted and in shock, but was in a healthy condition.[179] After being brought ashore he was interrogated and spent the rest of the war in a British prisoner of war camp. His interrogators left him thinking that he had hit a British mine, but actually *UC-11* had ended up in a German minefield which the British had left untouched. This had been a ruse they had already used several times, which had also destroyed *UC-6*.

A rare photo showing *UC-11* in the Ostend dry dock (Jörn Jensen)

The wreck of *UC-11* was quickly discovered after its sinking and two days later dived upon by Royal Naval divers. She lay on her port side with a large gash in her hull, 6 m abaft the tower. All her mines were still in their shafts. Damant suggested to the Admiralty to open up the wreck with explosives, although there was nothing further to prove. A 100-pound charge was detonated within the tower. Several explosions followed the firing of a second charge, when part of her cargo went up in sympathy. Large pieces of wreckage and important documents came to the surface and were salvaged.

The wreck of *UC-11* was re-discovered in the Shipwash area by diver Bob Hickson. She lies at a depth of 30 m and shows the obvious destructions of 1918. Up to now, only one exploratory dive could be made on the location as most of the year there is no visibility on the site.

UC-14

Before *UC-14* made any career in the *Flandern Flottille*, she had already seen service in the Mediterranean. She was completed and launched on 13 May 1915 and transported by rail to the harbour of Pola in the Adriatic where she joined the *K.u.K Marine* (*Kaiserliche und Königliche Kriegsmarine* of the Austro-Hungarian empire) as *U-18*. Her first mission as U-18 was a munitions- and weapons transport on 7 July destined for Constantinople (Istanbul). After this one and only transportation mission *U-18* was used during 15 minelaying patrols to mainly destroy Italian troop ships off the Albanian, Ionian and Apullian coasts and in the Gulf of Trente. The mines of *U-18* proved to be quite successful and managed to sink 15 ships. One of the most spectacular was the sinking of the heavy Italian cruiser *Regina Margherita* (13.427 BRT)

A somewhat fantastic depiction of the oversized *UC-14* in Helmut Lohrenz' book (Lohrenz)

UC-15 lies with fully laden shafts alongside her mothership (U-Boot-Archiv Cuxhaven)

UC-14 as U-18 in the Austro-Hungarian naval base Pola (TT)

Sketch of the wreck of *UC-14*, mined in the Westpit (TT)

off Valona, near Bari, on 12 April 1916. Due to stormy weather only 270 men could be saved. 675 others perished, including the captain of the ship and the commander of the 16th division, Lieutenant-General Bandini.[180]

By the end of October 1916, the task of *U-18* in the Mediterranean seemed to have come to an end. The U-boat was broken up into sections and sent to the Flanders front. At the Ostend wharf she was put back together, made watertight and went into service as *UC-14*.

UC-14 would be able to complete 20 minelaying operations in the Thames Estuary area and on the east coast between 24 February and 17 September 1917. The U-boat did not seem to achieve the same successes as she had did in the Mediterranean and only six ships, all of them British naval trawlers, were mined and sunk.

UC-14 left Zeebrugge on 1 October 1917 for her 21st and final mission. Two weeks earlier, command had been given to *Oberleutnant z. S. d. Res.* Adolf Feddersen and he managed to deposit *UC-14*'s mines in the Stanford Channel, off Lowestoft, and return home. From that moment the U-boat and her crew have been missing. On 3 October, at 22h15, the lookouts of the signal stations at Zeebrugge and Knokke observed a large explosion accompanied by a flash of light at sea. It is possible that it concerned *UC-14* which had struck a mine. British fast motorboats had laid a small field of only five mines on 14 September in the area of the Vlakte van de Raan. Some months later, Feddersen's body washed ashore on the island of Texel and was buried there.

The wreck of *UC-14* was discovered and dived by Dirk Termote in 1993. The wreck lies totally severed in two parts at a depth of 18 m in position 51° 31' 205 N 03° 12' 981 E. *UC-14* was hit by a mine abaft the control room and is totally cut in half. Both segments lie close to each other at 3 m and stand upright. The mineshafts are empty and the periscope partly protrudes out of the housing.

UC-16

UC-16 was the first minelayer of the type UC-II which would enter a Flemish harbour. She started her operations in September 1916 and would venture much further than the estuary of the Thames. On her first patrol, between 21 and 24 September 1916, her captain, *Oberleutnant z. S.* Egon von Werner, was able to stop 11 British trawlers. They were all sunk to the south of the Spurn lightship with the 8.8 cm deck gun or the use of explosive charges. Another 11 patrols were made during the period between 17 October 1916 and 13 September 1917. Under the command of von Werner a total of 19 ships were sunk, mainly in the bay of the Seine. Some of these were the Italian S*S*

Oberleutnant z. S. d. R. Adolf Feddersen, captain of *UC-14* (WZ-Bilddienst)

Taormin, the Norwegian *SS Reinunga*, *SS Theresda* and *SS Anna* on 18 January 1917. All were carrying victuals for England. On 16 April 1917, *UC-16* was the first UC-boat to encounter a British Q-ship. In the bay of the Seine a sailing ship was spotted and fired upon. Suddenly the innocent looking sailing ship produced two artillery pieces which opened fire on *UC-16*. *UC-16* escaped in the nick of time, dived below the surface and escaped the shells from the Q-ship *Glen*. After this, not uninteresting patrol, command was handed over to *Oberleutnant z. S.* Georg Reimarius who made his first patrol in the area of the Hoofden. *UC-16* destroyed six Dutch trawlers which found themselves in the forbidden zone. During the following two patrols another five ships were sent to the bottom.

On 2 October 1917, *UC-16* left Zeebrugge on her final patrol, which was to mine the area off Boulogne. This patrol was completed but *UC-16* disappeared shortly afterwards. About three weeks later, on 26 October, the body of her first officer, *Lt. z.* S. Rolf von Beczwarzowsky, washed ashore on the beach of Noordwijk, Holland.

The wreck has not been identified, but most likely concerns one of three known UC-II class submarines discovered in the area to the west of the Fairybank. Also the discovery of the body of the first officer on the Dutch coast and not on the British coast also can point out that the U-boat was sunk closer to home. See *UC-66*.

UC-17

Oberleutnant z. S. Ralph Wenninger would prove the full potential of the UC-II class submarine when he obtained command of *UC-17* on 23 July 1916. Between 1 October 1916 and 21 May 1917 Wenninger was able to carry out seven successful patrols in the western area of the Channel. By using mines, the deck gun and explosive charges he was able to sink a total of 66 ships. The largest of these were the British *SS Belgier*, *SS Rotorua* and *SS Galicia*. The 4,588 ton *SS Belgier* was sunk off Belle Île on 23 February 1917, with her cargo of 8,800 artillery shells from America. The larger *SS Rotorua*, 11.140 BRT, laden with 100,000 heads of slaughtered New Zealand cattle was torpedoed and sunk on 21 March. *SS Galicia*, a postal carrier of nearly 6.000 BRT, struck a mine laid by *UC-17* and sank off Exmouth on 12 May. After his seventh patrol Wenninger fell ill and had to be replaced by another ace, *Oberleutnant z. S.* Werner Fürbringer. *UC-17* was able to complete one mission in the second half of June 1917 sinking a total of eight ships. One was the 6,486 ton *SS Clan Davidson* with a mixed cargo and 3,000 tons of butter from Sydney. She was stopped and boarded on 24 June and sank with explosive charges. Due to the buoyant cargo, it took hours before the ship finally went to the bottom.

Three more captains followed Fürbringer and 12 patrols between 16 August 1917 and 17 October 1918 were completed. *UC-17* seemed to still be a successful

Leutnant z. S. Rolf von Beczwarszowsky, 1st officer of *UC-16*, was killed when his boat was sunk (TT)

UC-17 in Bruges docks (Nic Owen)

U-boat and managed to sink 22 ships with mines or torpedoes. On 19 October *UC-17* was taken to Brunsbüttel, as the Flemish ports were no longer in use. Normally *UC-17* would have been added to the *V U-Flottille* in Bremerhaven, but this did not materialise. On 25 November 1918 she was taken with the *5th Flottille* as prize to Harwich and was scrapped in 1920 in Preston by Thomas W. Ward Ltd.

UC-18

UC-18 was one of the many new UC-II U-boats which had crossed from the North Sea ports to Zeebrugge to join the *U-Flottille Flandern*. She arrived on 19 October 1916 and four days later headed to the British east coast for her first minelaying operation. British minesweepers were the first to suffer and three ships were mined in a field off Great Yarmouth. As it only concerned smaller tonnages of ships, her captain, *Oberleutnant z. S.* Wilhelm Kiel, wanted larger prey to sink. In the following three patrols, *UC-18* would concentrate her efforts off the Brittany coast and the western part of the Channel. Between 4 November 1916 and 25 January 1917 Kiel was able to sink 29 ships mainly by means of explosive charges and the deck gun.

On 16 February 1917, *UC-18* left Zeebrugge on her final patrol. Kiel wanted to lay mines off Boulogne, Le Havre and Le Vierge, but *UC-18* was lost with all hands. According to British sources, *UC-18* encountered the Q-ship *Lady Olive* (*Q-18*) on 19 February off the Channel Islands. When the unsuspecting *UC-18* had approached *Lady Olive* up to 100 m, the enemy opened fire with a 10.2 cm and four 7.5 cm guns. The shooting of the British gunners was very accurate and eight shells hit *UC-18*. The guncrew of *UC-18* fought back with their 8.8 cm but she was still heavily damaged and sank with the loss of her 28-man crew. The *Lady Olive* had also been heavily damaged and later started to sink. The French destroyer *Dunois* came on the scene and managed to save the crew of the sinking Q-ship. According to British sources, *UC-18* was sunk in position 49° 15' N 02° 34' E. It could be that *UC-18* was sunk instantaneously, but it is also possible that the heavily damaged U-boat managed to escape, but sank later.[181]

No wreck, which matches that of *UC-18,* has been found, but is most likely to be discovered somewhere in the area between Guernsey and Jersey.

UC-19

The minelayer *UC-19* would only have a short lifespan with the *U-Flottille Flandern*. She went into service on 22 August 1916 and was captained by *Oberleutnant z. S.* Alfred Nitzsche. It seemed to be the habit of first time captains of UC-II boats to carry out one patrol off the British east coast. On her first minelaying mission, on 25 November, she headed for Great Yarmouth where *UC-19* dropped her 18 mines. Three ships were sunk in this field. Nitzsche seemed to be ready for his big step towards a patrol in the western area of the Channel. On 27 November he left on his second patrol to lay mines off Bassure de Bas, Boulogne, Dieppe and Le Havre. On 6 December 1916 a lookout on the destroyer *HMS Ariel* spotted the tower of *UC-19*. She was then 12 miles to the southwest of Bishop Rock. But *UC-19* had also seen *HMS Ariel* and dived below the surface. When the destroyer came near the location she fired a depth charge in the path of the fleeing *UC-19*, but it failed to explode. After this failure she

Leutnant z. S. Henry Meyer, 1st officer of *UC-19* (TT)

set out an explosive paravane which detonated at a depth of 10 m. This seemed to have more success, as oil and wreckage bubbled up to the surface. No survivors of *UC-19* were found. *UC-19* is said to have been sunk in position 49° 39' N 06° 21' 2 W at a depth of 100 m.[182] Numerous attempts to locate the wreck have been undertaken in recent years, but with no luck. It could also be that *UC-19* was sunk closer to home, near the Dover Straits.

UC-21

Oberleutnant z. S. Reinhold Saltzwedel would make history with *UC-21* before being transferred to *UC-71*. On 15 September 1916 he received command over *UC-21* and brought her from Germany to Zeebrugge. It would only be two months later that *UC-21* would be ready for her first patrol and headed for the Channel area. Saltzwedel gave the British an unpleasant surprise in the shape of three minefields in the areas off Folkestone and Dungeness, a second near the Nab- and Owers lightships and a last one off the Isle of Wight. The mines only sank two trawlers and a sailing ship, but *UC-21* showed more of her worth with the deck gun and explosive charges. Another 19 ships, most of which had been stopped and checked on that one single journey, were sunk. One of the most important ones was the 4,387 ton British merchant ship *SS King Bleddyn* which had come from New York with 6,000 tons of war materials. Saltzwedel was showing his worth and that a

UC-21 sinks *SS Illinois* (Dirk Termote)

The Norwegian *SS Reinunga* sinks after being torpedoed by *UC-21* on 18 January 1917, near the Scillies (TT)

The end of the bark *Ville de Dieppe* (TT)

minelaying UC-II submarine proved to be a lethal weapon in his capable hands. He undertook another five patrols with *UC-21* between 17 January and 3 June 1917 and mainly operated off the Brittany coast where he managed to sink the staggering amount of 70 ships in just six months time! Some of these ships concerned the 5,225 ton American tanker *SS Illinois* which was sunk on 16 March off Alderney, and several sailings ships such as the Norwegian bark *Ville de Dieppe* and the American schooner *Percy Birdsall* on 22 April. The impressive American, five-masted bark *Harwood Palmer* of nearly 3.000 BRT, went to the bottom, off St. Nazaire. She was on her way from Boston to France with a cargo of steel beams. *UC-21* would cross the path of the French Q-ship *Marguerite VI* during that same trip. When *UC-21* was south of the Gironde, Saltzwedel observed a small merchant vessel sailing under Spanish flag. He approached cautiously to about 400 m in her wake. In the meantime the ship had set out its lifeboat with a number of crew. When *UC-21* had approached to about 300 m, the Tricolor was hoisted and machineguns opened fire on the U-boat. The camouflage fell off the guns and *UC-21* was bombarded. But Saltzwedel was an old fox and he reacted fast by letting *UC-21* dive below the surface immediately, with only a couple of bullets ricochetting off the bridge. Before *UC-21* could be readied to sink the French vessel, she had set course for La Rochelle. *Marguerite VI* already had become famous in March for a short battle with *UC-70*. On the same trip *UC-21* destroyed two Greek ships, *SS Aristides* and *SS Efstathios* as they had on board cargoes destined for the Allied front. On board *SS Efstathios* were 67 aircraft and engines which had come from New York and were destined for Bordeaux.

On 10 June 1917 *UC-21* came in hands of a new captain: *Oberleutnant z. S.* Werner von Zerboni di Sposetti. Between the end of June and early August *UC-21* was only able to carry out two short patrols during which she managed to sink three ships and another, the sailing ship *Roelfina*, was brought as prize into Zeebrugge. Von Zerboni di Sposetti saw potential in broadening his hunting ground to the area where Saltzwedel had known most of his successes: the Channel. On his third patrol he was only able to sink three ships and due to a leak caused by an aircraft bomb had to cut short the patrol. On 13 September 1917, *UC-21* left on her tenth and final patrol. Nothing further was heard of *UC-21* or her crew. The sinking of the Portuguese sailing ship *Maria Alice* on 30 September and *SS Memling* on 3 October could be accounted to her kills. *UC-21* was most likely lost on her return trip in one of the newly laid British minefields near the Westhinder, which already had claimed four other U-boats during that same year.[183]

It is possible that the wreck of *UC-21* lies to the west of the Westhinder (see *UC-66*).

UC-26

UC-26 was commisioned on 28 July 1916 and would serve her short life under *Oberleutnant z. S.* Mathias Graf von Schmettow. After sailing *UC-26* to the Flanders front she went on her first mission on 17 September. As it seemed to be habit, every new UC-II boat undertook a first minelaying operation off the British east coast. Mines laid off the Outer Dowsing lightship did not sink any ships, but just damaged a Swedish merchant vessel. It seemed that the life of *UC-26* would be plagued by many mechanical problems. After her first patrol the engines had to undergo a serious two-month long overhaul and nearly every patrol was accompanied by small breakages.

But von Schmettow would attain more success in the Channel, which came about during his second patrol. At the end of September, mines were laid off the harbours of Boulogne, Le Havre and Cherbourg resulting in the sinking of three enemy ships. *UC-26* would further hunt for enemy ships on the surface, sinking five ships between Cap de la Hague and the Scillies.

Between 24 October 1916 and 20 April 1917, *UC-26* was able to carry out five missions in the Channel. Von Schmettow managed to sink 25 ships, two of which proved to be hospital ships. The 6.772 BRT *HMHS Galeka* sank on 28 October 1916 after hitting a mine off Cherbourg. The other hospital ship was the 7.284 BRT *SS Salta*, which went to the bottom off Le Havre on 10 April 1917. On board were no wounded

In February 1917, *UC-26* is rammed by the paddlesteamer *Mona's Queen*. She lies in Ostend Harbour with a heavily damaged bow (TT).

An interesting photo, on which has been written following explanation: '5 captured Irish seamen and a negro, taken on board UC-26' (TT)

troops, but 86 crew and members of the Royal Army Medical Corps were drowned.

On 5 February 1917 *UC-26* narrowly escaped death. After dropping her cargo of mines off Boulogne she confronted a ship in blackout. This had now been identified as the paddle minesweeper *PMS Mona's Queen*. A torpedo was fired, but this failed to explode. *Mona's Queen* changed course and went straight for the submerging *UC-26*. *UC-26* was too slow in diving, was rammed on the bow and suffered heavy damages. The damages were so heavy that von Schmettow had to abort the patrol and head back to Ostend. The damage done to the bow of *UC-26* was patched up quickly, but the damaged fuel tanks were not used and her damaged torpedo tubes were crudely repaired. This led to her missing several targets as the forward torpedoes could not be fired. These problems caused much damage to the morale of her crew.

On 8 April 1917, *UC-26* left on her eighth and final patrol towards the Caen Roads. Here she deposited half the cargo of mines on 2 May and on the same day *HMS Derwent* was lost to the field. It was suspected that *UC-26* sank another three ships in the days that followed. On 9 May, after only a moderately successful patrol, von Schmettow decided to head back home. He wanted to cross the Dover Barrage on the surface, close to the French side. Around midnight, when off Cap Griz Nez, *UC-26* was observed by three destroyers. She immediately dived in position 51° 03' N 01° 40' E, but *HMS Milne* still managed to ram *UC-26*. *UC-26* was mortally hit in the pressure hull, just in front of her tower and crashdived to the bottom at 46 m. The surviving crewmen managed to shut off water gushing in, but could not make their U-boat lift up. When the electrical lighting broke down, the survivors knew that their U-boat would never make it back up to the surface. Escape through the hatches would be their only option. They divided themselves in two groups, one in the after compartment, a second in the control room. When this had been done, pressure within the submarine was equalised with the pressure outside, water was let in and the hatches were opened. Some of the survivors were forced to the surface in an air bubble and eight managed to breathe in fresh air again. This was a feat in itself, as they were able to reach the surface from a depth of 46 m, in total darkness, without the aid of diving gear. The British only managed to save two men from the sea, these were *Leutnant z. S.* Petersen and *Maschinistenmaat* Acksal. Versions of the rescue differ, whereby the survivors spoke of the fact that the British just left the six others behind.[184] British sources say that only two survivors made it alive to the surface.[185] Sadly enough, the ever-optimistic Graf von Schmettow was not amongst the survivors.

The wreck of *UC-26* was discovered by British diver Bob Peacock in position 51° 01' 740 N 01° 41' 207 E at a depth of 35 m. This is about 1.6 miles to the southeast of the then given historical location. Diver and researcher Alain Richard describes the wreck as being more or less intact, whereby *UC-26* is resting on her keel with an inclination over starboard. The tower is present, as are both forward torpedo tubes. On her visible, starboard propeller the inscription '*VULKAN AG HAMBURG, 15.05.1916, U-26*' was legible. This is probably a printing error by the wharf, as the '*C*' in the lettering was omitted.[186]

UC-31

As was the case with most of the newly built, large minelayers, *UC-31* was enlisted on 2 September 1916 with the *I U-Flottille* at Brunsbüttel. A total of 11 patrols were carried out under *Oberleutnant z. S.* Otto von Schrader, mainly on the British east coast, Scottish shores, the Shetlands and Irish south coast. It would only be on 14 June 1918 that she was ordered to join the *II. U-Flottille Flandern* at Zeebrugge. Luck did not seem to be on the side of *UC-31* and she was forced into dock for repairs after heavy damage to one of her engines. It was only on 1 October that all problems on board had been solved, but then the war was almost over. After four months of being laid up in the yard, she left Zeebrugge for Brunsbüttel once again. On 26 November 1918 she was delivered to England and scrapped in 1923 by the yard G. Cohen & Sons, Swansea.

UC-36

From the '30' -series of *UC-II* class submarines, only three of them would serve with the *Flandern Flottille*. *UC-36*, under command of *Oberleutnant z. S.* Gustav Buch, would only be able to complete three patrols, one of which was on the British east coast, which led to the sinking of just one vessel. The next two patrols in the Channel and off the Brittany coast saw more success. Between 15 March and 2 May 1917, *UC-36* was able to sink a total of 14 ships. On 16 May 1917 Buch and his crew left with *UC-36* on their final patrol from Zeebrugge. It is said that he managed to squeeze through the Dover Barrage to lay a minefield near the Nab lightship, which caused the loss of four British vessels. Around 30 May, all trace of *UC-36* vanished and it was assumed by German, as well as British sources, that she was mined near the Isle of Wight.

UC-39

Oberleutnant z. S. Otto Ehrentraut became captain of *UC-39* on 1 December 1917 after she was launched more than half a year earlier. He brought *UC-39* into Zeebrugge on 3 February and a week later made his first and only patrol with her. On the North Hinder, the Norwegian *SS Hans Kinck*, sailing in ballast, was sunk by gunfire and the next day on 8 February, *SS Hanna Larsen* en *SS Ida* were sunk off the south coast. The captain of *SS Hanna Larsen* was taken aboard as prisoner. Around noon, *UC-39* stopped the British *SS Hornsey* and opened fire. An alert lookout on the torpedo boat *HMS Thrasher* noticed the gunflashes. She altered course immediately and went full speed for UC-39 on which she opened fire at 1.5 miles distance with her 12-pounder quick-firing gun. Surviving *FT-Obergast*, Lassig later on said that the torpedo boat had attacked her from astern. *UC-39* was able to submerge in time, but *HMS Thrasher* dropped one depth charge in her wake,

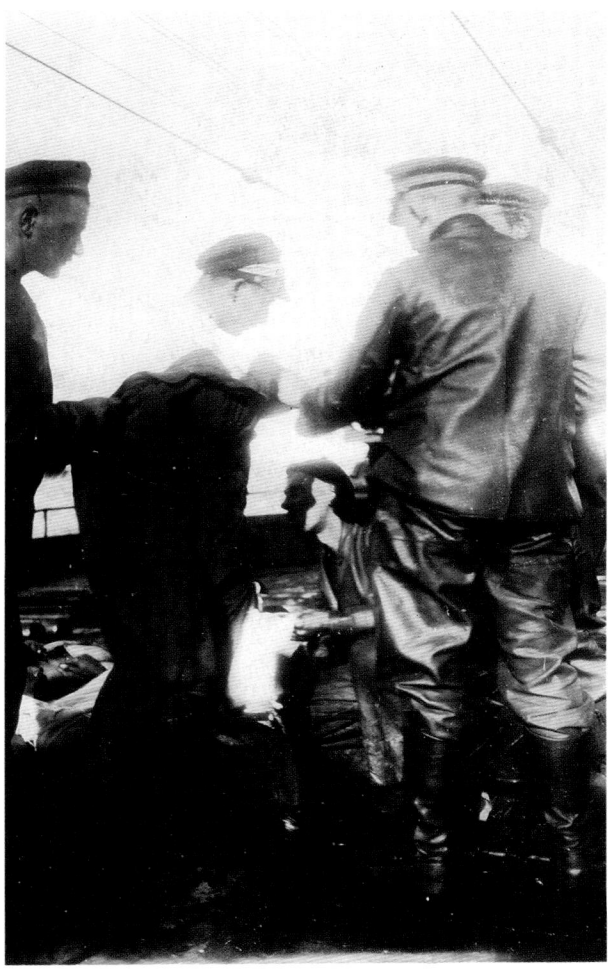

When there would be room on board a U-boat, enemy officers would be taken prisoner (TT)

Oberleutnant z. S. Otto Ehrentraut (middle, right), amongst part of his crew on *UC-39* (TT)

which detonated. *Steuermann* Eschenbach described how *UC-39* was heavily shaken by the explosion when they had reached a depth of 17 m. The explosion was so powerful that Eschenbach saw the engine room hatch drop inwards, followed by a waterfall of gushing water. *Heizer* Sauer stated later on that the explosion had fractured the glass of a porthole in the conning tower which resulted in water gushing into the control room which was not separated from the tower with an internal hatch. This resulted in the effect that all deck hatches were blasted open and most of the depth gauges fractured. Ehrentraut gave the order to blow the ballast tanks and make *UC-39* come to the surface. The torpedo boat immediately opened fire the moment *UC-39* had surfaced. In the end it was the captured British captain, Thomas Reid of the *SS Hanna Larsen*, who crawled up the tower ladder with a white handkerchief to wave their surrender. Ehrentraut followed him up the ladder but was killed on the bridge by a shell fragment. Sauer recounted that the torpedo boat came at them at full speed at 150 m distance. They had reopened their gunfire even though the entire crew of *UC-39* had gathered on deck. The captain of *HMS Thrasher* ordered *UC-39* to stop, as her electric engines were still running and the rudder forced her to sail in a circle. It was only after she stopped that the British launched a lifeboat. The British managed to rescue 17 Germans and two British prisoners from the sinking *UC-39*. A British officer stepped on board *UC-39*, which was already taking on water, jumped onto the tower and took a pair of binoculars as souvenir. The body of Ehrentraut was also taken off *UC-39* and buried in a Hull cemetery. *HMS Itchen* took *UC-39* in tow, but she foundered and sank at 16h20 about 3 miles south of Flamborough Head in position 53° 56' N 00° 06' E. More than a year later, on 7 June 1918, the wreck of *UC-39* was discovered and dived by Royal Naval divers. This chance discovery was caused by air bubbles seeping to the surface.[187]

UC-39 starts to sink despite being taken under tow by *HMS Thrasher* off Flamborough Head (Abrahams & Sons)

The wreck of UC-39 lies 8.5 miles to the east of Hornsea, north Yorkshire, in position 53° 55' 523 N 00° 04' 562 E at a depth of 22 m. She is largely intact and lies on an even keel. Graham Garner, a Leeds diver, stated in 2001 that all mineshafts were empty and several parts, such as a hatch, shells and brass junction boxes lay scattered over the seabed. The wreck was positively identified by the numbering 'UC-39' on the hub of the propeller. One of the propellers and a shell case are now on display at Bridlington Harbour Heritage Museum. The steering column can be seen at the Ship Inn, Sewerby.[188]

UC-40

UC-40 spent most of her life with the *I U.Flottille* in Brunsbüttel, after her launch on 5 September 1916. She was able to complete 14 patrols, mainly off the British east coast, Scottish coast, Orkneys and Shetlands. UC-40 sank 36 ships, many of which were naval trawlers and cargo ships which had been laden with pitprops. On 24 September 1918, UC-40 was sent to join the *U-Flottille Flandern*. After *Oberleutnant z. S. d. Res.* Bernhard Wischhausen had brought her to Zeebrugge, UC-40 did not have the opportunity to prove her worth for the *U-Flottille Flandern*. Just a week later, on 2 October, he received the order to return her to Brunsbüttel and join the *I-U. Flottille*. On 20 February 1919, UC-40 was sailed to Harwich with the 10th Group. She never made it that far, but sank to the east of the Dogger Bank in position 54° 55' N 04° 47' E, after an accident.

UC-46

UC-46, under command of *Oberleutnant z. S.* Fritz Moecke, entered the harbour of Zeebrugge at the end of November 1916. In his short career he managed to carry out three patrols off the British east coast and in the Bristol Channel. His first patrol, between 4 and 9 December 1916, was the laying of 18 mines between Spurn Point and Flamborough Head. This intensive action only resulted in the mining and sinking of the Norwegian *SS Modig*.

UC-46 opens fire on a British sailing ship (TT)

Patrol 2 ran over Christmas and New Year, and mines were laid off Dartmouth and Swansea. A British merchant ship was damaged, but could be saved and a French sailing ship was sunk. On this trip Moecke was able to sink a further four ships before returning back to the safety of Zeebrugge.

UC-46's third and final patrol was from 25 January to 8 February 1917 in the same area. In her minefield near the Breaksea lightship, only the naval trawler Longset was lost. By means of gunfire, Moecke was able to sink one steamship and two sailing ships between Lands End and the Isles of Scilly. His last victim was the 12,000 ton *SS Argyllshire* which was torpedoed near Start Point, but could sail on her power to Plymouth. On 8 February, *UC-46* undertook the crossing of the Dover Straits below the surface. Moecke was probably not at ease because halfway he decided to let his U-boat surface. It was a very clear night and he did not make an observation through the periscope. It proved to be a fatal mistake as the destroyer *HMS Liberty*, which only was half a mile away, had not been spotted. Her captain, *Lt. Cmdr.* King, immediately ordered her forward gun to open fire on *UC-46*, but the flashes blinded the lookouts on the bridge. King then ordered full speed ahead to ram the U-boat. *HMS Liberty* succeeded in hitting *UC-46*'s hull just forward of the conning tower, at a speed of 24 knots. The destroyer momentarily came to a standstill, but moments later glided over the submarine. *HMS Liberty* dropped a depth charge over the location where *UC-46* had disappeared beneath the waves. Nothing more was seen of *UC-46* and her crew. *HMS Liberty* was heavily damaged from the collision, but managed to limp to Dover where she was dry docked. During the analysis of the hull it was observed that about 4 feet of the bow must have sliced through *UC-46*. For the destruction of *UC-46*, King was awarded the Distinguished Service Order.

The wreck of *UC-46* was discovered by divers in position 51° 06' 902 N 01° 37' 081 E, and lies on a bottom of fine sand and gravel on a maximum depth of 35 m. It lies only 11 miles to the east of Dover pier. Dave Batchelor and Bob Peacock describe the wreck as listing slightly to port with six empty mineshafts. Just in front of her tower stand the 8.8 cm gun. Alain Richard has noticed a large tear in the pressure hull, measuring 30 cm in width, just abaft the gun.[189] This is obviously the spot where *HMS Liberty's* bow had lethally hit *UC-46*.

UC-47

About two weeks before *UC-46* would meet her end, the brand new *UC-47* entered Flemish territory, on 23 January 1917. *Oberleutnant z. S.* Paul Hundius had command and would prove to be much more successful than Moecke. Between 27 January and 9 October 1917 he was able to complete nine patrols in the Bristol Channel, Irish south coast and the western Channel area. Times had become difficult for U-boats in early 1917 and Hundius would experience this on several occasions. During the time he commanded *UC-47*, he came in contact with three Q-ships. One of these was *SS Gaelic* on 21 April, near Fastnet Rock. A heavy firefight ensued between the British and German gunners, but *UC-47* managed to register several hits on *SS Gaelic*. The Q-ship was only saved from sinking because the evening had come. Two days later *SS Vala* was met at Trevose Head and she immediately

A torpedoed merchant ship breaks in half and sinks (TT)

bared her teeth. After a short and powerful firefight both opponents left the scene without suffering any notable damage. A last confrontation was met on 28 September. In St. George's Channel, *SS Cullist* showed her guns, but Hundius did not want to risk his U-boat too close to the enemy. After exchanging fire for a few minutes, he decided to leave the area.

The heightened presence of the US Navy was also felt. During the same patrol the American sailing ship *Annie F. Conlon* was stopped south of the Scillies. Before an explosive charge could be put in her hold, *UC-47* was forced to dive as four American destroyers hove into view.

Although times proved to be difficult, Hundius still managed to prove himself as a very apt captain. In total he sank 49 ships, mainly through gunfire and torpedo, but also with explosive charges. The dropping of mines in enemy areas had some success but did not score on the top list. On 11 March, *UC-47* was able to make a repeat of successes against the British fleet in 1915. Ten trawlers were stopped off Trevose Head and collectively destroyed. The ships sunk by *UC-47* were of varying nationalities and often had all kinds of cargoes, such as sugar, coal, iron ore, general cargo and fuel. The British steamship *SS Brika* had come from Santiago de Cuba and was heading for London with a cargo of 6,280 tons of sugar. Hundius was able to torpedo and sink her in St. George's Channel. The Norwegian *SS Solferino* and *SS Wilfred* were sunk off Wissant on 15 March with explosive charges. On board were cargoes of coal destined for the Royal Navy in Gibraltar. The Italian *SS Medusa*, with a cargo of Spanish iron ore from Huelva was sunk in the same area. The American tanker *SS Motano*, despite having an escort of four destroyers, was torpedoed on 31 July to the southeast of Start Point.

Hundius had proven his worth and he gave over command of *UC-47* to *Oberleutnant z. S.* Günther Wigankow in October 1917. Early in 1918, Hundius was issued with the larger *UB-103*. He would serve the navy further as a very successful captain, but was killed in August 1918 when *UB-103* disappeared with all hands in the Dover Barrage.

Wigankow would not be able to prove his worth like his predecessor. Between 16 October and 13 November 1917 he was able to complete two patrols off the British east coast. Oddly enough, *UC-47* had left on both patrols without a cargo of mines and he was ordered to attack shipping with his torpedoes. In just under a month he was able to sink six enemy ships. On 17 November, *UC-47* left Zeebrugge for her final mission in the area off Flamborough Head. Wigankow did not even get the chance to go into action, as the day after he had left port he was already spotted by lookouts on the patrol vessel *HMS P-57*. *HMS P-57* headed full spead on ramcourse for the now surfaced *UC-47* and rammed her between the tower and gun. The pressure hull had been hit, water gushed in, and *UC-47* immediately sank in position 54° 03' N 00° 22' E. *HMS P-57* dropped a further two depth charges on the location, making oil and air bubbles come to the surface. The wreck

The waves washing over the gun deck of the UC-II boats was one of their main problems (TT)

311

was buoyed and dived by Royal Navy divers who managed to retrieve documents identifying the wreck as that of *UC-47*.

The wreck of *UC-47* was rediscovered in the late 1990s by divers from Bridlington, at a depth of 50 m. Later on, the wreck was designated a war grave by the Ministry of Defence. The U-boat is fairly intact, with the bow sanded up, but with both torpedo tubes lying loose in the sand. The tower hatch is open, but the interior is totally filled with sand. Just in front of the tower, heavy damage to the pressure hull is also visible. The gun is still in position and several shells are scattered around the area. The stern has severe damage to the port side and on the stern torpedo tube. This was probably caused by the explosion of one of the depth charges. Both propellers stand free and are visible in a 6 m deep scour. The wreck is hard to locate as she lies in an area of sandwaves which sometimes protrude higher than the remains.[190] In 2004, propellers, gun and a torpedo were removed from the site.

UC-48

It would only be on her third patrol that *UC-48* would know of any successes. After entering the navy on 6 November 1916, *UC-48* was commanded by *Kapitänleutnant* Kurt Ramien and added to the *U-Flottille Flandern*. Ramien proved to be a successful captain and was able to complete eight missions between 6 February and 18 October 1917. His area of operations was mainly the western part of the Channel, the Bristol Channel, the south coast of Ireland and the Spanish north coast. *UC-48* sank 33 ships, mainly with her torpedoes and deck gun. On his second patrol, on 15 March, a problem arose with the depth rudders and mid-Channel *UC-48* sank to a depth of 100 m. The strength of a UC-II class pressure hull proved its worth and no water entered. During her fifth patrol, *UC-48* twice had bad luck when trying to sink a ship. The 9,179 ton British *SS Westmeath* was torpedoed off Cherbourg, but the ship refused to sink, as her cargo of grain kept her afloat until she was able to reach the harbour. The American bark *Florence Creadick* was stopped during the same patrol near the Île de Batz. On board was a cargo of petrol destined for Le Havre. As it concerned a highly flammable cargo, Ramien decided to save a torpedo and sink the sailing ship with explosive charges. The charges detonated, but were not able to sink the ship! Oddly enough, the barrels of petrol kept the hull buoyant until towage help arrived on the scene. Despite a few problems, Ramien was still able to sink quite a few British, Spanish, French and Greek ships with cargoes destined for the Western Front.

Ramien relented command of *UC-48* on 21 October to *Oberleutnant z. S.* Helmut Lorenz, after which four unsuccessful patrols were carried out. Lorenz was only able to sink one ship, the Norwegian *SS Modemi*, off Whitby. *UC-48* left Zeebrugge on 17 March 1918 on her final patrol. She headed for the French Channel coast where mines were laid off the harbours of Tatikou and Cherbourg. Two days later *UC-48* was surprised on the surface by the destroyer *HMS Loyal*. *UC-48* was able to dive in time, but was heavily damaged by the detonations of several depth charges. Lorenz was skilled enough to navigate his U-boat away from the danger, but all *UC-48's* diving tanks had been damaged. He did not want to risk the return journey through the Dover Barrage with a vessel that could not submerge. Lorenz decided to run to the Spanish harbour of El Ferrol to have his U-boat interned. The Spanish put the captain and most of the crew in Alcala de Henares near Madrid as prisoners to prevent an escape back to Germany. Only the first officer, chief engineer and five crewmen were allowed to stay on board to keep *UC-48* in working order. *UC-48* remained in a corner of El Ferrol Harbour, beneath the vigilant guns of the cruiser *Rio De La Plata*, until November 1918. Even the propellers had been removed as a precaution. In February 1919 the interned *UB-23* and *UC-48* both had to be handed over to France. *UB-23* still had engine trouble and was to remain. On 19 March *UC-48* managed to commence the journey to France on her own. On board were Lorenz and nine men, five of which were engine room crew of *UB-23*. Finally Lorenz, in a last move of defiance, had the seacocks of *UC-48* opened, making her sink in the El Ferrol Harbour entrance. During this action *Oberheizer* Hartling drowned after falling overboard before *UC-48* had left the harbour. The remaining crew was later on repatriated to Germany via Holland.[191] France put in a complaint about suffering damages by the loss of *UC-48* and demanded to be compensated with the 90% completed U-boats *U-137*, *U-138* and *U-158*. As the whole process took lots of time, all three U-boats had by then been scrapped. France had to negotiate heavily and as compensation she was given the engines of the completed *UC-117*.

The wreck of *UC-48* must still lie in her original place of sinking, in about 21 m of water depth.

UC-49

UC-49 would spend the early months of her career with the *I. U-Flottille* from 2 December 1917 until 4 March 1918. *Oberleutnant z. S.* Hans Kükenthal brought her over to Zeebrugge on 25 May 1918 to add her to the *U-Flottille Flandern II*. *UC-49* had arrived in Flanders fairly late in the war, but still knew some moderate successes. On her tenth patrol, the first she would make out of a Flemish port, three ships were sunk, one of which was the 6,103 ton British merchant cruiser *SS Patia* off Hartland Point. *UC-49* was pursued and rewarded with a rain of depth charges from two escort vessels. She managed to give them the slip, but a heavily damaged fuel tank forced Kükenthal to cut short the patrol. On 1 August 1918 *UC-49* left on her final patrol, which was to lay mines in the Plymouth area. Two days out of Zeebrugge, Kükenthal made a painful error. Near the Owers lightship a ship was observed in thick fog, and, assuming it was a troop ship, Kükenthal had her torpedoed. In reality, it was the hospital ship *SS Warilda*, with on board 700 wounded. The ship sank after two hours with the loss of 123 men. *UC-49* would pay a heavy price for this mistake and a week later she was sunk by depth charges from the destroyer *HMS Opossum* near Start Point. *HMS Opossum* had been in company with seven motor launches which had hung hydrophones over board to locate the telltale sound of U-boat engines. *HMS Opossum* chanced upon *UC-49* and dropped a whole string of depth charges on her. The engine noises had halted, but the British stayed and waited. Some time later the sound continued, because *UC-49* had stayed on the bottom, and the British dropped another volley of depth charges. This game of cat and mouse carried on threefold, but *UC-49* finally had to surface and was taken under fire. She dived again and was pounded with depth charges, but this last time would be deadly and *UC-49* was destroyed with her entire crew. Confirmation of the sinking was made by the gruesome discovery of a severed, gloved hand and a lightbulb which had been manufactured in Vienna.[192]

A wreck which possibly corresponds to the identity of *UC-49* was found by divers in position 50° 19' 9 N 03° 30' 00 W. The wreck is intact and has heavy damage to the midship section. The remains concern a UC-II class U-boat, but up to now nothing decisive has been found concerning its positive identification.

UC-50

Just like her numerical predecessor, *UC-50* had first been enlisted in the *I. U-Flottille*, in Brunsbüttel, from 18 February to 6 June 1917. Her captain, *Oberleutnant z. S.* Rudi Seuffer, brought her after this period over to Flanders. *UC-50* was ready for her fourth patrol, her first from Zeebrugge, on 22 July 1917. Seuffer brought his U-boat to the Bay of Biscay area, where he was able to torpedo *SS Carmarthen*. To the west of Wissant, the helmsmen of *UC-50* lost control over their U-boat due to a fault in the engine room, forcing *UC-50* on a crashdive to 96 m. Evidently U-boat construction and toughness varied from U-boat to U-boat. In contrast with the case of *UC-48*, where control had been lost over the hydroplanes, resulting in the U-boat diving down to 100 m but without doing damage, certain areas of the hull had not been resistant to almost 11 atmospheres of pressure and water gushed inside damaging multiple batteries. Seuffer and his crew managed to bring *UC-50* up to the surface, but had to cancel the rest of the patrol.

After reaching home safely, repairs were carried out and another three patrols were completed in the same area, resulting in the sinking of eight ships. *UC-50* left Zeebrugge on 7 January 1918 for her eighth and also final mission. Nothing more was heard of *UC-50* and her crew, and to all probability she was destroyed by depth charges from *HMS Zubian* off Dungeness. This was during the night of 4 February in the then indicated position 50° 50' N 01° 26' E. The date of sinking was quite late for a patrol of a UC-II class U-boat, amounting to more than three weeks. We can only assume that problems on board had occurred and the patrol had to be extended.

Divers recently discovered a wreck of a UC-II class U-boat in position 50° 52' 800 N 00° 57' 13 E. The wreck showed extensive damage to the midship section and had probably been caused by impacts from depth charges. The wreck lies to the north of the historical position given by the captain of *HMS Zubian*.[193] The Royal Navy dive team was sent out shortly after the sinking, but no remains were found, as they had searched in the wrong location.

UC-51

UC-51 was initially employed in 1917 to attack shipping off the Scottish east coast, Shetlands and Irish south coast. During those months she was not based in Flanders, but with the *I. U-Flottille* and had Helgoland as homeport. *UC-51* was technically part of the *U-Flottille Flandern* when she had left Helgoland on her third patrol. Her captain, *Oberleutnant z. S.* Hans Galster managed to sink six enemy ships during this patrol. At the end of this mission, on 20 August 1917, *UC-51* entered the port of Zeebrugge. *UC-51* managed to complete another two patrols in the Irish Sea and Bristol Channel, sinking a total of 16 ships. *UC-51* left Zeebrugge on 15 November for her sixth patrol, but would not return. It is assumed that she was lost two days later on a British mine to the south of Start Point, in position 50° 08' N 03° 42' W. German suspicions over her loss were justified, as the British had laid 680 deepwater mines to the south of Start Point in early November 1917, to serve as a trap for U-boats. The crew of the trawler *Lois* was witness to an enormous explosion on 17 November. After the surge had passed, a U-boat surfaced, floated around for a while, rolled on its side and went under. Shortly afterwards a mine popped to the surface, accompanied by oil and wreckage. The crew of *Lois* were able to destroy the floating mine. When sailing through the wreckage, wooden flotsam, human intestines and a boot were spotted. The boot was fished out of the water and on the inside was a label with the name 'Metzger'. Later on, the owner was identified as Ewald Metzger, a crewman of *UC-51*.

According to Innes McCartney, the wreck of *UC-51* had been found in July 2000 by a UK-based diving team in position 50° 11' 52 N 04° 17' 18 W.[194] The team was led by experienced diver Bill Reid, who was accustomed to the Salcombe area. *UC-51* lies at a depth of 68 m and has damages to her stern. On the bow a net cutter still stands and her six shafts are filled with mines. This is additional proof of her identity as *UC-51*. As she was only sunk two days after her departure, she most likely did not get the opportunity to release all or any of her mines.

View on the bow of a UC-II boat during heavy weather (TT)

This photo shows a UC-II boat engaging in diving trials in a German port (TT)

UC-56

Before *UC-56* started her career with the *U-Flottille Flandern* in 1918, she saw service in the Baltic with the *U-Flottille Kurland*. Her captain, *Kapitänleutnant d. Res.* Wilhelm Kiesewetter, seemed to be unsuccessful, even after completing five patrols. The only ship *UC-56* managed to sink was the hospital ship *SS Glenart Castle,* which sank 10 miles to the west of Lundy Island with the loss of 153 lives. Kiesewetter had made a capital mistake caused by limited visibility and had mistaken the vessel as a merchantman. *UC-56* also seemed to be plagued by ill-fortune. On her fifth and final patrol, the starboard diesel engine drive shaft broke just after they had slipped through the Dover Barrage. On 21 May Kiesewetter wanted to attack a convoy near Le Four, but *UC-56* was bombarded with depth charges from the armed yacht *USS Christabel*. Shortly afterwards, the starboard electric engine failed and further engine damage made *UC-56* totally unmanageable. Kiesewetter decided to sail to the Spanish port of Santander to have his U-boat interned. Once in the port, he and his crew were taken to the town under guard. All weapons and ammunition were taken off and stored in a barracks. Both propellers were dismounted, the radio equipment and several shafts and couplings were disabled to make any escapes impossible. The largest part of the crew were later transferred to Madrid where they remained interned until early May 1919. *UC-56* had already been declared French war booty earlier, in March, and brought to Cherbourg. In 1923 the former minelayer was taken to Rochefort and scrapped.

The crew was repratriated back to Germany on the Dutch liner *SS Frisia*, via Falmouth to Rotterdam. For *Kapitänleutnant d. Res.* Kiesewetter there awaited an unpleasant surprise in the shape of a long stay in a British prison. On 7 May, the *SS Frisia* stopped in Falmouth to let on an armed guard which escorted Kiesewetter from the ship. Without any explanation he was brought to the Tower of London and incarcerated. Explanation still stayed out, despite his protests and he was only greeted with the icy silence from his guards. The arrest concerned the act of war crime which the British had said that he had committed with *UC-56* against a hospital ship. After 80 days of incarceration he was brought to Cologne under guard and released on 25 July.[195]

315

UC-61

UC-61 and her crew would have the unfortunate fame to be the only U-boat to have been captured by a Belgian cavalry unit! The brand new UC-61 arrived in Zeebrugge at the end of February 1917 and was commanded by *Oberleutnant z. S.* Georg Gerth. Gerth and his crew would only experience a very short career, completing only four patrols in five months. As was the case with all new arrivals, they made their first mission close to home. On 5 March, the British packet *SS Copenhagen* was torpedoed and sunk near the North Hinder lightship.

It would be six weeks later that UC-61 left on her first minelaying mission in the direction of western approaches. Mines were laid in groups of two and four near the Needles, Anvil Point and St. Alban's Head, but had only as result the sinking of the trawler Arfon. On the same patrol a further four ships were sunk, one of them the Italian cargoship *SS Giovannina*. The French vessel *SS Nelly* was stopped on 8 March in the Bay of Biscay, but she immediately opened fire on UC-61. The French gunner scored a hit on the ready-use ammunition stored on her stern. This ignited and UC-61 suffered slight damage and had to cease the attack. On her return journey, another two merchant ships were sent to the bottom.

Docking time for the received damage would be long and it was only by the end of June that UC-61 was again fit for sea. Mines laid on her third patrol seemed to have had much more success than the previous ones. Near Brest Harbour entrance, a small field of six mines was laid and resulted in the sinking of the French armoured cruiser *Kléber*. The 7,578 ton cruiser was coming from Dakar and would be added to the Channel fleet. The *Kléber* sank shortly after hitting a mine, with the loss of 38 men. The remainder of UC-61's patrol continued without further incident, but three ships were still sunk, one of which was a British destroyer.

UC-61 left Zeebrugge on 25 July on her final patrol. In the early hours of the next day, after Gerth had made calculations to cross the Dover Barrage on the French side, a thick fog appeared. Instead of letting UC-61 down to the seabed and awaiting their time, Gerth decided to brave the fog. This decision would mean the end of his career with the U-boat division. At 2 am they passed a flock of French patrol vessels, which had picked up their engine sounds, but could not locate her. At 04h20, UC-61 hit bottom. The captain thought that they had hit the shallows of La Bassure de Bas, but at the crack of dawn the situation looked totally different. UC-61 had come stuck at high tide on the Wissant beach, not even 800 m distance from the dunes! The rising sun soon cast light on the villas and houses, which were grouped around the small church. Gerth desperately tried to refloat his U-boat by ordering his men to jettison topload. They rolled two torpedoes overboard and numerous shells. As much as they tried, UC-61 would not budge an inch. The tide was dropping and the minelayer was totally exposed. A radio signal was sent to Bruges to inform them of their dire situation. After this, Gerth told his crew to evacuate after having placed explosive charges in the engine room. In the meantime, a French customs officer and three colleagues came to investigate with a trawler. They were totally surprised, came closer and yelled to the seamen on the bridge of the U-boat if they spoke any French. Gerth answered yes and initially they thought it concerned a British submarine! The customs officer jumped ashore and ran towards the nearest telephone to inform the military authorities at Calais. A Belgian cavalry unit was warned and ordered to investigate. History so dictated it that 40 cavalrymen of the 5th Lancers arrived to take 25 German seamen prisoner. When the lancers arrived, the explosive charges exploded and ignited the fuel tanks. The resulting explosion blew the entire stern to bits and severed it from the engine room area. Oddly enough, none of the 18 mines exploded and one torpedo had still been spared. A heavy fire spread and was only put out by the incoming tide around noon.

The Allies had enough material evidence to start an investigation. Eight mines, 300 shells and a new type of periscope were recovered and brought to Calais for further investigation. They also found a logbook and complete documents which had a connection to mined areas. Gerth obviously had not taken the time to destroy the codebooks and it informed the British that the Germans had partly deciphered their codes. The crew of UC-61 was taken that same day, on foot and under guard, by the Belgians to the Calais citadel.

On 28 August, a month later, a heavy storm occurred. Through the effects of wind, waves and tide, the wreck of UC-61 dug itself 1.5 m deeper in the

The wreck of UC-61 on the beach of Wissant (TT) ▶

sand. Due to her being buried, the authorities did not manage to recover the remaining mines or torpedo. Finally the site was used as target for the testing of a newly invented Belgian mortar. On 4 September, a projectile hit the remaining ammunition on *UC-61*, which ignited and blew the remains of the wreck to pieces.[196] Alain Richard did extensive research on the fate of *UC-61* on the Wissant beach. He found out that the wreck had been sold in 1920 to a certain Mr. Honvault of Wissant. Together with an old serviceman of a coastal battery they dismembered the remaining bronze, iron and copper parts. Up to now nothing has been found of the wreck, but we may assume that there are still parts buried beneath the sand. The French Hydrographic service, the SHOM, gives the location of the wreck in position 50° 53' 614 N 01° 39' 865 E, but has been taken out of the list as non-existent.

French sailors pose on the tower of the stranded UC-61 (ECPAD)

The story spreads to the other side of Channel: in the mid-1990s a copper ring was discovered in excavation works in the west of England. This had the inscription: 'U.61 Wissant August 1917'. The ring probably concerns a fragment of tubing which a British seaman had taken as a souvenir from the wreckage and made into a memorial piece.

UC-62

UC-62 was launched on 9 December 1916 and would only serve ten months in the navy before meeting her fate on the Thornton Bank. Her captain, *Oberleutnant z. S.* Max Schmitz, did not excel during this period as a successful commander. He took *UC-62* on her first three patrols to the North Hinder hunting grounds, after which he left for the western part oft he Channel.

A view on the destroyed stern and engine room of *UC-61* on the Wissant beach (ECPAD)

A brass ring with inscription 'U-61 Wissant August 1917' (TT)

The North Hinder proved to be moderate in successes and only the schooner *Noordzee* and the cargoship *SS Neptunus* were sunk. On 19 April *UC-62* got herself in an awkward situation, which was quite a rarity for the war at sea. *UC-62* found herself in position 52° 10' N 02° 30' E at a periscope depth of 11 m. Oddly enough, the U-boat bumped into an obstruction and stopped. Suddenly the U-boat was pushed upwards from the forward end and the depth indicator showed 5 m, in an area where it normally should be about 40 m depth in average! Schmitz bounded for the periscope and saw the bow of *UC-62* tilted up to an angle of 60° to 70°, lying on the bow of a surfaced British submarine! Schmitz was the first to react and ordered full astern, making his U-boat slide off the British one. The British submarine did the same and both slunk away from the scene. It came out later that it was *HMS E-50*.

Schmitz carried out another five patrols in the western part of the Channel during the following six months and sank 11 ships. The American sailing ship *A.B. Sherman* was a lucky vessel. On 27 June she was boarded to the southwest of the Scilly Isles and explosive charges placed in her bilge. During this operation, a cargo ship armed with two guns came towards her, forcing *UC-62* to dive. The explosive charges went off but her cargo of cotton kept the ship afloat and the American was able to reach the port of St. Mary. Luck did not seem to accompany Schmitz on this patrol when he went to periscope depth to shadow the British *SS Don Arturo*. Lookouts on the vessel spotted the periscope and the captain turned his ship 180° and headed straight for *UC-62* with the intention to ram. *UC-62* had to veer off-course, but Schmitz desperately wanted to sink his prey. *SS Don Arturo* now had turned and started to speed away from *UC-62*, but Schmitz pursued and after a chase lasting several hours managed to torpedo her around midnight. A heavy explosion followed and *SS Don Arturo* disintegrated and sank in a few seconds, taking all 34 crewmen down with her. In the following months, July to September, *UC-62* was able to sink *SS Neotsfield*, the bark *Vaarbud*, the schooner *Carmela*, *SS Glenstrae* and the bark *Chacma* in the Western Approaches.

UC-62 left Zeebrugge on her ninth and final patrol, on 11 October 1917, and headed for the southwestern coast of England. Schmitz wanted to lay mines off St. Alban's Head and Portland, as well as take on merchant shipping in the same area. All contact with the U-boat and her Bruges base was lost after she had

A UC-II boat on the canal towards Bruges (TT)

Oberleutnant z. S. Müller-Schwarz (*UC-64*), *Leutnant z. S.* Holm and *Leutnant z.S.d.R.* Lohmeyer (1st officer *UC-62*), in front of their lodging in Bruges (TT)

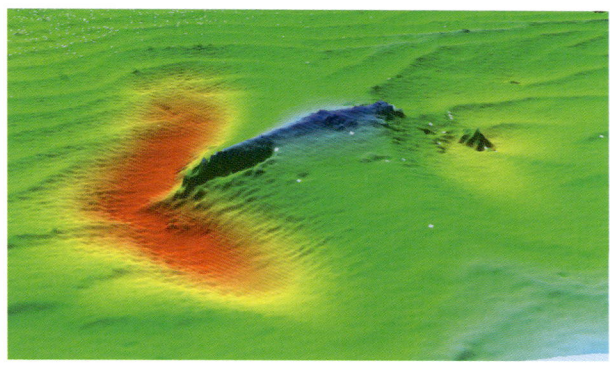

Multi-beam view of the wreck of *UC-62* (MDK-Vlaamse Hydrografie)

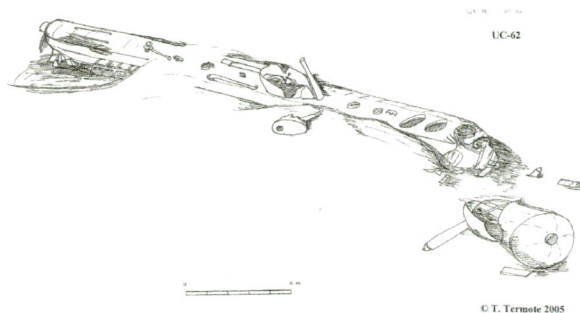

Sketch of the wreck of *UC-62* (TT)

left. According to British sources, a newly laid minefield was discovered off St. Alban's Head, causing the ships *SS Hartburn* and *SS Hazelwood* to sink. Off Portland *SS Ionian* was sunk. A number of U-boat mines appeared and were cleared by the British. It was suspected that *UC-62* had completed her assignment, but as nothing was heard from her for 16 days, it was presumed that the vessel had been lost with all hands. The German Admiralty suspected that she had been lost in a British minefield off Portland.[197] The British too suspected that they had caused *UC-62* to be sunk by their recently laid deep minefields.[198]

The mystery of *UC-62*'s disappearance would be solved almost 80 years later by the author and his research group. The location of the wreck of a UC-II class submarine north of the Thornton Bank and the diary of a British submarine captain would bring light upon her fate. The British submarine *HMS E-45* was on patrol near the Thornton Bank on 19 October 1917. At 06h29 her captain observed through the periscope a vessel to starboard steering an erratic course. Gunfire from a surfaced U-boat was spotted shortly after. The ship was struck and started sinking at around 07h00. The unsuspecting U-boat changed course and headed straight for *HMS E-45*. Her captain, Lt. Commander G.S. Watkins, fired a stern torpedo from *HMS E-45* at 07h08 at a distance of 400 m. Three minutes later he fired another torpedo, now *from* the bow tube. At 07h12 a heavy explosion was picked up and nothing more was seen on the surface.[199] This was later confirmed by the British Admiralty: *UC-62* had been torpedoed on the surface whilst engaging a Dutch merchant vessel.[200] Identification of the U-boat wreck on the Thornton Bank would confirm British sources.

Starboard view of the conning tower of *UC-62* (TT)

Irregular shrapnel holes in the portside of the tower (TT)

Starboardside propeller guard on *UC-62* (TT)

Starboard propellor (TT)

Port propellor (TT)

The wreck of *UC-62* lies in deeper water north of the Thornton Bank at a maximum depth of 36 m. She lies upright, but is heavily sanded up around the tower, up to the first mineshaft and abaft the tower just up to her lifting hook. Bow and stern both have a deep scours beneath their remains. Until 2004 the tower had been in an intact condition and showed on her port side penetration damage from shell or shrapnel impacts. Her gun is not present. About 8 m in front of the forward part of the wreck lie the remains of the torn off bow section. A heavy explosion was obviously the cause of this as well as the sinking of *UC-62*.[201] The irregular holes in the port side of the tower could have been the reason why *UC-62* was on the surface at that moment. Perhaps caused by a firefight with an armed merchant ship the pressure hull was hit and the U-boat was unable to submerge. UC-II class U-boats did not have a second hatch shutting off the tower section from the internal control area.

UC-63

The '60'-boats of the UC-class seemed to be predestined to serve on the Flanders front. *UC-63* was completed and launched on 6 January 1917. She sailed into Zeebrugge three months later and was ready for her first patrol under command of *Oberleutnant z. S.* Karsten von Heydebreck. Von Heydebreck had served on torpedo boats as first officer, before the war. It was only in early 1916 that he volunteered for the U-boat division. After his training he received command of *UB-6*, before being assigned to the larger *UC-63*. In contrast with the other UC-II class U-boats, von Heydebreck carried out five patrols off the British

Heavily damaged and distorted mineshafts 4 and 5 on *UC-62* (TT)

east coast and Humber, before heading further west, to the Bay of Biscay.

UC-63 was responsible for sinking 26 ships in the period between 25 April and 16 August. It mainly concerned British trawlers and cargo ships laden with coal. Without realising it, *UC-63* had also sunk two Q-ships off Yarmouth on 12 August. They concerned *Nelson* and *Ethel and Millie*, both of only 60 tons, but armed with a 4.7 cm and 5.7 cm gun. Von Heydebreck also proved to be very daring. During the night of 2 August he had the French sailing ship *Marie Jesus Protegez Nous* boarded by his crew. It was shortly after midnight, the sea was flat calm and *UC-63* found herself deep in enemy territory off the Humber Estuary. He ordered the Frenchman to drop anchor and let *UC-63* berth alongside. During the following hours the almost empty batteries of the U-boat were reloaded. The French sailing ship, as gratitude for her services rendered to the German navy, was sunk, after the crew had been left in the lifeboats.

UC-63 then moved to a new hunting area, after a few patrols on the east coast, which was now the Bay of Biscay. During 13 September and her sinking on 1 November 1917, she was able to sink ten ships. The ships that von Heydebreck came upon here were of a different calibre than those on the British east coast. They were mainly large ships with varying cargoes such as corn, saltpeter, iron ore and pitprops for the trenches.

On 1 November 1917 *UC-63* found herself on the western side of the Dover Barrage. After a moderately successful patrol in the Channel she was on the return route. Around 01h00 a radio message was sent to Bruges from their location (in 069 Beta VI, 51° 20' N 02° 05' E) and her possible arrival time in Bruges. Not even a quarter of an hour later *UC-63* was hit beneath the tower by a torpedo from the British submarine *HMS E-52*. *UC-63* immediately sank in position 51° 23' N 02° 00' E to the east of the Goodwin Sands. *U-boot-matrosenmaat* Fritz Marsal was the sole survivor, being picked up by *HMS E-52*. *UC-63* had been on the surface during the attack, with a full bridge watch. Marsal said that the atmosphere was relaxed, as they were going home, even though they still found themselves deep in enemy territory. Three men had been on watch on the tower, whilst *UC-63* was being steered from the control room. The first officer, *Leutnant z. S.* Brandt, kept watch to port. Marsal had the starboard section and a sailor had to keep an eye

Oberleutnant z. S. Max Brandt (right) would also perish when *UC-63* was torpedoed and sunk (TT)

Oberleutnant z. S. Karsten von Heydebreck, captain of *UC-63* (WZ-Bilddienst)

on the stern area. He remembered that it was a very cold but clear night. Brandt requested coffee and the sailor went down to the galley to fetch a cup. In the meantime, from beneath the waves, they were being watched by Lt. P. Phillips, captain of *HMS E-52*. *UC-63* had been spotted at 01h12 by her lookouts at 1,200 m from their port side. It surprised Phillips that the Germans had not seen them on such a clear night. But on board of *UC-63* it seemed that they were elsewhere with their thoughts. Engineer Danker had joined them and began to speak to Brandt. Brandt had made a crucial mistake not to keep an eye on his sector. Marsal looked over to port and spotted a surfaced submarine which was bearing on them with the bow torpedo tubes. He warned Brandt who immediately ordered the helm hard over to starboard. The order came too late as *HMS E-52* had just fired two torpedoes at a range of only 200 m! A column of water shot up 30 m high, followed by an explosion. The shock waves which reached *HMS E-52* were so heavy that a loaded torpedo was released by accident from a side tube. *UC-63* had just begun her turn, but it was too late. Marsal was flung against something hard and seconds later he was in the water. He was dragged under, but was able to kick himself free and reach the surface. Brandt also lay in the water and desperately tried to stay above. He was drowning because his clothing and boots had been soaked and were dragging him under.[202] Marsal was the only survivor from the 26-man crew. He was picked up by *HMS E-52* which had arrived on the scene.

The wreck has not been found or has not been formally identified as one of the known UC-II class U-boats. It is possible that *UC-63* lies 10 miles closer to shore than the then given position 53° 23' N 02° 0' E.

UC-64

UC-64 was added to the *U-Flottille Flandern* after arriving in Zeebrugge on 13 May 1917. She was commanded by *Oberleutnant z. S.* Ernst Müller Schwarz, who able to carry out three patrols in the North Hinder area. Just as was the case for the other UC-II class U-boats, this area proved to be fairly poor and only five Dutch ships, which had on board cargoes destined for Germany's enemy, were sunk. These were the smacks *Voorwaarts*, *Alberdina* and *Hendrika* and the small coastal cargo ships *SS Telegraaf XVIII* and *SS Timor*. *UC-64*, oddly enough, also experienced a collision with an enemy submarine. She had been cruising on the surface during the night of 8 July and wanted to submerge. When she was nearly totally submerged, *UC-64* was pushed back up to the surface by a British submarine which was just beneath her. Müller Schwarz ordered full astern, making his U-boat glide off the other. Both submarines were able to escape the scene unscathed. In August 1917, he was able to experience one more patrol with *UC-64*, this time in the Channel area. *UC-64* dropped her mines off Dieppe which resulted in the sinking of two ships.

On 13 September, command was given to *Oberleutnant z. S.* Erich Hecht, who wanted to test his new U-boat on the British east coast. He was able to sink three ships, but he was more ambitious and eager to sink larger targets in the western Channel area. Between 11 October 1917 and 30 January 1918 *UC-64* was able to complete four patrols in the Channel. Several minefields were laid, without result and she only managed to sink eight ships with her torpedoes and deck gun.

UC-64 changed captain for the third and last time in her career, this time being *Oberleutnant z. S.* Ferdinand Schwartz. As was habit, he first undertook a number of patrols off the British east coast. The catch was pretty meagre and he only managed to thin down the British fishing fleet with the loss of four trawlers and also sinking four cargo ships. His fourth patrol found him in the Bristol Channel, where luck did not seem to be on his side. Off Cornwall, *UC-64* had fired a

The rear of the photo reads: 'Amidst my crew' (Müller-Schwarz)

◄ Von Heydebreck (below left) and Brandt (with helmet) stand amongst the crew of *UC-63* in the Zeebrugge lock (TT)

UC-64 photographed whilst leaving Zeebrugge on patrol (BArch)

The small Dutch *Alberdina* sinks at the North Hinder after being sunk with explosive charges from *UC-64* (TT)

The sailing ship *Hendrika* is stopped at the North Hinder by *UC-64* on 21 June 1917 (TT)

After explosive charges are detonated, *Hendrika* sinks below the surface (TT)

A watery fate awaits the Dutch sailing barge *Voorwaarts* on the North Hinder (TT)

The rear reads: 'UC-64 in battle with British trawlers' (Müller-Schwarz)

An unknown cargo ships, after *UC-64* hits her several times with her deck gun (TT)

The bent periscope of *UC-64* shows the evidence of being hit by an enemy patrolship (TT)

torpedo which turned back on her, but luckily missed them! The next torpedo went deep and exploded on the bottom. On the final leg of the patrol, *UC-64* managed to sink the Norwegian *SS Mefjord*, but a lookout on a patrol ship had spotted her periscope and a course to ram was set. The periscope was hit and bent, making Schwartz cancel the rest of the patrol.

UC-64 left Zeebrugge on her final mission on 18 June 1918, after repairs had been carried out. Schwartz wanted to lay mines off the Gironde, but they never got so far. Whilst crossing the Dover Barrage, she hit a British mine in the early hours of 20 June, to the east of the Varne bank. The explosion was seen at 04h15 by a lookout on the armed trawler *Ocean Roamer*. She immediately altered course and went full steam to the location where a dark shadow was spotted below the surface. The shadow advanced slowly in northeasterly direction and in its wake was a trace of oil and air bubbles. The trawler dropped two depth charges and a second one, *Loyal Friend*, did the same. Oil and air bubbles kept rising to the surface in the following hours and it was not a big problem for Royal Naval divers to locate the wreck. The wreck was examined on 6 July and identified as a large UC-II class submarine. On board were still its cargo of mines, as well as spare torpedoes just abaft both bow torpedo tubes. There was an 8.8 cm deck guns and the U-boat had camouflage paint. Damant said that the bottom layer looked new, matt black to dark red in colour.[203] All hatches were shut, except that of the tower, which stood slightly ajar, but would not budge. It was deemed too dangerous to examine the wreck because of the presence of the mines, as well as a British mine which was swaying up and down with the tide, just next to the wreck. *UC-64*'s entire underbelly had been forced inwards by an explosion and the interior was a mixture of destroyed batteries, hammocks, clothes, mangled corpses and other wreckage. The floor of the control room had been so heavily pushed upwards that access to the radio room was not possible. Only the stern was directly recognisable. Explosives were used on the tower hatch on 16 July to gain further access to her interior*. The discovery of a wallet on one of the bodies would identify the wreck as *UC-64*.

---

* UC-64 had probably just come out of refit before her sinking.

The wreck of *UC-64* still holds stowed mines. The photo shows a close-up of one of the Hertzhorns (André Lugiez)

UC-64's portside propeller shows two of her three blades (Alain Richard)

UC-64 was able to sink a total of 27 ships, amounting to 25,038 tons, in a career which had lasted almost one and a half years.

Diver Dave Batchelor was able to dive the wreck a few years ago. *UC-64* lies about 9 miles to the south southeast of Dover, on the Varne bank in position 50° 58' 536 N 01° 23' 210 E at a depth of 43 m. He describes the control room as totally opened up. The conning tower is not on the wreck anymore but was blown off to gain access.(204) It had been obvious that Damant's diving team did not just want to blow off the hatch! Alain Richard describes her as lying on her starboard side on a white bed of sand. In the bow are six shafts with the entire cargo of mines, as well as both torpedo tubes. Just abaft is the deck gun, with numerous rounds of 8.8 cm ammunition. Some of the shells are still stored in their zinc ready-use cases.(205) The midship section is totally destroyed and flattened, and in most areas covered by lost trawls. The stern is intact and the starboard propeller, depth rudder and torpedo tube are visible.

UC-65

In not even a year's time, *UC-65* would become a very successful U-boat under the skilful command of *Oberleutnant z. S.* Otto Steinbrinck.

She arrived in Zeebrugge on 3 February 1917 and three days later she headed for the hunting grounds of the Bristol Channel. Steinbrinck did not deem it necessary to test his U-boat in waters closer to home.

Between 6 February and 1 August 1917, Steinbrinck carried out seven patrols in the western part of the Channel, Irish Sea and Bristol Channel. His success would not be equalled in the sinking of 96 ships and the damaging of a further five. The high results were gained mostly with use of the deck gun and the explosive charges. Large ships, or ships sailing in convoy had to be torpedoed. Mines laid by *UC-65* proved to know less results and only two large cargo ships, *SS Lapland*, of 18.565 BRT, and *SS New York*, of 10.798 BRT, were hit but did not sink. One of the largest warships sunk by *UC-65* was the escorted cruiser *HMS Ariadne*, of 11.000 BRT, which sank near the Royal Sovereign light ship after being struck by two torpedoes.

After his seventh patrol was finished, Steinbrinck handed over control to *Kapitänleutnant* Max Viebeg, who carried out just one patrol, sinking six ships.

UC-65's last captain was *Kapitänleutnant* Claus, 'Lala', Lafrenz, who took over command late August 1917. Lafrenz was, like his two predecessors, a very skilled captain, who enjoyed a high regard from his fellow officers and crew. Along with many officers in the U-boat service, he had been a volunteer after serving as first officer on torpedo boats. Before commanding *UC-65* he had captained *UB-18* and *UB-33*, and received the Housorder of Hohenzollern for his successes. This was awarded to him by the Kaiser after being the first man to photograph a British Q-ship.

On 3 November *UC-65* was on the way home from her second patrol under Lafrenz. During the previous

UC-65 stops a British tanker in order to destroy her (TT)

patrol he had to content himself with just three sinkings, one of which was the American bark *Paolina* with a cargo of steel thread and oil originating from New York. The current patrol had been even less successful, whereby only one ship had been sent to the bottom. He had been able to torpedo the British *SS Branksome Hall*, but she remained afloat until being saved. *UC-65* was cruising on the surface on her homeward leg. They were off Beachy Head, where Lafrenz and four of his crew were keeping a concentrated watch for patrol vessels and mines. But, danger lurked from beneath the waves in the shape of the British submarine *HMS C-15*. By sheer coincidence, both submarines spotted each other at exactly the same moment. Instead of immediately submerging, Lafrenz told the others about the periscope he had seen and kept on course for home. He was planning to dodge an enemy torpedo by his faith in *UC-65*'s manoeuvrability. The captain of *HMS C-15*, Lt. E.H. Dolphin, had in the meantime prepared his torpedo tubes for firing. At 16h45 the German lookouts spotted a torpedo heading towards them. Lafrenz rapidly ordered an alteration in course and was able to evade it. But *UC-65* did not prove to be as manoeuverable as he had hoped, as another torpedo exploded a few seconds later against her stern, sinking *UC-65* immediately. Dolphin had, unexpectedly, fired two torpedoes simultaneously. Through his overconfidence Lafrenz lost his U-boat and the lives of 22 men. Miraculously enough, he and his bridge crew were flung into the air and landed unscathed in the sea. They were then picked up by the British and spent the remainder of the war in a prisoner of war camp.[206]

The '60'-numbers of the UC-II class were unfortunate enough to encounter quite a few British submarines. *UC-62* and *UC-64* ended up on the decks of E-class submarines after accidently colliding, fortunately for both parties without deadly consequence. *UC-62*, *UC-63* and now also *UC-65* would in the end be sunk by the impact of perfectly fired British torpedoes. British submarine captains proved to be excellent shots as one should consider that these were moving targets of only 50 m length!

The wreck of *UC-65* lies in position 50° 30' 25 N 00° 28' 37 E, about 20 miles south-southwest from Hastings. The wreck is at a depth of 41 m and is broken in two in the engine room. Both halves lie 20 m separated from each other, with the foreship on its port side. The mineshafts, as well as one of the torpedo tubes are very recognisable. The 8.8 cm deck gun has fallen from its support and is partially buried by sand. Around it are several zinc containers with stowed 8.8 cm munition. In the stern section it is possible to get a glimpse of the MAN diesel engines.

UC-66

UC-66 arrived at Zeebrugge on 3 February 1917 and was commanded by *Oberleutnant z. S.* Herbert Pustkuchen. She was immediately added to the *U-Flottille Flandern*, but would only enjoy a career lasting four months, as she would be sunk with her entire crew by depth charge.

Pustkuchen did manage to carry out four patrols in the Irish Sea and on the Irish and French western coasts. On his first patrol he was able to torpedo and sink the 12,000 ton White Star Liner *SS Afric* mid-Channel, just off the Eddystone. A further 14 enemy ships were sunk by *UC-66* on her first patrol, making Pustkuchen a skilled, but also cautious captain. This he proved when he had ordered a tanker to stop on 17 February to the south of Wolf Rock. After a short battle, the tanker blew off steam, slowed down and launched two lifeboats. Pustkuchen did not come closer, despite the tempting situation, and had *UC-66* sink below the surface till only the tower was still visible. The tanker, which later proved to be the Q-ship *SS Penshurst*, Q-7, opened fire and scored a hit. After this, *Penshurst* turned and attempted to ram *UC-66*, which by now had submerged entirely. She had narrowly escaped the decoy vessel which had only recently surprised and sunk *UB-19* and *UB-37*. On three following patrols *UC-66* managed to sink another 21 ships and damage a further two. One was the hospital ship *HMHS Asturias* which was able to reach Plymouth under tow, minus her stern.

UC-66 left Zeebrugge on 22 May 1917 to lay mines off the Welsh coast, but nothing further was heard of her. She would have completed this task and on 25 May commenced hunting shipping. *UC-66* stayed away from home for a long time, and according to British sources she was chanced upon by an armed trawler. The trawler, *Sea King*, under command of Lt. Godfrey Herbert, lay to the south of the Lizard on anti-submarine patrol. It was known that this was a resting place for U-boats and a location where they could find single, unescorted cargo ships. The *Sea King* lay dead in the water and had a hydrophone hanging outboard on both sides to pick up the telltale hum of a U-boat's electric engines. Now and then a depth charge was detonated, with a lucky shot on *UC-66* in position 49° 56' N 05° 10' W. She surfaced, dived under, and was attacked by the trawler which dropped a string of depth charges on the place where she had disappeared. A number of explosions followed which was said to be the detonation of the remaining cargo of mines. Although there is no doubt about the confrontation of the trawler and a U-boat, it is unprobable that it concerns *UC-66*. Firstly, there is no material evidence found of a UC-II class U-boat wreck having been discovered in this area. More important is the fact that the confrontation was much too late in her patrol. *UC-66* was already expected back home on 8 June. The most probable scenario is that *UC-66* was able to complete her patrol, crossed the Dover Barrage, and most likely fell prey to a minefield in the area between the Varne and Fairy bank.

UC-68

Oberleutnant z. S. Hans Degetau would not get the necessary time to prove his worth as captain of *UC-68*. *UC-68* was launched on 12 August 1916 and joined the *U-Flottille Flandern* in February 1917. Degetau took *UC-68* on her first patrol towards the Channel on 10 March, but failed to return. A British source suggests that she was torpedoed on 5 April, off the Schouwenbank by the British submarine *HMS C-7*.[209] According to German sources this was a wrong identification and concerned the failed attack on *UB-10* by *HMS C-7*. The torpedo had exploded prematurely and *UB-10* was able to reach Zeebrugge unscathed.

Both the British and the Germans suggest the possibility that *UC-68* was sunk in the area between Dartmouth and Plymouth. A heavy underwater explosion was detected on 13 March, roughly 6 miles to the northeast of Start Point. Minesweepers were able to clear four German mines.[210] No UC-II class U-boat wreck has been found in this area up to now. It is possible that *UC-68* will be discovered in this area as several sinkings of ships proved that *UC-68* had partly fullfilled her orders. On 14 March *SS Orsova* ran onto a mine in a newly laid field to the southeast of Plymouth. *HMS Foyle* succumbed to the same field the

330

Oberleutnant z. S. Hans Degetau, captain of *UC-68* (WZ-Bilddienst)

following day. If it would not have been for the newly laid fields and the two mined vessels, then it could be assumed that *UC-68* was sunk closer to home.

UC-69

This minelayer would bring the war on merchant shipping deep into enemy territory. Her captain, *Kapitänleutnant z. S.* Erwin Wassner, took *UC-69* to the Bay of Biscay and to the Spanish and Portuguese coasts. Wassner was an experienced commander and before this had captained *UC-3* and *UB-38*. During five patrols, between 10 March and 4 August 1917, he was able to sink 42 ships with *UC-69*. Nationalities and cargoes were diverse, such as the British *SS Thracia* with iron ore, the Norwegian *SS Morild I* with wood, the Swedish *SS Hasting* with oil from groundnuts and the Portuguese *SS Cabo Verde* with wine and victuals. Besides Greek, Italian and Spanish ships, there was also the Japanese *SS Kagoshima Maru*. The 4,687 ton passenger ship was on her way from the East to Great Britain when she was torpedoed and sunk. On board was a large cargo of copper, rubber and general cargo. Wassner not only proved to be a successful captain, he was also able to save his submarine from perilous situations. On 17 June, *UC-69* came in contact with the French Q-ship *SS Marguerite* which was disguised as a Danish cargo ship. A gun battle ensued, resulting in both ships being hit. *UC-69* had received a hit in her tower but it did not threaten her diving capabilities. Instead of turning tail and returning back to port,

UC-69, commanded by *Kapitänleutnant* Erwin Wassner, is berthed in Bruges (TT)

DISCOVERY OF THREE UNIDENTIFIED UC-II CLASS U-BOATS
IN THE AREA WEST OF THE FAIRY BANK

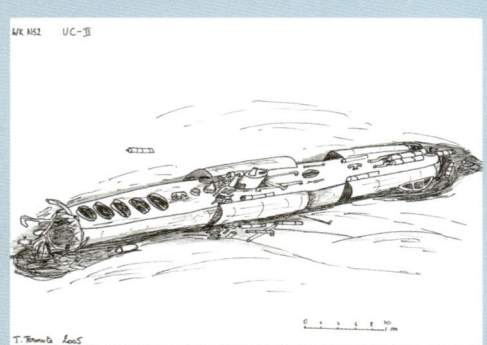

Sketch of wreck 2, a UB-III type boat, sunk to the north of the Fairy Bank (TT)

In the area described under *UB-54*, the location known as the Fairybank, there was not only the discovery of 2 UB-II and 3 UB-III class U-boat wrecks, but also 3 UC-III class submarines. The U-boats remain unknowns and are very similar as sites. They are fairly intact, they lack their cargoes of mines and were probably on the return journey from a patrol when they hit a mine and sank. Extensive investigation of the area by Dirk Termote in the mid-90s revealed the three UC-boats in close proximity to each other.

Wreck 1 is located in position 51° 24' 134 N 02° 05' 700 E in the middle of the north bound shipping lane and a few miles east of the Foxtrot 3 light ship. The wreck is keeled over to port and lies at a depth of 40 m. Heavy damage to the stern was observed, the mineshafts are empty and both torpedo tubes have fallen from the wreck. An 8.8 cm deck gun is also present but has also fallen from the wreck and lies also on the seabed, on the portside. Several empty shell cases, as well as dozens of full, zinc ammunition containers are spread around.

Wreck 2 was found in position 51° 29' 300 N 02° 04' 396 E and is located on the other side, in the south bound shipping lane. The wreck heels over to port and lies at a depth of 42 m, missing the top of the bow, as well as her first mineshaft. The other five shafts are empty and a 8.8 cm gun still stands on deck. On deck, around the tower, as well as on the sandy bottom, lie numerous sealed zinc containers with unfired rounds. Conning tower and stern remain

A stack of heavily overgrown ready-use ammunition canisters lie on a wreck of the UC-II class near the Foxtrot 3 lightvessel (TT)

intact. It was possible to clean the hub of the starboard propeller which revealed a number of interesting details. It was marked: '*Kaiserliche Werft Hamburg STB U-74, 13.10.16*'.[207] It could be that it concerns the propeller of *UC-74*, but it certainly does not concern this U-boat as it had survived the war.[208] In 2005 a trawl from a large, Dutch trawler was snagged on the stern loading hatch on the wreck. After many hours of tugging and pulling, the hatch had been wrenched free, and ended up, together with part of the net, in the scour under the stern. Hereafter it was possible to get a glimpse in the interior of the engine room. Between both engines lay a shifted torpedo on which were human remains. Two telegraphs, several gauges, tubing, a workbench and lockers could be seen. It took nature just a month to fill this part of the U-boat up to the top with sand.

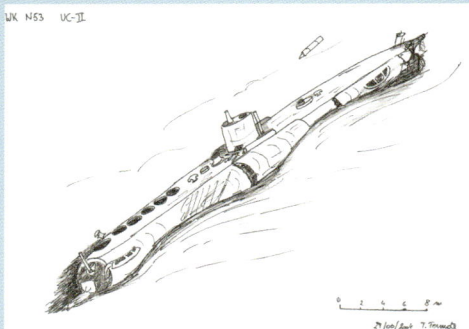

Sketch of wreck 3, a UC-II type boat, also to the north of the Fairy Bank (TT)

Wreck 3 lies only several hundred metres to the east of wreck 2, also in the south bound shipping lane. It is located in position 51° 29' 272 N 02° 03' 791 E, at a depth of 44 m and is keeled over to starboard. No damages were seen on first inspection. The bow is intact with her six, empty mineshafts, which are partly filled with sand. In front of the tower stands the foot of the 8.8 cm gun, but the barrel is missing and has probably been dragged off due to fishery activities. As with the other two wrecks, also this one is littered with unfired shells. The hatches of tower and stern are gone and have probably been torn from the wreck as a result of fishermen's snags. Identification through the propellers was not possible due to several lost trawls lying over this area.

The three minelayers were lost in 1917 or 1918 due to mine explosions. We can assign possible identities as *UC-16*, *UC-21*, *UC-66* or *UC-78* to the locations. Many of the wrecks do not contain mines, but it certainly does not mean that they were on their return journeys. Towards the end of the war more U-boats would leave port without their deadly cargo and just made use of the gun or torpedoes to attack an enemy.

Base and beginning of the barrel of the 8.8 cm gun on wreck 1, of a UC-II type boat (TT)

Wassner (3rd from right) sits amongs the crew of *UC-69*, Bruges (TT)

The Q-ship *Penshurst* scored hits on the mineshafts and tower of *UC-66* after a short gunbattle (TT)

Wassner decided to continue on his rampage and sank more merchant ships.

After his fifth patrol, he was given command of a new U-boat: *UB-59*. By the end of the war he had changed command once more, to *UB-117* and would be awarded the *Pour le Mérite* on 5 March 1918. By the end of the war Wassner had managed to sink 86 enemy ships, totalling 150.000 BRT.

After Wassner, command of *UC-69* went to *Oberleutnant z.S.* Hugo Thielmann, who carried out four patrols and sank eight ships. On 4 December 1917 *UC-69* left Zeebrugge on her final patrol. Thielmann wanted to lay mines off Cherbourg Harbour. He did not reach his destination because two days after his departure he came into collision with a submarine! This time it did not concern a British one, but the German *U-96*. *U-96* lay on the surface, at 20h, about 8 miles to the north of Cap Barfleur. Suddenly they hit an object, all lights fell out and the engines stopped. Part of the crew went above deck and looked at the U-boat which they had hit abaft the tower. *UC-69* had been hit at engine room level, but on board *U-96* they managed to get the engines running again. The bow of *U-96* was kept in the breach so as not to let the damaged U-boat sink immediately. Thielmann had not been on the bridge at the time of the collision, so the captain of *U-96* was forced to order her crew to evacuate the now sinking *UC-69*. Eighteen men got to safety before the stern broke off and *UC-69* finally sank below the waves. Thielmann was amongst the survivors but fate would not escape him and he would ultimately drown when *UB-106* was sunk in the Kiel Bight in March 1918.[211] *UC-69* would be the only U-boat sunk by accident in the Channel. Up to now the wreck has not been discovered.

UC-70

UC-70 was launched at the end of 1916 and, as was the case with most UC-II class minelayers, only arrived several months later in February 1917 in Flanders. Command was given to the successful *Oberleutnant z. S.* Werner Fürbringer who could carry out four patrols. Fürbringer gave the French fishing fleet on the Gironde a heavy blow when he had 12 trawlers sunk on 18 March. This was actually a repeat of his *modus operandi* when he had captained *UB-2* he sank a large number of British trawlers. When *UC-70* wanted to attack another group of fishing vessels, she was engaged by the 43 ton French naval sailing ship *Hyacinthe Yvonne*. The surprised *UC-70* was hit seven times at short distance by a concealed gun. Two crewmen were heavily wounded and three others suffered light injuries. A few of her dive tanks were hit as well by the precise French fire. But Fürbringer answered back with his 8.8 cm and managed to sink the brave French ship. *UC-70* still managed to dive and reach Zeebrugge despite having suffered damage. Fürbringer was able to sink a total of 25 ships between 27 February and 1 June 1917. After returning from her last patrol, *UC-70* was put into the Ostend dockyard for general repairs. When she lay in dry dock, she had the ill fortune of being hit by shells fired from British monitors which intended on bombarding the harbour installations on 5 June. *UC-70* was heavily damaged and sank in the harbour. She was lifted from the bottom, but had to undergo extensive repairs and only by the middle of April 1918 was she fit for duty.

By then she was assigned a new captain, *Oberleutnant z. S.* Kurt Loch, who carried out just two patrols on the British east coast, sinking two motorsailors.

Her last commander was *Oberleutnant z. S.* Karl Dobberstein who took on *UC-70* on 9 June 1918. He made two patrols in the area of the Hoofden and Flamborough Head. Dobberstein would experience the difficult months of 1918, where it had become much harder to find apt targets. Twice he attacked a convoy, sinking just five ships, but was attacked by escort ships which gave *UC-70* a rain of depth charges. *UC-70* would fail to return from her ninth patrol.

UC-70 was in the Whitby area on 28 August 1918, intending to lay a minefield and attack shipping. On her outbound journey she had obviously been damaged and left a long oilslick on the surface. At 15h30 she was spotted by Pilot Officer Waring, RAF, from his aircraft, a Kangaroo bomber (serial number

UC-70 and her crew in Zeebrugge (TT)

Oberleutnant z. S. Dobberstein, captain of *UC-70* (TT)

UC-71 photographed at full speed on the surface (BArch)

B9983) of 246 Squadron. The visibility seemed to be excellent, as he had observed beneath the surface a long shape from where the oil slick originated. Waring dropped a 125 kg bomb on what he thought was the front of the U-boat, in position 54° 32' N 00° 40' E. Large bubbles of air and oil boiled to the surface. The destroyer *HMS Ouse* arrived on the position and dropped a further ten depth charges which exploded at a depth of 16 m. More oil and wreckage floated to the surface. It was only on 14 September that divers were brought on the scene, letting Dusty Miller enter the wreck of the U-boat through an enormous gash in the hull, directly into the control room. Inside it was full of wreckage, destruction and floating corpses. Miller pushed through and came upon the watertight metal strongbox which contained logbooks, codebooks and charts of the route that the U-boat had taken. The wreck was positivily identified as that of *UC-70*.[212]

Diver Brian Clarkson was able to locate and identify the wreck of *UC-70* in the late 1980s. This news he gave Horst Bredow, founder of the *U-boot Archiv Cuxhaven*, already in October 1988. The wreck lies on a hard, sandy bottom at a depth of 25 m. She is fairly intact with six empty mineshafts and a deck gun on its original position. Diver Don Foster observed that two hatches are open and inside the tower it is possible to recognise cables and instruments.

UC-71

UC-71 would serve from her launch, on 12 August 1916, until the end of the war and end her life at the bottom of the sea, near the island of Helgoland in 1919.

Before finishing her two year-long career, she would be commanded by six different captains, one of which was the ace *Oberleutnant z. S.* Reinhold Saltzwedel. Between 10 March 1917 and 13 August 1918, *UC-71* carried out 19 patrols in the Channel, resulting in the sinking of 60 ships.

Oddly enough, it had become the habit to leave on a patrol without filling up the shafts of the UC-II class minelayer with mines. It seemed that more successes were obtained with the use of torpedoes, the deck gun and even explosive charges if the enemy ship could be boarded.

A close-up of the periscope and top of the helm on *UC-71*, scuttled near Helgoland (Norbert Thiel)

Saltzwedel proved to be her most successful captain with 17 ships sunk under his command. Through his bold actions he also encountered two Q-ships. These were two French three-masted barks, *Normandy* and *Kleber*, both equipped with four 7.5 cm calibre guns. After briefly exchanging fire, both parties left the scene without any significant damage.

A large cargo ship came into her sights on 8 August 1917, when *UC-71* found herself 120 miles to the west of Wissant. Because *UC-71* could not come close enough to fire a torpedo, she surfaced and stealthily approached her prey. Saltzwedel ordered to open fire at 3,000 m and his gun crew scored hits in the engine room and on the poop deck. A fire started and the enemy replied with a small calibre gun on her stern. The ready-use ammunition exploded shortly afterwards, destroying the stern. The English ship had kept her cool and had her true identity hidden from Saltzwedel. She was the Q-ship *Dunraven* and her captain, Gordon Campbell, thought that they had waited long enough, and had his five guns uncovered. He ordered to open fire on *UC-71*, but the suspicious Saltzwedel reacted fast enough to let his submarine dive. He had not let her dive before firing a torpedo at the unfortunate *SS Dunraven*. The cargo ship was hit in the engine room and slowly started to fill with water. The crew had to take to the lifeboats when the sea started to overflow the aft hatches. *UC-71* surfaced once again and opened fire on her superstructure and hull. She dived again and circled the stricken enemy whilst observing her at periscope depth. Suddenly, the sound of a torpedo was audible on board *UC-71*. The track of bubbles had passed close to *UC-71's* periscope and originated from approaching torpedo boats. Saltzwedel continued to follow the whole scene from periscope depth. The British put a tow on the *Dunraven*, but she sank two days after the action. Saltzwedel was able to sink, besides several cargo ships and tankers, the large 7,017 ton Belgian Congo boat, *SS Elisabethville*, off Belle Île. She had come from Congo and part of her cargo consisted of 10 tons of ivory.

UC-71 ended up in a mine net on her way back to base in early December 1917. It was a dangerous situation, but the net tore and *UC-71* was able to reach Zeebrugge on low revolutions. After arriving in the harbour about 40 m of net, including two mines which had been woven in it, had to be carefully cut free from her hull!

Towards the end of her career *UC-71* would hit a mine on 13 August 1918, making her unfit for diving. She had to return on the surface back to Zeebrugge, but was spotted and attacked several times by enemy aircraft. The crew was able to keep the aircraft away by using the machine gun. She reached home safely but had to travel to Bruges where the Imperial Dockyard carried out the necessary repairs. This would be the last of her missions and by the time she was ready for action she was forced to leave Flanders on 5 October and arrived a week later in Brunsbüttel.

UC-71 left with the 10th flotilla to England on 20 February 1919 for the compulsory handover. She never made it that far but sank on the same day half mile from the southern entrance to Helgoland Harbour, in position 54° 10' N 07° 54' E after an accident.

The wreck of *UC-71* was discovered almost 80 years later, in 1997, dived and identified by the author. This was part of a project to identify unknown wrecks around Helgoland, together with the *U-boot Archiv Cuxhaven* and the *Bundesinstitut für Seeschiffahrt und Hydrografie*,[213] *Hamburg*. *UC-71* is a well preserved example of a UC-II class minelayer. A large part of her outer hull still survives, torpedo tubes are still fixed on their original locations and even the net cutter on the bow is present! The good circumstances of conservation are due to its location. *UC-71* lies in a protected nature zone where fishing or diving is prohibited. This was positive news for the dive team, as we knew we would be the first divers ever on the site. The wreck lies on an even keel, at a maximum depth of 17 m. The deck gun has been removed, probably already before she left for her final voyage. No munition is present and all six shafts are void. The U-boat had most likely been sunk on purpose as all hatches are open, as well as all watertight doors. *UC-71* was also unique in my diving career. As all interior doors were open and there was little sand inside, it was possible to enter through the forward hatch and exit through the engine room. In the forward part there was a passageway next to the mine room and the radio room was well recognisable. Collapsed metal beds showed where the mens' quarters used to be. In the control room, all instruments were still fixed in position and even the seats for the helmsmen were still intact.[214]

UC-72

UC-72 joined the *U-Flottille Flandern* on 17 February 1917 and was commanded by *Oberleutnant z. S.* Ernst Voigt. Voigt followed the same trail that his colleagues took and found an excellent hunting ground near the western entrance of the Channel. Between 25 February and 12 August 1917, *UC-72* carried out seven patrols, resulting in the sinking of 41 enemy ships.

Her victims were diverse: from Spanish and French fishing vessels sunk between Cap Barfleur and Arcachon to large cargo ships, barks and troop transports torpedoed mid-Channel. The troopship *SS Sequana* was sunk near the Gironde mouth with the loss of 190 lives. The French sailing ship *Ceres* was one of the smaller vessels, laden with wine and sardines, coming from Lisbon and heading for Brest. *SS Anglo Patagonian*, of 5.017 BRT, was one of the larger ships, with a cargo of aircraft and other war materials originating from New York.

But *UC-72* would finally meet her end to the southwest of the Scillies, in position 46° 00' N 08° 48' W. On 21 August a cargo ship was spotted at great distance and fired upon. Voigt then had *UC-72* submerge to study the actions of the cargo ship before approaching her. The crew of stricken ship had jumped into the lifeboats, launched them and were pulling away from their ship. *UC-72* once again appeared on the surface to finish off the damaged ship, but was surprised by two concealed guns and four torpedo tubes which suddenly swung outboard. The innocent looking vessel was the Q-ship *HMS Acton, Q-34*. *UC-72* was utterly taken by surprise and did not stand a chance.

She sank, burning, after taking several well-placed hits, with all hands.

UC-75

Before seeing service with the *U-Flottille Flandern*, *UC-75* first was part of the *I U-Flottille*, with Helgoland as base. Her first captain, *Oberleutnant z.S.* Johannes Lohs, would operate on the British and Scottish east coasts and also in the Irish Sea. By the end of his fourth patrol he did not return to northern Germany, but arrived at Zeebrugge in August 1917. During those few patrols he had already managed to sink 29 ships.

Between 20 August 1917 and 8 January 1918 Lohs carried out another five patrols with *UC-75* before receiving the larger *UB-57*. During those six months he sank another 23 ships.

By the end of January 1918, *Oberleutnant z. S.* Walter Schmitz went on board as second and final captain of *UC-75*. He undertook three patrols in the same area, sinking nine ships and damaging three. By the end of May, *UC-75* had laid mines near the Outer Dowsing light ship, but came into difficulties off Flamborough Head. At 01h55, on 31 May, Schmitz attempted to engage a convoy at periscope depth but was accidentally run over by the cargoship *SS Blaydonian*. She was hard hit on her stern and tower. The point of the stern was bent over and when the tower got hit, the hinges of a hatch were dislocated. They were not able to shut the hatch watertight and water gushed inside, giving Schmitz no choice but to surface. *UC-75's* bad luck had not ended when two other ships in the convoy, *SS Tronda* and *SS Peter Pan*, also hit the drifting U-boat by accident. Lookouts on the destroyer *HMS Fairy* had heard a loud crash and arrived ten minutes later near the damaged U-boat. The captain of *HMS Fairy*, Lieutenant G. Barnish, was full of disbelief that a German U-boat could possibly be in this position! It was an area scattered with rocks and shallows and a U-boat could not possibly risk itself right amidst a convoy… Still Barnish called twice to him and let off two signal flares, as he suspected that the vessel may be British. Barnish did not get any answer and had the stern rammed. In making this manoeuvre, if it concerned a British submarine, then the crew would be given the chance to escape. After the first collision, many survivors appeared through the hatches. *HMS Fairy* turned in a brief circle and Barnish had her make a second approach to ram and destroy the German. A voice on the conning tower resounded with '*Kamerad! Kamerad!*', and Barnish hesitated and wanted to halt the second ramming. But at the same time the deck gun of *UC-75* fired a shell. Now the Englishman was ready for battle and ran at full speed to the damaged U-boat, whilst the guncrew on the stern 6 pounder registered about 40 hits on *UC-75*. The German crew on the tower jumped into the sea when the bow of *HMS Fairy* cut through the hull just abaft the gun. The small, 370 ton, *HMS Fairy* was not tough enough to resist the impact into the heavier built U-boat and started to sink, bow first. In the meantime, the U-boat had sunk and two Germans stood calmly on the sinking bow of *HMS Fairy* with their hands raised. Twelve other crewmen, Schmitz included, were also fished out of the sea by an approaching trawler. *UC-75* sank in position 53° 57' N 00° 09' E with the loss of 19 men.[215] *HMS Fairy* sank an hour later due to the mortal damage it had inflicted upon it. The 14 German prisoners ended up in the sea again an hour later. All British crewmen, but only five Germans, were saved by *HMS Greyhound*. Schmitz survived and was transferred to Skipton prisoner of war camp, but died in March 1919 of the flu epidemic.

The wreck of *UC-75* was found and dived upon by the Hull branch of the BSAC[216] in 1989. She lies on an even keel in a maximum depth of 31 m. *UC-75* is fairly intact and is to be found in position 53° 56' 478 N 00° 09' 036 E, about 13 miles to the south-southeast of Flamborough Head. The deck gun, one of her propellers and both torpedo tubes have been recovered.

UC-77

UC-77 was brought to Flanders and added to the *U-Flottille Flandern* on 2 July 1917, after having spent the first three months of her life with the *I. U-Flottille* in Helgoland. She was able to undertake nine patrols from Zeebrugge between July 1917 and her sinking, almost exactly a year later, on 11 July 1918. *UC-77* would know two captains, *Oberleutnant z. S.* Reinhard von Rabenau and *Oberleutnant z. S.* Johannes

Oberleutnant z. .S. Martin Troch, was first officer on board *UC-77* from December 1916 until January 1918 (TT)

Mines still fill the shutes on the wreck of a UC-II type boat sunk in the Westpit (Vic Verlinden)

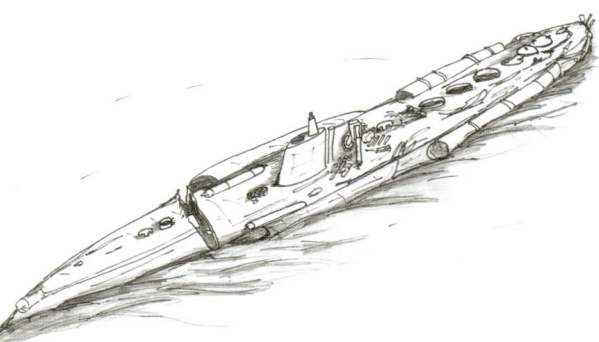

Sketch of the unidentified UC-II type boat in the Westpit (TT)

Ries, during her short career. Von Rabenau was able to sink a total of 14 ships in the Channel and the Bay of Biscay. Ries took over command on 6 March 1918 and carried out three patrols in the same areas. He was able to sink seven ships with *UC-77*. Ries had bad luck at the beginning of his third patrol when he was discovered by an aircraft. In the early hours of 9 June, *UC-77* was in Lyme Bay after sinking the British *SS Moidart*. When the aircraft spotted her, she closed in and dropped two bombs on *UC-77*. They were both lucky hits and the explosion damaged the pressure hull as well two diesel tanks. The crew could only make a temporary repair with the materials at hand. Ries decided to continue his patrol, despite the suffered damage to *UC-77* and was able to torpedo the French *SS Barthelemy* near Portland. After the attack the hydroplane jammed as well and *UC-77* was forced to return. She got back to port safely, but would have to remain for a month in dry dock as the damage was quite extensive. After having completed repairs, *UC-77* left Zeebrugge on 11 July 1918 on her final patrol towards the Channel. Nothing more was heard from her or her crew.

The wreck of a UC-II class U-boat was discovered in 1999 and dived upon by Dirk Termote in the area known as the Westpit, to the north of Zeebrugge, in position 51° 31' 545 N 03° 09' 039 E. It concerns an intact minelayer, sunk on even keel at a maximum depth of 27 m. The bow shows no obvious damages, with both torpedo tubes present and all mineshutes filled with a cargo of deadly mines. In front of the tower stands an 8.8 cm deck gun, barrel pointing downwards to the bottom on starboard. The stern shows damages beneath the hull, with a heavily crushed bottom just below the engine room. There is a also a large tear which runs over the whole breadth of this area. The U-boat most obviously suffered from the impact of a mine. The stern is visible, with the stern tube protruding, but further identification is not possible as both propellers are completely buried. It concerns a U-boat which was on an outward bound voyage from Zeebrugge. Oddly enough, there are several stowed, fired shells below deck near the gun. It could have been that the crew did not take the time to offload the fired rounds on land, before departing on their next mission.

Initially it was thought that it could concern the wreck of either *UC-21* or *UC-68*. *UC-21* disappeared in September 1917 after leaving Zeebrugge. *UC-68* would normally have laid her mines near Start Point and would have also been lost in the same area. As no wreck has yet been found, it

This label on the inside of a shell container gives us a *terminus postquem* date after which the UC-II type boat might have been sunk: July 1918 (TT)

was thought that *UC-68* was possibly sunk shortly after leaving in March 1917. All doubt disappeared after examining dates on the scattered shell cases on the wreck of the unidentified UC-class boat in the Westpit. Many of the shells date from before the war, but show inspection dates of June and July 1918. This gave an unrefutable *terminus post quem*. No other UC-II class U-boat, other than *UC-77*, was given up as missing after July 1918. It is very much possible that this concerns the wreck of *UC-77*.

UC-78

Before joining the *U-Flottille Flandern I* in early 1918, *UC-78* had seen a year of service in the Baltic. Her service time in the North Sea would be very brief, with only three patrols without much result. Her captain, *Oberleutnant z. S.* Hans Kukat, took *UC-78* on her 12th and final patrol to the Channel area on 2 May 1918. The intention was to lay mines near Boulogne and Newhaven, but nothing further was heard of *UC-78* and her crew.

Oberleutnant z. S. Hans Kukat, captain of *UC-78* (WZ-Bilddienst)

Initially it was believed that the loss of *UC-78* was due to a number of underwater explosions near Le Colbart ridge on 2 May 1918. In a location on the sandbank large amounts of oil boiled up to the surface and it was assumed to have come from *UC-78*. Several months later, on 7 August, Commander Damant's Dive team dived on a minelayer off Cap Gris Nez. The wreck was totally overgrown and it was estimated that she had sunk before June of that year. Automatically it was assumed that it concerned *UC-78*. It could also have been *UC-79* which had disappeared in April 1918. It is also possible that *UC-78* lies amongst one of the three unidentified UC-II class U-boats in the area to the west of the Westhinder (see *UC-66*).

UC-79

UC-79 arrived in Zeebrugge on 7 August 1917, after having served for four months with the *U-Flottille Kurland* in the Baltic. Her captain, *Oberleutnant z. S.* Werner Löwe, was intent on targeting shipping on the French coast. During three patrols he managed to sink a total of eight ships, mainly concerning small sailing ships, a few cargo vessels and two naval trawlers. *UC-79* was nearly sunk twice at the end of the patrol. After Löwe had engaged a coastal convoy in the bay of the Seine, he was attacked by British destroyers. A couple of dive tanks and a fuel tank were damaged after two depth charges exploded dangerously close to her hull. *UC-79* managed to slip away from her attackers, but was forced to return home. But during the night of 5 February, Löwe made a mistake in navigation and assumed that the buoys he saw were Ostend, but instead he steered straight for the Nieuwpoort Harbour mouth. The harbour defences immediately opened fire, bringing Löwe to his senses and making him turn about. An enthusiastic patrol boat sailed full steam out of the harbour to attack *UC-79*, but the German gunners answered with 8.8 cm shells, making the French vessel turn tail and run for cover. Finally, *UC-79* got back onto the correct course and arrived the next day safely in the harbour of Zeebrugge.

UC-79 left on her final mission on 20 March 1918 towards Brest and the Channel area. *Oberleutnant z. S.* Alfred Krameyer had taken over command from Löwe, but would disappear with all hands. German high command could make out from intelligence gathered from intercepted enemy radio traffic that

Underwater photos show markings on the starboard propeller of *UC-79* as *UC-77*, whilst the port one has *UC-79* as marking (Alain Richard)

Krameyer had been able to deposit his cargo of mines off Brest.

The wreck of *UC-79* was dived on by the Royal Navy dive team on 7 August 1918, but was indicated mistakenly as the wreck of *UC-78*. It was heavily overgrown, which would match a wreck which had been submerged for about half a year. Divers describe a UC-class U-boat with free-standing propellers, a deck gun and a torn-off bow. Damages were also observed beneath the radio room and officers' mess. Access to the wreck was difficult and during the first inspection no bodies were seen. Judging at the amount of growth it was then said that the wreck had to date from before June.

The wreck in question was rediscovered by fisherman Jean-François Baillet and dived upon in 2000 by Alain Richard and Jean François Jeu's team of divers. The wreck stands on an even keel, at a depth of 38 m, with a slight inclination to starboard. The conning tower with two periscopes is intact, with an 8.8 cm gun just in front. The wreck if broken by an explosion just in front of the gun. The entire forward section with her six mineshafts and two torpedo tubes has been detached, but lies close to the main wreck on her port side. The mineshafts are empty and shafts 4 and 5 are even totally accessible from deck to bottom. Both propellers are totally accessible and oddly enough, both carry a different number of identification. Port propeller has been stamped with number 'UC-79' and starboard has 'UC-77' as marking![217] It obviously concerns the use of a propeller of a similar U-boat. It cannot concern *UC-77* as she was only sunk in July 1918. The U-boat in question was discovered on 7 August 1918 and had been described as been heavily overgrown, most likely dating to about half a year.

UC-79 was the last in the series of UC-II class U-boats. Of the UC-III class, only six were assigned to the *U-Flottille Flandern*, but never saw any action. They were handed over to the Allies to be scrapped in the early 1920s. These were *UC-93*, *UC-94*, *UC-95*, *UC-96*, *UC-98* and *UC-100*.

THE EVACUATION OF THE FLANDERS BASES

When the order for the German navy to retreat out of Flanders was given, a total of nine U-boats were able to reach Germany on their own accord. A number of U-boats and surface craft, which still lay in the three ports, were found not to be seaworthy enough and destroyed, together with lots of infrastructure on land. The plan of destructions had a two-fold intent. Firstly, the Germans did not want their material to fall into Allied hands and secondly, they wanted to obstruct the reconstruction programme as long as possible.

Most piers, jetties, quays and bridges at Ostend were damaged or destroyed in one or other way. The sea station, adjoining buildings and offices had been turned into ruins. Most of the supplies had been taken with the retreating Germans and fuel depots were empty. Wrecks were strewn in every corner of the port. *HMS Vindictive* lay half sunk close to the easterly pier, as well as several dredgers, a trawler and a mine sweeper. In dry dock lay the remains of the exploded U-boat *UB-40*.

In Zeebrugge Roads lay a dredger close to the Mole, as well as the burnt out wreck of the accommodation vessel *SS Brussels*. The ships sunk during the St. George's Day attack, amounting to three blockships, several tugboats and several pontoons were piled up at the mouth of the canal.

Ships and facilities of the Imperial Dockyard Bruges are destroyed by engineers of the 31st Infantry Regiment in October 1918 (TT)

Three captured ships lie sunken in Bruges Harbour (TT)

In the eastern basin of the Bruges docks lay the remains of a semi-sunken drydock. Near the eastern wall of the western basin were a sunken British merchantship with alongside it the capsized remains of a German torpedo boat. Some distance away were two more sunken dry docks, one of which still had a torpedo boat docked in her and the other with a blown up UB-III class U-boat. The U-boat concerned *UB-59*, which had been destroyed with explosive charges and was nearly totally wrecked. The power of the explosion was so big that a 10 m long stern section was blown clear of the dock. After somersaulting through the air it ended up, rudders, shafts and propellers still in place, upside down on land, about 100 m away from the dock. Near the workshops lay heaps of hydrophones, rudders and radio masts which had been intended to be fitted to U-boats. A large, four-part dry dock lay to the northwestern corner of the main dock, where lay the wrecks of the sunken ferry *Princess Joséphine* and the captured ships *Brugge, Lestris, Gelderland, Midsland, Zaanstroom, Rio Pardo* and *Niobe*.

German sources mention the destruction and abandonment of four U-boats in Flanders. Possibly, this number is more likely to be five. In Ostend, *UB-40* was blown up in dry dock and *UB-59* underwent the same fate in Bruges. Two U-boats were taken in tow out to sea during the Zeebrugge evacuation. These were most definitely *UB-10, UC-4* and there is a possibility that an unidentified UB-III class U-boat joined them. These U-boats were all being repaired and would not have been able to reach Germany on their own, so it was decided to destroy them. *UB-10* was sunk by gunfire from battery Braunschweig (also known as battery 'Zoute') in the area to the east of the harbour, about 1 km from the shore off Heist. *UB-10* was salvaged in 1980 by the crane barge *Norma* of the *Tijdelijke Vereniging van Bergingswerken*. Divers Piet Lagast and Johan de Vent, then present during the operations, witnessed a relatively intact wreck, only missing its outer skin and conning tower. It could have been that the tower had been hit by a shell from the Braunschweig battery. *UB-10* was buried after her recovery and to this day lies beneath the modern container port of Zeebrugge.

UC-4 and the UB-III class U-boat were sunk about 5 miles to the north of Zeebrugge. Possibly they too were sunk by gunfire, but it would have been more logical that the seacocks were opened to be rid of them easily. The identification of the UB-III class remains a mystery to this day.

Bruges docks are a chaos of wrecks and destroyed structures (TT) ▶

.K, BRUGES

Bibliography

PRIMARY SOURCES

BUNDESARCHIV-MILITÄRARCHIV FREIBURG IM BREISGAU, GERMANY

RM104/216, *Luftfahrwesen Marinekorps, Tagesmeldung.*
RM 20/277, *Akten der Waffenstilstandskommission.*
RM 27 XIII/9: *Kriegsgabe für U-boote 1915-1918.*
RM 27 XIII/75: *Militärische Angelegenheiten der U-Flottille Flandern 1915-1918.*
RM 27 XIII/119: *Militär. Ausbildung der B-und C-boote.*
RM 27 XIII/120: *Abgabe der B-und C-boote.*
RM 27 XIII/122: *Signalwesen auf U-booten.*
RM 27 XIII/153: *Personal für U-boote bd.1: 1914-1918.*
RM 27 XIII/160: *Persönliche Angelegenheiten der O.A. 1915-1917.*
RM 27 XIII/168: *Offiziersangelegenheiten 1919.*
RM 27 XIII/246: *Handwaffen.*
RM 27 XIII/252: *Munitionsunterbringung november 1918.*
RM 27 XIII/279: *Taucherausbildung bd.3: 1912-1914.*
RM 27 XIII/284: *Sprengausrüstung der U-boote 1914-1918.*
RM 27 XIII/283: *Ärztlicher-Berichte, SM U-156, SM U-152 und UB-62.*
RM 27 XIII/283: *Die Grundlagen der U-bootshygiene (Lüftungshygiene) für den ärztlichen Dienst auf U-booten.*
RM 27 XIII/282: *Hygienische Angelegenheiten auf U-Booten 1913-1918.*
RM 27 XIII/173: *Urlaub, Krankheit 1918-1919.*
RM 27 XIII/266: *Stützpunkt Kanalküste 1914-1915.*
RM 27 XIII/246: *Handwaffen.*
RM 27 XIII/286-287: *Nautische Instrumente bd1-bd2.*
RM 27 XIII/287: *Nautische Instrumente bd2.*
RM 104/58: *Netze für U-boote: bd.4.*
RM 104/223: *Kriegsgliederung des Marinekorps (Seekriegsführung), 23.5.1918.*
RM 104/224-225: *Berichte über die Tätigkeit der Kaiserliche Werft Brügge bd.1-bd.2, juni 1915- april 1917; nov. 1914 – apr. 1915.*
RM 104/226: *Allgemeine U-boots-Angelegenheiten.*
RM 104/229: *UB-Boote jan. 1915-1917.*

◄ With a steam tug, the last occupation troops leave Bruges Harbour and head to Ghent (TT)

RM 104/230: *Geheim-Akten Vers. Stelle dez. 1914-febr. 1918.*
RM 104/234: *Bombenschutz Ostende febr. 1915 – sept. 1915.*
RM 104/235: *Dock in Ostende jan. 1915 – aug. 1915.*
RM 104/236: *Kaiserliche Werft Allgemeine Geheim Angelegenheiten bd. 1.*
RM 104/236: *Kaiserliche Werft Allgemeine Geheim Angelegenheiten bd. 2.*
RM 104/237: *Kaiserliche Werft Allgemeine Geheim Angelegenheiten bd.2.*
RM 104/ 252: *Hafenbau Ostende dez. 1914 –aug. 1918.*
RM 120/138: *Postalische Angelegenheiten bd.1.*
RM 120/41: *See-Operationen Unterseeboote.*
RM 120/42: *U-bootsbau und Reparaturen, Bootskörper und Einrichtung.*
RM 120/43: *U-boot KTB's anschreiben.*
RM 120/44: *U-boot KTB's anschreiben.*
RM 120/61: *Untergang S.M. Unterseeboot UC-62, 10/1917.*
RM 120/85: *Prisenangelegenheiten 1917-1918.*
RM 120/87: *Kriegsbeute.*
RM 120/95: *Stützpunkte, Bau und Reparaturen von U-booten bd.1 1914-1915.*
RM 120/96: *Stützpunkte, Bau und Reparaturen von U-booten bd.2 1915-1916.*

U-BOOT ARCHIV CUXHAVEN

C.B. 01378 O.X.O. '*U.C. 63*' *Report of Interrogation of Survivor*, November 1917.
C.B. 01379 O.X.O. '*U.C. 65*' *Interrogation of survivors*, November 1917.
Obermaschinist Arthur Enigk, *UC-5, verhandlung and personel documents.*
S.M. UB-57: Letter from Heinrich Lohs to the Reichsmarineamt, 5 October 1937.
S.M UB-81: *Auszug aus dem KTB des Marine-Ing. d. R. Hans Denker, 11 January 1918*

PUBLIC RECORDS OFFICE, LONDON

ADM 53/46075: *Diary of H.M. Submarine E-45*, October, 1917.
ADM 137/3060/90098: *Interrogation of Acting Warrant Officer Bernhard Haack, captured from German submarine UC-32.*

ADM 137/3060/90098: *Interrogation of survivors of UC-55.*

ADM 137/3060/90098: *Report of Examination of survivors from UC-65, sunk by C-15 on 3 November 1917.*

ADM 137/3060/90098: *Interrogation of prisoners captured from the German submarine UB-35 on 25 January 1918.*

ADM 137/3060/90098: *UC-11 Interrogation of survivor, July 1918.*

ADM 137/3060/90098: *Report of Interrogation of Survivors of UB 110, sunk on 19 July 1918.*

ADM 137/3060/90098: *UB 109 Interrogation of survivors, september 1918.*

AIR/677/21/13/1930: *R.N.A.S. Home waters 1917, part III: Belgian coast operations.*

AIR1/526/16/12/43

SECONDARY SOURCES

Bacon, R., *The Dover Patrol*, 2 vols., London, 1919.

Bartz, K., Zeebrügge. *Der Englische Angriff auf die deutsche U-Boot-Basis*, Berlin, 1938.

Bendert, H., *Die UB-Boote der Kaiserliche Marine 1914-1918. Einsatz – Erfolge – Schicksal*, Mittler, 2000.

Bendert, H., *Die UC-Boote der Kaiserliche Marine 1914-1918. Minenkrieg mit U-Booten*, Mittler, 2001.

Böhmig, 3. Unterseebootsflottille 'Lohs'. Wer war Johannes Lohs?, in *Wehrmacht*, heft 19, 1937.

Brooks, G., (ed.), *Fips. Legendary U-Boat Commander 1915-1918*, Barnsley, 1999.

Carpenter, A., *The Blocking of Zeebrugge*, London, 1922.

Chatterton, E.K., *The Auxiliary Patrol*, London, 1923.

Chatterton, E.K., *Q-Ships and their story*, London, 1922.

Chatterton, E.K., *Fighting the U-boats*, London, 1942.

Chatterton, E.K., *Beating the U-boats*, London, 1943.

De Schaepdrijver, S., *Bolwerk Brugge. Bezette stad in 14-18*, Bruges, 2014.

Deseyne, A., *De Kust Bezet 1914-1918*, Bruges, 2007.

Friedman, N., *German Warships of World War I*, London, 1992.

Gibson, R. en Prendergast, M., *The German Submarine war 1914-1918*, London, 1931.

Göthling, W., Lörscher, O. en S. Schnetzke, *Ausgeliefert. Die deutschen U-Boote 1918-1920 und ihr Verbleib – Eine Dokumentation*, Erfurt, 2012.

Grant, R.M., *U-boats Destroyed*, London, 1964.

Grant, R.M., *U-Boat Intelligence*, London, 1969.

Gray, E., *A Damned Un-English Weapon. The Story of submarine warfare 1914-1918*, London, 1971.

Haag von, *U-boot Flottille Flandern. 1. Weltkrieg Kommandant UC-7 Georg Haag. Ein Leben in Briefen*, Stuttgart, 1930.

Hall, N., *All Washed Up, Surviving First World War U-boat Wrecks around Britain's coastline*, in *Britain at War*, issue 14, June 2008.

Hermann Historica, *Auction 61: Motortechniek*, München, 2011.

Herzog, O. *Kapitänleutnant Otto Steinbrinck. Die Geschichte des erfolgreichsten U-Boot-Kommandanten in den Gewässern um England*, Krefeld, 1963.

Hocking, C., *Dictionary of disasters at sea during the age of steam. 1824-1962*, London, s.d.

Jacobsen, H., *Trutzig und Treu. Kämpfe der Deutschen Marine an Flanderns Küste 1914-1918.*

Koerver, H.J. (ed.), *Room 40: German Naval Warfare 1914-1918. Volume I: The fleet in Action*, Berlin, 2009.

Koerver, H.J. (ed.), *Room 40: German Naval Warfare 1914-1918. Volume II: The fleet in Being*, Berlin, 2009.

Koerver, H.J. (ed.), *German Submarine Warfare 1914-1918 in the Eyes of British Intelligence. Selected sources from the British National Archives, Kew*, Berlin, 2010.

Lambrecht, E., *Gruss aus Flandern!*, Kortrijk, 2004.

Lambrecht, E., *Versteende vleugels*, Kortrijk, 2005.

Larn, R. & B., *Shipwreck Index of the British Isles*. Vol II. Hampshire, Isle of Wight, Sussex, Kent, Goodwin Sands, Thames, Lloyd's Register of Shipping, London, 1995.

MacOrlan, P., *La Nuit de Zeebrugge*, Paris, 1934.

Mantey von, E., *Unsere Marine im Weltkrieg 1914-1918*, Berlin, 1926.

McCartney, I., *Lost Patrols. Submarine Wrecks of the English Channel*, Penzance, 2003.

McCartney, I. *The 'Tin Openers' Myth and Reality: Intelligence from U-boat Wrecks During WW I*, s.l., 2014.

McDonald, K., *The wreck of UB-30*, in *Diver Magazine*, March 1995.

Mcdonald, K., *The Tin Openers. The secret underwater war against the U-boats 1914-1918*, Worthing, 2003.

Messimer, D.R., *Verschollen. World War I U-boat losses*, Chatham Publishing, 2002.

O'Driscoll, P., *WW I Medway U-Boats*, in *After the Battle*, 36, 1982, pp. 39-42.

Outry, V.F., *Merkwaardige bladzijden uit de geschiedenis van Oostende*, Antwerp, 1938.

Pitt, B., *Zeebrugge, St. George's Day 1918*, London, 1958.

Philips, F., *14-18 op zee. Belgische schepen en zeelui tijdens de Grote Oorlog*, Lannoo, 2013.

Rau, J.A., *Geschiedenis van de Brugse rand: Koolkerke-Sint-Jozef*, Bruges, 1990.

Richard, A., *Plongées en Côte d'Opale*, Tome 1, 2007.

Richard A. & A. Lugiez, *Plongées en Côte d'Opale*, Tome 2, 2010.

Rössler, E., *Die Auslieferung der deutschen U-Boote nach dem Ersten Weltkrieg und ihre Hintergründe*, in *Marine-Rundschau*, 1, 1975, pp. 21-27.

Rössler, E., *Die Deutschen U-Boote und ihre Werften*, Vol I, Munich, 1979.

Stoelzel, *Ehrenrangliste der Kaiserlich Deutschen Marine 1914-18*, Berlin, 1930.

Termote, T., *U-Boote, Q-Ships, Kanonenrohre und Torpedos: Die Geschichte von SM UC-71*, in *Das Archiv*, Heft 10, März 1998.

Termote, T., *Verdwenen in de Noordzee. De geschiedenis van Duitse U-boten aan de Belgische kust in de Eerste Wereldoorlog*, Erpe, 1999.

Termote, T. & D., *Schatten en Scheepswrakken*, Leuven, 2009.

Thomas, L., *Ritter der Tiefe*, vertaling uit het Engels, Berlin, 1931.

Van Damme, P., *De haven van Brugge*, Bruges, 1946.

Woodward, M., *Reinhold's last stand*, in *Sport Diver*, s.d., pp. 12-14.

Young, R. & Armstrong, P., *Silent Warriors. Submarine Wrecks of the United Kingdom*, Vol. I, Tempus Publishing, 2006.

Young, R. & Armstrong, P., *Silent Warriors. Submarine Wrecks of the United Kingdom*, Vol. II, The History Press, 2009.

WEBSITES:

www.kenthistoryforum.co.uk
www.wikipedia.org
www.uboat.net
www.canterburydivers.org.uk
www.divernet.com
www.pastscape.org.uk
www.ub88.org
www.ecpad.fr
www.machuproject.eu
www.stocktondivers.co.uk

ACKNOWLEDGEMENTS

My father Dirk Termote (Oostende)

Without the help of my friends and colleagues from my dive group it would not have been possible to gather so much detailed information concerning the wrecks. My thanks goes out to Luc Commeine (Kortemark), Philippe and Carine Depoorter (Zulte), Kristof Temmerman (Mechelen), Donald Roland (Hamme), Sven Souris (Middelkerke), Didier Grunewald (Oostende) and Cedric Soete (Oostende), Johan Samyn (Oostduinkerke), Jean Paul Samyn (Oostduinkerke), Gilbert and Koen Allewerelt (Nieuwpoort), Daniël Devriendt (Oostende).

Further, I am indebted to fellow divers Harry Klerks (Brussel), Fons Schoonis (Veurne), André Ruissen (Vlissingen), Nicolas Mouchart (Brussels), Dirk Johansen (Aarhus), Vic Verlinden, Martin Woodward (Bembridge, Isle of Wight), Nic Owen (Ramsgate), Innes McCartney, Alain Richard, André Lugiez, Norbert Thiel, Coen Onstwedder, Arie Visser, Martin Bakker, Paul Dekeijzer, Jean Paul Bellart, Bob Hickson and Garry Eggleton.

Alex Deseyne (Ghent)

Luc Louwagie (Nieuwpoort)

Piet Lagast (Heist), Marcel Rutjens (Bruges) and Johan De Vent

Heiko Hermans, Bremen (Germany)

Peter Tamm, Hamburg (Germany)

In far away California: Gary Fabian, Kendall Raine and John Walker

Wolfgang Göthling, Trevor Young, Patrick Verbeke, Christoph Van der Beke and Danny Van Severen.

Dr. Noël Geirnaert and Jan Dhondt, Archives Bruges

Horst Bredow, U-boot Archiv Cuxhaven (Germany)

MDK, Flemish Hydrographic Department (Belgium)

Johan Opdebeeck, Rijksdienst voor het Cultureel Erfgoed (the Netherlands)

Provincial Domain Raversijde (Belgium)

ECPAD, Paris (France)

Internationales Maritimes Museum Hamburg (Germany)

Tyne & Wear Archives & Museums (Great Britain)

Jörn Ankersen Jensen (Denmark)

Gert Normann Andersen (Thorsminde, Denmark)

WZ-Bilddienst Wilhelmshaven (Germany)
Bundesarchiv-Militärarchiv Freiburg (Germany)
National Archives London (Great Britain)
Hermann Historica München (Germany)
Rijkswaterstaat Nederland (the Netherlands)

NOTES

1 Koerver, 2010, p. 20.
2 Koerver, 2010, p 32.
3 Litterarily 'U-boat cruiser'. These were enormous submarines provided with torpedo tubes and two 15 cm artillery pieces.
4 RM 120/41, pp. 1-5.
5 RM 27 XIII/266, pp.1-4.
6 RM 27 XIII/266, pp. 5-8.
7 Brooks, 1999, p. 13.
8 Gibson and Prendergast, 1931, p. 50.
9 Gibson and Prendergast, 1931, pp. 38-39.
10 RM 104/236.
11 ADM 137/3060/90098, p. 6.
12 McDonald, 2003, pp. 8-12.
13 Young, 2006, p. 176.
14 Bendert, 2001, p. 18.
15 RM 120/ 42.
16 Termote, 1999, p. 118.
17 Friedman, 1992, p. 276.
18 Koerver, 2009, p. 166.
19 Grant, 1969, p. 40.
20 McDonald, 2003, p. 17.
21 Fürbringer, 1933, p. 53.
22 O'Driscoll, 1982, p. 41.
23 Hermann Historica, lot 6901, May 2011.
24 Admiralty, Naval staff, report 1920, p. 26.
25 RM 27 XIII/ 287, bd. 2.
26 Techel, 1940, p. 45.
27 RM 27 XIII 287, bd.2.
28 RM 27 XIII/284 p. 77.
29 Friedman, 1992, p. 292.
30 Grant, 1969, p. 94.
31 Admiralty, Naval staff, report 1920, p. 28.
32 RM 27 XIII/252.
33 RM 27 XIII/282.
34 TNT= Tri Nitro Tolueen
35 The horn was named after its inventor, Dr. Heinrich Hertz, who designed it in 1868.
36 Bendert, 2001, p. 15 and Termote, 1999, p. 57.
37 RM 27 XIII/284, p. 1.
38 RM 27 XIII/246.
39 RM 27 XIII/284.
40 RM 27 XIII/284, p. 27.
41 RM XIII/279.
42 RM 27 XIII/168.
43 ADM 137/3060/90098, p. 6.
44 Bendert, 2000, p. 20.
45 Admiralty, Naval staff, report 1920, p. 26.
46 RM 27 XIII/282, p. 84.
47 ADM 137/3060/90098, UC-65, p. 17.
48 RM 27 XIII/160.
49 U-boot Archiv, UC-65: Interrogation of survivors.
50 Koerver, vol I, p. 167.
51 Thomas, 1931, p. 88.
52 Thomas, 1931, p. 234. '*Just cross on the surface, as the patrol vessels are all blind. They totally don't see anything, so I pass them directly beneath their very noses.*'
53 U-boot Archiv, letter from Heinrich Lohs to the Reichsmarineamt, 1937.
54 ADM 137/3060/90098, UC-65, p. 17.
55 Fürbringer, p. 101, 1999.
56 Lit.: 'drowning command'
57 RM 27 XIII/283.
58 U.C. 63 Interrogation report, p. 3.
59 Evans, 1986, p. 178.
60 Brooks, 1999, p. 54.
61 Thomas,1931, p. 83.
62 Fürbringer, 1933, p. 93.
63 RM 27 XIII/282, p. 63.
64 RM 27 XIII/282, p. 64.
65 Stoelzel, 1930, p. 198.
66 RM 27 XIII/173 and Stoelzel 1930.
67 RM 27 XIII/168.
68 RM 27 XIII/283.
69 U-boot Archiv, Obermaschinist Arthur Enigk, UC-5.
70 RM 120/43.
71 RM 120/44.
72 ADM 137/3060/90098, UB-35, p. 14.
73 Oral information Christoph van der Beke.
74 Koerver, 2009, p. 167.
75 Oral information Christoph van der Beke.
76 RM 104/237.

77 RM 27 XIII/9.
78 RM 104/236.
79 Grant, 1969, p. 50.
80 'Hurrah: for our number 1, may you live long! Hurrah! For all (on board).'
81 'Thoughts during the watch.'
82 Lit.: pain of being separated (from one's loved ones)
83 Brooks, pp. 50-51.
84 RM 120/87.
85 Koerver, 2009, p. 58.
86 Mcdonald, p. 16.
87 Grant, 1969, p. 51.
88 Bendert, 2000, p. 64.
89 Van Damme, pp. 26-29.
90 RM 27 XIII/266, p. 14.
91 RM 104/58.
92 Van Damme, p. 48.
93 Bruges Imperial Dockyard.
94 Litt.: 'Eight blisses'.
95 RM 120/85.
96 Small, square windows.
97 Thomas, p. 212.
98 AIR/677/21/13/1930.
99 Thomas, p. 212, 'There was (in Bruges) an ancient bar room, a cellar whose vaults were supported by Gothic arches, with walls a metre thick. This was the nightly meeting place for a valiant gang, who ventured beneath the surface of the seas.'
100 'Enjoy life, as it is oh-so brief.'
101 Admiralty, Naval staff, report 1920, p. 16.
102 Litt.: Ostend port construction.
103 RM 104/226.
104 RM 104/236.
105 RM 104/224-225.
106 RM 120/97, p. 4 and pp.17-19.
107 RM 120/97, pp. 4-41.
108 RM 104/235.
109 RM 104/224-225.
110 RM 120/97, pp. 6-9 and 27-41.
111 *Lager* meaning 'storage' or mine-storage-area.
112 Grant, 1969, p. 11.
113 De Schaepdrijver, pp. 83-86.
114 Bendert, 2000, p. 99.
115 Bendert, 2001, p. 146.
116 Chatterton, 1922, p. 56.
117 Chatterton, 1922, p. 65.
118 Chatterton, 1922, pp. 109-131.
119 McCartney, 2014, pp. 1-2.
120 Mcdonald, p. 23.
121 Mcdonald, p. 14.
122 Mcdonald, p. 3.

123 Deseyne, p. 76.
124 Young, 2006, pp. 162-163.
125 Mcdonald, pp. 13-15.
126 Herzog, p. 37.
127 Litt. Temporary Salvage Association
128 Bendert, 2000, p. 57.
129 Gibson and Prendergast, p. 91.
130 Young, 2006, p. 193.
131 Grant, 1964, p. 122.
132 Evans, p. 78.
133 Grant, 1964, p. 68.
134 McCartney, 2003, p. 62.
135 Bendert, 2000, p. 74.
136 Thomas, p. 235
137 Grant, p. 54
138 Terraine, p. 76
139 Göthling, Lörscher and Schnetzke, pp. 188-189.
140 Gibson and Prendergast, p. 90, Grant, 1964, p. 32 and Bendert, 2000, p. 83.
141 Gibson and Prendergast, p. 193 and Bendert, 2000, p. 85.
142 Bendert, 2000, p. 87.
143 Grant, 1964, p. 128.
144 McDonald, 1995, p. 38.
145 Bendert, 2000, p. 92 and Grant, 1964, p. 88.
146 Bendert, 2000, p. 94 and Grant, 1964, p. 63.
147 Bendert, 2000, p. 95, McCartney, 2003, p. 150, Richard and Lugiez, p. 189 and McCartney, 2014, p. 8.
148 Young, 2006, p. 324.
149 Bendert, 2000, p. 101.
150 Richard, 2010, p. 178 and McCartney, 2003, p. 148.
151 Bendert, 2000, p. 136 and Grant, 1964, p. 120.
152 McCartney, 2003, p. 132.
153 Termote, 1999, p. 139-144 and 2009, p. 292.
154 Oral information from Patrick Eeckhout.
155 Richard and Lugiez, p. 184.
156 Richard and Lugiez, p. 168.
157 Hydrographic department, dossier B125/306b and interview with Piet Lagast 2008.
158 Termote, 2009, p. 286.
159 Young, 2006, p. 321.
160 McCartney, 2003, p. 151.
161 Distinguished Service Cross.
162 Young and Armstrong, p. 183.
163 U-boot Archiv: SM-UB-81, KTB belonging to Denker, pp. 4-6.
164 Young, 2009, p. 120.
165 Young, 2006, pp. 114-117.
166 Young, 2006, pp. 291-293.
167 Young, 2006, pp. 84-86.
168 Grant, 1964, p. 93.

169 McCartney, 2014, pp. 10-12.
170 Gibson and Prendergast, p. 192.
171 Gibson and Prendergast, p. 90.
172 Termote, 2009, pp. 283-284.
173 Hocking, p. 446.
174 Gibson and Prendergast, p. 214.
175 'Greasing tube for capstan'.
176 Grant, 1964, p. 57.
177 Young, 2006, p. 243.
178 McCartney, 2003, p. 162.
179 ADM/137/3060/90098: UC-11
180 Hocking, p. 583 and Bendert, 2001, p. 81.
181 McCartney, 2003, p. 65.
182 McCartney, 2003, p. 21.
183 Grant, 1964, p. 56.
184 McCartney, 2003, p. 157.
185 Grant, 1964, p. 46.
186 Richard, 2007, p. 143.
187 Grant, 1964, p. 66.
188 Young, 2006, pp. 135-137.
189 McCartney, 2003, p. 158 and Richard, 2007, p. 146.
190 www.divernet.com/UC-47
191 Göthling, Lörsscher and Schnetzke, pp. 332-333
192 McCartney, 2003, p. 61.
193 McCartney, 2003, p. 145.
194 McCartney, 2003, p. 39.
195 Göthling, Lörscher and Schnetske, pp. 334-337 and BAMA, RM 20/277
196 Richard, 2007, pp. 148-150.
197 BAMA/RM 120/61
198 Grant, 1964, p. 58.
199 PRO ADM 53/46075.
200 Gibson and Prendergast, p. 220.
201 Termote, 2009, pp. 327-328.
202 Messimer, p. 302; U-boot Archiv C.B. 01378 O.X.O ; and Young, 2006, p. 246.
203 Young, 2006, p. 333.
204 McCartney, 2003, p. 153.
205 Richard, 2007, pp. 151-153.
206 ADM 137/3060/90098 and McCartney, 2003, p. 133.
207 Imperial Dockyard Hamburg, Starboard propeller, U-74, 12 October 1916
208 Bendert, 2001, p. 184.
209 Gibson and Prendergast, p. 167.
210 Grant, 1964, p. 69.
211 Stoelzel, p. 321.
212 Grant, 1964, p. 128 and Young, 2006, pp. 100-103.
213 German Hydrographic Department.
214 Termote, 1998.
215 Grant, 1964, pp. 123-124.
216 British Sub Aqua Club.
217 Richard, 2007, pp. 156-161.